FREEZE!

FREEZE!

THE GRASSROOTS MOVEMENT TO HALT THE ARMS RACE AND END THE COLD WAR

HENRY RICHARD MAAR III

CORNELL UNIVERSITY PRESS

Ithaca and London

First published 2021 by Cornell University Press

Library of Congress Cataloging-in-Publication Data

Names: Maar, Henry Richard, III, author.
Title: Freeze!: the grassroots movement to halt the arms race and end the Cold War / Henry Richard Maar III.
Description: Ithaca [New York]: Cornell University Press, 2021. | Includes bibliographical references and index.
Identifiers: LCCN 2021011508 (print) | LCCN 2021011509 (ebook) | ISBN 9781501760884 (hardcover) | ISBN 9781501760891 (pdf) | ISBN 9781501760907 (epub)
Subjects: LCSH: Reagan, Ronald. | Antinuclear movement—United States—History—20th century. | Nuclear arms control—United States—History—20th century. | Nuclear weapons—Government policy—United States. | Cold War. | United States—Foreign relations—1981–1989. | United States—Foreign relations—Soviet Union. | Soviet Union—Foreign relations—United States.
Classification: LCC JZ5574 .M33 2021 (print) | LCC JZ5574 (ebook) | DDC 327.1/747097309048—dc23
LC record available at https://lccn.loc.gov/2021011508
LC ebook record available at https://lccn.loc.gov/2021011509

For the Maar family

And for Tom Layton: teacher, mentor, friend

In a world where children are still not safe from starvation or bombs, should not the historian thrust himself and his writing into history, on behalf of goals in which he deeply believes?
—Howard Zinn, *The Politics of History*

CONTENTS

ABBREVIATIONS

ABC	American Broadcasting Corporation
ABM	anti–ballistic missile
ACDA	Arms Control and Disarmament Agency
ACU	American Conservative Union
AEC	Atomic Energy Commission
AEI	American Enterprise Institute
AFSC	American Friends Service Committee
AFSCME	American Federation of State, County, and Municipal Employees
ASCF	American Security Council Foundation
CALC	Clergy and Laity Concerned
CALS	Citizen Action for Lasting Security
CIA	Central Intelligence Agency
CND	Campaign for Nuclear Disarmament
CNN	Cable News Network
CPD	Committee on the Present Danger
DOJ	Department of Justice
END	European Nuclear Disarmament
FAS	Federation of American Scientists
FBI	Federal Bureau of Investigation
FCO	Foreign Commonwealth Office
FOR	Fellowship of Reconciliation
GE	General Electric
HFAC	House Foreign Affairs Committee
ICBM	intercontinental ballistic missile
IDDS	Institute for Defense and Disarmament Studies
IKV	Interchurch Peace Council (Interkerkelijk Vredesberaad)
INF	intermediate-range nuclear forces
MFS	Mobilization for Survival
MIRV	multiple independently targetable re-entry vehicle
MIT	Massachusetts Institute of Technology
MTV	Music Television

NAE	National Association of Evangelicals
NATO	North Atlantic Treaty Organization
NCCB	National Conference of Catholic Bishops
NPT	Nuclear Non-proliferation Treaty
NSC	National Security Council
NTS	Nevada Test Site
NVA	Non-Violent Action to Abolish Nuclear Weapons
NWFTF	Nuclear Weapons Facilities Task Force
PAC	political action committee
PSR	Physicians for Social Responsibility
PTBT	Partial Test Ban Treaty
RI	Rockwell International
SALT	Strategic Arms Limitation Talks
SANE	National Committee for a Sane Nuclear Policy
SDI	Strategic Defense Initiative
SDS	Students for a Democratic Society
SEC	Securities and Exchange Commission
SIPRI	Stockholm International Peace Research Institute
SLBM	submarine-launched ballistic missile
START	strategic arms reduction talks
TMI	Three Mile Island
UAW	United Auto Workers
UE	United Electrical
UN	United Nations
UNC	University of North Carolina
VFW	Veterans of Foreign Wars
VVA	Vietnam Veterans Association
WILPF	Women's International League for Peace and Freedom
WRL	War Resisters League

FREEZE!

Introduction

Grassroots Diplomacy

As the sun rose in New York City one brisk June day, it appeared to be just another morning in Ronald Reagan's America. Paul McCartney and Stevie Wonder sat atop the *Billboard* charts with their single "Ebony and Ivory," while Steven Spielberg's science fiction blockbuster *E.T.* was smashing box office records. In baseball, the New York Yankees were struggling to stay above .500 in the standings after a World Series appearance the year before, while in the world of boxing WBC heavyweight champion Larry Holmes had just defeated challenger Gerry Cooney in a bout with racially charged undertones. In the realm of politics, President Reagan struggled to stay even in the polls. Having survived an assassination attempt a year before, the president's poll numbers were now down 20 percent, with the country split evenly over his performance. Adding to the misery, the country remained in the grip of the worst economic downturn of the postwar period, with unemployment numbers nearly reaching double digits.

Yet, looming over it all was the threat of nuclear Armageddon. US-Soviet relations had deteriorated following the Soviet Union's invasion of Afghanistan in 1979. Reagan's subsequent election in 1980 brought with it a new cycle of nuclear fear and anxiety. Defense budgets soared to record highs as the new administration pushed for a modernization of nuclear forces, including the placement in Western Europe of the controversial Pershing II and cruise missiles (colloquially dubbed the Euromissiles)—intermediate-range nuclear forces

(INF) that many viewed as potential first-strike weapons. Fear of a nuclear confrontation with the Soviets was exacerbated by open and reckless talk among members of the administration about "limited" and "survivable" nuclear war.

On Saturday morning, June 12, 1982, more than one million people took to the streets of New York City, marching, chanting, and shouting. They came from across the United States and from around the world: from New York to Nebraska, from Japan to Australia. They came as representatives of various faiths: from Jews to Catholics, from Quakers to Buddhists. They spanned generations, with babies and toddlers mingling with teenagers, adults, and representatives from the Gray Panthers. They waved signs with messages such as "No Nukes!" and carried banners reading "FREEZE!" Starting from the plaza outside the United Nations (UN) Building, they marched through the streets of midtown Manhattan to a rally on the Great Lawn in Central Park. There were performances by popular acts; speeches by prominent activists, congressional allies, and religious figures; and appearances by the survivors of the atomic bombings of Hiroshima and Nagasaki (the *Hibakusha*) as well as President Reagan's rebellious daughter Patti Davis. The demonstrators came with a demand for the world's leaders: stop the madness and end the nuclear arms race.

Although the June 12 Disarmament March and Rally was organized by leaders across peace organizations, the massive turnout—the largest political demonstration in the nation's history—was due to support for the Nuclear Weapons Freeze Campaign. The Freeze campaign offered a modest and easy-to-understand solution to the arms race: a bilateral halt (or freeze) between the United States and the Soviet Union on the testing, production, and deployment of nuclear weapons. This "Call to Halt the Arms Race" would become the rallying cry of the largest peace movement in US history. Originating in discussions among arms control advocates and peace activists, the Freeze campaign emerged in Massachusetts and soon spread into small communities across the northeast. As the campaign grew nationally, questions about nuclear war became as morally controversial as abortion in Catholic circles. Popular evangelical preachers Billy Graham and Jerry Falwell feuded over it. The campaign drew support from prominent scientists, such as Carl Sagan, and influential statesmen, such as Averell Harriman, while receiving the endorsement of professional organizations of all stripes. In the popular and political culture, nothing short of the fate of the Earth was at stake. Over one hundred million viewers watched *The Day After*, a made-for-TV movie wherein the residents of Lawrence, Kansas, grappled with the cataclysmic effects of a nuclear exchange. Freeze debates dominated radio and television talk shows, as movie stars and celebrities, prominent intellectuals and scholars, bishops and reverends, and governors and congressional leaders lined up for and against the idea. In the US Congress, Republicans and Democrats debated a nuclear freeze resolution, with the House of Representatives endorsing it. Those at the highest levels of the Reagan administration privately conceded that the antinuclear backlash was potentially the most important national security challenge facing the administration.

The Freeze movement appeared to be an unstoppable force. It was poised to take control of Congress by the 1982 midterm elections, receiving bipartisan support in divisive times. Committed Cold Warriors, the Reagan administration rejected a nuclear freeze and even attempted to link the movement to the Soviet Union. The Freeze, however, resisted such easy labeling, in part because of its alliance with arguably its most important ally: the United States Conference of Catholic Bishops. The Catholic bishops represented a powerful voting bloc that could not be simply dismissed or maligned. Their intervention in the public dialogue by means of a pro-freeze pastoral letter left the Reagan administration with no choice but to treat the bishops—and, by extension, the Freeze movement—with respect. No longer would the administration dismiss or redbait the movement. Instead, it offered empathy over the fear of a nuclear war while peddling a solution in the Strategic Defense Initiative (SDI) that psychologically appealed to the desire to end the threat of nuclear war but in reality maintained support for military Keynesianism.

The nuclear question, however, remained an essential feature of public political dialogue. During fall 1983, US-Soviet relations hit their nadir, as misunderstandings and misinformation brought the world to the brink of nuclear war. Just days after millions watched *The Day After*, the Reagan administration went forward with the deployment of Euromissiles, over antinuclear opposition. As a result, the Soviet delegation promptly walked out of ongoing arms control talks in Geneva, leaving the administration without an arms control treaty heading into an election year. With opinion polls demonstrating the overwhelming fear of nuclear war alongside the popularity of a nuclear weapons freeze, Reagan's opponents in the Democratic Party primaries sought to exploit his lack of arms control progress while pledging their support for a freeze. The forthcoming 1984 election would be a pivotal moment for the burgeoning New Right, with the entire Reagan revolution resting on the president's reelection.

To blunt the Freeze movement and offset the lack of progress on arms control, Reagan reinvented his public image to become a champion of peace, nuclear abolition, and open dialogue with the Soviet Union—a reversal from the Cold Warrior persona he had exemplified for much of his political life. The Reagan administration was thus forced to co-opt the antinuclear message or continue to face a growing backlash with potential electoral repercussions.

With the election of the youthful Mikhail Gorbachev as general secretary in the Soviet Union in 1985, dire predictions that a second Reagan term would lead to a nuclear war proved unfounded. By 1988, with Reagan and Gorbachev strolling through Moscow's Red Square, the Cold War appeared over in all but name.

But just how and why the Cold War ended is a subject of much debate in historical scholarship. In the first instance, conservative intellectuals and former White House staffers have argued that Reagan's defense buildup and deployment of the Euromissiles ultimately drove the Soviet Union to the bargaining table. These get-tough policies, followers of the Reagan victory school aver, resulted in the elimination of an entire class of nuclear weapons, revolutions across Eastern Europe, and, eventually, the collapse of the Soviet Union itself.[1] Other scholars place the emphasis on the collapse of the Soviet Union and the end of the Cold War on the leadership and reforms of Gorbachev,[2] while, more recently, historians have attempted to bridge the two dominant narratives, crediting the reforms and leadership of both Reagan and Gorbachev.[3] But whether the end of the Cold War was a by-product of the diplomacy of Reagan, Gorbachev, or some combination of the two, these top-down narratives remain severed from the dynamic social forces that underpinned diplomacy.

Scholarship on the Freeze campaign can be split into two camps: those who argue that it effectively influenced the Reagan administration and those who see it as a passing fad with no significant achievements. Most accounts supporting an effective Freeze campaign, however, were written by participants themselves, and, with few exceptions, were published before the declassification of much archival material. In recent years, serious scholarship on the Freeze campaign—and the broader antinuclear campaigns of the period—has begun to reemerge. Nevertheless, the Freeze campaign remains vastly understudied and its influence on policy underappreciated.[4] This neglect is surprising but perhaps understandable: while the campaign garnered one million protesters in the streets of New York City in 1982, it appeared politically irrelevant by 1985. The campaign's meteoric rise followed by its sudden collapse has led to the dismissal of pro-Freeze scholarship, creating what J. Michael Hogan calls a "Great Freeze Myth: the notion that the American public suddenly 'awakened' from some historical stupor to overwhelmingly embrace the Freeze initiative, only to just as suddenly lose interest after 1984."[5] Moreover, even Noam Chomsky suggested that while the Freeze was "probably the most successful campaign ever carried out in the US peace movement," it had "essentially zero impact on American politics."[6]

But the Freeze movement was important, both for the outcome of the Cold War and within the history of the US left, and neither the Freeze nor the role of public opinion on national security matters should be so easily dismissed. Indeed, as historian Thomas Bailey observed, "An angered electorate is an awesome thing."[7] This work demonstrates the significant role the Freeze played in mobilizing society against the arms race and in shaping the political battlefield on which arms control diplomacy played out, creating political pressure on the Reagan administration to engage the Soviet Union both in arms control diplomacy and in dialogue to prevent nuclear war. From an examination of the archives of the Ronald Reagan Presidential Library, it becomes clear that the White House took the Freeze movement seriously—and so should historians.

This work reexamines the influence of the Freeze campaign across US society. It challenges traditional Cold War historiography while bridging the growing gap between the Freeze and the historiography of the Reagan presidency. In so doing, it forces historians to reconsider both traditional narratives surrounding the end of the Cold War and its periodization. This work uses the Freeze as a case study to demonstrate how public opinion shapes foreign policy, measuring its sway through the categories of religion, popular culture, and domestic politics. Moreover, it offers the first full treatment of the campaign from its roots following the Vietnam War through its merger with the Committee for a Sane Nuclear Policy (SANE). Although the Freeze appeared to lose politically in 1984, I conclude that the movement played an important role in shaping the peaceful outcome of the Cold War.

We think we know how the Cold War ended, but as this work demonstrates, it took more than just the willingness of Reagan to break with the hawks surrounding him and more than just the new thinking of Gorbachev to make the peaceful outcome possible. The diplomatic achievements that defined the end of the Cold War were a by-product not just of two giant personas of the era but of a discourse between the United States and the Soviet Union that was transformed by the direct pressures of antinuclear activism and public opinion. By decentering the narrative away from a top-down focus on the personalities of statesmen, we gain a better understanding of the political, social, and cultural forces that both underscored that diplomacy and made it possible.

The Influence of Peace Activism

Peace and antiwar activism have a long history in America. From Henry David Thoreau's refusal to pay a poll tax and his subsequent jail sentence protesting the Mexican-American War, to Eugene Debs and the conscription dissidents in World War I, to the demonstrations against the wars in Vietnam and Iraq, nearly every war the United States entered was accompanied by outbursts of dissent. Policymakers themselves, however, are often quick to dismiss public opinion and to deny any role antiwar and social protest movements has had on their decisions, even when they are secretly plotting to undermine these movements (as Richard Nixon did during the 1969 Vietnam War moratorium).[8]

But social movements matter. They manifest the voices of dissent and channel public anxiety. They generate awareness and raise issues that policymakers cannot ignore. Activists can furthermore hold considerable sway in the arena of public opinion and in domestic politics, where both their effectiveness and their victories can often be found. As sociologist David Meyer observes, social movements can "lastingly change political debates, governmental institutions and the wider culture"; they are "complex, veiled, and take far longer to manifest themselves than the news cycle that covers a single demonstration, or even a whole protest campaign."[9] By situating the Freeze campaign in the larger history of antinuclear activism and the Cold War, a pattern emerges: even the most sensitive national security issues are shaped by public opinion and domestic political considerations.

Opposition to nuclear weapons, however, has not always been in line with prevailing public attitudes. In the wake of the atomic bombing of Japan, poll numbers overwhelmingly supported the decision, with a notable 22 percent suggesting the United States should have dropped "many more" atomic bombs prior to the Japanese surrender. Likewise, less than 5 percent of Americans objected to the atomic bombings.[10] Those few who did composed two often-overlapping groups that historian Milton Katz calls "nuclear pacifists": one-worlders and atomic scientists. One-worlders believed the atomic bombings of Hiroshima and Nagasaki made an old idea for world government an "immediate, urgent necessity, unless civilization is determined on suicide."[11] Atomic scientists proved to be the most influential of the nuclear pacifists, with Chicago's Federation of Atomic Scientists claiming the support of 90 percent of scientists from the Manhattan Project. It would soon merge with the Federation of American Scientists (FAS), which continued to publish the Chicago organization's *Bulletin of the Atomic Scientists*. Plagued with guilt over having built the atomic bomb and over the subsequent arms race, FAS members felt the United States had "a peculiar responsibility," a "special duty": "We first used the bomb; we alone manufacture it." Moreover, "The bombs are marked 'Made in the USA.'"[12]

From the onset of the Cold War, FAS members were influential in the debate on atomic weapons. At the Moscow Conference in December 1945, Secretary of State James Byrnes and Soviet premier Joseph Stalin agreed to a proposed plan that would hand control over atomic weapons to the United

Nations. To prepare for the first meeting of the UN Atomic Energy Commission (AEC), Byrnes created a committee headed by then undersecretary of state Dean Acheson to draft the proposal. Alongside David Lilienthal (chairman of the Tennessee Valley Authority), Acheson would report his findings to the State Department by March. The *Report on the International Control of Atomic Energy* (or, colloquially, the "Acheson-Lilienthal report") sketched out "a scheme for world cooperation in the peaceful development of atomic energy," historian Paul Boyer observed. The plan proposed giving the UN AEC the authority to "survey and control all fissionable ore deposits on earth; license, construct, and monitor all national atomic energy facilities"; and give the agency "broad powers to detect any diversion of atomic resources to military purposes." The Acheson-Lilienthal report was warmly embraced by the atomic scientists, "for it seemed to give an official imprimatur to what they had been saying for months."[13] As historian Lawrence Wittner writes, "The Acheson-Lilienthal Plan represented the zenith of the movement's impact on public policy," and while the plan could not "prevent a nation from developing nuclear weapons if it were determined to do so," its provisions would "make the building of new ones difficult and dangerous."[14]

In June 1946, at the first meeting of the UN AEC, longtime presidential consultant and philanthropist Bernard Baruch warned that the world faced a choice between "the quick and the dead." Baruch was committed to the abolition of war but moreover distrusted the Soviet Union. Thus, while pledging the United States' commitment to world peace, Baruch usurped the Acheson-Lilienthal plan, modifying it in ways neither Acheson nor Lilienthal had envisioned. As the Baruch Plan outlined, the United States would not turn over its atomic weaponry until the UN survey of raw materials was complete and the plan for an inspection system could be fully implemented. Until that time, the United States would continue to build and test atomic weaponry. Distrusting the United Nations and the Western powers, the Soviets rejected the seemingly magnanimous offer, suggesting instead that the United States unilaterally destroy its nuclear weapons as "the first step towards nuclear disarmament." Secure in their nuclear monopoly, the United States rejected the Soviet counteroffer and "clung doggedly to the Baruch Plan, refusing to accept its modification."[15] Debate over the Baruch Plan would continue through 1948, but with the Soviets pursuing their own atomic arsenal and the United States accelerating its creation of atomic weapons, the debate became effectively moot.

Harry Truman's presidential victory in 1948 would fracture postwar liberalism, leaving establishment liberals to rally around Truman and the warfare state. With US intervention in Greece and Turkey, liberal Cold Warriors shunned pacifists and more radical elements of the Left. Meanwhile, the United

States continued to test atomic weapons in the Pacific. On March 5, 1954, the United States tested a massive thermonuclear device in the Bikini Atoll. Code-named Castle Bravo, it was the first test of a hydrogen bomb—the largest weapon the United States had ever tested and far more powerful than scientists had predicted. Radiation from the blast drifted for thousands of miles across the Pacific. Ninety miles downwind of the test, a Japanese fishing vessel, ironically named the *Lucky Dragon*, received a massive dose of radiation, showering the crew with white ash and contaminating the vessel's catch. In Japan, the *Lucky Dragon* incident galvanized an emerging antinuclear movement, as fear spread concerning lethally radioactive fish in Japanese markets. The aftermath of the Castle Bravo test furthermore coincided with the downfall of Joseph McCarthy, opening the door to criticism of postwar national security.

As nuclear testing shifted to the Nevada Proving Grounds, efforts to stop the United States and the Soviet Union from testing nuclear weapons united both nuclear pacifists and mainstream Cold War liberals. In July 1955, Albert Einstein joined Bertrand Russell and nine others in issuing a manifesto urging world leaders to put humanity first and find a peaceful resolution to the Cold War. In short order, the international community came out against nuclear testing, with criticisms emanating from the governments of India and Indonesia as well as from the Vatican, where Pope Pius XII called for the United States and the Soviet Union to agree to a treaty to stop testing nuclear weapons and, moreover, renounce their use. In the US presidential election of 1956, Democratic candidate Adlai Stevenson introduced the test ban as a campaign issue, bringing it "out of obscurity and into the forefront of public discussion."[16]

A debate was now open in American society over the health hazards posed by radioactive fallout—a debate that would last the next nine years. While the US government claimed fallout had little impact on human health, scientists from Washington University in St. Louis published the results of their study on the effects of fallout on human anatomy through the examination of baby teeth. Led by a team that included biology professor Barry Commoner, the baby tooth survey concluded that the element strontium-90 (Sr-90, a by-product of radioactive fallout) was contaminating milk supplies. This was particularly dangerous for children, whose bodies mistook Sr-90 for calcium, lodging the element in their bones, where it would "continually expose victims to internal radiation for years to come." Moreover, by the end of the decade, studies would conclude that the United States had the greatest concentration of Sr-90 anywhere on the planet.[17]

One of those alarmed by the results of the baby tooth survey was Norman Cousins. Cousins had been the editor of the *Saturday Review* since 1942 and was a prominent pacifist. In the wake of the atomic bombing of Hiroshima,

Cousins felt deep guilt and wrote a famous editorial, "The Modern Man Is Obsolete."[18] The Hiroshima bombing "marked the violent death of one stage in man's history and the beginnings of another," Cousins lamented. By 1957, Cousins was actively involved in discussions with leading pacifists to form a provisional committee of the American Friends Service Committee (AFSC) that would work to stop the testing of nuclear weapons in the atmosphere. Seeking a name, the committee found inspiration in the writings of psychoanalyst and German refugee Eric Fromm, who declared that the Cold War was overwhelming the "normal drive for survival" and that informed citizens must "bring the voice of sanity to the people."[19] The committee thus adopted the name SANE.

Although SANE was not originally intended to be a permanent membership committee, its membership soared following an advertisement in the *New York Times* opposing the atmospheric testing of atomic weapons. The committee separated from the AFSC, drawing membership from one-worlders, pacifists, and mainstream liberals alike. Hundreds of local SANE chapters sprang up across the country. SANE's campaign against atmospheric testing received endorsements and praise from mainstream social-political figures, such as Eleanor Roosevelt and Martin Luther King Jr.; leading physicists, such as Leo Szilard and Edward Teller; and Hollywood luminaries, such as Steve Allen and Marlon Brando. With SANE's rapid growth in membership, the debate over atmospheric nuclear testing came into the mainstream.[20]

Outside SANE, radical pacifists sought to move people "from opposition to action." At the Nevada Test Site (NTS), activists from Non-Violent Action to Abolish Nuclear Weapons (NVA) called for "unilateral disarmament and direct action against the bomb." On the twelfth anniversary of the bombing of Hiroshima, thirty-three NVA activists attempted to enter the NTS to halt the atomic bombings; they were arrested, tried, and released, receiving only probation. In February 1958, NVA peace activist Albert Bigelow attempted to sail his thirty-foot ketch *The Golden Rule* to the Marshall Islands to protest impending nuclear weapons tests. Bigelow and his crew, however, were quickly apprehended, tried, and convicted. While sentenced to probation, Bigelow and his crew decided once again to attempt the journey, only to be apprehended again and this time sent to prison following their conviction at trial. Bigelow's voyage, however, inspired others, such as Earle Reynolds, to attempt a similar protest. In April 1958, following the Soviet Union's announcement of a unilateral halt to atmospheric nuclear tests, SANE held its first protest rally, attracting marchers from across the New York City metro region and as far away as Philadelphia and New Haven, converging at UN Plaza. Two months later, the Eisenhower administration announced it, too, would suspend nuclear testing, and agreed to meet the Soviet Union in Geneva for a conference to begin negotiations on a test ban treaty. SANE soon expanded its cause to include nuclear disarmament.[21]

SANE shared a similar youth with the Freeze campaign of the 1980s, marked by rapid growth that jolted the public into action while also mobilizing Hollywood star power. And just like Freeze activists, SANE faced similar attacks about its alleged ties to communism. On the eve of a massive rally in New York City, Senator Thomas J. Dodd (D-CT)—a strong opponent of the test ban—demanded that SANE "purge their ranks ruthlessly of Communists." While SANE did not turn over its membership lists to the Senate, it did seek resignations. By caving in to pressure from Dodd, SANE lost significant membership numbers following resignations from prominent pacifists, such as A. J. Muste, and from youth organizations whose members joined the newly formed Students for a Democratic Society (SDS).[22]

While SANE wrestled internally over its communist dilemma, at the global level, test ban talks stalled following the downing of the U-2 spy plane in 1959. With Eisenhower reluctant to continue discussions of nuclear testing during the 1960 presidential campaign, the issue would fall to his successor, President John F. Kennedy. Although a committed Cold Warrior who campaigned on a fictitious missile gap, Kennedy's promise in his inaugural address to "begin anew the quest for peace" led to an optimistic view among SANE activists. Addressing the United Nations during his first year in office, Kennedy cautioned, "Every man, woman and child lives under a nuclear sword of Damocles, hanging by the slenderest of threads, capable of being cut at any moment by accident or miscalculation or by madness." With an ally in the White House, SANE would petition President Kennedy, alongside Soviet premier Nikita Khrushchev and British prime minister Harold Macmillan, to continue test ban negotiations. Likewise, SANE led demonstrations across major US cities, called for a "peace race" (a phrase President Kennedy would later borrow), and took leadership in pushing Congress to establish the Arms Control and Disarmament Agency (ACDA).[23]

International tensions from Berlin to Cuba, however, continued to thwart progress on a test ban while threatening to turn the Cold War hot. With tensions mounting, the Soviet Union resumed its testing of nuclear weapons in August; the United States would follow suit in September. In October, the Soviets tested the largest thermonuclear device ever made, the fifty-eight-megaton TSAR BOMBA. In the United States, more than fifty thousand women from more than one hundred communities walked out of their workplaces, forming Women Strike for Peace. In Boston, physicians determined to present the facts about Sr-90 and fallout formed Physicians for Social Responsibility (PSR).

In fall 1962, however, the world came just one word away from nuclear Armageddon. That October, reconnaissance photographs uncovered the construction of a launch pad in Cuba capable of firing nuclear missiles at nearly any place in the continental United States. As the Cuban Missile Crisis unfolded, SANE praised Kennedy for working through the UN but also urged the president to adhere to previous vows not to undertake military action. SANE held both sides accountable for the crisis but nevertheless sought to broker peace. SANE urged colleagues in Moscow to request that the Soviet leadership suspend arms shipments to Cuba while further requesting that the Kennedy administration both suspend the blockade of Cuba and close "American missile bases in Turkey in exchange for the dismantling of Soviet bases in Cuba." The crisis would end peacefully thirteen days after it began, with the Soviets agreeing to withdraw its missiles from Cuba and the Kennedy administration pledging not to invade.[24]

US-Soviet tensions eased following the crisis. By the end of 1962, however, the two powers remained stalled on test ban negotiations. On behalf of the Catholic Church, Norman Cousins would privately meet with Khrushchev to discuss issues of human rights and religion in the Soviet Union. Khrushchev, however, was familiar with Cousins's peace advocacy and had previously written to Cousins expressing his support for SANE's cause. Although the meeting only briefly touched on the stalled test ban negotiations, "at the very least," as historian Allen Pietroban writes, "the meeting helped break the ice." Following his meeting with Cousins, Khrushchev sent a lengthy letter to Kennedy "devoted entirely to the test ban issue." Khrushchev had "gone out on a limb" persuading members of the politburo to accept up to three inspections a year, but Kennedy's initial optimism over the letter quickly waned as he continued to insist on eight to ten inspections. After six years, the two sides remained aloof regarding a test ban agreement.[25]

Dismayed but still optimistic, Cousins set out to help obtain a test ban treaty. After a second visit to the Soviet Union in spring 1963, Cousins returned to explain to Kennedy Khrushchev's concerns over nuclear war and the internal needs for his "'peaceful coexistence' policy to bear fruit." With Khrushchev having expended all his political capital, it was up to Kennedy to take the next steps. Cousins met with Kennedy, laying out a "bold proposal" wherein the United States would call not for a total test ban but a six-month trial period. At the urging of Cousins, Kennedy would make a bold speech at a commencement address at American University. Based on a draft written by Cousins, with parts taken nearly verbatim, Kennedy spoke of "genuine peace" and a reexamination of American attitudes toward the Soviet Union and moreover the Cold War. Secretary of State Dean Rusk would soon meet with Khrushchev in Moscow to sign the Partial Test Ban Treaty (PTBT). Although the treaty did not stop testing completely (allowing nuclear tests to continue underground), it was a major step toward peace. While the treaty was the by-product of years of negotiations, as Pietroban observes, Cousins intervened at a pivotal moment, "helping to clear the air," supplementing through "a parallel track . . . what the negotiators . . . had been unable to achieve."[26]

From Armageddon to Quagmire

As the debate over the test ban treaty demonstrates, antinuclear activism and public pressure have held considerable sway over diplomacy, but in the years following the PTBT, a feeling of apathy over nuclear weapons enveloped the United States. With nuclear weapons testing driven underground, concerns over nuclear war largely faded into the background as the United States became entangled in Vietnam. But just as the atomic scientists influenced debates over nuclear weapons in the 1940s, and just as peace activists helped shape the PTBT, in the era of Vietnam and détente peace activists were central to policymaking.[27]

By 1968, the Vietnam War had become the most unpopular war in US history. Over the course of the 1960s, the energy of peace activism would merge with civil rights to form a broad antiwar coalition. Against this backdrop, the presidential race of 1968 lurched forward, forcing both major candidates to address questions over de-escalation and exit from Vietnam. Vice president and Democratic Party presidential nominee Hubert Humphrey told antiwar crowds that the United States could begin withdrawing from Vietnam toward the end of 1968. His opponent, Republican Party presidential nominee Richard Nixon, promised an "honorable end to the war in Vietnam." Nixon's statement, however, was deliberately vague. In reality, Nixon surreptitiously relayed a message to the South Vietnamese leadership that a better peace deal could be obtained under his administration. The Paris Peace Accords subsequently collapsed. With his electoral victory over Humphrey, Nixon would inherit the Vietnam quagmire.[28]

To co-opt the rising tide of peace activism and temper public opinion, President Nixon and his National Security Advisor, Henry Kissinger, would embrace arms control and détente with the Soviet Union. For Nixon and Kissinger, initiatives on arms control were not undertaken for their intrinsic value but were forced on them, as new advances in missile technology had the potential to send the arms race spiraling upward. Multiple independently targetable reentry vehicles (MIRVs) were the culmination of a decade of enhancements in missile technology. A MIRVed missile allowed multiple miniature warheads on a single missile, with each warhead capable of being fired separately and aimed at separate targets. This created several US advantages, including the potential for a first strike. In the event of a nuclear exchange, if the United States launched its missiles first, targeting Soviet missile silos, a first strike could destroy much of the Soviet arsenal, thus limiting or entirely negating a retaliation strike.

Proponents of MIRV argued for its necessity to counter another emerging controversial technology: the anti–ballistic missile (ABM) defense system. Since the Sputnik shock of 1957, the United States had been working simultaneously on miniaturizing warheads (culminating in MIRVs) and on developing ABM systems. Amid antiwar fervor, growing distrust of government, and concerns over US defense spending, ABMs came into the crosshairs of Congress, merging with antiwar activism. Anti-ABM scientists lobbied Congress and informed the public about what was often perceived as too technical an issue for the average person. An expanded ABM program, scientists warned, would escalate the arms race and further impart an illusion of safety from the threat of nuclear weapons. As the Nixon administration went forward with Sentinel ABM construction, "fear of 'bombs in the backyard'" led to a "massive public outcry."[29] From Chicago to Seattle, Los Angeles to Boston, and in every community building a Sentinel ABM, a diverse coalition of scientists, arms control advocates, peace activists, religious groups, and liberal political organizations mobilized against the system.[30]

The Strategic Arms Limitation Talks (SALT) commenced in Helsinki, Finland, in November 1969. Nixon's private recordings demonstrate that when it came to SALT, domestic politics and public perception were always at the front of his mind. Nixon routinely dismissed the arms control process, telling Kissinger, "I think it's basically what I'm placating the critics with."[31] Nixon further said the agreement "wasn't worth a damn" and called the negotiations "a bunch of shit," but with the pending "Vietnam War Out Now" rally producing headlines, he confessed, "We could use something like this at this time."[32] Nixon further believed any agreement would appease "peace-loving" Americans because "they think agreements solve everything." Therefore, if the administration could get an agreement for "political reasons," it could carry the "peace issue" in 1972 and thus "survive" the election.[33]

On May 26, 1972, Nixon and Soviet general secretary Leonid Brezhnev signed the Interim Agreement (SALT I) and the ABM Treaty in Moscow. The ABM Treaty limited both the United States and the Soviet Union to just two ABM deployments, one around the capital and the other to protect a missile field. Unlike the ABM agreement, however, SALT I was a treaty of finite duration. The five-year Interim Agreement froze US ICBMs at 1,054 and Soviet

ICBMs at 1,618. Under the agreement, the United States would be limited to forty-four nuclear submarines and 710 submarine-launched ballistic missiles (SLBMs), while the Soviets were limited to sixty-two nuclear submarines with 950 SLBMs. Although the agreements received criticism from hawks, the SALT agreement and the ABM Treaty passed the Senate overwhelmingly.[34]

With Nixon's reelection and the end of the Vietnam War, the peace movement faded into the background. Committed peace activists organized locally against individual weapon systems while calling for the peaceful conversion of the economy as a means of stopping the broader militarism that had caused the Vietnam War. Treaties such as the NPT (Nuclear Non-proliferation Treaty), SALT, and ABM appeared to place limits on nuclear weapons while surrounding arms control with a haze of acronyms and seemingly arcane technical jargon. Despite their flaws, these arms control agreements reflected the institutionalization of what international relations scholar Nina Tannenwald calls "the nuclear taboo": an acceptance that nuclear weapons were only for deterrence and not for use.[35]

But as the 1970s progressed, détente became a politically dirty word. While arms control seduced activists, major loopholes within the agreements, combined with the US political establishment's apathy toward constraining advances in missile technology, allowed neoconservatives to successfully midwife a new arms race. By the 1980 presidential election, the cracks in détente had become major fissures, exposing its crumbling façade. Amid a renewed threat of nuclear war, a new cycle of antinuclear activism would emerge. From the grassroots to the grasstops, it took the power and courage of ordinary individuals to band together and pressure world leaders to change the thinking on both sides.

CHAPTER 1

The Lost Years

The Peace Movement, from Vietnam to Nuclear Freeze

As the 1970s set in, disillusionment ran through former sixties radicals.[1] By the decade's end, many prominent activists from the Vietnam generation had moved on to new causes, while still others underwent radical political transformations. Jerry Rubin turned from Yippie antiwar activist to clean-cut yuppie capitalist, while fellow Yippie Abbie Hoffman went underground, changing his name and appearance to avoid a drug trafficking conviction. SDS's Tom Hayden would join with his new wife, Jane Fonda, in opposing nuclear power while working within the electoral system for change. SDS would essentially dissolve in 1969, while its more radical wing would form the Weather Underground, an organization that embraced "violent revolution" as a means to "bring the war home." But, like other antiwar organizations, following the US disengagement from Vietnam, the Weather Underground dissipated, having no issue to hold it together. Former Black Panther leaders Eldridge Cleaver and Huey Newton split over the necessity of armed struggle as a response to the FBI's COINTEL program, with Cleaver finding evangelical Christianity (later Mormonism) while transforming politically into a conservative Republican. Important alternative periodicals, such as *Liberation*, *New Times*, and *Ramparts*, all met their demise, with *Ramparts* coeditor David Horowitz later coming out in support of Ronald Reagan.

With the fervor over ABMs subsiding and the sterilizing effect of détente on Cold War tensions, fear over nuclear war gave way to more imminent concerns about the safety of nuclear power and the state of the economy. Indeed, for the post-Vietnam left, new causes were front and center, from gay rights to second-wave feminism and the push for an equal rights amendment to the constitution. The budding environmental movement of the 1960s expanded in the 1970s with the emergence of new activist environmental organizations such as Greenpeace, Friends of the Earth, and the Natural Resources Defense Council, among others. These larger environmental organizations allied with local movements such as the Clamshell Alliance and the Abalone Alliance to fight nuclear power.

The end of American involvement in Vietnam did not, however, mean an end to empire or military Keynesianism. Indeed, historian William Appleman Williams observed four "mundane" traits of the relationship between militarism and the federal budget in the years following Vietnam: (1) 50 percent of those employed as scientists or engineers were engaged in military work; (2) an additional 53 percent of every tax dollar paid for "past, present, and anticipated military operations"; (3) federal budget expenditures provided 418 dollars per person for the military but only two hundred dollars per person for health care and a measly thirty-two dollars per person for education; (4) and the federal budget did not fund "even one person whose primary responsibility is to think about stopping and reversing the arms race."[2]

Unlike other, more visible elements of the US left, the peace movement faced an uncertain future. As David Cortright reflected, by 1974 "you could hardly find the peace movement. Once the United States had withdrawn from Indochina, there was little or nothing going on in the peace community."[3] Cortright, a Vietnam War veteran and activist within the GI movement, became the executive director of SANE in fall 1977, inheriting a shrunken staff, record-low membership, and an organization with debt upward of fifty thousand dollars. Although membership in peace organizations declined following Vietnam, several older peace organizations continued to function, including the American Friends Service Committee (AFSC), Clergy and Laity Concerned (CALC), Fellowship of Reconciliation (FOR), the Women's International League for Peace and Freedom (WILPF), the War Resisters League (WRL), and Women Strike for Peace.[4]

In 1977, labor leader and political activist Sidney Lens would publish *The Day before Dooms Day* as a warning about the possibility of nuclear warfare. Alongside several prominent peace activists, Lens cofounded a new organization, Mobilization for Survival (MFS). Loosely modeled on the defunct National Mobilization Committee to End the War in Vietnam, MFS featured 280 affiliated groups alongside forty national organizations and sought to unite both the environmental and peace wings of the antinuclear movement under

FIGURE 1.   David Cortright was executive director of SANE (the Committee for a Sane Nuclear Policy) from 1977 to 1987. When SANE merged with the Nuclear Weapons Freeze Campaign to become "SANE/Freeze: Campaign for Global Security," Cortright stayed on as codirector. Cortright worked closely with Randall Forsberg and the Nuclear Freeze Strategy Committee. He played an active role in the broader antinuclear and peace movement of the 1980s. Courtesy of the family of Ray Pinkson, SANE, Inc. Records, Swarthmore College Peace Collection.

one umbrella. MFS's mission, as Lens proclaimed, was to "put back on the agenda what had been lost in the Vietnam years: an awareness of the threat of nuclear holocaust."[5] In an era where the New Right was taking center stage, peace activists pushed back on the escalating arms race while making the question of war and peace central to US politics. Thus, in these lost years, activists sought to launch a peace conversion campaign as the answer to US militarism, for which Vietnam was only a symptom. Amid conflicting activist goals and agendas, it would take a new idea from an outsider to unite peace activists.

Peace Conversion and the B-1

As the war in Vietnam raged at home and abroad, the Pentagon quietly planned for the modernization of its existing nuclear forces. At the center of this proposed modernization was the B-1 bomber. Unlike the active but aging B-52, the proposed B-1 would be smaller, sleeker, and faster, "carrying twice as many nuclear weapons."[6] It would boost America's defenses while strengthening its position in arms control negotiations with the Soviets. The production of the B-1 came during a period of rising unemployment, economic downturn, and defense budget cuts. With the aerospace industry ailing, Nixon's election in 1968 brought hope of a financial windfall to companies such as Boeing, Grumman, Lockheed, and General Dynamics (among other defense industry titans). The B-1 contracts had the potential to more than offset losses these companies faced in the commercial airline downturn of the period, putting them in the black for years to come. The Nixon administration, however, awarded the contract to a heavy contributor to its 1968 campaign, Rockwell International (RI).

The plane and the Rockwell contract were not without controversy. Within the defense community, experts questioned whether a new bomber needed to be as technically complicated as the B-1. Within the US Congress, Representative John Seiberling (D-OH) and Senator George McGovern (D-SD) fought the B-1 in its early stages, concluding in a 1970 study that the B-52 still served the nation's "strategic deterrent bomber role." Inside the Nixon administration, Richard Stubbing of the Office of Management and Budget sought to stop production of the B-1, gaining support from National Security Council (NSC) staff, analysts within the Pentagon, and the White House Office of Science and Technology, all of which shared a desire to see the bomber canceled because of fears of rising costs and technical inefficiency. For a short period, even Nixon seemed on the fence over the program. Ultimately, the decision to build the B-1 hinged on domestic politics; its production would bring thousands of jobs and millions of dollars to California—a state Nixon thought crucial to his reelection chances in 1972.[7]

Despite the peace agreement in Vietnam, the manufacture of the B-1 continued. Fears of rising costs and delays in production proved clairvoyant. As journalist Nick Kotz writes, "After three years of development, the estimated cost of each bomber had risen from $27 million to $50 million." Those who sought to strip the "goldplated bomber" or the "Supersonic Swingwing Swindle" (as critics dubbed the B-1) of its excesses won few concessions, while still other dissenting voices were threatened with the termination of career advancement. With Nixon's resignation following the Watergate scandal, Gerald Ford's new administration would inherit a program with a total price tag that now exceeded nineteen billion dollars, with rising costs, projected at one hundred million dollars per plane. The bomber was thus a leading example of the "revolving door between the Pentagon and private corporations" that was creating both a "permanent war economy" and "corporate influence over national security policy," as peace activist Pam Solo observed.[8]

In the wake of the Vietnam War, peace activists mobilized around the concept of peace conversion of the economy. The 1.3 trillion dollars the United States had spent on the military since 1945 had transformed the nation's economic system into what peace activists called a "planned warfare economy," with "frightening concentrations of power in the Pentagon, White House and multi-national corporations."[9] The continued funding of this warfare state would only lead to future Vietnams. Support for such levels of militarism, activists argued, meant higher taxes; inflation; less money for education, the environment, health care, and mass transportation; and a dearth of resources to address problems plaguing inner-city America. Peace conversion, however, meant the creation of a stable economy that supported "peoples' needs." Peace conversion meant fewer jobs in defense and more jobs for civilians, ending the giant profits made from war and militarism, supporting human liberation abroad, and ending aid to dictators and privileges for multinational corporations. In short, peace conversion sought a "better society and a more peaceful world."[10]

As progress toward the B-1 rollout continued, grassroots opposition fomented, beginning in the New England chapter of the AFSC. To make peace conversion a reality, Massachusetts AFSC activist Peter Barrer envisioned a national campaign that would target a weapon system built by a corporation that produced both commercial and military parts, making the company subject to a consumer boycott. B-1 parts were manufactured by General Electric (GE), so the bomber was the perfect target. In Barrer's vision, the campaign would block production of the B-1, "educate consumers about GE's role in the military-industrial complex," "recapture the spirit of the antiwar movement," and "advance the idea of peace conversion." At an AFSC meeting in Germantown, Ohio, activists from AFSC and CALC initiated a campaign against the bomber. The campaign's name, "Stop the B-1 Bomber / National Peace Conversion Campaign," was to reflect both the short-term goal of defeating production of the bomber and the long-term goal of establishing an alternative to the US war economy and the power structure that maintained it. A campaign headed by both CALC and AFSC would combine "hundreds of the most experienced Vietnam protest organizers." With fifty chapters between them, spread out across the country, AFSC and CALC believed they "had the resources to make the bomber a major issue" across the nation while simultaneously reigniting and rallying the antiwar movement to a new cause.[11]

The Stop the B-1 Bomber / National Peace Conversion Campaign was organized by numerous peace activists of various generations. These included Fay Honey Knopp (AFSC), a Quaker peace activist who could trace her affiliation with the Society of Friends to a peace rally in 1939; Mary Adams, a feminist dating back to the 1930s and a lifelong political and social activist; Marita Heller, a nun who was a full-time coordinator for Nebraskans for Peace; George Lakey (AFSC), a veteran of the civil rights movement, who, as a protest against the Vietnam War, sailed a Quaker peace ship into a war zone to deliver medicines for suffering Vietnamese; Richard Boardman, cochair of CALC, who spent eighteen months in prison as a conscientious objector and draft resister to the Vietnam War; and Terry Provance, an ordained minister with the United Church of Christ and AFSC activist, who worked "nonstop" against the Vietnam War between 1969 and 1973 while also serving on the

Harrisburg Defense Committee and working alongside Daniel Ellsberg on the Pentagon Papers. In December 1973, Provance was named by the AFSC Peace Education and B-1 staff as the coordinator of the National B-1 Campaign.[12]

Between 1974 and 1976, peace activists formed a sophisticated grassroots campaign, organizing activities around the rollout of the B-1, the first flight, and Tax Day, with emphasis on the financial constraints of building the B-1 on state budgets. A three-part campaign slideshow would focus on national security, military corporation production and profits, and peace conversion; likewise, a three-part radio series would cover the same topics. In Cincinnati, Ohio, activists planned a conversion conference in October and a vigil at the Wright-Patterson Air Force Base, while an activist in San Francisco worked on a poster for the rollout campaign. To build enthusiasm, activists planned on one hundred vigils nationwide. As Provance recalled, "The B-1 was a good image because people remembered the carpet bombings of the B-52 and it could sustain peace movement work while doing education on corporate power." Although the campaign was scheduled to last for one to two years, it lasted four.[13]

To "expose and challenge" the role of corporations in the production of the B-1, the campaign actively sought to engage its major manufacturers. Campaign activists sent letters to RI and GE requesting an audience. Whereas Rockwell proposed various meeting dates, GE denied all requests. When activists submitted two proxy resolutions for GE to take up at their shareholder meeting in Chicago in 1974, GE rejected them, claiming they did not conform to the standards required by the Securities and Exchange Commission (SEC). An appeal to the SEC, however, overturned GE's decision. Over fifty activists from CALC and AFSC attended the shareholder meeting, while activists leafleted and picketed outside, with some holding a gold-painted model B-1 bomber that caught the attention of the press and shareholders. Inside, as activists attempted to introduce the resolution, they were met with boos and hisses. Although the resolutions received two-and-a-half million votes, with a total of 145 million votes, it amounted to less than 2 percent of the total vote. Activists nevertheless considered it a victory, given how heavily skewed proxy procedures were in management's favor. The resolutions and the direct actions further succeeded in drawing the attention of the press, both the local television stations and newspapers as well as the national press.[14]

Shareholder actions, however, had little value at the national level and were mostly successful only in the regions where defense contractors held their meetings. While actions at shareholder meetings would remain part of local campaign strategies, the joint council of the national coalition against the B-1 decided to embrace labor as "the primary constituency for work around corporations." This meant targeting employees of RI, GE, and Boeing while also appealing to those former employees who had been laid off. The campaign made alliances with major labor unions. The international vice president of United Electrical (UE) pledged the union's support "to help stop the B-1 bomber, and to spend for people, not for war." Jerry Wurf, president of the American Federation of State, County, and Municipal Employees (AFSCME), lent his support to the campaign. Wurf linked the costs of bomber production to the destruction of public needs across the country, calling into question a paradox at the heart of military Keynesianism: "What good is it to be able to destroy Moscow ten times over if our own cities die in the meantime?"[15]

While the more radical UE lent its support for the campaign, the United Auto Workers (UAW) disappointed peace activists. UAW local 887 spokesman Tom Whalen defended the need for the B-1 as a "deterrent weapon." In Washington, D.C., representatives from the UAW joined Rockwell in lobbying Congress for its continued development. Dissident local 887 rank-and-file activists alleged that UAW leaders made a "sweetheart" deal with RI, ensuring that inevitable layoffs would mean employees with seniority would not "bump" equally skilled employees of lesser seniority who worked on the company's line of executive jets. Furthermore, the dissidents charged that UAW's contract with RI froze wages at the 1973 level through October 1977, allowing RI to pay new employees $1.30 less per hour than they were entitled to. This pay gap meant rank-and-file workers subsidized the B-1, saving Rockwell over fifteen million dollars per year. Despite UAW's cozy relationship with RI, both union leaders and rank-and-file activists expressed desires for peace conversion, but with corporations more interested in "violence and death," as one rank-and-file member suggested, peace conversion took a back seat to the continued subsidization of the warfare state.[16]

Beyond labor unions, the campaign created further alliances with a broad array of nonprofits. The Coalition for Human Needs would initiate forums to discuss budget priorities, while the Washington Environmental Action Group agreed to study the environmental consequences of the B-1. Peace organizations were a natural constituency. While AFSC and CALC led the coalition, the Stop the B-1 campaign also received support from the War Resisters League (an older, secular, pacifist organization), Common Cause (a civics organization formed in 1970 that pledged to make B-1 opposition "a major grassroots effort") and the National Action/Research on the Military-Industrial Complex (a younger AFSC project aimed at exposing the impact of the military-industrial complex on the US and the World). Arms control advocates and defense watchdogs lent their support, with the Center for Defense Information dedicating an issue of its quarterly publication *The Defense Monitor* to urge cancellation of the bomber. Although the older antinuclear organization SANE did not prioritize opposition to the B-1, members were kept informed about the campaign through news releases and legislative updates and were further urged to send letters opposing the bomber to Congress. The coalition also included religious organizations (such as the Catholic Peace Fellowship), as well as the National Taxpayers Union, which opposed the B-1 on the grounds of fiscal responsibility.[17]

Peace activists forged a unique coalition representing a cross section of influential interest groups while further aligning with sympathetic members of Congress. The coalition began work on a congressional strategy early, with an eye toward key votes. Among its activities, the coalition developed an anti–B-1 citizen lobby, organized at the district level to target key swing districts and districts of committee members, initiated a letter writing campaign, and testified before key committees and hearings, while urging members of Congress to vote against all B-1 appropriations. The campaign worked with Senator McGovern's office to defeat B-1 legislation, while Representative Les Aspin (D-WI) sought special hearings for the B-1 to give activists the chance to speak out against the bomber. The campaign formed an alliance with the bipartisan Congress Members for Peace through Law, while dozens of members of congress and their aides helped the coalition strategize and organize within Congress.[18]

On April 8, 1976, the House voted on the annual military appropriations bill. It was the first chance to gather the sense of Congress on the military spending on and commitment to building the bomber. Representative Seiberling introduced an amendment to delay production funds for the B-1 until February 1977, but facing what activists described as "a well-planned and coordinated Administration propaganda-extravaganza," the amendment was defeated by a narrow vote. Nevertheless, activists felt good about having created "a huge wave of public sentiment against the B-1 program" three months sooner than expected.[19]

Following the loss in the House in April 1976, activists proposed a shift in campaign strategies to emphasize direct action, or "bringing the war home." At its board meeting that month, the coalition agreed to a limited number of specific direct-action proposals of varying militancy to "deliver a clear public message" that the money GE, RI, and Boeing were making off the B-1 was "coming out of *our* pockets and *our* services." The new plans were not considered a fundamental shift in strategy but relied on local actions targeting RI and GE offices, Air Force bases, congressional offices, the FBI, and the Pentagon. Members of the coalition further desired to expand the message and not limit it to "stop the B-1."[20]

The Stop the B-1 campaign continued its work at the national level while local campaigns implored direct-action tactics. In Los Angeles, B-1 opponents occupied the office of Senator Alan Cranston (D-CA). Although Cranston was an opponent of the Vietnam War and one of the more progressive voices both in the Senate and within the Democratic Party, he supported production of the B-1 because it would bring jobs to California. As Cranston was flying to Los Angeles to meet with activists and others about the B-1, another group of activists occupied his San Francisco office to hold a peace vigil. In Pittsburgh, sixteen activists occupied the national offices of RI. In Boston, activists leafleted RI workers while working through local churches to bring in allies from the black community. In Knoxville and Memphis, activists also organized in black churches while pressuring Congressman Harold Ford Sr. (D-TN). In Ohio, activists leafleted a luncheon talk by Defense Secretary Donald Rumsfeld, handing out bomb-shaped flyers reading, "Let them eat bombs." In congressional offices in Arkansas, Louisiana, and Texas, however, activists were bluntly told to "go to hell!," leading campaign organizers to describe opponents as "Rednecks with a capital 'R!'"[21]

At their fourth annual meeting, activists extended the Stop the B-1 campaign through 1977. Although the campaign was committed to focusing on the B-1 through the 1976 election and up to the release of the military budget, the campaign would also broaden its focus to include other defense weapons and the expansion of military bases. Over the next six to eight months, the campaign would focus on the theme of "Peace, Jobs, and Human Needs." Activists articulated long-range goals, such as terminating military programs and cutting defense spending, while planning for "human needs spending and production in military facilities" and ensuring job security for employees of military plants. Finally, the campaign wanted to ensure that as the peace conversion plan was implemented, local communities would retain the tax dollars to use them to "meet their human needs." Transitioning from the B-1 campaign to a long-term goal of combating militarism presented a host of difficulties, with some activists fearing the dissolution of the coalition. In the interim, however, with a presidential election just over the horizon, the campaign sought to persuade the candidates on the B-1 and peace conversion.[22]

Carter and Arms Control

On the campaign trail in 1976, AFSC activists in Iowa pressured Democratic presidential candidate Jimmy Carter to take a stance on the B-1 bomber. Carter knew little about the bomber but openly criticized it as "an example of a proposed system which should not be funded" and a waste of taxpayer dollars. Carter furthermore proclaimed that "all nations should reduce atomic weapons to zero." Likewise, activists followed the other Democratic candidates on the campaign trail, even forcing defense hardliner Senator Henry Jackson (D-WA) into expressing reservations on the effectiveness of the B-1.[23]

Although Carter represented the centrist wing of the Democratic Party, his eventual election victory over President Ford brought with it a new sense of hope among peace activists. As David Cortright reflected, "There was . . . a feeling on the public mind of less concern about the nuclear threat" and "a sense that the bad, nasty people—Nixon and company—were out, and that there was, perhaps, a new period of more openness and decency in government that we might look forward to. And, at least with Carter's election, it appeared that that was what was happening." Peace activists continued to pressure Carter over campaign promises for a nuclear-free world. Following the election, activists staged demonstrations against the B-1 and held vigils in two hundred cities, including outside the Carter family home in Plains, Georgia. SANE vowed to "watch" Carter. On Inauguration Day, members of SANE greeted him with a twelve-foot banner reading "Zero nuclear weapons." The White House was soon flooded with "telephone calls, letters, and appeals, including an anti-B1 petition signed by twenty-nine mayors."[24]

The influence of peace activists on the Carter campaign was felt early on. Carter appointed several prominent critics of the Vietnam War to his cabinet while offering a full pardon to thousands of Americans who had evaded the war's draft. Carter raised hopes for arms control and renewed détente, advocating for a "quick freeze" on the production of warheads, missiles, throw weights, and for "qualitative weapons improvement." Following such a freeze, Carter envisioned a series of "step-by-step mutual reductions," culminating in a world with zero nuclear weapons.[25]

But if Carter was to make good on pledges to curtail the arms race, improved US-Soviet relations were not just important but necessary. Less than a week after his inauguration, Carter wrote a letter to Soviet general secretary Brezhnev expressing his desire to improve relations and "avoid a new armaments race." Carter's NSC began work on a detailed study of arms control issues for SALT II and what he hoped would be SALT III. Carter filled his cabinet with arms control advocates. As secretary of state, Carter appointed Cyrus Vance, a proponent of global détente, who told *Newsweek* in December 1976 that there was nothing more important than "getting SALT out of the doldrums." As national security advisor, Carter appointed Zbigniew Brzezinski, who favored SALT I as an "important step forward," criticized the force levels agreed to at Vladivostok as "too high," and felt very strongly about low-

FIGURE 2. On Inauguration Day, January 20, 1977, President Jimmy Carter and First Lady Rosalynn Carter walked from the swearing-in ceremony at the Capitol Building over to the White House. Along the route, Carter was greeted by activists from SANE who held a twelve-foot banner reading "SANE SUPPORTS ZERO NUCLEAR WEAPONS." Courtesy of SANE Inc. Records, Swarthmore College Peace Collection.

ering nuclear stockpiles on both sides. Though Vance and Brzezinski would later become rivals with contradictory opinions, at the outset of the Carter administration, they both supported further efforts on arms control. Incoming secretary of defense Harold Brown had a mixed record on arms control but was a member of the SALT delegation and, like Brzezinski, urged deeper cuts to both the Soviet and US arsenals. As UN ambassador, Carter selected Congressman Andrew Young (D-GA). A former aide to Martin Luther King Jr., Young opposed the war in Vietnam and was the cochairman of SANE.[26]

Perhaps most symbolic of Carter's commitment to arms control, however, was the appointment of Paul Warnke to head both ACDA and the SALT II delegation. Warnke's time as assistant secretary of defense in the Johnson administration was marked by his opposition to the Vietnam War and his support for arms control. In 1975, Warnke had argued in *Foreign Policy* magazine that the United States and Soviet Union were "apes on a treadmill." Warnke believed that negotiating from strength was preposterous and proposed instead that the United States could be "the first off the treadmill . . . the only victory the arms race has to offer." Warnke, however, was a controversial appointment, facing fierce opposition from members of the recently revived hawkish Committee on the Present Danger (CPD). As SANE reflected, the drama over the Warnke nomination would be "a test, not of a person, but a philosophy of arms control." Tensions over Warnke's nomination began even before the hearings started, when an anonymous memo quoted Warnke extensively to paint him as an advocate for unilateral disarmament and as someone who did not understand the threat from the Soviet Union. As the memo circulated inside the Beltway, Senator Jackson called for additional hearings for Warnke to explain his views. A coalition of conservatives and defense hawks formed the Emergency Coalition against Unilateral Disarmament, flooding the Senate with an estimated one million letters in opposition to Warnke.[27]

Over the course of two days, Warnke underwent grueling cross-examination by the Senate Armed Services Committee, where he was attacked for past statements that appeared "dovish" toward the Soviets. A typographical error that left out a comma before the word "which" from a prior statement to the Senate touched off Commagate. Senator S. I. Hayakawa (R-CA), a former professor of English, jumped on the deleted comma as evidence of Warnke's duplicity and vowed not to vote for him. Prestigious career diplomat and CPD chairman Paul Nitze testified that Warnke's views were "absolutely asinine . . . screwball, arbitrary, and fictitious" and even suggested he might be a better American than Warnke. One member of Congress accused Warnke of colluding with the World Peace Council (a Moscow organization that advocated Western disarmament). Under assault, Warnke modified his views somewhat, telling the Senate Foreign Relations Committee that he would not advise "parallel restraint" amid negotiations. When asked about Carter's goals for zero nuclear weapons, Warnke explained that the idea was "so far from current reality as to be in the realm of prayer."[28]

Although the Warnke nomination proved a hostile and bitter battle, the Senate voted seventy to twenty-nine to approve his appointment to ACDA. Warnke's appointment to lead the SALT delegation, however, was much closer (fifty-eight to forty). The two vote tallies, as SANE noted, were evidence that the campaign against Warnke focused on his role as head of the SALT delegation over fear that as chief negotiator he could "give everything away to the Soviets." But amid the assault on Warnke and arms control, SANE remained optimistic: "For the first time in 14 years there is a chance to move in the right direction. We have to grab that chance."[29]

With the war over Warnke behind them, the Carter administration moved quickly to reach agreement on a SALT II Treaty. Carter sought to move the stalled SALT talks forward with what SANE described as "that most elusive of proposals—an actual arms reduction." The two options proposed went further in their cuts than what Brezhnev had agreed to at Vladivostok and what he had suggested the two sides agree on both publicly and in a series of letter exchanges. To reach Carter's proposed larger cuts, Brezhnev insisted on reaching an agreement on the unfinished business from Vladivostok. Although the Soviets took umbrage at President Carter's very public handling of the negotiations, what ultimately sank the proposals was not Carter's style but their very substance. Under proposal A, both sides would make significant cuts to their ICBM forces—the very foundation of Soviet nuclear defenses. Furthermore, the United States offered no cuts to the cruise missile, a small but portable, fast, and accurate missile that raised alarms for arms controllers *and* the Soviets because of the difficulty in detecting it via satellites. Under proposal B, the two sides would agree to the terms of Vladivostok but exempt the Soviet Backfire bomber and the US cruise missile. The Soviets rejected both proposed agreements as "worthless and one-sided" and concluded that "Carter was not serious." Far from creating the unity he hoped for, Carter sowed the seeds of division. The one-sided proposals received blessings from arms control opponents such as Henry Jackson, but when Carter's initial proposal failed and he returned to a less ambitious SALT II approach, Jackson and others treated him as an enemy for his alleged retreat. The "bruising Warnke nomination fight obviously left its scars," observed SANE.[30]

With arms control talks still stalled, Carter continued to face pressure from antinuclear activists. Women Strike for Peace marched on the White House, believing "nothing had changed."[31] On May 18, 1977, President Carter wrote representatives from CALC, promising a decision on the production of the B-1 that summer. CALC activists, however, believed this was Carter's way of "'fudging' the decision until it's too late—until it can be argued that to stop full production would be to waste the billions already invested." With the B-1 costing taxpayers three million dollars every day, CALC activists promised supporters that they would make one last "big push" against the bomber. Activists opposing the B-1 flooded the White House with calls and inundated it with letters. The B-1 was "such a hot issue," observed peace activist Jeanne Kaylor, that the White House could not "keep up in correspondence with phone callers and letter writers protesting the bomber."[32]

On a muggy and rainy June day in D.C., over two hundred B-1 opponents from fifteen states gathered in front of the White House to ask President Carter to decide against its production. Activists held placards, read the "B-1 Liturgy," and called on the president to "Honor your word. Stop the B-1 NOW!" From morning to early afternoon, activists remained in good spirits, chanting, marching, and singing, while others leafleted and spoke to passersby. After hours of discussion and a break, a core group of activists felt the conviction to use civil disobedience tactics at a sit-in in front of the White House. Organized by Provance, activists marched up the White House driveway, carrying signs and statements, blocking Secretary of State Vance's limousine in the process and forcing him to enter around the back. In all, eighteen activists (including Provance) were arrested; while half paid a fifty-dollar collateral fee, the other half were sent to the federal district court. The following day, prosecutors dropped all charges, after concluding that the arrestees were part of the larger protest, which had previously obtained a permit for their demonstration. CALC concluded from the incident that "Carter does not want the media focusing on the growing opposition to the B-1." B-1 opponents left the demonstration feeling "exhilarated" and "boosted by a sense of common purpose."[33]

On June 30, 1977, Carter made what he called "one of the most difficult decisions" of his presidency. Citing its cost and lack of strategic necessity, Carter canceled the B-1. Carter's stunning decision was met with "loud cheers and rebel yells" that "bellowed through the White House West Wing offices and hallways." Carter's closest aides celebrated the decision, believing he was keeping a campaign promise. Senator McGovern praised it as Carter's "finest hour." Activists printed t-shirts reading "WE stopped the B-1." But not everyone was happy with the cancellation. Gerry Whipple of the UAW called the decision "a betrayal of the workers." The termination of the B-1 would eliminate the positions of ten thousand employees at RI. The campaign to stop the B-1, however, created an important bridge from the Vietnam antiwar movement to the antinuclear campaigns to come. As Provance reflected, "It gave an agenda to peace organizing and led into antinuclear weapons work."[34]

An Uneasy Coalition

Although the peace movement found short-term success against the B-1, there was no guarantee that the broader peace conversion campaign could continue to find victories. As Pam Solo noted, "Not every community was home to a major B-1 contractor." Born and raised in a devout Catholic household in Denver, Solo became a nun in the order of the Sisters of Loreto. By her mid-twenties, she had taken part in social justice activities and protested the war in Vietnam, but by the mid-1970s she had turned her attention toward the nuclear arms race. In 1974, as a staff member at the Denver AFSC, she co-organized the Rocky Flats Action Group, whose goal was to close the Rocky Flats nuclear weapons production facility just outside Denver while "putting

disarmament and peace conversion on the public agenda." The group succeeded in pressuring the Colorado political establishment to appoint a citizens' committee to directly oversee the facility—the first such committee in
the nation. As Len Ackland writes, the Rocky Flats Action Group became "a
unique marriage between environmental and peace activism," blending "en-
vironmentalism's popular appeal and focus on changing policy with peace activism's community-organizing skills and campaigning experience."[35]

Based on the success of the Rocky Flats campaign, a national coalition was
formed to bring coherence and vision to the burgeoning antinuclear movement. By mid-1977, veteran peace activists had joined with labor activist and
author Sidney Lens to found a new antinuclear and peace organization, the
Mobilization for Survival (MFS). It was designed around four slogans: Zero
Nuclear Weapons, Ban Nuclear Power, Stop the Arms Race, and Fund Human
Needs. In 1977 alone, it sponsored over one hundred gatherings in commem-
oration of the atomic bombings of Hiroshima and Nagasaki and coordinated
over two hundred teach-ins across the country. MFS attracted prominent speakers from the peace and environmental movements, including pediatrician
Benjamin Spock, ecologist Barry Commoner, antiwar Catholic priest Philip
Berrigan, and Daniel Ellsberg, the former Pentagon war planner who became
a household name after he leaked the Pentagon Papers in 1971. By its first national conference in December, MFS claimed 330 affiliates, reflecting broad-
based national and regional representation, as well as sister movements from
Japan and Western Europe. MFS further played the central role in organizing
demonstrations outside the UN Special Session on Disarmament in May 1978,
attracting over twenty-five thousand people.[36]

The merger between peace and environmental activists, however, was "not
a welcome initiative," as Solo observes. Environmentalists "mistrusted the
peace groups and felt that the success of campaigns focused on commercial
nuclear power would only be set back by any link to nuclear weapons." Environmental activists thus sought to avoid any mention of nuclear weapons or
the Soviet Union. The uneasy coalition erupted into "ferocious struggles." At
the national level, peace and environmental organizations sparred over the differences between nuclear power and nuclear weapons, while local antinuclear activists saw them as two heads of the atomic hydra. These local activists
proposed a political action satisfactory to both peace activists and environmentalists: a national demonstration. On April 29 and 30, 1978, thousands demonstrated at a commercial nuclear power plant in Barnwell, South Carolina,
and at the Rocky Flats nuclear weapons facility.[37]

The success of the demonstrations raised the profile of the movement and
led to another joint effort between AFSC and FOR: the Nuclear Weapons

Facilities Task Force (NWFTF). NWFTF was a critical stepping-stone on the way to the creation of the national Nuclear Weapons Freeze Campaign. It relied on Pam Solo (AFSC) and Mike Jendrzejczyk (FOR) as facilitators for their respective organizations and was chaired by Steve Ladd (WRL). In the years to come, Solo and Jendrzejczyk would play important roles in the national Nuclear Weapons Freeze Campaign, while Ladd would form the Northern California chapter of the Freeze campaign, serve on the national and executive committees, and become the national cochair of the Freeze campaign from July 1984 to September 1986. While the NWFTF was affiliated with MFS during its first year, like other members of the MFS coalition it would soon branch out on its own, acting as a national source for activists to share information, tactics, and national publicity. Its New Left ethos of acting locally to stop global threats helped it circumvent turf wars and "bureaucratic inertia." By creating local networks across the nation, NWFTF helped lay the groundwork for the expansion of the Freeze campaign in the coming decade.[38]

Although the new peace movement defeated the B-1, its cancellation opened the door for new weapons projects, including the cruise missile and the Trident submarine. By the late 1970s, Trident basing sites became a battleground, pitting peace activists against the military-industrial complex. On May 22, 1978, approximately four thousand protesters marched on the naval base in Bangor, Washington. While nearly three hundred antinuclear activists from the Live without Trident organization were arrested for scaling the fence, they vowed to return. In April 1979, the Trident Conversion Campaign and the Clamshell Alliance jointly protested the launching of the Trident in Shoreham, New York. Two months later, fifteen thousand people protested the Shoreham Nuclear Power Plant. In fall 1979, actions against the Trident took place across the nation. Activists once again scaled the fence in Bangor, while four activists in Groton, Connecticut, attempted to climb the roof of the General Dynamics Electric Boat Division's south guardhouse and replace a sign reading "Defense Plant" with a wooden plaque reading "Death Plant." That same day, actions against the Trident took place in St. Louis, Missouri; Detroit, Michigan; Pittsburgh, Pennsylvania; and Kings Bay, Georgia (selected in May 1979 as the preferred East Coast basing site for the *Ohio*-class submarine).[39]

While regional peace and antinuclear campaigns flourished in the mid- to late 1970s, perhaps the largest of the peace campaigns besides the B-1 revolved around the basing of the ten-warhead mobile MX ICBM. Approved for full development in 1979, the MX basing plan called for massive slow-moving trucks to transport the MX between four thousand new concrete shelters along a racetrack in the deserts of Utah and Nevada. The objective of this shell game was to leave the Soviets guessing as to where the missile was at any precise moment, thus eliminating the possibility of a Soviet first strike on the US ICBM force.

By summer 1979, however, opposition to the MX had soared in Utah and Nevada. Fear reigned among the populace, as residents worried about becoming the targets in a nuclear war and over the possibility of a derailment causing a nuclear accident. Politicians in Utah and Nevada recognized the sway the court of public opinion held. In Utah, Frances Farley, the first female state senator in twenty years, left her meeting with the US Air Force feeling "physically ill" and determined to stop the MX. In Nevada, State Senator Rick Blakemore, a Democrat in whose district most of the Nevada MX installations would be based, raised issues of privacy and the death of small-town community. Utah governor Scott Matheson (a Democrat) and Nevada governor Robert List (a Republican) created a bistate management committee to share information and concerns about the MX project. After the office of Governor Matheson was flooded with letters opposing the MX, he came out against its basing in Utah and later called his initial support a source of "embarrassment." Facing reelection in 1980, Senators Paul Laxalt (R-NV) and Jake Garn (R-UT) treaded precariously over the issue. In light of public opinion, Laxalt transformed himself from "a wrathful hawk to an ardent Nevada environmentalist." Laxalt and Garn, prominent Senate hawks, soon became the Senate's leading opponents of Carter's MX basing plan.[40]

The environmental wing of the "No Nukes" movement received its most dramatic spark when the reactor core overheated at the Three Mile Island (TMI) nuclear power plant near Harrisburg, Pennsylvania, in March 1979. Pregnant women, infants, and toddlers within twenty miles were urged to evacuate, while all those within ten miles of the plant were told to stay indoors. The nation stood on edge for a week, fearing a total meltdown. In the wake of the TMI accident, "No more Harrisburgs!" became a rallying cry. Hundreds of protests were held around the world, with many connecting nuclear power with nuclear weapons. Peace activists from CALC jammed the White House phone lines, requesting an emergency shutdown of all operating nuclear reactors, a moratorium on building new nuclear plants and nuclear weapons, job security for nuclear employees, and the rapid development of safe energy.[41]

From California to New Hampshire, opposition to nuclear power bloomed while boosting membership in both SANE and the newly revived Physicians for Social Responsibility (PSR). Initially formed in 1961, PSR sought to address the mounting threat of nuclear war between the United States and the Soviet Union, and its medical consequences. While PSR helped mobilize popular opinion against the aboveground nuclear tests and spoke out against the Vietnam War, by 1973 the organization had been largely disbanded.[42]

Its revival was largely due to its new president, a fiery young Australian pediatrician named Helen Caldicott. Caldicott was an activist in Australia, where she was involved in campaigns to stop the French nuclear tests as well as campaigns to stop uranium mining. Practicing medicine in Boston in the 1970s, Caldicott sought to organize a campaign against nuclear power, viewing it as a "medical problem." Since PSR was still incorporated in Massachusetts, it was easier to use the existing PSR incorporation than to establish a new one. With PSR revived, Caldicott published *Nuclear Madness* in 1978, boosting the stateside antinuclear power movement. In an act of serendipity, PSR published an advertisement in the *New England Journal of Medicine* one day after the TMI incident, garnering it five hundred new members. Caldicott soon traveled to Harrisburg to educate the residents on how nuclear reactors work; to her surprise, she found herself educating the medical community on the dangers the radioactive isotopes posed to the nearby food supply. In the months and years to come, Caldicott would traverse the nation, giving lectures, speaking at churches of various faiths, and warning of the dangers of both nuclear power and the arms race. As a result of Caldicott's efforts, PSR attracted over twenty thousand new members while spurring the formation of other professional antinuclear organizations.[43]

Three Mile Island brought new attention to concerns over nuclear power, but the peace wing of the antinuclear movement still suffered from a lack of a cohesive message. "We lacked a narrative framework that would engage our audience," noted MFS activist Patricia McCullough, adding "we struggled for the message that would indeed 'mobilize' people to resist an arms race that was literally threatening 'survival.'" Furthermore, despite growing attention to the antinuclear cause in general, activists from the broader peace and environmental movements did not have the political or financial clout of their hawkish counterparts. While MFS would continue as a separate peace organization, as Solo observed, "there was, in fact, nothing to naturally keep [MFS] together—no political program, no set of demands." Although religious peace organizations and others promoted a nuclear moratorium, it was not specific enough to "ignite and inspire those who wanted to take action, who wanted more than a symbolic statement." Thus, by spring 1979, an "unspoken consensus" had emerged within the peace movement: to go further, they would need coordination and "a policy proposal with some teeth to it."[44]

In 1979, the Boston Study Group, comprised of military analysts and scientists, published *The Price of Defense*, a study that questioned the values of the arms race while calling for a 40 percent reduction in military spending. Among the six coauthors of the study was an arms control advocate named Randall Forsberg. A middle-aged divorced mother, she self-identified as a "different kind of arms control advocate." After receiving her bachelor's degree in English at Barnard College, she became a teacher of English literature, but she grew wary, believing there were subjects more relevant to the world. In 1968, Forsberg married a young Swede and moved with him to Switzerland. Although having participated in two demonstrations against the Vietnam War, she considered herself "apolitical," but even in Sweden, she could not escape America's war in Vietnam, as deserters soon arrived, riveting the Swedish public with the conflict. Seeking to make a contribution to world peace, the Swedish government created the Stockholm International Peace Research Institute (SIPRI). Because SIPRI wanted an international staff, Forsberg was hired as a typist. In typing statistical material for SIPRI, Forsberg became "amazed by the enormous amounts of money spent in peacetime on arms and the military by industrial nations." Even more shocking was her discovery that the United States and the Soviet Union "were not serious about arms control negotiations," pointing to their failure to compromise over onsite inspections during the 1963 nuclear test ban negotiations. "We probably wouldn't have an arms race today if they had hammered through an agreement then," Forsberg later told the *Boston Globe*. Forsberg would spend seven years at SIPRI, discovering her passion for educating others about the arms race while advancing from typist to editor, researcher, and, finally, writer. By 1974, Forsberg had left SIPRI for graduate work in arms control and security studies at MIT.[45]

Forsberg was "very intelligent" and "very influential," as Caldicott remembered. Since Caldicott did not know as much about nuclear weapons as she did about nuclear power, she was shocked to find out from Forsberg that "nuclear war could happen in half an hour." An astonished Caldicott reflected, "My eyeballs fell out. I had no idea." But whereas Caldicott was a dynamic speaker, Forsberg was no fiery orator or even, as she confessed, a sharp dresser. Forsberg, however, regularly spoke to peace organizations such as the AFSC and CALC. What she found were organizations scattered in their goals and demands, with some even advocating unilateral disarmament if it would prevent a nuclear war. To unify the various peace organizations, Forsberg focused her talks around a single goal that would enable peace activists to "have the more powerful public outreach and would represent an acceptable kind of medium between their most modest goals and their most ambitious goals."[46]

In December 1979, Forsberg accepted an invitation from MFS to speak at their second annual meeting, held in Louisville, Kentucky, at the University of Louisville. With an estimated 200 to 250 peace activists gathered, Forsberg spoke not on stopping the conventional arms trade, as she was asked to do, but on stopping the nuclear arms race. In the wake of the Vietnam War, peace organizations were advocating for a unilateral moratorium on nuclear weapons

FIGURE 3. Randall ("Randy") Forsberg drafted the "Call to Halt the Arms Race." In simple language, the proposal called on the United States and the Soviet Union to bilaterally halt (or "freeze") the testing, production, and deployment of nuclear weapons. This "Call" became the founding document of the Nuclear Weapons Freeze Campaign. Courtesy of Rick Reinhard.

production. Forsberg urged the groups to instead make the moratorium bilateral, for then "the great majority of the American people would completely agree with you, and you could change the world." Forsberg's talk lasted only ten minutes, but the idea resonated with audience members such as Patricia McCullough who called the response "electric" with attendees "talking about how much sense Randy's proposal made." Following Forsberg's talk, representatives from AFSC, FOR, and CALC, enthusiastically embraced the idea of a bilateral moratorium and approached Forsberg to draft such a statement. Forsberg's talk became, as MFS national secretary Reverend Bob Moore recollected, "the primary impetus for the launch of the Nuclear Weapons Freeze Campaign." Forsberg would soon take a hiatus from her doctoral studies at MIT to found the Institute for Defense and Disarmament Studies (IDDS).[47]

In April 1980, after months of drafts and revisions, Forsberg and IDDS, with the support of AFSC, FOR, and CALC, jointly published the "Call to Halt the Nuclear Arms Race." The four-page proposal suggested in plain language that the United States and Soviet Union simply "stop the arms race" and instead "adopt a mutual freeze on the testing, production, and deployment of nuclear weapons and . . . missiles and new aircraft designed primarily to deliver nuclear weapons." The proposal identified the security and economic benefits of a freeze, in addition to detailing its scope and verifiability. It could be started unilaterally by the United States or the Soviet Union, with either side taking steps to "demonstrate its good faith, start movement in the right direction, and make it easier for the other country to take a similar step."[48]

The idea was at once both conservative and radical: conservative in that it did not ask either side to make major cuts to its arsenal; radical in that, if implemented, it would stop the deployment, testing, and production of nuclear weapons—a billion-dollar industry. The idea furthermore was far outside the mainstream political discussion. Unlike many other nuclear freeze proposals made over the years, Forsberg's freeze was intended not just as an arms control proposal but also as "the centerpiece of a protest movement." As Solo observed, peace groups flocked to Forsberg's freeze proposal because "they saw its potential as a policy proposal and as a grassroots organizing vehicle."[49]

In 1980, the idea of a nuclear freeze was not new. Debate over freezing weapons can be traced back at least as early as 1922, when the United States, Great Britain, and Japan agreed to cut their battleship forces in half and negotiated a ten-year freeze on the construction of new battleships. The Johnson administration proposed a freeze on building nuclear weapons at a time when the United States held a considerable advantage over the Soviet Union. (The Soviets, naturally, rejected the offer.) During the SALT I negotiations, lead negotiator Gerard Smith privately advised President Nixon to propose a "Stop

Where We Are" plan that would freeze the arms race in place at a position of parity. (Nixon ignored the proposal.) During the debate over SALT II, Senator Mark Hatfield (R-OR) introduced an amendment offering a mutual US-Soviet freeze on strategic weapons deployment. Hatfield's freeze amendment, however, died with the withdrawal of SALT II from the Senate. In the Spring 1979 issue of *Foreign Affairs*, activist-scholar Richard Barnet outlined a "freeze on new strategic systems" as a step toward "a significant demilitarization of the U.S.-Soviet competition and to a demonstrably safer world." President Carter would later claim that he, too, had proposed a mutual nuclear weapons freeze to the Soviet Union during the SALT II negotiations.[50] Likewise, in 1977, a group of over twelve thousand prominent professionals and Nobel laureates signed onto a "Declaration on the Nuclear Arms Race," which recommended that the United States unilaterally stop the testing of nuclear weapons and the deployment of "*new* strategic nuclear weapons, nuclear weapons systems, and missile defense systems for 2 to 3 years," provided the Soviet Union did likewise. (The declaration was signed by many who would endorse the Freeze campaign during the 1980s.)[51]

While one potential nuclear freeze idea circulated within the arms control and foreign policy community, peace activists also began thinking about a bilateral moratorium. In fall 1979, a peace delegation traveled to the Soviet Union to meet with the Soviet SALT II negotiators. Represented by Terry Provance, Helen Caldicott, Reverend William Sloane Coffin, and Pam Solo, the delegation urged the Soviets to accept a moratorium on the production, testing, and deployment of new nuclear weapons "with or without the ratification of SALT II." Although the Soviets expressed interest, as Solo recollected, their "interest needed to be tested, their seriousness challenged." The peace delegation therefore returned to the United States prepared to lobby the government and raise public awareness for a bilateral nuclear weapons freeze.[52]

The following spring, peace activists formed the Ad Hoc Task Force for a Nuclear Weapons Freeze to build what would become the Nuclear Weapons Freeze Campaign. To create visibility for the campaign, they distributed thousands of copies of the "Call" while seeking endorsements from scientists, arms control advocates, politicians, and others who could both raise awareness and add credibility to the emerging campaign. Peace organizations such as CALC and FOR formally endorsed the idea at their national conferences in 1980, as did the AFSC board. At a special meeting of the National Council of Churches in April 1980, the freeze proposal received "a very positive reception . . . as a basic approach for disarmament issues."[53] Surprisingly, the one constituency the campaign had difficulty gaining the support of were liberal arms control advocates. Herbert Scoville (Arms Control Association), Jeremy Stone (Federation of

American Scientists), and Eugene LaRocque (Center for Defense Information) all initially declined to endorse a nuclear weapons freeze, citing its broadness, comprehensiveness, and problems of verification, among other objections.[54]

By summer 1980, CALC had mobilized activists on the "interrelated issues of the nuclear menace, the arms race and human needs." As CALC unified its base around opposition to nuclear energy and nuclear weapons and in support of peace conversion and a bilateral nuclear freeze, MFS undertook a new initiative: Survival Summer. Modeled after the 1964 Freedom Summer organized by the civil rights movement and the Summer of 1967 organized by the Vietnam antiwar movement, Survival Summer would be chaired by former CALC national director Reverend Richard Fernandez. CALC would soon embrace the initiative, making it the primary focus of its "Human Security Program." During summer 1980, volunteers canvassed door-to-door, led teach-ins, organized community group presentations and neighborhood forums, and participated in local political dialogue, while CALC worked to mobilize congregations and church groups to "reach a much broader segment of the religious community than [they had] before." Survival Summer sought to challenge candidates for national office on the arms race and gather endorsements for a "new comprehensive proposal for a nuclear weapons freeze." CALC urged its members to study Forsberg's "Call." Thus, on the eve of the fall 1980 presidential campaign, peace activists sought to make opposition to the arms race and the new Cold War a defining issue.[55]

Peace and Presidential Campaigns

By the end of Carter's second year in office, the rightward drift of the administration was becoming increasingly evident. The attacks on Paul Warnke never let up, and in fall 1978 he resigned as head of ACDA and the SALT II negotiating team. To aid the passage of SALT II, Carter appointed Army lieutenant general George Seignious to ACDA. Seignious, however, was a member of the Coalition for Peace through Strength, which openly opposed SALT II and arms control. As SANE noted, Seignious retained his membership in the organization until *after* he was offered the ACDA position. To sidestep, Seignious wrote a letter to John Fisher, president of the American Security Council and a mover within the coalition, blasting the coalition's views on SALT II and arms control as "distorted and untrue." But the letter had the opposite effect, uniting both SANE and neoconservatives against his nomination.

Testifying before the Senate Foreign Relations Committee, SANE executive director David Cortright urged Seignious's rejection, calling the appointment "an improper choice" while questioning Seignious's "judgment and independence of thought." Cortright made a blistering assault on ACDA, claiming that the agency had "reneged on its promise and betrayed its original mandate" and was no longer a serious arms control body. With the Pentagon employing millions in the "business of war" and with the arms race spiraling "recklessly out of control," Cortright charged that no one from the agency or the government took seriously the responsibility of reversing the arms race: "Ought not the ACDA provide at least some opposite balance and live up to its original mandate as an agency for peace—an advocate of arms reduction?" Despite opposition, Seignious was confirmed by the Senate in a far less controversial vote than Warnke's had been.[56]

After much delay, Carter and Brezhnev finally signed the SALT II Treaty at an anticlimactic ceremony on June 19, 1979. Under the two-year protocol period, both parties were prohibited from testing or deploying mobile ICBMs while further placing restrictions on the range of deployed cruise missiles. The treaty furthermore placed sublimits on the arsenals of both parties and placed ceilings on MIRVed ICBMs and SLBMs, and heavy bombers equipped with long-range cruise missiles. Among other provisions, the treaty allowed both sides to deploy one new type of missile.[57] The treaty was subsequently sent to the Senate with the hope of ratification, but by fall 1979, détente was on life support.

In early December, the Carter administration approved a plan to place a new generation of nuclear weapons in Europe. The decision was a response to the Soviet Union's SS-20 (a mobile intermediate-range missile with three MIRVed warheads). Although the SS-20 was accepted in its initial deployment in 1976 as simply an upgrade from its predecessors, as Cold War tensions ratcheted up, the SS-20 came to symbolize the Soviets' intent on military dominance. In reaction to this, NATO offered immediate negotiations to the Warsaw Pact to ban intermediate-and medium-range missiles from Europe completely. If these negotiations failed, the United States would deploy Pershing II and ground-launched cruise missiles in Western Europe to assure mutual destruction. The offer became known as the dual-track decision. While it assured some NATO governments of a US commitment to their defense, the decision frightened many Europeans. The decision furthermore enraged the Soviets. The Pershing II was not just an upgrade but rather an entirely new system, which had been under development since the late 1960s, well before SS-20s were even conceived. The Soviets viewed the Pershing II as a first-strike weapon because of its pinpoint accuracy, high yield, and range of up to two thousand miles. From Europe, the Pershing II could penetrate the Soviet Union within four to six minutes, destroying command and control centers before Soviet radar and satellites even noticed a strategic launch from the United States.[58]

The final blow to détente came on Christmas Eve, 1979, when the Soviet Union invaded neighboring Afghanistan to save the Marxist government that was under increasing pressure from the mujahedeen (a CIA-financed Islamic jihadist rebellion). Though the Soviets had considered intervening in Afghanistan the prior March, members of the politburo recognized that such actions would be disastrous for détente and arms control and spur international opposition. But recent commotions over Soviet troops in Cuba alongside NATO's dual-track decision "tipped the scales in favor of intervention," as historian Vladislav Zubok writes.[59]

The Soviet invasion of Afghanistan created major ripples in US politics. Among the first casualties of the Soviet invasion was the SALT II Treaty. Facing certain defeat in the Senate, Carter withdrew it from consideration. Carter further canceled a wheat deal intended to ease Cold War tensions. An ultimatum soon followed, demanding that the Soviets withdraw from Afghanistan within one month or face a US-led boycott of the 1980 Summer Olympic Games in Moscow. In July, Carter signed one of the most controversial documents of the Cold War: Presidential Directive 59 (PD-59). If deterrence failed and a nuclear conflict occurred, PD-59 called for the United States to be "capable of fighting successfully," preventing an adversary from "achieving his war aims," and ensuring the enemy would "suffer costs that are unacceptable." The doctrine changed the nuclear targeting strategy, placing less emphasis on all-out retaliation against cities and greater emphasis on limited strikes aimed at military forces as well as political and military command centers. Designed to give the president flexibility beyond massive retaliation, PD-59 was in essence a blueprint for fighting and winning a nuclear war.[60]

Although PD-59 was classified, parts leaked to the press almost immediately. The *New York Times* reported that the Carter administration envisioned "fighting a prolonged nuclear war, lasting weeks, even months." In the Soviet Union, *Pravda* called the new doctrine "a prescription . . . for stimulating the arms race." SANE denounced PD-59 as "completely bankrupt, morally obscene and completely unrealistic." The Federation of American Scientists suggested the doctrine would "make nuclear war itself more likely; make it more difficult to prevent nuclear wars once begun; and make the arms race more difficult to stop." There was nothing accidental about the leak of PD-59. With the Republican Party formally nominating Ronald Reagan while simultaneously rejecting the concept of MAD, leaking parts of PD-59 could counter Reagan's attacks and create an image of President Carter as a strong Cold War Democrat.[61]

In recognition of deteriorating US-Soviet relations, the hands of the Doomsday Clock of the *Bulletin of the Atomic Scientists* moved forward two minutes to read seven minutes to midnight, the closest the hands had been to midnight in over a decade. In a message to the membership of SANE, Cortright ominously warned, "We are closer to war now than at any time in recent history." From Soviet actions in Afghanistan to the withdrawal of SALT II and the subsequent escalation of the arms race, it was clear that the era of détente was dead. In its wake lay a more dangerous world and a renewed Cold War.[62]

Against this backdrop, foreign policy, nuclear diplomacy, and the larger question of war and peace would all become central components of the 1980 presidential election. In the Democratic primary, President Carter faced a bitter fight with Senator Edward "Ted" Kennedy (D-MA), but it was foreign events from Afghanistan to Iran that shaped its outcome. Following the Iran hostage crisis, public approval for increased defense spending jumped from 27 percent to 46 percent, while President Carter enjoyed a rally-round-the-flag popularity boost. Although Kennedy would continue a bitter nomination fight through the summer and into the Democratic convention, with less than half the delegates of Carter, it was a lost cause.[63] The highlight of the convention, however, was Carter's acceptance speech. Carter hit Reagan and the Republicans hard on the question of war and peace. Whereas Carter claimed he was restoring military strength, he charged that Reagan and the Republicans would go too far and "launch an all-out nuclear arms race." By abandoning arms control treaties such as SALT II, Carter charged, Reagan and the Republicans offered a "radical and irresponsible course" that would "threaten our security—and put the whole world at peril."[64]

Although Reagan surged in the polls following the Republican convention, Carter was quickly catching him. The Reagan campaign watched the issue of war and peace with great care. The campaign polled voters, asking, "Which of the two candidates would be most likely to get us into war?" As Reagan pollster Richard Wirthlin observed, "Reagan ranked considerably higher on that dimension than did Carter." To counter Carter's claim that he was the candidate of peace, the Reagan campaign sought to dramatize the perceived loss of US power and prestige since Carter's election, all while avoiding "anything that would heighten the already fairly strong perception that Reagan was not only more aggressive in foreign affairs and the development of strong defense but also would be more likely than Carter to get us into war."[65]

While the Reagan strategists recognized the importance of the war and peace question, the Carter team saw it as the defining issue of the 1980 election. Carter aides believed that if the question of war and peace remained the central focus of the campaign, "the guy [Reagan] loses big." At a town hall meeting in Independence, Missouri, Carter suggested Reagan would "start a massive nuclear arms race" that could lead to war with the Soviet Union. By contrast, Carter emphasized his belief in "peace . . . arms control . . . controlling nuclear weapons." In a speech to the AFL-CIO, President Carter would frame the election as one that "will determine whether we have peace or war."[66]

If Carter was simply trying to frighten voters, the Reagan campaign gave him plenty of ammunition. On the campaign trail, Reagan advocated abandoning SALT II in favor of an arms race, the "one card that's been missing in these [SALT II] negotiations." Vice presidential candidate George H. W. Bush criticized Carter for not deploying the B-1 bomber or the MX quickly enough, but he, too, would come under fire for comments about survivable nuclear war. At a campaign stop at a hog farm in Iowa, the Des Moines chapter of MFS greeted Bush with a large white banner with bright blue text reading, "Iowa's Farms Won't Survive a Nuclear War." Bush climbed onto the back of a pickup truck, gestured toward the sign, and told the activists he could not help but "empathize," but the activists soon confronted Bush and demanded to know how to survive nuclear war. The question was in reference to an interview Bush gave to the *Los Angeles Times* in January. When pressed on whether a nuclear buildup was overkill, Bush responded, "Yes if you believe there is no such winner in a nuclear exchange . . . [but] I don't believe that." On the hog farm in Iowa, Bush denied the remarks, but when activists pushed him to answer whether nuclear war was survivable, Bush could only muster a befuddled reply: "Well, if—ah—I hope that we won't ever have to have one."[67]

By October 14, Carter had moved ahead of Reagan in the polls. For the sake of the election, Reagan's campaign advisers muted him. The campaign deliberately toned down the rhetoric; when candidate Reagan returned to the spotlight, he began stressing his abhorrence of war. Even that, however, failed to change perceptions. A frustrated campaign staffer complained, "We are getting bombed on the 'war monger issue' and all we are doing to counter it, so far as I can see, is use the word 'peace' in ever more improbable contexts and speeches." But Carter's framing of the election as a choice between war and peace obscured the fact that there really was no peace candidate among the major candidates. Although independent nominee Congressman John Anderson (R-IL) supported SALT II, he still advocated placement of the Euromissiles and backed the neutron bomb. While Anderson criticized the MX, he voted to fund it in 1979 and further supported higher defense spending. The only candidates thoroughly opposed to the arms race and militarism were minor third-party candidates. While there were significant differences in the Republican and Democratic platforms, on the question of war and peace, voters may as well have been voting for "Jimmy Reagan or Ronald Carter," as Coleman McCarthy observed.[68]

Despite the dearth of peace candidates, the 1980 election remained, as the *New York Times* editorialized, a "political war over peace," with the main candidates dancing around the "question of questions": "whether a president knows how to advance American interests without war." In the only debate between Carter and Reagan, Carter attempted, but failed, to portray Reagan as "a threat to peace." When the discussion turned to arms control, Carter insisted it was the most important issue of the campaign—largely because his thirteen-year-old daughter Amy told him so. In contrast to the warmonger image, Reagan appeared "reasonable and commanding."[69]

That November, Reagan won an overwhelming number of votes in the Electoral College, turning a close contest into a landslide. Reagan's victory, alongside the Republican takeover of the Senate, created the impression of "a national consensus in favor of defense expenditure, and a much firmer military posture," as Eugene Rostow boasted.[70] But pointing to Reagan's victory as a basis for a mandate or a new national consensus neglects the actual political strategies Reagan used to win. During the 1980 campaign, Reagan stopped talking about war and peace and focused instead on the economy and jobs. To change his warmonger image, Reagan used his wry sense of humor. By late October, with polls showing he was losing women voters who viewed him as too hawkish, Reagan announced that as president he would "immediately open negotiations on a SALT III Treaty" and would seek reductions to the nuclear arsenals.[71]

While Carter lost the election to Reagan, the central tenet of his campaign—war and peace—struck a chord with American society at large. In September 1980, the famous antiwar Catholic priests Philip and Daniel Berrigan, alongside six others, broke into the General Electric plant in King of Prussia, Pennsylvania, seeking to significantly damage the MX's Mark 12A reentry vehicle. The "Plowshares Eight" managed to evade the lax security, sprinkle fake blood on security documents, and hammer nuclear warhead cones.[72] A group of scientists and physicists warned the public that nuclear war "was not inevitable, but that it is highly likely and becoming more so." Helen Caldicott stressed the possibility of a nuclear war within the next decade. Opinion polls in 1980 suggested most Americans feared a nuclear war. In Nevada, over two-thirds voted against deployment of the MX, while all three members of Congress who served on SANE's board of directors won reelection.[73]

The most serious challenge to the emerging new Cold War, however, took place in western Massachusetts. Paralleling, but not linked to, Forsberg's "Call" was a similar campaign that would place the idea of a mutual nuclear weapons freeze on the ballot in Massachusetts, led in part by Randy Kehler, a member of the WRL and a conscientious objector who served twenty-two months in prison for noncooperation during the Vietnam War. Kehler's concerns over the arms race led him to leave his job as a high school teacher to help found and direct the Traprock Peace Center in Deerfield, Massachusetts. Kehler soon learned of the success of the peace organization Sojourners in getting Senator Hatfield to sponsor a proposed nuclear freeze amendment to the SALT II Treaty. But after the treaty's withdrawal from the Senate, Kehler and the Traprock Center concluded that the best way to mobilize public support for a nuclear moratorium was a ballot referendum.[74]

With the support of peace, church, community, and labor activists, Kehler organized a campaign to place a nuclear freeze referendum on the ballot. Over the next nine months, with the aid of activists, Kehler collected over twelve thousand signatures to put the issue on the ballot in three districts, covering four counties. The ballot referendum ("Question 7") asked voters to instruct their state senator to vote in favor of a resolution requesting that the president "propose to the Soviet Union a mutual nuclear weapons moratorium, immediately halting the testing, production, and deployment of all nuclear warheads, missiles and delivery systems, and requesting congress to transfer the funds that would have been used for those purposes to civilian use."

Ballot supporters, however, were worried that the referendum would not pass. In a traditionally conservative, Republican-voting region, the western Massachusetts ballot already contained antitax measures alongside the presidential options. To succeed, the campaign would rely greatly on volunteers and resource donations. Approximately three hundred volunteers handed out sixty thousand "Yes on 7" flyers, while paid advertisements appeared on eleven radio stations and three television stations. The campaign's main source of income came from the approximately 125 individuals who donated a total of fifteen thousand dollars. It further benefited from the owner of an advertising company who donated space on seven large billboards urging citizens to "Vote for a Mutual Nuclear Weapons Moratorium." Daniel Ellsberg undertook a speaking tour of western Massachusetts in support of the referendum, while campaign volunteers circulated sign-up sheets and recruited hundreds of new volunteers.[75]

As a result of their efforts, Question 7 passed with 59 percent of the vote in three districts. Moreover, the initiative passed in thirty of the thirty-three communities in which Reagan was victorious. The Massachusetts results were the first victory of the emerging Freeze campaign and further evidence that the 1980 election was not a triumph for a resurgent Cold War so much as it was a rejection of Jimmy Carter.

CHAPTER 2

Igniting a Movement

The Reagan Administration's War on Peace

At the dawn of the 1980s, two seemingly contradictory ideas regarding national security germinated in American society. The first was promoted by the neoconservatives and trumpeted by the newly elected Reagan administration. Armed with the (now discredited) Team B report, which questioned the accuracy of the National Intelligence Estimates on the Soviet Union, promoters of this idea argued that America's national defenses were weak and vulnerable and thus invited potential nuclear blackmail from the Soviet Union.[1] The other idea concerned the danger and folly of the unabated arms race. Seeking a way to unify various strands of the peace movement, activists called for a simple national security goal: a mutual freeze on the production, testing, and deployment of nuclear weapons between the United States and the Soviet Union. The Reagan administration's overt discussion of winnable and survivable nuclear war, alongside its pursuit of first-strike weapons, ignited a grassroots movement, captivating the American public and millions of others across the globe. By summer 1982, an estimated one million people would march through the streets of New York City calling for the freeze of the arms race.

New Hostilities

As 1980 closed, the question of war and peace hung like a dark storm cloud over society. The hands of the Doomsday Clock leaped forward three minutes to read "four minutes to midnight." Doomsday, it seemed, was approaching with increasing rapidity. On Inauguration Day 1981, thousands of dissidents flocked to the capital, with one group hauling a mock MX missile on the back of a mule wagon in protest of the new "bigger nuclear stick" the Reagan administration planned to wield. While Reagan may have won the election, he still had to manage the question of war or peace.[2]

But at the top of the agenda of the new administration were tax cuts for the wealthy and an unprecedented increase in military spending. Everything else, as White House Communication Director David Gergen explained, was "deliberately de-emphasized." President Reagan insisted such policies would create jobs and subsequently end the recession. Several studies, however, pointed to defense jobs as being the least effective way to stimulate the economy.[3] In the final days of Carter's presidency, as a parting shot at Reagan, he increased the defense budget significantly, believing this would prevent the incoming Reagan administration from increasing defense spending. But the Reagan administration did not acknowledge Carter's increases and insisted on an even higher "get well" package for the military. As President Reagan told Director of the Office of Management and Budget David Stockman, "Defense is not a budget item. You spend what you need." Because of fatigue and a calculator error, Stockman "mistakenly agreed to use the recently inflated Carter budgets plus the Reagan 'get well' package as a base line upon which subsequent increases would be added." This resulted in actual defense increases that were, as David Meyer observes, "fully twice what Reagan promised during the campaign." Reagan nevertheless backed the request. The defense budget soon soared to new heights, exceeding military spending during both world wars, the Korean War, and the Vietnam War, subsequently creating massive budget deficits over the course of the administration.[4]

The Reagan administration continued to peddle the myth of Soviet military superiority. In his first statement as secretary of defense, Caspar Weinberger insisted his mission was "to re-arm America"—a plan that would include two hundred thousand more soldiers, millions in special tax breaks for the military-industrial complex, and an extensive plan to "regain atomic superiority."[5]

But most Americans simply were not convinced that weapons such as the MX would have prevented tragedies such as the Iran hostage crisis. Indeed, prominent individuals within the Cold War defense establishment believed the accelerating arms race actually made Americans less secure. Upon accepting the 1981 Albert Einstein Peace Prize, George F. Kennan, the father of the containment strategy, encouraged the administration not to expand the nuclear arsenal but to cut it—by 50 percent—immediately. The two superpowers, Kennan warned, were drifting toward nuclear collision, "piling weapon upon weapon, missile upon missile" as if they were "victims of some sort of hypnosis, men in a dream, like lemmings headed for the sea." Kennan argued that deterrence could be maintained with just 20 percent of the existing arsenal. The rest, Kennan concluded, was simply overkill, reaching such "grotesque dimensions as to defy rational understanding."[6]

To convince the public of its own insecurity and to raise support for higher defense spending, neoconservative think tanks launched a propaganda campaign. At the forefront of this effort was the American Security Council Foundation (ASCF), a hawkish defense lobbyist organization originally formed in 1955 as a personnel security and consulting firm. The ASCF, as SANE observed, specialized in "scare tactics, distortions and outright lies about the strength of the American military" and was at the forefront of the campaign against détente and SALT II. Its 320,000 members included 231 members of Congress and President Reagan. Located in Boston, Virginia, the ASCF privately stored over six million files on so-called dissidents, "the largest known private collection on American progressives" that is "not available for public scrutiny," as a detailed report on the ASCF observed.[7] Having organized a congressional coalition dubbed "Peace through Strength," the ASCF recruited hundreds to lobby against the SALT II Treaty during "Peace through Strength Week" in 1980. With a budget of over four million dollars, ASCF relied heavily on thousands in contributions from some of America's largest defense contractors. They funded aggressive direct mailings and bankrolled propaganda films such as *The Price of Peace and Freedom* (1976) and *The SALT Syndrome* (1979), the latter so misleading that the Pentagon was forced to issue a point-by-point refutation.[8]

Nevertheless, such films found their way to television audiences across the United States regularly in the late 1970s and early 1980s, with *The SALT Syndrome* airing over two thousand times. ASCF president John Fisher estimated their message had reached at least 137 million Americans by 1980. Thus, by Reagan's election, neoconservatives had thoroughly and successfully propagandized Americans into the belief that arms control and détente had weakened American security. Following the election, the ASCF earmarked another five million dollars for production of the series *Project Survival*, aimed at generating support for Reagan's military buildup. These fear tactics were designed not just for "some incremental changes in (military) spending," Fisher explained, "but a major change in national attitudes."[9]

Like many presidents, Reagan had little background in national security affairs. Because of his lack of knowledge on these issues, historian Ronald Powaski observed, Reagan "relied on his advisors to a much greater extent than most Cold War presidents." Many of them, however, came from the highest ranks of the Committee on the Present Danger. A self-described group of "concerned citizens," the CPD had originally formed in the 1950s to raise an alarm about the Soviet Union while mobilizing the public to support troop deployment in Europe, increased militarism, and Truman's containment policy. The 1970s reiteration would share not just the alarmism or support for higher defense appropriations but also members.[10]

Within the Reagan administration, the CPD claimed thirty-two officials, not counting the president himself. Since nearly all Reagan's "top foreign and military advisers were members of the Committee," CPD executive director Charles Tyroler II boasted, they controlled the "whole hierarchy."[11] These appointments included Eugene Rostow (chairman of the CPD's executive board and critic of the SALT and ABM Treaties) as head of the Arms Control and Disarmament Agency. Leading SALT II critic Paul Nitze became chief INF negotiator. Neoconservative defense intellectual Colin Gray was appointed to an advisory role with the State Department and ACDA. In Summer 1980 issue of *Foreign Policy*, Gray and coauthor Keith Payne lamented that too many commentators and government officials considered nuclear war "a nonsurvivable event," but, they countered, "an intelligent U.S. offensive strategy, wedded to homeland defenses," could reduce US casualties to an acceptable "20 million." As Robert Scheer observes, the CPD brought the administration "a patina of intellectual respectability to what otherwise might have seemed to voters no more than out-of-date and primitive anti-Soviet rhetoric."[12]

Outside the CPD, Reagan's staff included members from his days as California governor and choices from within the Republican Party establishment. The "troika" was representative of this. Edwin Meese and Michael Deaver, two aides of Reagan from his time as California governor, were appointed counselors to the president, while James Baker III, a personal friend of and campaign manager for Vice President George H. W. Bush, became chief of staff. While former Nixon aide George Shultz was considered at the top of many lists to become secretary of state, because of his more moderate views on détente and the Soviet Union, as well as his perceived hostility toward Israel, the position was given to General Alexander Haig. The former chief of staff to Presidents Nixon and Ford, Haig was chief executive of United Technologies (the third-largest military contractor in the United States) prior to joining the Reagan administration. An establishment Republican who believed in "hard headed détente," Haig was neither a neoconservative nor a member of the CPD, but his involvement in the Vietnam War, his role in the bombing of Cambodia, and his close ties to Nixon led many in the mainstream press to question the selection, while peace activists picketed outside his confirmation hearings.[13]

As the Reagan administration took office, US-Soviet relations sank to their lowest levels in nearly twenty years. At his first press conference, President Reagan told Sam Donaldson of ABC News that the Soviets "reserve unto themselves the right to commit any crime, to lie, to cheat." When Soviet ambassador Anatoly Dobrynin attempted to exercise his long-held privilege of driving into the State Department garage, he was turned away and told to use the front entrance like everyone else. Though Reagan claimed to know nothing about the snub, the media, tipped off, awaited Dobrynin at the garage, airing the embarrassing footage on television that evening. Within the first six weeks of the Reagan administration, Secretary of State Haig linked the Soviets to terrorism in El Salvador and other Latin American nations and condemned them for "training, funding, and equipping international terrorists," but, as *Congressional Quarterly* reported, "Haig offered no concrete evidence to support his assertions." As George Shultz reflected, "Relations between the two superpowers were not simply bad; they were nonexistent."[14]

Among the more troubling aspects of the Reagan administration's defense buildup was the frequency with which members—including President Reagan himself—spoke of limited and survivable nuclear war. This was matched with an often profound and dangerous ignorance of nuclear weapons. As Strobe Talbott observes, Reagan was "a detached, sometimes befuddled character" who "frequently did not understand the basic aspects of the nuclear weapons issues and of the policies promulgated in his name." Indeed, Reagan would falsely claim the United States had unilaterally disarmed over the previous decade while insisting submarine-launched ballistic missiles could be recalled after launch.[15]

President Reagan's provocative comments, however, were just the tip of the iceberg. Major General Robert Schweitzer, a military adviser in Reagan's NSC, warned that because of the Soviets' nuclear superiority and readiness to attack, the United States was in the gravest danger since its independence. Although Schweitzer was soon fired, Reagan did not reassure the public or allies when he told reporters, "I could see where you could have the exchange of tactical weapons against troops in the field without it bringing either one of the major powers to pushing the button." Reagan's comments on a potential limited nuclear war on European soil received "prominent play" in the European media, with an internal NSC cable describing the coverage as "essentially negative" and "coming at a time of heightened Norwegian interest in peace initiatives."[16]

Loose talk of nuclear war became the norm. At his confirmation hearing, Haig told the Senate that the United States had to show the Soviet Union "our willingness to do whatever is necessary to protect our vital interests," which "must include the arsenal of nuclear weapons." Haig later testified that in the event of a conventional war in Europe, the United States might "fire a nuclear weapon for demonstrative purposes" over Europe to deter the Soviets. At Eugene Rostow's ACDA confirmation hearing, Senator Claiborne Pell (D-RI) asked Rostow if he believed the United States could survive a nuclear war. Rostow cited the experience of Japan in World War II as an example of a nation that "not only survived but flourished after a nuclear attack." When pressed further whether America could survive a full nuclear assault and not just two primitive atomic bombs, Rostow optimistically observed, "The human race is very resilient" and "depending upon certain assumptions, some estimates predict that there would be ten million casualties on one side and one hundred million on another. But that is not the whole population."[17]

Perhaps the most alarming comments to the public were those of Thomas "T. K." Jones, the administration's undersecretary of defense for European Nuclear Theater Forces. In an interview with the *Los Angeles Times*, Jones explained that "nuclear war was not nearly as devastating as we had been led to believe." The United States, Jones elaborated, "could fully recover from an all-out nuclear war with the Soviet Union in just two to four years." For Jones, surviving a nuclear attack was quite simple really: "Dig a hole, cover it with a couple of doors and then throw three feet of dirt on top. It's the dirt that does it." "The major obstacle" in the United States, Jones continued, "is we've conditioned our people to believe that once the first nuclear bomb goes off, everybody's going to die." But, Jones optimistically explained, if Americans simply built makeshift shelters and took essential goods (such as food and water), more than 90 percent of the population would survive: "If there are enough shovels to go around everybody's going to make it."[18]

These casual discussions of fighting and surviving limited nuclear war, in conjunction with the pursuit of new potential first-strike nuclear weapons and an increasingly abysmal US-Soviet relationship, chafed at the American psyche. As Jeffrey Knopf observes, Americans were left with the perception that the Reagan administration was contemplating and planning "a nuclear war in an entirely cold blooded way." Jones's comments were likewise derided in Europe: "I'm not sure how you're supposed to cover the door with earth while you're lying underneath it," European Nuclear Disarmament (END) chairman Dan Smith wondered.[19]

Embarrassing leaks from the Pentagon soon revealed that the administration accepted the premise of a protracted nuclear conflict with the Soviets.

Secretary of Defense Weinberger quickly denied that the administration planned to launch a protracted nuclear war, claiming the word "protracted" was "wrenched out of context." Weinberger nevertheless contended that if the Soviets started a nuclear war, the Reagan administration planned to prevail. Later that summer, the Pentagon approved a secret plan to replace PD-59 of the Carter administration: National Security Decision Directive-13. The new plan envisioned fighting a protracted nuclear war lasting up to six months.[20]

Intent on modernizing the nuclear arsenal, on August 6, 1981 (the thirty-sixth anniversary of the atomic bombing of Hiroshima), the Reagan administration announced plans to produce neutron bombs. An enhanced radiation weapon, the neutron bomb produced more lethal radiation but less heat and blast destruction than a fission bomb. In essence, it was designed to save property but destroy lives. Domestic opponents derided the weapon as a "Republican bomb," while the Soviets mocked it as a "capitalist bomb," but the neutron bomb was no joke. The throng of protests in Europe against the placement of the weapon pressured the Carter administration to delay its production to an unspecified later date. The Reagan administration's decision to pursue the weapon rekindled European opposition while boosting long-dormant antinuclear organizations stateside. SANE soon circulated a letter of protest addressed to Reagan and Weinberger signed by more than twenty-four organizations and representing environmental and peace groups as well as numerous religious denominations. In Texas, twelve Catholic bishops adopted a statement condemning the weapon.[21]

The Reagan administration, however, did not stop with the neutron bomb. Although Reagan had criticized Carter's MX basing proposals, his lack of interest in stopping the project allowed the controversy not just to continue but to thrive. Mail concerning the MX missile flooded Reagan's office. A coalition of activists from SANE, Friends of the Earth, the National Taxpayers Union, and several arms control and other environmentalist organizations implored Reagan to cancel the weapon. Though a *Salt Lake Tribune* poll indicated very high approval ratings for President Reagan in Utah, the MX continued to generate strong opposition. A letter to the editor of *Deseret News* claimed the only people in the region in favor of the MX were those "highly visible merchants and Chamber of Commerce types," while the proposed basing plan "would probably harm the country more than if the Russians took over."[22]

Major religious figures in Utah and Nevada openly spoke out both against basing the MX in the Great Basin region and the missile itself on moral grounds, including the traditionally conservative Church of Jesus Christ of Latter-day Saints (Mormons, or LDS). Following Reagan's election, approval of the MX among Mormons had increased 12 percent, leaving them nearly equally split over the project. But on May 5, 1981, Spencer W. Kimble, the First Presidency of the LDS, issued a letter warning against the "terrifying arms race," deploring the "building of vast arsenals of nuclear weapons," and pleading for "national leaders to marshal the genius of the nation to find viable alternatives" to the MX. In the wake of Kimble's letter, opposition in Utah to the MX soared from a simple majority to 67 percent.[23]

The Emerging Global Antinuclear Revolt

Opposition to nuclear weapons continued to expand across the globe, especially in Europe following NATO's dual-track decision. In Britain, the older Campaign for Nuclear Disarmament (CND) saw its membership rocket from 3,500 to 70,000 in less than two years. In continental Europe, European Nuclear Disarmament (END), led by famed Marxist labor historian E. P. Thompson, sought in the short term to stop the placement of NATO's Euromissiles and further placement of Soviet SS-20s; in the long term, END sought to make Europe a nuclear-weapons-free zone. In Belgium and Norway, the Interchurch Peace Council (Interkerkelijk Vredessberaad or IKV) led the opposition. In West Germany, sixty thousand marched against the NATO decision to deploy 108 Pershing II and 464 cruise missiles. Over seventy thousand protested in London's Trafalgar Square, with five hundred thousand signing a petition to remove all cruise missiles from Europe.[24]

In the United States, on the day after Reagan's electoral victory, activists representing various national and peace organizations met for two-and-a-half hours at the Philadelphia offices of the WILPF to strategize on expanding the Freeze campaign nationally. The nascent organization had a tall task in front of it. Short-range goals such as stopping the MX or passing SALT II would become much more difficult with Reagan's election and a Republican-controlled Senate. The advantage of a nuclear freeze, as peace activists saw it, was in its simplicity. A freeze was easy to comprehend, bilateral, "conservative and modest," and "might even be discussed with some of Reagan's new advisers to find out what their objections might be."

As the Reagan administration rolled out its plans to cut federal spending, peace activists reasoned that the economy would only get worse. Therefore, exposing what the Pentagon budget was "really doing to people—unemployment, inflation, lack of services, etc."—would be "crucial to gaining support for the freeze from new groups." Activists believed new ideas, such as a nuclear freeze, would attract both new allies and moderate Democrats, the latter of whom might be more willing to criticize the new president. While some activists expressed hope in getting the bilateral nuclear freeze proposal into the Democratic platform, others wanted to work with third parties, including a new Black Party.

Peace activists also strategized on foreign policy. In the short term, if the MX and a fleet of Trident submarines were deployed, it would make a freeze "less meaningful and harder to verify." In the long term, the nuclear freeze proposal was one step in fighting military Keynesianism. Activists still had to confront fears of the "Soviet threat." Without downplaying genuine concerns, activists would need to change "people's attitudes" toward the threat in "personal discussions" armed with "concrete facts and statistics."

As the meeting ended, activists planned to introduce a strategy proposal for the first Nuclear Freeze conference that consisted of six components that would address (1) legislative and congressional issues, (2) various nuclear weapons facilities campaigns, (3) economic issues, (4) US nuclear policy, (5) outreach approaches to scientists, feminists, the religious, labor, minorities, and others, and, lastly, (6) the Soviet threat.[25] Although the conference was initially scheduled for that January, organizers pushed it back to March to give the committee more time to prepare the agenda, outreach, and strategy. While the executive committee for the Freeze considered several venues, they decided on the Executive House Hotel in Washington, D.C.—a larger venue that had the advantages of a downtown location and extensive conference room options. The committee projected the total cost of having the conference at five thousand dollars—a hefty sum considering the campaign was already having difficulty paying staff members.[26]

The cost and the location became a sore point for some activists, who questioned the nature of the Freeze campaign. "This is a *bullshit* proposal," read an internal note from an MFS activist named Harold. In another memo, the same activist fumed, "More bullshit!! $5000 for 200 people? Wow what a waste of money." Harold had serious doubts that the Freeze proposal would draw any "'grass-roots' support" and wondered why a "'grass-roots' campaign" was holding a conference at the Executive House Hotel. Likewise, Cynthia from MFS did not think a mutual freeze should be the focus of the 1984 campaign but that the antinuclear movement should "stick with the human needs/rights aspect of our goals: strengthening the connections, helping the peace movement to realize how *we* have to change in order to broaden our base—how we may have to give support on other issues, change our style, etc., to connect with the 'grass-roots.'" Like Harold, Cynthia did not see the Freeze campaign generating a mass base but thought it would instead "be a terrible drain of energy away from what matters."[27]

Other activists expressed cautious optimism over the freeze. In MFS's newsletter, *The Mobilizer*, Dan Ebner of the Fellowship of Reconciliation noted that the freeze provided a "common goal for disarmament activists and 'mainstream America.'" A nuclear weapons freeze was a "specific, attainable goal" that was "easy to explain to anyone." A freeze, however, did not go far enough for proponents of "unilateral disarmament," as Ebner self-identified. While disarmament proponents could support a freeze as a *"first step"* to say *"Stop producing,"* it needed to go on to say, *"Start reducing."* Ebner nevertheless saw in the Freeze campaign an umbrella to unite "a broad spectrum of activists," including those opposed to specific programs such as the MX, Trident, and cruise missile.[28]

The Freeze campaign would modify its agenda, meeting at Georgetown University instead of the plush hotel. The change in venue meant limiting registration, but organizers still expected 275 Freeze activists from thirty-one states. The First National Strategy Meeting was a seminal event in the Freeze campaign, marking, as Forsberg noted to invitees, "the beginning of a national concerted effort to stop the nuclear arms race."[29] The conference endorsed Forsberg's "Call" while focusing on creating both a national strategy for stopping the nuclear arms race and the optimal structure for implementing that strategy. Activists projected a campaign of two to five years to achieve their goals, emphasizing work done "on a local, decentralized basis" during the first year. During phase one, the Freeze campaign would "demonstrate the positive potential of the freeze proposal for stopping the arms race." In phase two, it would "build broad and visible public support for the freeze." Phase three would "focus public support for the freeze on policy-makers so that it becomes a matter of national debate." Finally, phase four would see the Freeze campaign win the debate "so that the freeze is 'adopted as a national policy objective.'"[30]

The campaign would establish the National Freeze Clearinghouse in St. Louis, Missouri, giving the Freeze campaign the image of being "anchored in middle America," Kehler noted. The clearinghouse would house twelve full-time staff and use funding from churches to monitor Freeze activities. Several task forces comprised of volunteers were created to carry out specific functions (such as monitoring public opinion polls or pursuing nonviolent tactics). Regional caucuses would also be formed to "insure representation throughout the country." The clearinghouse would maintain lists of activists, organizations, prominent individuals and members of Congress, and outreach contacts. Likewise, it would coordinate information requests from the media and activists, act as "a consulting and referral service," publish a national newsletter, and coordinate with multiple Freeze task forces that worked on "specific freeze functions" (such as raising funds, developing educational materials, or coordinating national events).[31]

A strategy synthesis group made several recommendations for the Freeze campaign in the early stages. It recommended a stronger connection between the Freeze and budget questions, particularly regarding the funding of human needs. The campaign needed to broaden its base and bring in the "working class, minority groups, and other constituencies not typically involved in disarmament work and not adequately represented at the conference." The national committee should add "specific, immediate goals," such as organizing for the UN Special Session on Disarmament in June 1982 (where the campaign hoped to put a nuclear freeze vote before the UN General Assembly) or the November 1982 elections. The group further recommended that the Freeze not limit itself to nuclear weapons but "remain mindful of the relationship between the Freeze and other issues," such as intervention in El Salvador. Other recommendations included creating a one-page Freeze petition, creating a more readable version of "The Call," tracking and using public opinion polls, and considering the "possibility of nonviolent direct action" as "a viable tactic."[32]

A structure synthesis group outlined a proposal for the structure of the Freeze campaign in the first year, focusing largely on the role of the national Freeze campaign and its relationship to the local level. The group made two recommendations: (1) that the "Freeze effort . . . be nationally coordinated, with locally-based determination of what gets done" and (2) that the national structure should "facilitate local actions, tying them together, eliminating duplication . . . and not dictating from top-down." A national Freeze conference would be held twice annually (but more often if necessary), where final authority for review of the Freeze strategy would rest.[33]

Between conferences, a national committee would be empowered to "carry on the work of the Freeze," making all major decisions, including hiring, firing, and management of the clearinghouse staff. The national committee meetings would be open to all Freeze workers, but only official delegates would receive voting privileges. To make sure no single constituency within the Freeze campaign dominated the national committee, it would be limited to one person from each task force and one person from each regional caucus, with a specific number of seats allocated both for major constituency groups and for "contributing organizations" (defined as "any group that has contributed and will continue to contribute to move forward the work of the Freeze"). The national committee would further appoint an executive committee that would oversee the interim decisions made between meetings of the national conference.[34]

In the months following the first Freeze conference, the campaign continued to gain momentum across North America. In April 1981, thousands rallied against nuclear weapons across the United States in over twenty-five states. At a rally in Denver, Colorado, eight thousand protested the Department of Energy's plan to expand operations at the Rocky Flats plutonium fabrication plant. Two thousand rallied in the rain and cold at the GE Electric Boat Company in Groton, Connecticut, to protest the launching of the Trident submarine *Corpus Christi*, while local Catholic bishops expressed their ire at naming an attack submarine after the Body of Christ. Further antinuclear actions took place at eight naval installations in the San Francisco Bay Area; the Titan II missile silo in Damascus, Arkansas; Grissom Air Force Base in Indiana; the Bendix H-bomb plant in Kansas City, Missouri; outside the White House; and at the corporate headquarters of Rockwell International on both coasts. Likewise, thousands rallied across four provinces in Canada, where Project Plowshares, a coalition of Canadian disarmament groups, had launched a three-year campaign advocating the establishment of Canada as a nuclear-weapons-free zone.[35]

To demonstrate the potential of a nuclear freeze and marshal "substantial public support for the idea," Freeze activists hit the ground running in congressional districts across the country. The campaign set an immediate strategy in 1981 to collect five thousand signatures in each congressional district calling for a bilateral nuclear weapons freeze. The petition drive was under way in forty-seven states. In the early stages, activists sought to gather a minimum of five thousand signatures in seventy-five to one hundred congressional districts to build the campaign and from which to further draw a base of supporters. In Connecticut, a coalition of forty groups and six hundred individuals had already gathered 22,500 signatures across six congressional districts and presented them to their representatives and senators.[36]

In June 1981, following the lead of the state senate, the Massachusetts House of Representatives voted overwhelmingly to approve a resolution calling on President Reagan to propose to the Soviet Union a mutual and bilateral halt on the testing, production, and deployment of all nuclear warheads, missiles, and delivery systems. The resolution further requested that funds saved by such a halt be transferred for civilian use. Paralleling the Massachusetts state legislature's freeze resolutions, the New York State Assembly passed a proposal endorsing a nuclear moratorium. The New York resolution similarly called on Congress to transfer all funds saved by a nuclear freeze to civilian purposes. Later that month, the Oregon State Assembly approved a "Freeze memorial." Like the resolutions in Massachusetts and New York, the Oregon Freeze memorial called for the money saved by a nuclear freeze to be used for "peaceful, non-nuclear uses." The Oregon legislation strove for bipartisanship, even deleting a clause requesting "no first-use" since it alienated Republican allies.[37]

But there was more than meets the eye with these early legislative success stories. For instance, supporters in Oregon understood that the memorial would have no effect in D.C.; however, it was seen as symbolic, with its value coming in terms of organizing efforts. Although activists collected thousands of signatures in Illinois, the executive committees of the House and Senate voted against a Freeze resolution. Organizers there struggled to coordinate lobbying in the state capital of Springfield—several hours away from Chicago.[38] This led Freeze activists Gordon Faison and Randy Kehler to stress that they needed to avoid "the temptation to go directly to elected officials, at the state or federal levels, without first doing our homework—that is the work of organizing freeze support at home, in our local communities and local organizations." Without this base of support to pressure the policymakers, support for a nuclear freeze would "evaporate as soon as there is heavy pressure from the other side." There would be "no shortcuts on the way to halting the nuclear arms," and "only one [long] road," which "begins in our local churches and synagogues, in our union halls and town halls, in school auditoriums and our village greens." To build support for the Freeze campaign, Faison and Kehler emphasized building contacts across the globe, including the Soviet Union. Although the Freeze campaign had already scored political successes in state legislatures, the initial steps to halt the arms race favored "serious and sustained local organizing" over working within the political establishment.[39]

In fall 1981, the Freeze campaign was growing rapidly, with the Call to Halt receiving endorsements from multiple religious and peace organizations representing national, local, and regional organizations. Moreover, the Call received endorsements from a wide array of individuals, including Freeze leaders Randy Forsberg (IDDS) and Helen Caldicott (PSR); arms control experts, such as George Rathjens (ACDA) and Bernard Feld (editor of the *Bulletin of the Atomic Scientists*); feminists, such as Bella Abzug (cofounder of Women Strike for Peace) and activist folk singer Joan Baez; progressives, such as Adam Hochschild (cofounder and publisher of *Mother Jones*) and Jerome Grossman (director of the Council for a Livable World); intellectuals, such as professor Richard Falk (International Law, Princeton) and economist John Kenneth Galbraith (Harvard); religious figures, such as Rabbi Daniel Freelander (Union of American Hebrew Congregations) and several Episcopal and Catholic bishops; older peace and antinuclear activists Sidney Lens, Daniel Ellsberg, and Seymour Melman; and several elected officials from members of Congress to state and local elected officials representing both major political parties. That

October, the campaign organized a national call-in day, generating thousands of calls to Congress and the White House demanding a nuclear freeze.[40]

With activists appearing to offer a way out of the arms race, the antinuclear message gained traction, while the Reagan administration's arms control initiatives appeared nonexistent. After nine months in office, the Reagan administration had not yet proposed an arms control treaty. It was not until October 1981 that President Reagan announced the first of his arms control initiatives: the Zero Option. The Zero Option, or Zero-Zero, was a simple proposal: in exchange for the Soviets eliminating all SS-20 missiles, NATO would not deploy ground-launched cruise missiles in Western Europe or the Pershing II in West Germany. These theater or intermediate-range forces were of paramount concern in Europe. Although NATO allies wanted an upgrade to existing forces to counter the Soviet deployment of SS-20s, many antinuclear activists and arms control advocates raised concerns that NATO deployment of similar weapons in Europe aimed at the Soviet Union would be both destabilizing and provocative. In the event of a false alert, the Soviets would have only minutes to assess whether the threat was real or simply a faulty computer chip.

The Zero Option, however, did not originate from the Reagan administration but rather came from the Western European antinuclear movement. West German and Dutch Social Democratic parties embraced the idea of zero intermediate-range weapons as an alternative to the dual-track decision put forth by Carter. As the European antinuclear activists proposed, the Soviet Union was to remove its SS-20s unilaterally, while NATO should neither develop nor deploy a similar weapon, resulting in zero intermediate-range nuclear weapons in Europe. Reagan was quick to dismiss the European peace movement publicly. "Oh, those demonstrations," Reagan told journalist Ben Wattenberg, "Those are all sponsored by a thing called the World Peace Council, which is bought and paid for by the Soviet Union." A communist front organization, the World Peace Council had a long and contested history with Western peace movements. Although it opposed the placement of cruise and Pershing missiles in Europe, no American or European antinuclear organizations cooperated or organized with it.[41]

While Reagan publicly redbaited activists, his cabinet picked up on both the popularity of the Zero Option and its strategic co-optability. If the Reagan administration could make Zero *their* idea, it could both continue to build nuclear weapons *and* give the appearance of wanting arms control negotiations. As Gergen later conceded, the Zero Option "was designed to allay public fears . . . to convince people you were really serious about peace," further adding that it was "a way to buy off a wary Europe" and was designed to "humanize Reagan"—a public relations move sorely needed following loose talk of survivable nuclear war. But there was a catch to the proposal: the United States did not yet have an intermediate-range weapon deployed, making the proposal, as Haig reflected, "not negotiable," adding, "It was absurd to expect the Soviets to dismantle an existing force of 1,100 warheads, which they already put into the field at the cost of billions of rubles, in exchange for a promise from the United States not to deploy a missile force that we had not yet begun to build and that had aroused such violent controversy in Western Europe." The Zero Option, however, resonated with Weinberger, who saw "its potential for attracting public support."[42]

On October 13, 1981, at a top-secret NSC meeting, Weinberger formally proposed the Zero Option, framing it as "a bold plan, sweeping in nature," which could "capture world opinion." President Reagan was skeptical, and even Weinberger was certain the Soviets would reject it. Nevertheless, Weinberger concluded that "whether they [the Soviets] reject it or accept it, they would be set back on their heels. We would be left in good shape and would be shown as the White Hats." Although CIA Director William Casey and Edwin Meese both liked the idea, Haig remained opposed, telling the NSC staff, "'Zero-zero' will not be viewed as the President's initiative. It has already been proposed by the German Social Democrats and the [West German] Foreign Minister [Hans-Dietrich] Genscher in Moscow, and it is a subject of intense debate in Europe." Haig noted "serious problems with any 'zero-zero' option," including what to do if in two years it was time to deploy the weapons with the Zero Option still on the table.[43]

The administration would meet again to discuss the matter on November 12, 1981, with less than two weeks before the scheduled INF talks were to begin in Geneva. By then it was clear that Reagan had made up his mind: "One should ask for the moon, and when the other fellow offers green cheese, one can settle for something in between," Reagan told his cabinet. Haig continued to object, saying, "Asking for the moon could be turned against us and to our disadvantage." Reagan responded that the Soviet SS-20s were being deployed "at the rate of one per week and capable of destroying every population center in Europe. . . . It is my belief that we can begin negotiations with the hope that we can eliminate all of these missiles totally, verifiably, and globally." Discussion among the cabinet continued, with Haig voicing his concerns that proposing the Zero Option would "generate the suspicion that the United States was only interested in a frivolous propaganda exercise or, worse, that it was disingenuously engaging in arms negotiations simply as a cover for a desire to build up its nuclear arsenal." Despite Haig's opposition, the Zero Option won out.[44]

With the modernization of the nuclear arsenal under way, Reagan announced in a commencement speech at his alma mater, Eureka College, that his administration had "given up on SALT" and would instead pursue Strategic Arms Reduction Talks, or START. START called for each side to cut both ICBMs and SLBMs to equal levels. The emphasis on "reduction" over "limitation" was a direct response to the recent criticisms George Kennan had made of the arms race the prior fall and was written with the public in mind. As James Goodby, the State Department's representative at the START talks and one of the writers of the Eureka speech, explained, "I wrote it in Kennanesque language so it would have the same public appeal. I wanted it to look like the president was paying attention to public concern."[45]

Problems with Reagan's START proposal abounded. Whereas Kennan argued for a 50 percent reduction, Reagan's START proposal only called for reductions of about 35 percent. The sizes of the arsenals were not equal. For the United States, such a cut would amount to about one-half of then current forces, while for the Soviets it would have amounted to a nearly two-thirds reduction. The treaty would place limits on "medium" missiles, such as the MX, as well as "heavy" missiles, such as the Soviet SS-19, but place no restrictions on cruise missiles or bombers, which advantaged the United States. Furthermore, the Reagan administration sought to equalize missile throw weight to a ceiling of four million pounds each. This was yet another US advantage, as its total throw weight was just over four million pounds, while the Soviet throw weight was nearly three times that. The administration offered few concessions on reducing bombers and cruise missiles, but even these would only occur in the second stage of talks. Although Reagan campaigned against SALT II, the administration pledged to honor the treaty for the duration of the START talks as long as the Soviets reciprocated.[46]

Perhaps unsurprisingly, little progress was made. While Reagan blamed this on the Soviets, the Reagan arms control proposals appeared designed to fail, giving the administration a public relations boost while placing the onus for agreement on the Soviets. Indeed, most observers viewed both the Zero-Zero proposal and START as efforts to "stalemate arms control rather than as a sincere attempt to achieve the real reductions the two proposals professed to seek," as historian John Lewis Gaddis writes. The Zero Option asked the Soviets to eliminate an entire class of nuclear weapons in exchange for NATO not deploying a (then nonexistent) similar weapon, while START would maintain US technological superiority. A high-level Soviet official believed Reagan favored Zero because that was "as far as he can count." *Time* magazine's principal US-Soviet affairs correspondent, Strobe Talbott, declared the true acronym for START was "STALL." As historian Michael Sherry observes, "The few noises and proposals offered" by the Reagan administration on arms control "were insincere and defensive, often made to outmaneuver the nuclear freeze movement."[47]

A Political Wildfire

By 1982, with the perception that the Reagan administration was not serious about arms control and was perhaps leading the nation toward a nuclear confrontation with the Soviets, the sparks of antinuclear activism had created a political wildfire. "Over 18 months," the *Los Angeles Times* reported, the Freeze campaign emerged as "the inspiration for a coast-to-coast grass-roots crusade," drawing comparisons to the civil rights and antiwar movements of the 1960s. While President Reagan avoided the label of nuclear risk-taker during the 1980 campaign, by the end of his first year in office, more than half of those polled saw him as precisely that. Sixty-three percent of those surveyed by *Time* believed a nuclear war would break out in five years, whereas a *Newsweek* poll found a third of those surveyed believed the Reagan administration's policies were increasing the odds of nuclear war. Among those *Newsweek* surveyed, 60 percent were in favor of a nuclear weapons freeze, while a sizable 43 percent were unaware of the existence of the Freeze campaign itself. The campaign had room to grow.[48]

An ABC News / *Washington Post* survey asked respondents to place nuclear war among "a list of things in life that worry you personally," with the biggest fears first and the lowest concerns last. Thirty-six percent of respondents indicated nuclear war was at the top of their list, while an additional 26 percent indicated it was somewhere in between. While a third of those polled in the survey believed a nuclear war between the United States and the Soviet Union was "unlikely," more than a quarter thought it was "somewhat likely," while 23 percent believed it was only "less likely."[49]

A Harris Survey between March and May 1982 found 50–54 percent of those polled were "very concerned" over "the possibility the world will be plunged into a nuclear war." An internal survey by Richard Wirthlin from April 1982 found just over 50 percent of pollsters thought Reagan "believed we must build as many nuclear weapons as quickly as possible so that we won't be pushed around by the Russians anymore," while only 35 percent viewed Reagan as "a strong, militant . . . cowboy." By June, however, those numbers had reversed. "The Nuclear Freeze is now a runaway horse," *Washington Post* columnist Mary McGrory observed, "and the Rough Rider in the White House inadvertently applied the whip as he tried to bring it back into the stable."[50]

By early spring, the idea of a nuclear freeze had emerged as "the inspiration for a coast-to-coast grass roots crusade." Pro-freeze op-eds soon filled the nation's newspapers, and the liberal arms controllers who initially hesitated to back it now climbed on board. In the US Senate, Democrat Ted Kennedy and Republican Mark Hatfield championed a bilateral-freeze resolution, leaving conservative columnist James Kilpatrick lamenting how the conservatives did nothing "about the most awesomely important political question in the world." A nuclear weapons freeze received the support of past statesmen, such as Averell Harriman and William Colby, in addition to survivors of the Hiroshima bombing. Religious leaders of various faiths championed a nuclear freeze, as did Ronald Reagan's rebellious daughter Patti. Soviet general secretary Leonid Brezhnev also endorsed a nuclear freeze—albeit limited to Europe. Since Soviet SS-20 missiles were already deployed, implementing such a freeze would be advantageous to the Soviets. Antinuclear activists summarily dismissed Brezhnev's freeze proposal.[51]

But not everyone was in love with the idea of the activist-proposed bilateral nuclear freeze. The Reagan administration remained publicly opposed, believing such a freeze locked the United States into a position of inferiority. Conservative columnist George Will called the freeze idea "irresponsible" and "another example of posturing and wasted motion that the world can ill afford." In an essay in *Military Review*, Army captain David Petraeus railed against a nuclear weapons freeze, claiming it could not be verified, the Soviets could not be trusted, and a freeze was far more complicated than its supporters believed.[52]

Criticism of the nuclear freeze proposal came not just from Reagan's allies but also prominent news publications and mainstream liberal opinion. A *New York Times* editorial denounced the freeze proposal as a "simplistic diplomatic formula" designed to appeal to the popular masses. A freeze, the *Times* claimed, was unverifiable, "unworkable," would "prevent modernization," and would "carelessly throw away an already negotiated, verifiable and more favorable limit [SALT II]."[53] In the traditionally left-leaning *New Republic*, editor Charles Krauthammer claimed a freeze would "jeopardize deterrence," "delay arms control," and remove "any leverage we might have" fulfilling those goals. The *New Republic*'s attack on the freeze, however, resulted in "more canceled subscriptions than any other article in the magazine's history," Krauthammer later acknowledged.[54] In the Columbia University newspaper, the *Sun Dial*, a senior named Barack Obama criticized the Freeze campaign from the left, suggesting that "the narrow focus of the Freeze movement, as well as academic discussions of first-strike vs. second-strike," only aided "the military-industrial interests" and their "billion dollar erector sets."[55]

Although administration officials and freeze critics argued such a policy would leave in place a Soviet military advantage, it was not a view shared by the US military and past government officials. General David Jones (Reagan's first chairman of the Joint Chiefs of Staff) stated he "would not swap our present military capability with that of the Soviet Union." Likewise, when asked by the Senate Armed Services Committee whether he would trade arsenals with the Soviet Union, General John Vessey (Reagan's second chairman of the Joint Chiefs of Staff) curtly replied, "Not on your life." Former secretary of defense Robert McNamara believed the Soviets were "in a weaker position today [1982] than they were 14 or 15 years ago," while Secretary of Defense Harold Brown of the Carter administration believed the US military was "second to none." When asked during congressional testimony whether he would rather have the United States' nuclear arsenal or the Soviet Union's, Secretary of Defense Weinberger affirmed he would "not for a moment exchange anything, for we have a firm technological advantage."[56]

Nevertheless, claims of US vulnerability were repeated frequently as means to assail the freeze proposal. On ABC television's *Nightline* program, Richard Burke of the State Department repeated administration talking points that their arms control proposals already went beyond a freeze. A nuclear freeze, Burke argued, would "simply freeze the existing imbalance and capabilities" and provide "no incentive for the Soviet leaders to reduce their forces." While Helen Caldicott was given an opportunity to respond to Burke on *Nightline*, many Freeze activists were "disappointed" by her "failure to respond specifically" to many of Burke's claims. Freeze leaders needed to be prepared for increasing attacks. As Freeze activist Rod Morris put it, "Our honeymoon is over and we've got to be prepared to do ideological factual battle with our opponents who will come storming out of the woodwork with guns blazing!"[57]

Criticism of the Freeze campaign and the freeze proposal aside, American society remained gripped in fear over a potential nuclear conflict. A book by journalist Jonathan Schell about the aftermath of nuclear war marched to the top of the *New York Times* best sellers list. As Schell's *The Fate of the Earth* galvanized an anxious public, the nation underwent Ground Zero Week. Across the nation, during the week of April 18–25, 1982, millions of Americans began coming to grips with the devastating consequences of a continued arms race. In 650 communities, attendees listened to speeches, participated in teach-ins, held candlelight vigils, viewed films, or read Roger Molander's book *Nuclear War: What's in It for You?* (already in its third printing). In 1980, Molander, an NSC member under the administrations of Presidents Nixon, Ford, and Carter, formed the nonprofit Ground Zero organization. Though many members of Ground Zero favored an arms freeze, Molander and his organization did not explicitly endorse the campaign, aiming to stay above the political fray while educating the public about the effects of nuclear warfare.

During Ground Zero Week, President Reagan made public announcements urging Brezhnev to meet him at the United Nations for preliminary arms control talks, which, he emphasized, would not replace a summit meeting later on. As the *New York Times* reported, Reagan "also tried to extend an olive branch to the Ground Zero organization," declaring his "heart and soul" were in "sympathy with the people that are talking about the horrors of nuclear war." Although the president privately saw the need for nuclear abolition, given his extreme anti-Soviet rhetoric, his desires to modernize the nuclear triad, and the over-the-top rhetoric from within the administration about winnable nuclear war, as Knopf observes, "No one outside the administration had any reason to think that Ronald Reagan harbored a deep distaste for nuclear weapons." Reagan's public sympathy toward the Freeze movement, however, had less to do with his own private views and more to do with his poor poll numbers on arms control. Despite the Freeze hurting him in the polls, Reagan continued to object to a freeze, reiterating that it would leave a Soviet advantage (a view Reagan claimed Roger Molander shared). But, as Molander told the *Times*, Reagan "misrepresented" his views. "The freeze," Molander stated, "provides a badly needed vehicle for people to confront the nuclear issue" and "to express their concern, not just about nuclear war, but about the arms race itself."[58]

Inside the White House, staff had begun collecting campaign information on the Freeze and were following events such as Ground Zero Week closely. As a briefing memo prepared for director of the White House Office of Public Liaison Elizabeth Dole concluded, the Ground Zero organization was "a force to be reckoned with," with the "momentum of the antinuclear movement . . . clearly working to their advantage."[59]

Although Ground Zero Week had its setbacks, National Security Advisor William Clark warned that the "accelerating growth of anti-nuclear sentiment in this country and abroad make it imperative that the administration develop a comprehensive arms control and defense information effort on the important issues involved." In a memo to White House Chief of Staff Baker, Clark further advised that the dimensions of the Freeze movement, Ground Zero Week, and public opinion on defense issues in both the United States and Europe required that the administration "address the public affairs issues connected with defense and arms control in the most comprehensive fashion possible, and at the highest level."[60]

The Reagan administration had a dilemma: it could not ignore the antinuclear demonstrations, but neither did it wish to empower the movement further. "The fact that the activists have our attention should be kept secret," wrote Clark. To demonstrate to the public that they were "paying attention to the national message of concern," Clark advocated for "High Level meetings" with respectable arms control advocates such as Roger Molander. Clark, however, cautioned that the nuclear freeze issue "may be the most important national security opportunity and challenge of [the Reagan] administration."[61]

A longer memo from Deputy Assistant to the President for Public Liaison Red Cavaney to White House Deputy Chief of Staff Michael Deaver warned of the possibilities of summer demonstrations, propelled by "the grassroots strength of the nuclear freeze issue." With the success of best sellers such as *The Fate of the Earth*, and the projected success of Ground Zero Week, "the freeze issue," Cavaney warned, would be propelled "into the forefront of conventional folklore," thus making it "the catalyst for a number of summertime demonstrations." Cavaney's proposed strategy avoided a direct confrontation with the Freeze movement, seeking instead to work within the media to "counter the public momentum." This would be accomplished through the creation of a "Preparedness Working Group," which would allow the administration to "speak to the complex issues involved in the [nuclear freeze] debate." With a severe recession and unemployment plaguing the nation, Cavaney warned that the Freeze movement was "rapidly gaining a momentum" and "likely to capture the public debate at the expense of virtually everything other than jobs."[62]

The administration would also have to change its rhetoric. Privately, Gergen questioned Baker and Clark on the administration's freeze strategy, saying, "Do we really need to attack [the Freeze campaign] so vigorously? What are we gaining? . . . Given the fact that we are not going to be forthcoming on the freeze issue, can we be more forthcoming about START?" To "win the propaganda battle," Baker's assistant James Cicconi argued, the administration had to adopt the "freeze language" or else it would "not succeed in co-opting any significant part of the freeze movement."[63]

In May 1982, Gergen reported to Baker that a "Public Affairs Group on Nuclear Issues" had been established and was now meeting regularly. This Nuclear Arms Control Information Working Group was chaired by National Security Advisor Bud McFarlane and had been created in response to the Freeze campaign. As McFarlane notes, its purpose was to "bring together political-military experts such as [Richard] Perle and [Richard] Burt and the public affairs people from the White House and Cabinet to determine how to package and disseminate our policy." McFarlane's group sent out high-ranking members of the administration to major media markets across the United States. Administration officials appeared on editorial pages in major newspapers and could be heard on drive-time radio shows, in talks before civic-oriented groups, and within academic settings.[64]

To avoid "serious confrontations," the public had to perceive the president as "an honest man wrestling with a very real dilemma." Cavaney described the administration's battle with the Freeze movement as "a two-pronged war" on "the strategic national security threat and the domestic political threat," adding that any efforts to "totally neutralize" the movement would be "exceedingly difficult." "In the final analysis," noted Cavaney, "it may be best not to deride those who hold the freeze idea so closely, since their beliefs may be strongly rooted in the morals of the argument." Cavaney warned that the morality of the issue would help mobilize activist clergy and church attendees, lending "the thoughtful moral weight . . . critical to the success of the grassroots effort." In addition to McFarlane's anti-freeze group, Cavaney's warnings and suggestions helped formulate the strategic tenets of the Reagan administration's response to the Freeze movement. It would not reject the idea that nuclear war was cataclysmic or that the continued arms race was exceedingly dangerous. Instead, it sought to convince the public that by accepting "peace through strength," the danger of nuclear war would be lessened.[65]

As the Reagan administration privately deliberated its strategies to co-opt the Freeze campaign, it faced a critical juncture. A *New York Times* / CBS News poll found 72 percent in favor of a nuclear weapons freeze if it prevented the expansion of the Soviet arsenal. On the other hand, most Americans surveyed opposed a freeze if it gave the Soviets an edge. But if a mutual nuclear weapons freeze resulted in a state of parity between the two superpowers, approval rates soared to 87 percent; if a freeze allowed both sides to catch cheating, 83 percent were in favor. Even the conservative *National Review* acknowledged the polling results were impressive considering that "'freeze' was an uncoined political slogan less than a year ago." The nuclear freeze issue was "very much up for grabs," one White House official noted, but instead of lessening growing concerns over nuclear war, the administration pressed ahead with an unpopular idea focusing on evacuations. The plan entailed evacuating citizens from potential target zones (nuclear bases and metropolitan areas with over 50,000 people) to 3,040 locations in rural America. At a cost of 4.3 billion dollars over seven years, however, critics seized on the plan as yet another defense boondoggle.[66]

Days after the evacuation plan announcement, the second special session on disarmament began at the United Nations, with hundreds of members of parliament from across the globe demanding an immediate nuclear freeze. Reagan later took the podium, blending "appeals for peace with blunt denunciations of Soviet behavior." He championed his administration's arms control

proposals while accusing the Soviets of repressing Eastern Europe in violation of the Yalta agreement of 1945. He further castigated the Soviets for
their "vast buildup" over the "decade of so-called détente." Reagan, however,
was on the defensive from what many in his administration saw as "a coup of
sorts." The day before his UN address, Soviet foreign minister Andrei Gromyko
delivered a pledge from Brezhnev of no first use of nuclear weapons. Reagan
did not address the concern in his remarks, but the administration affirmed
there would be no change in its position on first strike. Reagan's twenty-six-
minute UN speech was greeted with minor applause, but no standing ovation
as often accompanies speeches by heads of state.[67]

The primary importance of Reagan's UN speech was to build support for
his arms control proposals while deflecting the expected protests that would
accompany his forthcoming European peace offensive. British prime minister
Margaret Thatcher's conservative government privately sought to "counter
any impression on the part of the President that Britain is dominated by antinuclear and anti-American elements," adding that Americans and Europeans
alike saw Reagan's visit to London as "an opportunity for him to demonstrate
the closeness of the ANGLO/US relationship." Furthermore, Reagan's address
to both houses of Parliament was "an opportunity to address himself through
Britain to Europe as a whole and to project himself as a strong leader as well
as a decent man, a peacemaker and not a warmonger." But faced with "public
disillusionment, particularly in the field of disarmament, the president never
looked like scoring an easy victory," British ambassador to the United States
Nicholas Henderson concluded. Inside Parliament, Reagan proclaimed he
would leave the Soviet Union in the "ash heap of history," while outside an
additional two hundred fifty thousand people protested in the streets. Reagan
would encounter protests from peace activists throughout his trip to Europe.
In advance of his speech in Rome, three hundred thousand took to the streets,
and another three hundred thousand rallied against him and the arms race the
day after his address to the West German Bundestag in Bonn. The message to
Reagan from Europe was "clear," as END noted: "We want active steps to disarmament now, not cosmetic talks."[68]

Stateside, the UN disarmament session was accompanied by major rallies
across the nation. From Los Angeles to San Francisco, Salt Lake City to Denver, at the US-Canadian border, and in Little Rock, Arkansas, hundreds of thousands rallied for a nuclear freeze and policies favoring disarmament. The
largest of these rallies, however, occurred on June 12, 1982, in New York City.
Dubbed the "March for Disarmament," peace activists from across the world
marched through the streets of Manhattan, carrying banners reading "Freeze
the Arms Race," singing "Give Peace a Chance," and chanting "No more

nukes!" The goals were twofold: call for a freeze in the arms race and convert military spending for human needs.

Planning for the June 12 march and rally had been in the works since April 1981, before the Freeze became a mass movement. As MFS activist Leslie Cagan recollected, "For over a year a coalition had met, planned, worked and struggled to build this massive outpouring of public sentiment." The inspiration to hold a massive rally in the United States, however, came from European antinuclear activists, who were already holding large demonstrations in opposition to the neutron bomb and cruise missiles and wanted their American colleagues to "step up." As Terry Provance returned from Europe, he brought the idea to a Freeze meeting at the Riverside Church in Manhattan. From there he "practically worked fulltime from 1981 to 1982" to help build the march and rally. At the annual MFS meeting in December 1981, Reverend Bob Moore encouraged members to come to the planned spring demonstration; he would later charter a fourteen-car New Jersey Transit train of over 1,400 people to the event. While MFS played a key role in organizing the March for Disarmament, the June 12th Rally Committee consisted of a diverse coalition of activists from various peace, antinuclear, labor, and religious organizations, including Freeze, Greenpeace, WILPF, the Riverside Church Disarmament Program, the Coalition of Black Trade Unionists, the Ministerial Interfaith Association, the Asian-American Caucus for Disarmament, and Hispanics for Survival and Disarmament (among others). By coming together to plan the demonstration, alongside various cultural and political activities that would surround it, activists hoped to "broaden and deepen" the movement to not only grow in numbers but further "reach into different constituencies and communities."[69]

As planning progressed at the UN Church Center, the coalition agreed on a call against all nuclear weapons and for the transfer of funds from military to social spending but could not agree on a statement against military intervention. Disagreements emerged over civil disobedience. Newer groups were unwilling to publicly associate with the tactic, while older peace activists from the WRL organized a civil disobedience action on June 14 that would include leaders from the West German Greens. The coalition also struggled with the issue of racism, both as a demand (antiracism) and surrounding "operative racism within the coalition." In an effort to break with "the old habit of letting white people set the terms for third world participation," the coalition assured that at least one-third of all participants would be third world groups or individuals chosen by third world constituents. Another weakness Cagan identified was "the lack of struggle around feminism and issues of sexual politics." For Cagan, the fact that there was "no overt, direct struggle around issues of

FIGURE 4. On June 12, 1982, over one million people from across the world protested against nuclear weapons in New York City as part of the June 12 Disarmament March and Rally. Demonstrators rallied at Central Park, where they called for a freeze in the arms race. Courtesy of Rick Reinhard.

sexism" was testament "not to how good things were but rather to how very far we still have to go before feminism is incorporated into the politics of other social change movements."[70]

The coalition may have struggled at times, but they created a stronger and even more diverse group of attendees. Those who came to demonstrate that June came from around the world, representing all walks of life. While rally organizers expected a large turnout, those expectations were far surpassed, with approximately one in every 220 Americans participating in the march and rally. At its peak, the crowd was estimated at one million—the largest single demonstration in US history. The march was covered by everyone from popular local New York cable channel host Coca Crystal to major journalists and news anchors from around the world.[71]

The March for Disarmament culminated in a rally on the Great Lawn in Central Park. Every hour of the rally would feature two different program emcees (billed as "Co-masters of Ceremonies"). These included union activists from national organizations such as the UAW and AFSCME, actors Ossie Davis and Paul Newman, actresses Lily Tomlin and Ruby Dee, author and broadcaster Studs Terkel, peace activist David Dellinger, and Reverend Jesse Jackson and Reverend William Sloane Coffin, among others. The emcees would introduce an array of speakers, including UAW president Douglas Frazer; civil rights activists Andrew Young and Coretta Scott King; Freeze activists Helen Caldicott and Randy Forsberg; retired admiral Gene LaRocque (Center for Defense Information); and former congressman and former ambassador to the Soviet Union Tom Watson. As part of the rally, the Dentures Art Club of New York City invited thousands of activists to participate in a balloon release. The club distributed three thousand helium-filled silver Mylar balloons, each imprinted with an atomic blast on one side and the message "Say Goodbye to Nuclear Weapons" on the other. The activity would culminate in a "final countdown to a nuclear arms-free world," with attendees releasing the balloons—a symbolic act to "'Say Goodbye to Nuclear Weapons' forever." Hours of speeches were interspersed with performances by contemporary popular musicians, such as Bruce Springsteen; older folk artists, such as Pete Seeger; reggae artist Rita Marley (widow of reggae legend Bob Marley); Latin artist Roy Brown; and rock artists James Taylor, Linda Ronstadt, and Jackson Browne, among others. Taking to the microphone to address the attendees, Randy Forsberg looked out at the massive crowd and announced, "We've done it. The nuclear freeze campaign has mobilized the biggest peacetime peace movement in United States history." "Until the arms race stops," Forsberg told the audience, "we will not go home and be quiet. We will go home and organize."[72]

CHAPTER 3

From the Streets to the Pulpit

The Catholic Challenge to the Arms Race

With the rapid growth of the Freeze movement came allies from across society. Perhaps the most significant of these was the National Conference of Catholic Bishops (NCCB, which later became the United States Conference of Catholic Bishops, USCCB). The bishops provided the moral backbone to the Freeze after debating and publishing a pastoral letter that condemned the arms race and lent support to the campaign. This created a major dilemma for the Reagan administration in that whereas it could publicly dismiss members of the broader antinuclear movement as "freeze-niks" or "unilateral disarmers," using the same terms to describe Catholic bishops could potentially alienate Catholic voters—a major voting bloc. If the administration could not position itself on the moral high ground on the arms race, it could lose the Catholic vote and with it possibly reelection in 1984 (thus resulting in the premature end of the Reagan revolution).

To prevent this, the administration adopted new strategies to combat the Freeze. First, it pushed important Catholic social issues, such as opposition to abortion and support for prayer in school, into the mainstream of US politics, helping sow the seeds of the modern-day culture wars. While administration officials privately worried about the political implications of the pastoral, publicly they were always cordial to the bishops. The administration watched the pastoral deliberations carefully but never expressed outright disapproval of the letter. Instead, it insisted the two parties held the same fundamental views on the arms race, differing only on minor matters. As NSC staff member Robert Sims later acknowledged, "There was every effort to handle the issue with kids' gloves, to not set up a hostile situation."[1] To avoid a dynamic wherein the administration was pitted against the bishops, more hostile critiques were left to Catholic allies and other mainstream conservative voices. Furthermore, the administration attempted to highlight and widen divisions among the bishops over nuclear weapons and the Cold War more generally, meeting with and using the statements of Archbishop Phillip Hannan as well as Pope John Paul II—both steeped in Cold War ideological hatred for the Soviet Union. To fend off critics, the administration pushed a new image of the president struggling with the morality of nuclear war, just as the Catholic bishops were. In so doing, it managed to evade the bishops' serious criticisms. In the larger picture, the bishops' intervention in the public dialogue surrounding the arms race underscored how the Reagan administration engaged its arms control critics and subsequently the Freeze movement.

Morality and Armageddon

In 1963, Pope John XXIII announced the opening of the Second Vatican Council. Vatican II ushered in numerous changes to the Church and led to four Apostolic constitutions (the highest decree a pope can issue to the public). The 1965 Pastoral Constitution on the Church in the Modern World ("Gaudium et Spes") was an overview of the Catholic Church's teachings about humanity's relationship to society, tackling a range of issues. The Church notably condemned methods of warfare that were "designed for the extermination of entire peoples, nations, and ethnic minorities" and further declared "every act of war directed to the indiscriminate destruction of whole cities or vast areas with their inhabitants" to be "a crime against God and man, which merits firm and unequivocal condemnation." From this came what Joseph Cardinal Bernardin later called "a consistent ethic of life"—an idea that would significantly affect the Church's relationship with the US government in the years to come.[2]

By the 1976 presidential campaign, Catholics found themselves in opposition to their government over another pro-life issue: the legalized practice of abortion (a practice the Catholic Church had been campaigning against for the past decade). Just three years earlier, in the *Roe v. Wade* decision, the US Supreme Court overturned restrictions on legalized abortion. The *Roe* decision created a national debate over a woman's right to choose and the definition of life, while altering US political dynamics. In 1976, many Catholic voters sought a president who would overturn the *Roe* decision. With neither party taking a strong stance against abortion, anti-abortion Catholics sided with Democratic presidential candidate Jimmy Carter. An openly born-again Christian, Carter persuaded Catholics that he would support a "stricter ruling" on the *Roe* case and would support a "national statute" on abortion. Catholics therefore overwhelmingly cast their lot with Carter, 57 percent to Ford's 42 percent. Once in office, however, Carter never supported stricter measures on abortion, let alone a constitutional amendment overturning *Roe*.

As the 1980 election approached, Catholics were primed for a split with the Democrats. Campaigning for the Republican Party nomination, Ronald Reagan embraced the pro-life movement and vigorously opposed *Roe*. In the years to come, the Christian right would proudly boast of making abortion a "litmus test" for anyone seeking office in the Republican Party.[3] Reagan won the Republican nomination and went on to edge out the Catholic vote from Carter, 47 percent to 46 percent. Although this only represented a 5 percent gain from President Ford's total in 1976, it was the highest percentage of the Catholic vote a Republican had received since Richard Nixon's 1972 victory over George McGovern. It further marked an 11 percent decline from Jimmy Carter's 57 percent of the Catholic vote just four years earlier.[4]

Most important to the Reagan administration was the increase in what it described as "ECBCs" (ethnic Catholic blue collars), "the most dynamic element in American politics today." Administration pollster Richard Wirthlin found that ECBCs jumped to the Reagan campaign, with Reagan picking up 17 percent more than Gerald Ford had in 1976. As Catholic journalist Jim Castelli concluded, "The normally democratic voters who voted for Reagan [were] more important to his administration's success and any plans for re-election than [were] most other groups." As such, Catholic views on the arms race were critical. Since the dawn of the nuclear age, the papacy had linked the role of nuclear weapons and the arms race to the teachings of peace. During Vatican II, the bishops labeled the arms race "an utterly treacherous trap for humanity, and one which injures the poor to an intolerable degree." Although the Catholic Church supported the SALT II Treaty in 1980, its perceived flaws led Catholic publications such as *Commonweal* to carry vigorous debates over whether it deserved support. Pacifist organizations such as PAX Christi claimed the treaty was not a "step toward arms limitation" but encouraged "arms escalation." Father J. Bryan Hehir of the Office of the United States Catholic Bishops argued it was possible to build a case for support of SALT II as a limited, but necessary, measure of arms control deserving the "support of all those, including Christians, who are committed to abolishing the nuclear threat to human life."[5]

Following the Soviet invasion of Afghanistan and the subsequent withdrawal of SALT II from the Senate in 1980, Catholic bishops began speaking out against the arms race. In an address at the United Nations, the auxiliary bishop of Baltimore, Maryland, P. Francis Murphy, declared, "There is a moral imperative to halt the arms race." As someone who believed in "God's gift of peace to the entire human family," Murphy was "terrified by the thoughts of the world's annihilation by nuclear warfare." He called on all religious leaders to "provide for the world a sign and source of hope that we can bring the arms race under control." Murphy pledged that, as a moral teacher, the Catholic Church would continue to condemn the arms race. Murphy concluded his rousing speech with a call to "make flesh the words of [Pope] Paul VI to the UN: 'No more war, war never again. Peace! It is peace that must guide the destinies of peoples and all humankind.'"[6]

In fall 1980, Catholic peace organization PAX Christi USA sponsored a five-page statement issued by three bishops and forty clergy members. Distressed by the rhetoric of militarism and the insistence that the United States must "continue to lead in the production of instruments of death," "A Catholic Call to Conscience" urged the Catholic Church to "undertake a major effort to mobilize effective opposition to modern war and weaponry on a scale at least equal to that now directed against abortion." The statement furthermore asked Catholics in the military "not to give or obey orders to use nuclear weapons" and asked those involved in the production of weapons of mass destruction to "seek other occupations."[7]

PAX Christi USA soon followed the Catholic Call to Conscience. A Lent mailing to its 3,500 members encouraged them to individually write to Freeze coordinator Randall Forsberg and personally endorse a nuclear freeze. Furthermore, PAX Christi began soliciting Catholic bishops to endorse the campaign and collected the signatures of those who did. In May 1981, PAX Christi International adopted a declaration in Vienna on "International Disarmament and Security." The declaration pleaded for a "new way of thinking and a new approach" about peace and disarmament, stating that, "We should rethink the concept of security, which cannot be interpreted as merely a military concept" but must be defined as including "socio-economic, political, and also ecological value." They welcomed unilateral proposals that could "evoke a bilateral and multilateral process towards disarmament and peace," such as the example of PAX Christi Netherlands, which proposed its own country be free of nuclear weapons "as an example to others and a realistic path to the peacemaking process." The Church "should be a leading force" in this new way of thinking, and, as a Catholic organization dedicated to peace,

PAX Christi saw itself with a special role to play in promoting "the process of disarmament."[8]

Catholics were a critical voting block for the Reagan administration. In recognition of their support, Reagan soon extended diplomatic relations to the Vatican (a move previous administrations had rejected).[9] Furthermore, as Paul Kengor writes, Reagan's cabinet "was surrounded by serious Catholics," such as CIA Director William J. Casey, speechwriter Tony Dolan, Secretary of State Alexander Haig, ambassador-at-large Vernon Walters, and Reagan's first two national security advisors, Richard Allen and William "Judge" Clark (the latter so devout that he once considered studying for the priesthood).[10] The administration did not simply court Catholics; it placed them in the highest positions of policymaking. But on matters of war and peace, Catholic opinion followed much of public opinion.

The question of nuclear war hung over American society like the sword of Damocles, but the Reagan administration's defense modernization plans clashed with the statements on arms control and nuclear war many of the Catholic bishops were making. Just days after Reagan's neutron bomb announcement, in Amarillo, Texas, Bishop Leroy T. Matthiessen made the front page of the *New York Times* in what was described as an "unpopular, one man campaign against the neutron bomb." Reagan's decision to pursue the dormant neutron bomb was just "the latest in a self series [*sic*] of tragic anti-life positions taken by our government," Matthiessen bemoaned. Following his condemnation of the neutron bomb, Matthiessen reiterated the Catholic Call to Conscience and urged workers at the nearby Pantex plant (home to production of the nation's nuclear weapons) to "consider resigning" and instead seek "employment in peaceful pursuits." The Amarillo branch of the nonprofit Catholic Family Services soon after offered ten thousand dollars in grants to help employees quit work at the Pantex plant, but the remarks and the offer by Catholic Family Services were not well received in the community and furthermore created serious repercussions for the Catholic charity. Ten percent of the Pantex employees (as well as numerous others from the surrounding Amarillo community) threatened to withhold contributions to the United Way, a prime donor to Catholic Family Services. Caving in to the pressure, United Way dropped a sixty-one thousand dollar grant to the nonprofit Catholic organization.[11]

While Matthiessen was making headlines, other bishops were equally driven to stop the arms race. A study paper by bishop Anthony Pilla of Cleveland condemned the use of nuclear weapons in war as violating Saint Augustine's principles of just war, therefore making modern war "morally reprehensible, and a crime against God." Pilla called on the Church to oppose modern war "as strongly as we oppose abortion, racism and poverty" and urged Catholics to join and support the Nuclear Freeze movement. In Seattle, Washington, Archbishop Raymond G. Hunthausen condemned the Trident II submarine as the "Auschwitz of the Puget Sound" and threatened to withhold half his income tax as a protest against the arms race. In Montana and Nevada, bishops expressed similar feelings condemning the MX missile. Within a week of Matthiessen's controversial remarks, twelve Catholic bishops had adopted a statement condemning the neutron bomb specifically and the arms race more broadly. From Alaska to California, Massachusetts to Illinois, bishops were condemning nuclear war, the arms race, and the possession of weapons of mass destruction.[12]

In fall 1981, Archbishop John R. Quinn, past president of the NCCB, publicly called on Catholics to take "concerted political action to stop development and deployment of nuclear weapons." Quinn urged Catholic hospitals to oppose a government plan to develop a "civilian-military contingency hospital system" since it might foster "the illusion that there can be an effective response" to a nuclear war. Finally, Quinn, like Pilla, urged Catholics to join the burgeoning national cause calling for an immediate "nuclear arms freeze" between the United States and the Soviet Union as a "realistic step toward bilateral disarmament."[13]

Just before year's end, Stockton, California, bishop Roger Mahoney added his voice to the "growing chorus of Catholic protests against the arms race." Mahoney contended that the arsenals and weapon policies of both the United States and the Soviet Union "exceeded the bounds of justice, and moral legitimacy," making it "impossible effectively to end the urgent crisis of world hunger," adding, "Each day we permit [the arms race] to continue without protest perpetuates itself by becoming embedded in our everyday habits and attitudes." Mahoney believed that what was needed instead was "a radical change of our hearts and our attitudes—a new awareness of our calling to be a people dedicated to peace." Thus, by the end of 1981, a sizable section of the Church hierarchy openly opposed a continuing arms race.[14]

A "revolution" was fomenting within the Catholic hierarchy. As Vincent A. Yzermans, a priest from Minnesota and former information director for the bishops, wrote in an op-ed in the New York Times, antinuclear activism had the potential to create "an explosion between church and state," making issues such as abortion, school aid, and the tax-exempt status of churches look like "a child's sparkler on the Fourth of July." By all measures, the bishops' annual meeting that November seemed to indicate that a revolution was indeed taking place within the Catholic hierarchy. "Never before had the bishops stood so firmly against the use of nuclear arms," reported the New York Times. Many bishops expressed complete opposition to nuclear weapons, and some began referring to the Catholic Church as a "peace church." Pro-life could no longer be reduced to opposition to abortion. Instead, it was to be blended with issues of poverty and disarmament to form a broader meaning, covering life from "womb to tomb."[15]

In April 1982, the Associated Press reported that nearly half the nation's Catholic bishops favored a nuclear weapons freeze, but the bishops' bold and open opposition to nuclear war, manifested in the writing of a pastoral letter, began quietly in 1980, when then archbishop Joseph Bernardin of Cincinnati was appointed to head a committee that would lay the foundation for a future pastoral letter on war and peace. Bernardin was pro-life in the broadest sense. From Vatican II, Bernardin came to the realization that he had been called not just to promote Catholic subculture within society but also to actively shape and engage the society he lived in. Like many other bishops, Bernardin was alarmed at the escalating arms race. "In Bernardin's judgment," his biographer Eugene Kennedy writes, life was to be defended "against all negative threats to its sacred character. Otherwise, the pro-life movement might seem distorted and could come under the control of the extreme right wing of anti-abortionist activists." If that happened, the challenge of both overturning the *Roe* decision via constitutional amendment and building a consensus in the nation against abortion would become crippled. Bernardin, however, was assigned to head the pastoral review committee not because of his philosophical positions but based on his past actions as a mediator within the Church. As even Catholic opponents of the Freeze acknowledged, Bernardin was well known as a consensus builder—and, on an issue with obvious political implications, there was no one in the Church more qualified.[16]

In 1981 and 1982, Bernardin's ad hoc committee would meet and solicit testimony from a variety of experts, including former government officials and members of the Reagan administration. From the outset, notes Castelli, Bernardin set "one firm ground rule for the committee—it would not under any circumstances support unilateral nuclear disarmament." Instead, the committee sought to develop existing Catholic thought on war in the modern world and, if necessary, develop new doctrine. Though the Catholic peace organization PAX Christi urged the committee to seek out a moral vision, the committee also sought out technical experts in the field to explain weapons systems and defense measures. The bishops listened to numerous experts on nuclear war but held off on meeting with members of the White House until they were further along in their deliberations. Bernardin assumed that members of the Reagan administration would stick to official positions, and he wanted

FIGURE 5. Joseph Cardinal Bernardin oversaw the drafting of the National Conference of Catholic Bishops' pastoral letter on war and peace ("The Challenge of Peace"). The final draft of the letter condemned the arms race as a threat to "the sovereignty of God over the world He has brought into being." Courtesy of the Archdiocese of Chicago's Joseph Cardinal Bernardin Archives and Records Center.

the committee to have a chance to develop its own thinking on the subject before hearing from the White House.

In February 1982, Bernardin's committee began corresponding with the White House. Bernardin wrote to President Reagan but did not receive a direct reply. Within a month, however, Bernardin received separate replies from Secretary of State Haig, Secretary of Defense Weinberger, and ACDA director Eugene Rostow. Though communications between the bishops and the White House were open, administration officials did not meet with the committee until May. Unable to meet with Haig, the bishops met with Undersecretary of State for Political Affairs Lawrence Eagleburger, but the meeting did not go so well. As Castelli wrote, "Eagleburger was called out of the room on business several times," leaving the bishops with Eagleburger's younger aides, who "chided the bishops for being too idealistic." On the other hand, meetings between the bishops and Rostow and Weinberger were "more cordial," with Weinberger being perhaps "a little too candid," telling the bishops that the administration was seeking nuclear parity with the Soviets—a process that Weinberger estimated would take "about eight years." Rostow followed up with a letter to Bernardin exclaiming how delighted he was "'to be a witness' before [Bernardin] and the members of the NCCB's Committee on War and Peace."[17]

In April 1982, however, Bernardin was still unsure whether to support a nuclear freeze. In a letter to Father J. Bryan Hehir, Bernardin enclosed editorials from local Cincinnati newspapers opposing a freeze and expressed concern over the arguments against it while expressing his own concerns over what to believe.[18] Inside the Reagan White House, however, staff had already drawn conclusions about where the Catholic bishops and their allies were heading. In an April 1982 memo to White House chief of staff James Baker, Thomas Patrick Melady, a prominent Catholic academic serving in the Education Department, suggested the Reagan administration should "seize the peace initiative in Catholic Circles." The "President's opponents in the Catholic community," Melady suggested, were "orchestrating a campaign" that would pit the Reagan administration against "the Pope, the Vatican, and the Catholic Church on the issue of nuclear force." Melady called on the administration to "begin now not only to defuse this sensitive issue, but to seize the initiative to prove that our position is the moral one for a responsible major power in an imperfect world, where aggressive communist-atheistic forces are out to destroy Judeo Christian values."[19]

Heeding Melady's advice, the administration began pushing issues of importance to the Catholic community. As a candidate, Reagan campaigned on a constitutional amendment that would ban abortion, but in his first year in office, Reagan suggested there might be no need for an amendment, so long as the Congress defined "when and what is a human being." President Reagan soon changed his position and pushed for a constitutional amendment that would limit or restrict legalized abortions. Likewise, he came out in support of a constitutional amendment that would allow prayer in school, further proclaiming May 6, 1982, a "national day of prayer." But, as *Time* magazine suggested, the Reagan administration "worked only halfheartedly in Congress for laws that would permit organized school prayer" as well as other issues important to social conservatives.[20]

In June 1982, the US Catholic bishops circulated the first draft of their new pastoral letter. From the outset, however, the draft was problematic in several ways. The title, "God's Hope in a Time of Fear," raised questions from other bishops, who thought it was "vague" or "confusing" or implied that "God hopes" could be discerned. Besides the title, there were more serious issues. The draft was hard to follow at times, with some points repeating themselves and others not connecting for several pages. The draft also sought to avoid "political 'red flag'" words such as "nuclear freeze" and "no first use." Though it did not specifically call for a "freeze," the letter did have a section backing its essential elements. Despite its problems, the draft staked out key claims that would form the basis of the bishops' critique of the arms race. In response to the draft, Bernardin received thousands of letters, and countless invitations from organizations asking him to address their group. While the conservative *Cincinnati Enquirer* published critical editorials and letters from prominent Catholics such as Patrick Buchanan and William F. Buckley, Bernardin received much support from lay Catholics, as well as nuns and priests. A letter from the Sisters of Charity of Nazareth praised Bernardin for the "extension of the pro-life stance into the areas of nuclear disarmament." Even the Communist Party USA (no friends of the Catholic Church) praised the bishops, hoping their "voices of reason" would be "heard above Reagan's call for a holy war."[21]

Coinciding with the development of the first draft but just prior to its public distribution, Pope John Paul II made two statements that would have major implications for the entire nuclear arms debate within Catholic communities. On June 10, 1982, the pope remarked that "the scale and the horror of modern warfare . . . makes [war] totally unacceptable as a means of settling differences between nations. War should belong to the tragic past, to history; it should find no place on humanity's agenda for the future." The following day, speaking on behalf of the pope at the UN Special Session on Disarmament, Vatican secretary of state Cardinal Agostino Cassaroli condemned the possibility of nuclear war while recognizing the "sincere and profound desire of peace" among the many movements developing across the globe. The pope's message, however, did not call for a freeze or for disarmament but instead argued that "in current conditions 'deterrence' based on balance, certainly not as an end in itself but as a step on the way toward a progressive disarmament, may still be judged morally acceptable."[22]

Deterrence as "morally acceptable" soon became keywords that Freeze opponents and opponents of the pastoral seized on, but was it a disavowal of the claims the bishops were staking out? Detroit's auxiliary bishop Thomas Gumbleton believed that the pope's words were being taken out of context. In a letter to Father Hehir, Gumbleton wrote, "We must use the whole quotation because he [Pope John Paul II] is, in fact, speaking about a certain kind of deterrent (and only this kind is morally acceptable), i.e., a deterrent that is intimately joined with genuine steps towards disarmament." But this clearly was not the case with the current deterrent, as Gumbleton observed, since one could not reasonably conclude that the United States' nuclear deterrent fit into "a framework where disarmament is going on." As further evidence, Gumbleton pointed to the "Weinberger 5-year plan for escalation," wherein the United States committed itself to developing a strategy for protracted and winnable nuclear war. The United States' nuclear deterrent, Gumbleton concluded, was "clearly something other than what John Paul was describing."[23]

Toward "Nuclear Heresy"

While it was one thing for liberal bishops such as Bernardin to openly oppose the Reagan administration's Cold War policies, the administration worried that the antinuclear message the US Catholic hierarchy voiced would resonate with lay Catholics. But rather than attack the bishops directly, President Reagan spoke in front of religious audiences of various faiths to dissuade them from accepting a freeze. In August 1982, in an address to Roman Catholics in the Supreme Council of the Knights of the Republic in Hartford, Connecticut, Reagan told his audience that they took "second place to none in the quest for peace through arms control and agreements," whereas the ideas put forward by the Freeze were "obsolete" and "sterile." While antinuclear voices were prominent outside the Hartford Civic Center, inside President Reagan fared no better when a protester interrupted him in the middle of his speech, shouting "No more nuclear weapons! Jobs for the poor!" It was a message that was coming directly from the teachings of the bishops.[24]

Antinuclear activism was flourishing in Catholic circles. In July 1982, the "Trident Nein" (a group of activists from the Catholic activist network Atlantic Life Community) broke into General Dynamics' Electric Boat Division shipyard in Groton, Connecticut, where the Trident submarine was manufactured. As Bruce Shapiro reported in *Nuclear Times* (the official newsletter of the Freeze campaign), "Four of the nine paddled in a canoe up to the U.S.S. *Florida,* an uncompleted Trident docked in the Thames River." There the activists "hoisted banners, spray painted the 560-foot submarine with the words 'U.S.S. Auschwitz,' poured blood down missile tubes, and hammered on hatch covers." The activists cut a hole in the chain link fence and "hammered and poured blood on uninstalled sonar equipment"—"the eyes and ears of the Trident monster."[25]

But Catholic opposition to the arms race did not always involve such dramatic acts of civil disobedience. In September 1982, the annual meeting of the National Association of Catholic Chaplains (a US organization consisting of 2,800 Catholic priests, deacons, religious, and laity serving in health care institutions) adopted a resolution calling on the US government to "uphold basic human rights by immediately adopting a policy and practice of a nuclear arms freeze, and more than that, a nuclear arms reduction." In Indianapolis, St. Thomas Aquinas Catholic Church began withholding its federal taxes on its phone bill as a protest against the arms race. Members of St. Thomas Aquinas were now frequently discussing the arms race, with many having "accepted the church's role in opposition to the arms race," noted one member of its Peace Education Committee.[26]

With the White House inundated with letters concerned about the arms race and the bishops' opposition to it spreading among the lay masses, the Reagan administration anxiously worried about the next step the bishops would take. National Security Advisor Clark took the lead in critiquing the pastoral. In a letter to former US congresswoman and ambassador Clare Booth Luce, a prominent Catholic and Reagan White House confidante, Clark expressed two "fundamental concerns" over it. First, Clark charged that the bishops had a "fundamental misunderstanding" of "existing nuclear deterrence policy." Second, though the letter called for alternative approaches to nuclear arsenals, it did so "without presenting the reader . . . with any information about the far-reaching efforts initiated by the United States to bring the world close to peace and reconciliation." Clark attempted to frame the issue as one in which there was no real conflict but only a simple misunderstanding. Clark concluded his letter to Luce by stressing that the pastoral letter actually was "remarkably consistent with current U.S. nuclear policy, with one notable exception—the issue of no nuclear first use." But even there, Clark added, the administration shared the "concern about the risk of escalation." Though there were no real disagreements, Clark concluded, since the administration's approach took consideration of the "full range of escalatory risk," it was "better and wiser."[27]

On October 26, 1982, in a memo to Bill Triplett of the Office of Public Liaison, Red Cavaney reported on a meeting of Bud McFarlane's Nuclear Policy Group, where the discussion focused on the bishops' stance "supporting a freeze, doubting deterrence, and suggesting to Catholic lay people that any participation in nuclear arms production or deployment may be morally wrong." These topics were certain to be on the agenda at the bishops' annual meeting, Cavaney reported, and thus "it was suggested that we may have to mobilize some of 'our political types like Jack Burgess [a deputy director in the White House Office of Public Liaison] to educate the bishops in this matter."[28]

Although Cavaney's memo was vague, the fears it expressed were well founded, given the timing. With the 1982 midterm elections just one week away, nine states and the District of Columbia had nonbinding resolutions calling for the United States and the Soviet Union to bilaterally freeze the arms race. The same morning Cavaney sent the memo to Triplett, the front page of the *New York Times* featured excerpts from the forthcoming second draft of the pastoral letter. Though the bishops would not formally meet until mid-November, the excerpts were leaked and appeared in several major newspapers. The letter criticized policies such as targeting civilians, called deterrence into question, and, "if [its ideas] passed," the *Times* reported, "would also shift concerns for arms reduction from the periphery to the core of the church's social ministry." The heart of the letter condemned the arms race as a threat to "the sovereignty of God over the world He has brought into being." Finally, in complete opposition to the administration, the letter urged "an immediate but verifiable freeze" of the arms race. At their annual meeting that November, the full body of US Catholic bishops began debating this second draft, now titled "The Challenge of Peace: God's Promise and Our Response."[29]

The Reagan administration did not sit idly by as the bishops made headlines but rather appealed directly to the Vatican. Ambassador-at-large Vernon Walters entered the Holy City unannounced, seeking an audience with the pope. While the exact nature of Walters's visit is disputed, conservative columnists Robert Novak and Rowland Evans suggested the "real purpose" of Walters's visit with the pope was to stem the bishops' "nuclear heresy." Novak and Evans reported concerns from many American Catholic laity that the antinuclear activism of the bishops had gone too far for even the pope to stamp out, but they believed the Reagan administration was more optimistic, thus explaining Walters's mission.[30]

The administration's optimism was related to recent interactions between the pope and Bernardin, who had been summoned by His Holiness the previous week. Though Evans and Novak implied the pope was bringing Bernardin in line with both the Church hierarchy and the Reagan administration, Bernardin's biographer Eugene Kennedy disputes this, saying, "Church officials in Rome were hesitant to endorse the work of the American bishops," not on political grounds but out of fear that the bishops could get out of control and threaten their "conception of central church authority." Indeed, Archbishop of St. Paul and Minneapolis John Roach suggested there had been "no direct pressure" from either the White House or the Vatican to weaken the pastoral letter. Roach did, however, express concern over "a little bit of the rhetoric" that the antinuclear movement was manipulated by the Soviets. This, Roach noted, was "a disservice," for if "ever there was a group of people with a pretty good track record when it comes to loyalty, it is this body."[31]

Archbishop Roach's comments were in response to Reagan's accusation that foreign agents were manipulating the Freeze movement. At a press conference, Reagan suggested there was "plenty of evidence" and "no question . . . the Soviet Union saw an advantage in a peace movement built around the idea of a nuclear freeze." But when asked a follow-up question about details of Soviet involvement in the Freeze campaign, Reagan refused to discuss it any further, claiming it was an "intelligence matter." While attempting to link the Freeze campaign with the Soviet Union in one breath, Reagan attempted to head off the movement, downplaying disagreements: "I want to emphasize again that the overwhelming majority of the people involved in [the Freeze movement] . . . are sincere and well intentioned and, as a matter of fact, are saying the same thing I'm saying."[32]

The Reagan White House nevertheless maintained an active watch over the bishops. In a memo to Cavaney, Burgess passed along an op-ed from Archbishop of New Orleans Philip Hannan. In it, Hannan called for the tabling of the pastoral letter, substituting instead the "splendid message made by the Holy Father on disarmament on June 11, 1982 to the United Nations" and the "message of the Holy Father on Peace from January 1, 1982." These messages, Hannan believed, were "vastly superior to the proposed pastoral in many respects," embodying a "much more universal concern for all human rights and spiritual needs." The pastoral, on the other hand, did not give "sufficient importance to the statement of the Holy Father on the morality of deterrence."[33]

Archbishop Hannan was a strident anticommunist. The Reagan administration had previously engaged Hannan, finding him "very supportive of the administration," while further recommending him to McFarlane's anti-freeze policy group.[34] Hannan was also part of a minority of bishops who opposed the pastoral letter, believing it indicated a lack of understanding of current nuclear policy and President Reagan's policy of first strike. Hannan quoted Reagan as stating that NATO policy was based on "restraint and balance" and that "no weapon, conventional or nuclear, will ever be used in Europe except in response to attack." Hannan furthermore doubted that a nuclear war would ever occur "as long as we have adequate defense" and reiterated his concerns for the "millions who suffer daily from the deprivation of their basic human rights"—a remark aimed at the Soviet Union.[35]

Not long after the bishops began their annual meeting, Clark went back on the offensive for the White House. In a letter to Bernardin, he repeated the mantra that there was no disagreement between the White House and the bishops. Clark took a critical but cordial approach. "We understood then that our comments would be fully considered by the committee," he wrote, reminding Bernardin of their past correspondence over the first draft while implying that the bishops had not taken the administration's critiques under full consideration. Quoting the pastoral, Clark noted, "We can agree that any moral theory of defense is 'not . . . to legitimize war, but to prevent it,' and this, of course, is what American deterrence strategy is designed to achieve," adding that the White House "welcomed the involvement of the Catholic Bishops in the effort to secure effective arms control and to reduce the risks of war." Because of this, Clark said, it was regrettable "that the Committee's latest draft continues to reflect fundamental misreadings of American policies, and continues essentially to ignore the far-reaching American proposals." His letter went on to critique the freeze proposal as removing "incentives for reductions," while stressing the administration's own proposals as "initiatives for reduction, or even elimination, of the most destabilizing systems."[36]

Clark's letter, however, was published in the *New York Times* before Bernardin even received it. By publishing the letter, the administration could publicly state its objections about the pastoral while pushing its own narrative. But Clark was not the only Catholic in the administration to publish a letter about the bishops. In an op-ed in the *Wall Street Journal*, Secretary of the Navy John Lehman suggested it was "possible to completely agree with the [pastoral] letter's assertions about the moral paradox of deterrence and to disagree with its specific recommendations," since the recommendations could "lead directly to immoral consequences." The letter from Lehman was published on the first day of the bishops' meeting.[37]

To further undermine the bishops, Dana Rohrabacher, a speechwriter and special adviser to President Reagan, suggested using the attempted assassination of Pope John Paul II the prior May. Rohrabacher asserted that the highest levels of the Soviet government knew of the plot to assassinate the pope, with Soviet general secretary Yuri Andropov perhaps having "directly approved the attempt on the Pope's life." "This information, if used correctly," Rohrabacher claimed, could influence the deliberations of the Catholic bishops, as any arms control progress would require that the administration "trust the same Soviet leaders who may have plotted to assassinate their Pope."[38]

Elsewhere, administration tactics to influence the pastoral and the broader reach of the bishops would bring strong condemnation. In a letter to Joseph F. Fogarty Jr., chairman of the American Marine Underwriters and a prominent lay member of the Catholic Archdiocese of Washington, D.C., Ed Rowny (chairman of the START Talks) shared his "deep concerns" over the direction the US Catholic hierarchy was heading regarding US defense policy, deterrence, and national security. Rowny called the pastoral's second draft "troublesome" and "potentially dangerous, both for our country and our church." A decorated three-star general and a veteran of three wars, Rowny was concerned that the draft did not adequately represent the threat the Soviet Union posed. Rowny insisted the pastoral embraced "unilateral measures" that would lead to "the martyrdom of unilateral surrender." If the bishops chose to "deviate from papal teaching, they should make that point clear, and provide sound rationale for differing with the Holy Father," Rowny concluded. Fogarty passed on Rowny's remarks to Archbishop James Hickey. Hickey was "pained" by Rowny's letter and unequivocally stated that the bishops were not calling for unilateral disarmament or deviating from the Holy Father or the teachings of the Church. "This transparent attempt by the administration to drive a wedge between the Pope and the bishops is one that we necessarily resent and one that is totally unacceptable," Hickey scolded, while urging Rowny "to argue the case on its merits and not to cloud the issue by such divisionary actions as trying to find the difference between the Pope and the bishops on the issue of nuclear disarmament."[39]

An anonymous but politically savvy letter circulated internally best captured the dilemmas the bishops were causing the administration. Dated December 12, 1982, the memo expressed extreme concern that the bishops were dragging out the pastoral debate in order to "keep the nuclear freeze issue and their opposition to President Reagan on page one and thereby influence the Catholic community on the freeze." To counter the "public relations goldmine," the memo suggested one solution: "THE ABORTION ISSUE." The bishops had a "house divided" over the "nuclear freeze versus the pro-life issue," and thus, by pushing the abortion issue, the administration could take the offensive away from the bishops. The memo painted a stark choice: "use the president's strong pro-life stand to counter [the bishops], or face deeper and deeper loses [sic] in the Catholic vote in '84." During the 1982 midterm elections, the Republican Party had already lost 7 percent of the Catholic vote, and with a final draft of the pastoral slated for 1983, the issue could continue to plague Reagan and ignite Catholic opposition to him based on support for a nuclear freeze.[40]

Outside the Reagan White House, the bishops' stance was controversial in the Catholic community at large. James Hitchcock, a contributing editor to the *National Catholic Register*, expressed deep concerns over the bishops' letter, fearing their focus on nuclear weapons would push abortion off the agenda. With the defeat of the abortion bill in the Senate in 1982, Hitchcock suggested, "It will be tempting for many people, including some bishops, to say in effect: 'We gave it a good try but we failed. All we can do now is move on to other things.'" Furthermore, Hitchcock suggested there was a better reason for the bishops to ensure abortion remained the chief priority of the Catholic Church: "Nobody has been killed in nuclear war since 1945; abortions are taking place every minute."[41]

Conservative Catholics were central to the administration's strategy to avoid confrontation with the bishops. "We may be blessed by the presence of Michael Novak," noted McFarlane. A prominent Catholic journalist and philosopher, Novak's views had shifted rightward from his days as a sixties antiwar activist. Novak was now a resident scholar at conservative think tank the American Enterprise Institute (AEI) and a theoconservative—blending the beliefs of neoconservatism with theology. Novak was outraged by the pastoral letter and wrote scathingly of what he deemed "war bishops" in conservative magazines such as *National Review.* As early as January 1982, Novak was featured in the *Wall Street Journal* opinion pages critiquing bishops Matthiessen and Hunthausen as "extremists" who did not mind "passing judgment on their fellow Catholics" while claiming "their own extreme positions represent the teaching of the whole church." Novak was "exactly the right interlocutor" in the administration's efforts to "cast the Bishops as inflicting something on the Catholic people." The administration, McFarlane noted, should "not be visually seen as fighting men of the cloth" but should instead allow the bishops to "duke it out among themselves."[42]

Novak was an adviser to and board member of the American Catholic Committee, a group formed to oppose the bishops on issues related to economic, social, and foreign policy questions. Also involved with the organization were several other prominent conservative Catholics with ties to the administration: Robert Reilly, who would become special assistant to the president in 1983; Philip Lawler of AEI, who did not have a formal role in the White House but was a reliable ally; and Joseph Dugan, a UN staff member for Jeane Kirkpatrick. The group held a counterconference in October 1982, where they insisted that the United States needed "a strong nuclear arsenal to deter aggression" and deplored the "anti-Americanism of the Catholic left."[43]

Conservative lay Catholics continued to scold the bishops. In the *Phyllis Schlafly Report*, Schlafly and the Eagle Forum took the bishops to task for supporting a freeze, while *Human Events* reprinted Archbishop Hannan's critiques of the pastoral letter. The Eagle Forum of Northern Illinois sent a letter to its members urging them to write to Bernardin and request a postponement on publishing the pastoral because of the concerns of Archbishop Hannan and many in Congress, such as Representative Henry Hyde (R-IL). Hyde, a conservative Catholic, took the lead in Congress in attacking the bishops' pastoral letter. In a "most extraordinary response," historian Andrew Preston wrote, Hyde "carefully attacked the bishops' terms point by point." Signed by twenty-three other Catholic members of Congress, Hyde's letter to the bishops argued that nuclear weapons curtailed "the very real threat of Soviet Communism." As Preston observed, "Rarely had the gap between clergy and laity been so wide."[44]

Criticisms of the bishops were not confined to the halls of Congress, nor did they just appear in conservative publications or at conservative conferences. Since the pastoral was crafted in such a public fashion, Bernardin received thousands of letters. Some letters politely asked Bernardin to delay the pastoral, allowing more time for discussion, while other letters challenged the expertise of the bishops on national security matters. Many believed the letter should have been about abortion, while another common criticism was the neglect of the Lady of Fatima's plan for peace.[45] Although most of the mail Bernardin received was cordial, even if critical, there were others who were far more antagonistic toward him. A real estate agent from New York wrote to Bernardin, "I cant [sic] believe the stupidity in your intellect. How in the name of Christ did a lightweight like you become a Bishop? It's unbelievable. . . . Please for the Church's sake get lost! You are one of the worst embarrassments to come along since the Radic/Left/Marxist 'Father' [Robert] Drinan."[46] Another letter writer to Bernardin was "appalled at the naiveté of the Catholic Bishop" and accused him of being "a quisling—the leader of the Revolution to hand my country over to the KGB and Andropov. . . . You, Archbishop Bernardin, are aiding and abetting the destruction of this nation. I do pray for you—you terribly misguided soul!" Bernardin often acknowledged letters sent to him. In this instance, Bernardin expressed his understanding over disagreements about the pastoral while calmly replying: "You called me a 'quisling.' Don't you think that is a little extreme? I shall pray for you."[47]

The Reagan White House also received numerous letters concerning the second draft of the pastoral. When popular syndicated columnist Ann Landers implored her readers to write to the White House and mail in her column in support of a nuclear freeze, one writer sent the article to the White House with a letter that denounced Landers and the "mis-guided" "Catholic priests" as leading the nation on a path to be "overrun and dominated by communists."[48] Another critical correspondence came from a Catholic priest who identified himself as a former prisoner in a Siberian concentration camp. The priest wrote Reagan expressing support for the deployment of the MX missile and to "apologize for the silly ramblings of the American bishops." President Reagan replied directly, thanking the priest for the letter and lamenting that "if only . . . the bishops could hear and heed the words of someone like yourself who knows firsthand the Godless tyranny of Soviet totalitarianism."[49]

Most of the letters the White House received on the pastoral letter, however, supported both the bishops and the Freeze. A letter from the Priest Senate of the Bellville Diocese pledged wholehearted support for the pastoral. Furthermore, they pledged solidarity with now Cardinal-elect Bernardin and expressed support for "the process by which the pastoral is evolving and its involvement of Catholics in awakening America to the moral issue of nuclear disarmament." "The letter writing promoted by the organized movement has had its effect," wrote President Reagan to Ambassador Earl T. Smith.[50] The administration was fighting an uphill battle against Catholics in the movement, with the final draft of the pastoral scheduled for publication in the spring.

To Curb or Halt

Following the second draft of the pastoral letter in January 1983, the Vatican announced a two-day conference at Old Synod Hall to discuss the pastoral. Although the US Catholic bishops sent the draft pastoral to various European bishops' conferences and to the Holy See in Rome seeking comments, the Reagan administration privately contended that the Rome Conference was a by-product of Vernon Walters's private meeting with the pope the preceding October. Writing to Clark, McFarlane claimed Walters's mission had "an effect" on the Vatican, also telling General Dick Boverie that the Rome Conference was "stimulated" by Walters's visit, a detail McFarlane had asked Boverie to "hold close."[51] The "Informal Consultation on Peace and Disarmament" was attended by bishops from the United States and across Europe. They were met at the Vatican by Cardinal Joseph Ratzinger (prefect of the Sacred Congregation for the Doctrine of the Faith), Cardinal Cassaroli (Vatican secretary of state), Archbishop Achille Silvestrini (secretary of the Council for the Public Affairs of the Church), and Father Jan Schotte (secretary of the Pontifical Council for Justice and Peace).[52]

The two-day exchange was conducted with great openness and vigorous debate. As the official Vatican synopsis of the conference noted, there was "general agreement that in the face of the threats of the present time to life, to basic human values and to the survival of the peoples," the Episcopal Conferences had to address these pressing problems. Moreover, the conference sought to establish basic agreement on these perilous matters "between the Episcopal Conferences and with the Holy See, in order to provide guidance along the path to peace for the People of God, and all people of good will."

The conference began with opening remarks by its moderator, Cardinal Ratzinger. Ratzinger's comments were followed by two presentations, one on the comments and reactions the Holy See received in response to the pastoral and the other outlining the "moral principles which underlie the nuclear debate." The conference then asked the US bishops to outline why their pastoral letter entered public discussion. Led by Cardinal-elect Bernardin and Archbishop Roach, the bishops first emphasized their role as teachers of religion and moral principles. The pastoral letter therefore was intended both to "provide guidance for the Catholic conscience and to help set the right terms for public debate on the morality of war." At the heart of the pastoral, however, was a call to erect "a barrier against the concept of nuclear war as a viable strategy of defense." To do this, the bishops saw the pastoral as the chance to "draw a strong and clear line politically and morally against resort to nuclear weapons." The pastoral restricted the "morally acceptable function of deterrence" to its sole purpose: "preventing the use of nuclear weapons in any form." It also made clear that the US bishops "cannot approve of any policy of deterrence which involves an intention to do what is morally evil."

Cardinal Ratzinger opened up the conference for discussion, with debate beginning around several questions pertaining to the authority of the US bishops' teaching. European bishops asked for clarification on several questions: What were the limits of a pastoral letter? Should it contain elements encouraging debate? With what authority can a pastoral letter address both Catholics and non-Catholics alike? When bishops speak out on problems that have world repercussions, can they do so at the risk of proposing views that might conflict with those of other episcopates who are equally involved in the problem? The US bishops acknowledged that their letter spoke to different levels of authority, and they were aware that this would need to be rectified in the final draft.

Another exchange surrounded the morality of nuclear weapons: their use in combat, their possession for use in combat, and their possession as a threat per se. The US bishops emphasized that the letter affirmed the right of self-defense and was based on the application of just war theory to modern nuclear policies and strategies. While the pastoral did not address the morality of a second (presumably) defensive nuclear strike, it did apply the moral principles of proportionality and discrimination to say "no" to attacks on civilian populations, first strike, and limited nuclear war. Some European bishops questioned whether bishops' conferences should take a stand on points subject to different evaluations. Other European bishops called into question the authority of the US bishops to make a moral judgment that reflects on the entire Church. Still others disagreed with the pastoral's stance against a nuclear first strike, declaring it "an apodictic moral judgment." The right of first strike, some European bishops believed, was "necessary at this stage within the context of deterrence."

Regarding nonviolence and the just war tradition, European bishops believed the pastoral offered a "double Catholic tradition," claiming a tradition of nonviolence and a tradition of just war. These bishops argued that the just war tradition was the only viable tradition in Catholic theology, and they dismissed the draft's argument that a tradition of Christian pacifism ran through the teachings and actions of St. Francis of Assisi, Dorothy Day, and Martin Luther King Jr. Although the conference body dismissed the argument for a tradition of Christian pacifism, it offered the caveat that the just war tradition was "subject to inner tensions coming from an ever desire for peace." The US bishops denied arguing that a nation could adopt a pacifist stance and vowed to study the draft pastoral's language about just war tradition.

Just how to interpret the pope's statement to the UN General Assembly the preceding June became crucial to the discussion surrounding deterrence. All participants agreed that all guidance on the subject must derive from this message. At the request of the meeting, Cardinal Cassaroli offered a personal commentary on how he interpreted the pope's message. Although Cassaroli was not the sole authorized interpreter of the pope's message, he was one of the pope's closest confidants and was perceived to have greater insights into the pope's thinking. The danger of nuclear conflict, Cassaroli stated, created implications of both a human and a moral nature. It endangered the independence and freedom of entire peoples and led to mutual suspicions of imperialism. Moreover, Cassaroli observed, in the West there was "fear . . . of the imposition of an ideology and of a 'socialist' regime." These two dangers guided any discussion about nuclear weapons. The Church had responsibility, Cassaroli argued, to "encourage, export, admonish, foster and promote" both the dangers of nuclear war and ideological imposition by "the use of political means" (such as arms control negotiations). To avoid the two fears of nuclear war and ideological imposition, Cassaroli reiterated the pope's earlier remarks on the moral acceptability of deterrence. According to the official Vatican synopsis, Cassaroli's explanation of the pope's message to the United Nations "was gratefully accepted by all." The Rome meeting concluded with Cardinal Ratzinger expressing his gratitude for the US bishops' discussion of the third draft of the pastoral and praising them for their "sensus catholicus" (Catholic sense) and "their willingness to put their teaching in a universal context."

As Bernardin and the committee set out to revise the letter, reports surfaced indicating the bishops were caving in to White House pressure. Made public in April 1983, the third draft of the pastoral substituted the word "curb" for the word "halt" in its discussion of the arms race. While many Freeze activists believed the Reagan administration pressured the bishops to remove the word "freeze," the internal record of the bishops may point us in a different direction. In a confidential memo from Bernardin to members of the War and Peace Committee, Bernardin reported the details of his personal lunch with the pope on February 3, 1983. The Holy Father conveyed his main message to Bernardin, that the various hierarchies must be united on the Church's "moral teaching," for if they became divided, it could result in confusion, with one Episcopal Conference (including the Holy See) disavowing what another has said. It was clear to Bernardin that the pope was "talking about the level of authority which would be attached to the specific points contained in the pastoral." Members of society at large were already "using the pastoral for their own purposes," whether that was in support of the Freeze or in "criticizing the Church for the points for which they were in disagreement." Bernardin promised to make every effort to "make a clear distinction between official, magisterial teaching and the application of that teaching to specific situations/ strategies; between principle . . . and the application of principle." In other words, Bernardin wrote, "We [the US bishops] would explicitly not give (or seem to give) magisterial authority practical judgments we might make."[53]

The pope further indicated his concern that "the Church was advocating a pacifist position generally." While pacifism was fine as a personal option, the pope made the distinction that "nations have not only the right but the obligation to defend themselves." Bernardin stressed that there was no disagreement between himself and the pope but a "misunderstanding" that the bishops would clarify in their final draft. Additionally, the Holy Father strongly emphasized the need for both superpowers to work toward a mutually verifiable and bilateral disarmament. Bernardin again stated his agreement and emphasized that while some US bishops may have advocated unilateral disarmament, it was not the position of the bishops as a whole.

For the pope, however, the true difficulty in grappling with the question of morality and nuclear deterrence rested with the Soviet Union. As he put it, "The Soviets do not subscribe to the same moral principles as we," so when the bishops speak, they may have some effect on the American people and the American government "but not necessarily the Soviet Union." Bernardin did not disagree but believed "the moral analysis" remained valid "regardless of the response or non-response of one side or the other." The pope emphasized, however, that if "one side does not accept the moral analysis and continues on its predetermined course, then the other side must take that fact into account in developing the strategy for the protection of its people." It was precisely this logic that led the pope to conclude that deterrence under present conditions was morally justifiable on the way to mutual arms reductions. The pope offered Bernardin no specific guidelines on the pastoral, nor did he instruct Bernardin to back away from nuclear freeze or specifically ask that the pastoral accommodate the Reagan administration's views. "Generally," Bernardin wrote, "the Holy Father did not ask that the basic thrust of the Pastoral be changed but that we keep in mind the points he had made." The pope specifically asked Bernardin to assume responsibility for the letter as chairman of the War and Peace Committee.

At the request of the pope, Bernardin met with Cardinals Ratzinger and Cassaroli. Ratzinger offered Bernardin three main points. First, he emphasized the need to "make a clear distinction between principle and application of principles, so that magisterial authority would not be attached to practical judgments about specific strategies, weapons," and so on. Second, he emphasized the need to clarify the relationship between pacifism and the just war tradition, noting there were not two traditions within the Church but only one. Finally, Ratzinger spoke of "the need of using Scripture better." Cassaroli emphasized that because the draft was public, "every change will be scrutinized carefully and at times assume more significance than warranted," thus making the revisions called for and agreed on "more difficult . . . because it will be done in the public forum." Like the pope, neither Ratzinger nor Cassaroli wanted to change the letter's basic thrust but sought clarifications, distinctions, and less selectivity when it came to Scripture. Although the Vatican hierarchy did not mention the US government, Bernardin wanted to "give more credit for what the United States is trying to do." The bishops would try to "represent correctly" the government's actual stance, but Bernardin could not see "the Government's being totally pleased with our document, no matter how the final nuancing turns out."

The substitution of "curb" for "freeze" came at the behest of New York archbishop John O'Connor. O'Connor was an illustrious two-star Navy rear admiral who had earned a PhD in political science under the mentorship of Jeane Kirkpatrick. A registered Republican, O'Connor was a friend of the White House whose nephew later worked for Reagan's reelection campaign.

As a member of Bernardin's War and Peace Committee, O'Connor was assigned to revise the section dealing with just war theory and pacifism. Without authorization, O'Connor scrapped the second draft's section on deterrence, rewriting it from scratch and attaching a forty-seven-page redraft. The new draft left out not just "freeze" but the section on no first use and the example of the MX missile while further giving "at least as much weight to finding possible uses of nuclear weapons," as Castelli observed. Members of the War and Peace Committee feared O'Connor's dissent over the pastoral or his possible resignation. Because of the media's attention, Bernardin himself had reservations about using "freeze," but he still insisted that the Vatican did not mandate its omission. While O'Connor compromised with the committee on many of his proposed revisions, he continued to assail the use of "freeze." Ever the diplomat, Bernardin set out to maintain consensus. Thus, a "deal was struck," and the word "curb" replaced "freeze."[54]

While using "curb" in place of "halt" may appear a minor linguistic substitution, its significance was symbolic. The word "halt" was linked to support for the Freeze, and by using the word "curb," Freeze critics and Reagan administration officials could reasonably argue that the bishops were backtracking on support—this amid the congressional freeze debate. If the bishops appeared noncommittal, the movement would be losing a crucial ally. A weakened pastoral could cause representatives who were only lukewarm about the idea to vote against it. Moreover, Freeze opponents, such as Congressman Hyde, could cite the shift in language as proof that the bishops "refused to endorse the nuclear arms freeze." The letter appeared just after Reagan had told evangelicals that supporting a freeze was "un-Christian" and "un-American," and the letter gave the administration a "boost" following Paul Nitze's remarks to the Senate Foreign Relations Committee that INF talks were "just about dead." Many letters to Bernardin expressed their dismay at the alleged cave-in. One read, "I sincerely hope the story in the *Washington Post* on the new draft of the pastoral letter on nuclear arms is not true. As I read it, the new draft has been completely Reaganized even to the extent of chopping endorsement of the nuclear freeze. I am scandalized and saddened by the ignoramus retreat from a strong position against the insanity of nuclear war and nuclear weapons."[55]

Because of the level of attention the pastoral received, Bernardin and Roach issued a statement on the third draft. Outlining several key points, Bernardin and Roach sought to emphasize the differences between the pastoral and the Reagan administration's policies: (1) the pastoral's moral critique was directed "not just to issues of the moment but to issues with a long history in our national life"—thus, its moral criticisms were applicable to prior administrations and administrations to come; (2) the third draft was "just that—a draft," adding there was "little doubt" it would be changed again; (3) the changes between the second and third drafts reflected a "conscientious effort" to respond to comments from other US bishops in addition to the comments from the Holy See and European bishops at the Rome Conference, as well as "helpful comments" from administration officials, but ultimately was a product of "reflection and dialogue within the Catholic community"; (4) Bernardin and Roach specifically addressed how the pastoral differed from US policy, which included a call for "no first use" and a "call to cap the arms race"; and (5) the third draft reflected "a conscious effort to acknowledge quantitative moral differences between policies and practices of the United States . . . and the Soviet Union." Bernardin and Roach welcomed further views on the document going forward but noted that the final decision would "rest with the bishops and only them."[56]

Bernardin and the bishops were seeking a third way—a position between those of the Reagan administration and the Freeze movement. "On the question of nuclear freeze," Bernardin and Roach stated, "neither the second nor the third draft advocates such a 'freeze' as such," with the third draft favoring the word "curb." They emphasized further that their "purpose in both drafts has been to state a central moral imperative: that the arms race must be stopped and disarmament begun." Inside the bishops' deliberations, some proposed the word "curb" be stricken and substituted with "cease," "freeze," "arrest," "terminate," "discontinue," or "prevent." While most bishops favored keeping the word "halt," the case was perhaps best made by Bishop of Memphis James Francis Stafford. In his response to Bernardin's committee, Stafford pleaded that the "entire thrust of the ethical reasoning used in the pastoral letter would favor the word 'halt' to 'curb.' Moreover, should the suggestion be that there is no real difference in the meaning of these two words, the following reflection could be offered regarding another ethical issue: we would certainly want to do more than 'curb' the numbers; our hope would be to 'halt' abortions."[57]

On May 4, 1983, the final draft of the pastoral letter was released to some controversy: did it offer a significant rebuke to the Reagan administration? Writing in *Commonweal*, John Garvey lamented that the "watered-down" final draft "moved away from a position which seemed to call for an immediate halt to the arms race to one which urges such a halt as a goal," while also backing away from language that made "a stronger condemnation of the possession and possible use of nuclear weapons." Indeed, even the *New York Times* ran two separate articles, both printed under the name of journalist Kenneth Briggs, who claimed in the New York edition that the pastoral made "some changes in emphasis" but retained "the main elements of the strong antinuclear stance that was evident in previous versions." The condensed story that ran over the wires and subsequently was carried in papers throughout the country claimed the bishops' letter was "more accommodating than earlier versions to the Reagan Administration." Actually, the two pieces were not both written by Kenneth Briggs. The condensed version had inappropriately listed Briggs as its author, while the real journalist was the *New York Times* military columnist, Richard Halloran. Though the *New York Times* made a mistake, *Nuclear Times* snidely reported that "perhaps the [*New York*] *Times* should have stuck with Halloran's account."[58]

The reason *Nuclear Times* believed the final pastoral letter was not strong enough correlated with the administration's strategy to co-opt the bishops' message. Throughout the battle over the pastoral, the Reagan administration claimed the bishops' letter said nothing it did not agree with. Indeed, when the final draft was released, the State Department claimed the revised letter had been "substantially improved," leaving the Reagan administration "pleased" since it "explicitly endorses many of the far reaching objectives which the Administration seeks." As Cortright notes, "If the administration could not persuade the bishops to change their views, White House officials hoped they could at least obfuscate the issue by claiming that the letter endorsed administration policy."[59]

The final draft of the pastoral once again brought a variety of responses from the public. Sixties activist Tom Hayden (then a California state assemblyman, and a devout Catholic) wrote to Bernardin, gushing about how "deeply gratified" he was to "see my Church take such a strong role in the critical debate over nuclear arms."[60] Less prominent lay Catholics also conveyed their joy with the pastoral. One letter writer expressed "renewed pride in being a Catholic," believing Bernardin and the pastoral letter had "given our religion meaning again."[61] But Bernardin also received a fair amount of criticism from allies. Father Roy Bourgeois, an activist Catholic priest and critic of US foreign policy toward Latin America, sent Bernardin a mailgram criticizing the changes as a betrayal of "the gospel and the poor."[62] Philip Berrigan called the final draft a retreat on disarmament, speculating it was in "response to possible confrontations with the government, in response to possible elements of taxation being proposed by the state against the Catholic Church," just one of the ways in which "Catholics have been kept in line over the years."[63]

Despite the Left's critiques of the pastoral letter, White House allies urged the administration to act cautiously. The conservative American Catholic Committee advised the administration not to respond, believing it would place them in a no-win situation, but instead of pretending the pastoral did not exist, the administration turned back to the strategy of co-optation of the bishops' message. At a question-and-answer session with reporters on domestic and foreign policy issues, Reagan was immediately asked whether the pastoral would complicate the administration's attempts to "head off the nuclear freeze movement." Reagan responded that he understood the pastoral as "a legitimate effort to do exactly what we're doing, and that is to try to find ways toward world peace." While the media focused on the debate over whether to "curb" or to "halt" the arms race, Reagan suggested "in reality, there are many things in there that we'll have no quarrel with at all." The administration did not want a public dispute with the bishops. By claiming the pastoral contained nothing it disagreed with, it deflected a delicate issue.[64]

Nevertheless, the pastoral letter still represented a serious critique of the Reagan administration and the arms race. The final draft condemned the strategy of first strike and, moreover, condemned any use of nuclear weapons, even in response to an attack on a US city. Its ultimate challenge to the White House, however, was its call for an "immediate, verifiable halt to the arms race"—a phrase nearly identical to the one used in the founding document of the Freeze campaign. Because of the high profile of the bishops and political importance of the Catholic vote, the administration was left with no choice but to treat dissenting bishops with respect and cordiality. The administration thus moved further away from the rhetoric of winnable nuclear war—a key component in claiming public opinion from the Freeze. By taking the moral high ground from the bishops, the administration undercut a key Freeze ally on the eve of a critical vote in Congress.

Chapter 4

With Friends Like These

Congress and the Nuclear Freeze Debate

Paralleling the voices of nuclear dissent in religious communities, the Freeze campaign became a dominant feature of the political culture of the United States during the early 1980s and a magnet for politicians in both major parties. With congressional midterm elections approaching, many representatives lined up to affiliate themselves as champions of a nuclear weapons freeze, peace, and arms control—and in opposition to President Reagan, who, given the state of the economy, appeared to be a lame duck. By October 1982, over eight hundred town meetings and seventeen state legislatures had passed resolutions in support of a nuclear weapons freeze. In ten states and the District of Columbia, voters weighed in on nuclear freeze ballot measures, with an estimated 25 percent of the population voting one way or another on a nuclear freeze by 1983. The antinuclear message was reaching its crescendo.

The fight in Congress for a favorable nuclear freeze resolution, however, is a cautionary example of how popular social movements can create alliances with factions that ultimately do not share the same goal. Although the Freeze drew bipartisan support, many in Congress embraced the popularity of the idea but cared little for the movement's larger objectives. As a result of the congressional embrace, the campaign took on a much more partisan and professional attitude, contrary to its original grassroots objectives. By the time the

House of Representatives passed a freeze resolution, the movement's internal divisions began splintering and dividing over its goals and purpose.

Despite the major flaws in the Congress-Freeze alliance, the push from congressional circles ultimately placed domestic political pressure on the Reagan administration to make arms control and diplomacy central to its foreign policy concerns. As Deputy Press Secretary for Foreign Affairs Les Janka observed, Congress was where the Freeze "really did catch fire," pressuring the administration to "do something, to show some progress, at least in terms of coming up with proposals that appeared to be reasonable."[1] As a result of Freeze pressure, the administration moved from arms control proposals seemingly designed to fail to an openness on arms control summits previously conditioned on Soviet actions.

Freeze and the 97th Congress

Ronald Reagan's 1980 electoral victory brought with it a conservative tide that swept through the 97th Congress. For the first time in twenty-six years, the Republican Party wrested control of the Senate, with a fifty-three to forty-seven majority. The conservative tide swept away prominent liberal senators, including George McGovern and Frank Church. New faces would now take over major committees. While moderate Charles Percy (R-IL) headed the Senate Foreign Relations Committee, Texas Republican John Tower (a staunch hardliner on defense and national security policy) would head the Senate Armed Services Committee. Although the Democrats maintained control of the House, Republicans picked up thirty-three seats, replacing many liberals and moderates with conservative Reagan Republicans.[2]

Reagan appeared to have a mandate, but he and his administration appeared more interested in arms racing than arms control. On the campaign trail in 1980, Reagan proclaimed that he was not against the SALT treaties and that, as president, he would "immediately open negotiations on a SALT III Treaty." Soon after the inauguration, however, Reagan told various journalists he had "no timetable" with regard to arms control negotiations and would meet the Soviets if they were willing to discuss "legitimate reduction of nuclear weapons." Meanwhile, conservative defense lobbyists pushed Reagan and the 97th Congress to abandon SALT II in favor of a "national strategy" that would eclipse the "overall military and technological superiority of the Soviet Union."[3]

Many in Congress were uneasy with the direction in which US-Soviet relations were heading and sought to reassure the world regarding the threat of nuclear war. A concurrent (nonbinding) resolution introduced in the House in June 1981 by Hamilton Fish (R-NY) expressed "the sense of the Congress that nuclear war represents a great hazard and should be prevented." The resolution urged President Reagan to propose arms control negotiations that would reduce the US and Soviet nuclear arsenals substantially while encouraging all nuclear nations to "propose annual reductions and gradual elimination of all nuclear weapons." That November, Senator Mark Hatfield introduced a bill expressing "the conviction of Congress that the United States should not base its policies on the belief that the United States can limit, survive, or win a nuclear war." Both bills were referred to committee, though neither made it out.

In the public realm, fiscal conservatives became uneasy with the ballooning defense budget and subsequent deficits, while anxious town halls and churches across the nation began endorsing a nuclear freeze. Despite the momentum, Freeze activists were not ready to align themselves with Congress. In their first-year "Structure Proposal," activists sought to work on "a local, decentralized basis," creating Freeze task forces that would coordinate contacts with government officials at home and abroad, raise funds for the Freeze, develop educational and promotional resources, and coordinate national events or projects. In acting locally and building support in each congressional district, the campaign hoped to secure bipartisan support from 150 representatives prior to the introduction of any resolution.[4]

But Freeze activists did not have the luxury of building a longer campaign in each congressional district. As SANE's David Cortright lamented, "The train was already leaving the station . . . and freeze leaders were powerless to stop it." Within a year of the First Annual National Nuclear Freeze Conference in Washington, D.C., eager members of Congress began courting the movement. One was Boston's Edward J. Markey (D-MA). A four-term representative, Markey was a major critic of nuclear power and opponent of nuclear proliferation, who garnered attention from the antinuclear movement in the wake of the TMI accident. By early 1982, Markey was in the early stages of writing a book outlining his opposition to nuclear power and his concerns about nuclear proliferation when his administrative assistant Peter Franchot discovered Randall Forsberg's "Call." An antinuclear activist himself and a former lobbyist for the Union of Concerned Scientists, Franchot repeatedly told Markey that the Freeze movement would "sweep the country" and there was no reason Markey's office "shouldn't be in the middle of it."[5]

While Markey's office began work on a freeze resolution, it soon ran into a major dilemma: Markey was on neither the House Armed Services Committee nor the House Foreign Affairs Committee (HFAC), making his claim to an arms control issue, such as nuclear freeze, a violation of legislative protocol. Markey's staff ran with the issue anyway, sending several draft resolutions to fellow members of Congress. Markey's draft resolution, however, was met with mixed reactions. Although several congressional offices favored it, many others saw the resolution as "symbolic but not practical" or "too radical an approach," while some worried that a nuclear arms freeze would undercut arms control negotiations or freeze the United States into an inferior position. In the Senate, Gary Hart (D-CO) appeared an ideal cosponsor. Hart's staff, however, had numerous detailed questions about a freeze and eventually passed on it.[6]

Renewed diplomacy on arms control was of clear interest to many in Congress, but in early 1982, Congress did not appear ready to embrace a nuclear weapons freeze. Congressman Markey remained unfazed. In February 1982, Markey sent a letter to his 434 House colleagues, announcing his intention to introduce a freeze resolution and to seek cosponsors. Markey specifically pointed to the "upsurge of concern" within the public, pointing to the statements of Catholic bishops on the threat of nuclear war. Markey's letter urged Congress to "respond to the voices of these religious groups, as well as business leaders and citizen organizations across the country, who are demanding to be heard." As Markey's aide Douglas Waller observed, the letter carried a simple political message for members of Congress: "It is time to halt the nuclear arms race on both sides, so reductions can be made." While the letter captured the spirit of the Freeze, it did not seem to carry much weight. Five days after its introduction, only twenty-eight House members (all of whom identified as liberal) signed on as cosponsors. In the weeks that followed, the resolution still attracted few cosponsors. As Waller reflected, "It was evident that a major educational effort would have to be launched in Congress on the freeze, with more experts trooping up the Hill to brief other members."[7]

The movement, however, was still reluctant to jump on board with Congress. At the Second Annual National Nuclear Freeze Conference, in January 1982, the Freeze campaign reaffirmed its strategy to first build local support, then seek a national policy in Congress. This strategy notwithstanding, the campaign did accelerate its congressional goals, seeking endorsement by 135 House members and 35 senators by 1982, but activists were unhappy with the freeze resolution circulating within Congress—they sought bipartisan legislation, not just endorsements by liberal Democrats. They took issue with Markey's call for a multilateral freeze, believing it would create confusion and thus jeopardize the bilateral freeze that activists had been organizing around for over a year.

Likewise, Freeze activists opposed a parallel bill being drafted by Congressman Jonathan Bingham (D-NY) that called for a freeze on the testing and deployment of nuclear weapons but not their production. In a letter to Freeze national coordinator Randy Kehler, Steve Ladd (WRL) feared "that some representatives will move [too] rapidly towards a vote in the house," before activists had built enough public support and pressure for the resolution. Pointing to past battles over SALT II and other legislative initiatives, Ladd cautioned there would be "a big fight to make the resolution as meaningless or as watered down as possible in order to get more votes." "Frankly," Ladd warned, "politicians can kill the Freeze right now, whether they support us or not. We have to be very careful all along about how we let politicians take off with the Freeze. The public must always [be] seen as the leaders of this movement, not the politicians." Without grassroots support, however, the freeze legislation in the House took a back seat to restarting SALT. Nevertheless, if the Freeze campaign sought successful legislation, the movement "had to get behind the Congressional resolution and vice versa."[8]

While the Freeze campaign and the Congress appeared aloof from each other, reconciliation appeared imminent when Senator Ted Kennedy embraced the Freeze movement. On March 10, 1982, Kennedy introduced a joint resolution to the Senate, S.J. Res. 163. It was a strategic decision that contrasted with the previous concurrent resolutions in the House that Markey and Bingham had introduced. The concurrent resolutions did not require a presidential signature but only carried the sense of Congress, whereas a joint resolution "would be perceived by Congress and the public as having more legislative bite . . . because it did have the force of law, whereas a concurrent resolution did not," as Douglas Waller writes, adding that "if both houses of Congress passed a joint resolution on the freeze, the president would have to either sign or veto it." Freeze supporters reasoned that Reagan would not veto an arms control initiative that carried the weight of the grassroots public and most of Congress.[9]

To make the resolution bipartisan, Kennedy enlisted Senator Hatfield as a cosponsor. A devout pacifist, Hatfield's views harkened back to his service with the USNavy during World War II, where he saw combat at the battles of Iwo Jima and Okinawa and walked through the remains of a decimated Hiroshima. Although Hatfield would credit the bomb with ending World War II, it was an experience that left him with "a sense of ambivalence about the kind of power that had been unleashed in the world." Announcing his support for a nuclear freeze, Hatfield argued that the United States and Soviet Union were "strategically equal" in nuclear armaments, but if the arms race continued, Hatfield warned, it would "make mincemeat out of the present strategic balance." For Hatfield, a freeze "would not be just a piece of legislation," as Waller writes, but "a sacred commitment." While the language of the Kennedy-Hatfield freeze resolution borrowed from Forsberg's "Call," there were significant differences. As David Meyer observes, "Kennedy deliberately wrote his proposal in vague language to attract moderate support." The resolution would appeal to a swath of supporters, including liberal arms controllers, moderate Republicans, and centrist Democrats, all of whom, Kennedy believed, were crucial to its political viability.[10]

Kennedy soon unveiled his bipartisan joint nuclear freeze resolution at a major press conference. Flanking Kennedy were several prominent freeze endorsers, including former statesmen Paul Warnke, W. Averell Harriman, William Colby, and George Kennan; major religious leaders and figures, such as Bishop James Armstrong (National Council of Churches), Rabbi Alexander Schindler (president of the Union of American Hebrew Congregations), Rev-

FIGURE 6.   Senator Edward "Ted" Kennedy (D-MA) questions a witness at a congressional hearing, flanked by Senator Mark Hatfield (R-OR) next to him on his right and Representative Edward Markey (D-MA) on his far left (with an unidentified person between them). Kennedy, Hatfield, and Markey led the fight for a nuclear freeze resolution in the US Congress. Photo courtesy of the Edward M. Kennedy Institute for the United States Senate, copyright United States Senate Photo Studio.

erend Timothy Healy (president of Georgetown University), Billy Graham (evangelical preacher), and Catholic bishops. They joined astrophysicist Carl Sagan, actor Paul Newman, civil rights activist Coretta Scott King, and a variety of other prominent societal figures. It was a symbolic show of strength and reflected the clout and attention Kennedy brought the Freeze. The site of the press conference, American University, also held symbolic value, for it was where President John F. Kennedy delivered a famous speech in support of the Partial Nuclear Test Ban Treaty in 1963. Within a month, Ted Kennedy and Hatfield had coauthored the book *Freeze: How You Can Prevent Nuclear War* to support their nuclear freeze resolution.[11]

The Kennedy embrace, however, acted as a double-edged sword: while it brought the Freeze significant attention and discussion, it also served as a platform for Kennedy's own political ambitions. Although Kennedy had not formally announced his campaign for the presidency, by the end of 1981, the Kennedy for President campaign was well under way, while "nuclear freeze" became attached to both Kennedy and the Democratic Party. Moreover, Kennedy's crafting of the resolution to appeal to moderates alienated the same Freeze activists who had brought the issue to Congress. From the outset, as Cortright observed, "the legislation crafted by Kennedy, Markey, and others fell far short of the political goals set by grassroots freeze leaders." Furthermore, collaborating with Kennedy and other congressional liberals had other disadvantages, as the media "increasingly turned to politicians and not to the movement itself for explanation of Freeze goals." Despite the many issues with the Kennedy resolution, the Freeze was left with no choice but to climb on board or get left behind.[12]

Following the introduction of the Kennedy-Hatfield resolution in the Senate, an identical bill was introduced in the House of Representatives, but who in the House would sponsor the legislation became an open question. Congressman Bingham did not want to be the lead sponsor but was also adamant that the sponsor not be Congressman Markey, given Markey's strong antinuclear views. Bingham wanted the legislation to appeal to members who were against the continued arms race but not necessarily opposed to nuclear power. Therefore, a more moderate figure was needed. Although initially reluctant, Markey turned to his Massachusetts colleague Congressman Silvio Conte. Conte, a Republican, was an early supporter of the 1980 Massachusetts nuclear freeze ballot referendum. Moreover, Conte was a "shrewd yet candid politician" as well as a "power-puncher in Congress," as Waller writes. A ranking minority member of the House Appropriations Committee, Conte was a Republican who congressional freeze advocates viewed as impervious to White House intimidation. Conte introduced the House resolution with 122 cosponsors.[13]

By the end of March, a bipartisan group of House members had begun debating the merits of a nuclear freeze under "special orders" that allowed discussion of an issue without voting. The debate raged on from midafternoon into the early evening hours and featured over thirty speakers, including the unusual appearance of House Minority Leader Robert Michel (R-IL) and House Speaker Thomas "Tip" O'Neill (D-MA). While Michel claimed a freeze would leave the United States in an "inferior position" and was a "threat to peace," O'Neill compared the House debate to the first debates over the Vietnam War moratorium in October 1969 and expressed the desire that the Markey freeze resolution "would provide the vehicle to stop this arms race." Unlike during the Vietnam War debate, however, the House galleries were practically empty, with few representatives listening in at any one time. But, as the *Washington Post* reported, outside, on the steps of the Capitol, "about 100 demonstrators stood silently, holding candles, in support of the freeze."[14]

Attacking, Co-opting, and Politicizing

While many Freeze activists had reservations about the joint resolution, the Reagan administration was quick to attack it. Secretary of State Haig took the lead at a Senate hearing, claiming a freeze would leave the Soviets with a possible six-to-one nuclear force advantage in Europe while further eliminating any possibility that they would bargain over nuclear weapons reductions. A nuclear freeze, Haig claimed, was "not only bad defense and bad security policy, [but] bad arms control." ACDA's Eugene Rostow suggested a freeze would "play entirely into the hands of the Soviet Union." Vice President George H. W. Bush warned, "The appealing, simple solution of negotiating a freeze at current levels would be harmful to our security and that of our allies." President Reagan himself claimed a freeze "isn't good enough because it doesn't go far enough." The United States, Reagan proclaimed, "must get beyond the freeze to insist on real reductions in nuclear arms." But the Reagan administration's attacks, however, simply were not effective since they appeared to have a "weapons policy, but not a peace policy," as Kennedy argued. The administration routinely repeated unfounded and easily disproven allegations that Freeze activists sought unilateral disarmament. As policy, a nuclear freeze would apply not just to Europe but globally, where the United States maintained a two-thousand-warhead numerical advantage over the Soviets. Such arguments against a freeze furthermore never considered missile accuracy, where the United States had a decisive advantage.[15]

The Reagan administration's arms control proposals and defense spending were coming under attack not just from nuclear freeze advocates but also from the administration's conservative allies. As the *Chicago Tribune* reported, conservative voices pressed the Reagan administration to present a "more convincing defense strategy, trim waste from the Pentagon budget, re-examine the more expensive new weapons programs and offer a more aggressive nuclear arms control program." With a record $1.6 trillion in defense spending planned for the next five years, conservative critics worried that the administration lacked focus on defense and was preparing to fight the Soviet Union across the globe. Even the conservative Heritage Foundation called the defense costs "staggering," asserting firmly, "Weapons cost must be lowered."[16]

Freshman Republican representatives also dissented from the Reagan defense plan. Although Democrats derogatorily called them "Reagan's Robots," these freshman Republicans were proving anything but. Reagan's proposed budget included a one hundred billion dollar deficit while ramping up the defense budget at the expense of social programs and education, so many freshman Republicans revolted. "I campaigned on the idea that we could increase defense spending, cut taxes, and balance the budget," Congressman John Patrick Hiller (R-IN) noted, "but it didn't occur to me that Reagan would increase the defense budget $60 billion in two years." Freshman congressman Hank Brown (R-CO), a Navy veteran and a volunteer combatant during the Vietnam War, found himself voting alongside liberal Democrats. "I never thought I'd be voting against the defense budget. I voted against the B-1 bomber too," Brown confessed.[17]

In the Senate, even staunchly pro-defense legislators appeared ready to pay lip service to Freeze advocates—particularly if it would help their political careers. That March, Senator Henry Jackson was informed by a Democratic pollster that his political strength had eroded. Jackson's opposition to a freeze became a political issue that, in a tough primary contest, Democratic and Republican challengers alike were using against him. In a savvy political move that could both bolster his reelection chances and counter the Kennedy-Hatfield resolution, Jackson, alongside Senator John Warner (R-VA), worked with the Reagan administration to develop a more conservative freeze resolution. Senate Joint Resolution 177 urged the United States to "propose to the Soviet Union a long-term, mutual, and verifiable nuclear forces freeze." The keyword of the proposal was, as Waller observes, "long-term." It thus called for a nuclear freeze "only after Mr. Reagan completed his arms buildup and after a reduction in Soviet forces."[18]

With the White House alarmed over growing support for a freeze among the public and Congress, Senators Jackson and Warner met with President

Reagan. Although the resolution was a tacit acknowledgment of public concern over the arms race, Reagan found the "basic thrust" of the resolution "acceptable" and "expressed a common interest." The Jackson-Warner resolution allowed the administration to build the MX, the B-1, and the Trident submarine, in addition to continued deployment of the Euromissiles. When the United States reached nuclear parity with the Soviets, the two sides would commit to a "mutual and verifiable freeze," with the eventual goal of eliminating all nuclear weapons. The resolution received fifty-eight cosponsors in the Senate, where it was offered as a substitute for Kennedy-Hatfield.[19]

Senator Kennedy immediately attacked the Jackson-Warner resolution, warning that it would offer "a blank check for the Reagan Administration to continue the nuclear arms race." Kennedy criticized Jackson-Warner as "dangerously deceptive," since it only paid "lip service to the concept of a freeze, while actually pushing the nation into yet another spiral of the arms race." A joint statement by Kennedy and Hatfield further criticized the resolution for offering "nothing more than a fig leaf over the nuclear arms race." Congressman Markey commented that Jackson-Warner allowed those who did not sincerely favor arms control to "jump on any resolution that contains the word 'freeze.'" Other backers of the Kennedy-Hatfield resolution sent telegrams to Capitol Hill deploring Jackson-Warner as "disastrous" because it encouraged the "production and deployment of dangerous, unnecessary new weapons."[20]

Anxious over the growing support for a nuclear weapons freeze, aides urged Reagan to "make a personal commitment to peace and to arms negotiations." In his first prime-time television press conference, Reagan addressed the freeze resolutions circulating in Congress. He hailed Jackson-Warner as "an important measure in the right direction" while assuring the public that his goal was to "reduce nuclear weapons dramatically, assuring peace and security." To no one's surprise, he rejected the goal of an immediate freeze that the Kennedy-Hatfield resolution proposed, claiming it would leave the United States vulnerable to a Soviet first strike while eliminating Soviet incentives to negotiate on arms control. Reagan offered assurances, pleading that the tragedy and destruction of war must be avoided while further hinting that, barring "unseemly" events (such as the Soviet invasion of Afghanistan), his administration could begin arms control talks as early as the summer. Nevertheless, Reagan may have inadvertently kept up the public alarm over nuclear war, suggesting the Soviets had "on balance . . . a definitive margin of superiority" and could "absorb a retaliatory blow by this country and still launch a nuclear attack on their own."[21]

Reagan's neoconservative allies, however, jumped on the president for his support of Jackson-Warner. In a memo to the president, William Clark noted fierce opposition to the Jackson-Warner resolution from the American Security Council Foundation, which believed it showed "tacit approval" of the Freeze campaign's "basic goal of a 'freeze' and zero nuclear weapons." Acceptance of a freeze, the ASCF warned, would "freeze the United States into its present position of nuclear inferiority" while ignoring conventional Soviet force advantages. In a handwritten note, Reagan suggested prodding Jackson and Warner to include a "conventional weapons reduction which could then open the door to zero nuclear weapons." In the neoconservative magazine *Commentary*, editor Norman Podhoretz also lamented Reagan's endorsement of Jackson-Warner and warned Reagan that adopting the Freeze campaign's rhetoric would not defuse the movement but "intensify demands for deep cuts in the defense budget and unilateral concessions in arms-control negotiations" that would "jeopardize [Reagan's] effort to restore parity, let alone the 'margin of safety.'"[22]

In the HFAC, the Freeze campaign made an uneasy alliance with Chairman Clement Zablocki (D-WI). Zablocki was "no fan of the freeze." Having represented the heavily Polish south side of Milwaukee in the House since 1948, Zablocki had built his reputation as a firm anticommunist and a hawk on foreign policy, who supported the Vietnam War on through the Nixon years. Irritated by "unclear and inconsistent" statements by the Reagan administration and the lack of progress on arms control, Zablocki began holding hearings on arms control within a subcommittee. Just three days before the House recess for the Fourth of July holiday, and just a week before the beginning of START negotiations in Geneva, the Zablocki-led HFAC met to mark up and vote on the Markey-Bingham freeze resolution. On June 23, 1982, the committee voted overwhelmingly and across party lines to endorse a marked-up resolution calling on President Reagan to seek a "mutual and verifiable freeze" on the testing, production, and deployment of nuclear weapons in conjunction with the approval of the SALT II Treaty. The Freeze thus claimed its first victory in Congress.[23]

Paralleling the gains in the HFAC, a nuclear freeze became a central component of the Democratic Party's midterm convention. While congressional Democrats remained divided over a freeze, the party's initial draft statement attempted an evenhanded approach, "welcoming" it but also emphasizing reduction plans. Fearing the party was weakening its support for a freeze, elderly Cold War statesman Averell Harriman spoke at the convention to assure Democrats, "We have absolutely nothing to fear from a freeze. We have absolutely adequate nuclear capability now." His speech received a standing ovation. Expected Democratic presidential candidates all spoke to the emotional issue of nuclear war and a nuclear freeze. Senator John Glenn (D-OH) repeatedly emphasized support for a *verifiable* freeze while cautioning that a nuclear freeze would "not do us any good . . . if another 10 or 20 nations get nuclear weapons in the meantime." Senator Alan Cranston (D-CA) received a major burst of applause for his call "to negotiate a fair and verifiable freeze," leading to "the total abolition of nuclear weapons." Former vice president Walter Mondale blasted the administration's talk of fighting nuclear war and firing warning shots. "Let the party of Ted Kennedy and Jimmy Carter and Alan Cranston commit this country to negotiating the freeze, reducing the arsenals and eliminating nuclear weapons from the earth," Mondale bellowed. The convention closed with Kennedy receiving multiple ovations for his stinging critiques of Reaganomics, his support for women's rights, and his commitment to a freeze. As Kennedy's rousing speech ended, he returned to the stage with his family, standing at the podium for an encore applause, as attendees waved placards reading, "Kennedy: Nuclear Freeze."[24]

By the end of the miniconvention, the Democrats had passed a compromise statement on arms control that called for "support" for a freeze but adding the ambiguous phrase "consistent with overall parity." Nevertheless, "nuclear freeze" remained at the top of their arms control agenda. As Waller concludes, "It was quite a political odyssey. In just 108 days, the freeze had moved from the political fringe to dominate the foreign policy plank of one of the country's two national parties." Although Freeze activists saw the campaign as bipartisan, by summer 1982, "nuclear freeze" was more partisan and more politicized than ever.[25]

With its passage in the HFAC, the nuclear freeze resolution (now dubbed the Zablocki freeze) was bound for the House floor, but despite Democrats' control over the House, as *Congressional Quarterly* noted, prospects for a "full-fledged nuclear freeze" remained "uncertain at best." The HFAC was not representative of the party as a whole. Of its five southern Democrats, only three voted in favor of a freeze. Furthermore, beyond lobbying against the resolution by members of the State Department, the Reagan administration did not apply pressure against its passage, but with the resolution now reaching the House floor, "the White House and the GOP leadership might hold a much larger proportion of uneasy Republicans in line."[26] The Republican House leadership soon joined the administration in promoting a counterfreeze resolution. A memo from Bud McFarlane reported that the House leadership was ready to move on a pro-administration substitute resolution but needed White House assurances that the president would both support the text and openly say so. House allies urged the administration to send a speaker to "rally the troops."[27]

For the Reagan administration, an alternative freeze resolution was critical. As Jeffrey Knopf observes, the administration feared that if Congress passed a pro-freeze resolution, "it might create an impression that Congress could vote against Reagan's defense programs with impunity or lessen administration leverage to extract arms concessions from the USSR." Inside ACDA, officials worried over the "danger of the wrong resolution from Congress." State Department officials feared the "spillover effects" a freeze would have on "congressional funding of the strategic modernization program." Chief START negotiator Ed Rowny conjectured that "a Congressional resolution calling for an immediate freeze would make it exceedingly difficult to achieve reductions which would lessen the risk of nuclear war." He furthermore praised a substitute amendment that Congressman William Broomfield (R-MI) planned to propose, believing it would "show the Soviet Union that the Congress is behind President Reagan's efforts to accomplish substantial arms reductions" while strengthening America's hand at the START negotiations. Inside the Reagan White House, David Gergen explained, there was a "widespread view . . . that the freeze was a dagger pointed at the heart of the administration's defense policies."[28]

On August 5, the House opened debate over the Zablocki freeze resolution. Zablocki spoke first, linking his personal reputation with support for the resolution while assuring the House that his resolution was "totally supportive of the best national security interests of the United States." Following Zablocki's remarks, Congressman Broomfield castigated the resolution as "political mischief" that "undercuts the President and cripples our negotiators at Geneva." Before yielding the floor, however, Broomfield introduced his substitute resolution, carrying 160 cosponsors and backing the START proposal over a nuclear freeze. The debate that afternoon was frequently bitter and contentious. Administration allies such as Congressman Henry Hyde claimed the Zablocki resolution would lock the United States into an inferior arms position. "If we freeze now, it's like freezing with the Soviets' hands at our throat," Hyde proclaimed. Congressman Larry McDonald (R-GA) accused freeze advocates of also supporting the Vietcong, the Palestine Liberation Organization, and "the Communist terrorists in El Salvador and Southern Africa." Given the nature of the remarks on the House floor, as Waller recollected, "It would be a misnomer to call what was happening . . . a debate."[29]

As the debate moved toward its conclusion, Congressman Bloomfield produced a letter directly from President Reagan that claimed the Bloomfield substitute would "significantly aid Ambassador Rowny" at the START negotiations in Geneva, while passage of the Zablocki freeze resolution "would undercut our negotiators." As the House debated the Bloomfield substitute, many Republican representatives continued to assail and redbait freeze supporters. Pushing back, Congressman Les Aspin (D-WI) asserted that if the president were "genuinely interested in arms control, perhaps it [the Zablocki freeze resolution] would not be necessary." "For 20 years," Aspin continued, "Ronald Reagan has opposed every step towards arms control by every President of either party. . . . Now they say they are for arms controls. Well, maybe, and maybe not. My guess is that a [freeze] resolution is necessary."[30]

With the electric clock overlooking the chamber ticking away into the late evening hours, there was just enough time left for two speakers: House Minority Leader Michel and House Speaker O'Neill. Spectators packed the congressional galleries. Phones in the Democratic and Republican cloakrooms rang off the hook while "Freeze lobbyists scrambled to convince last-minute holdouts to stand firm for the resolution." Michel spoke first "in his deep baritone voice," equating a nuclear freeze with "national suicide." Pounding his fist on the lectern, Michel claimed there was no arms race, only a "deadly nuclear arms predicament brought about by ten years of a Soviet nuclear arms buildup unanswered by the United States." Michel dramatically concluded that in his "over 30 years in Washington," he had never seen "a proposal so clouded by emotion, so fraught with danger . . . so attractive on the surface, yet so surely wrong, and so ultimately deadly to our national survival as House Joint Resolution 521." Michel's speech received a standing ovation from the Republican side of the House chamber. As O'Neill, who rarely took the floor, walked slowly to the lectern, a hush fell over the chamber. O'Neill lamented that the two concluding speakers were leaders of the two dominant political parties, leading to the impression that a nuclear freeze was "a party matter or party issue." For O'Neill, however, it was a matter of conscience. He recounted witnessing two atomic tests in Yucca Flats, Nevada, thirty years earlier. "Anybody that ever saw one of those bombs must wonder why we did not start this freeze movement years ago," O'Neill recounted. O'Neill compared the arms race to a driver placing a foot on a car's accelerator and not applying the brakes. A freeze at present levels, O'Neill believed, would enhance national security and protect future civilizations. "That is the duty of all of us as leaders," he somberly concluded.[31]

When O'Neill finished speaking, a vote on the Broomfield substitute resolution commenced. As congressional Freeze allies understood, a "no" vote was a vote in favor of an immediate bilateral nuclear freeze, while a "yes" vote was a vote for the Reagan administration. As the vote totals were displayed on the scoreboard, they "seesawed between victory and defeat for each side." At one point, Democrats and Freeze supporters cheered, as the vote read 200–198 against. Seconds later, the vote count flipped to read 200–199 in favor, drawing a thunderous cheer from Republicans. But the voting was not finished. Suddenly, the scoreboard displayed a deadlocked tally of 202–202.[32] As the freeze debate raged, the Reagan administration placed extreme pressure on north-eastern Republicans to vote against the Zablocki freeze and for the Broom-field substitute. In a high-level meeting in the Cabinet room earlier that day, Reagan, accompanied by Vice President Bush, Secretary of Defense Wein-berger, Secretary of State George Shultz, and several other top White House aides, attempted to persuade key members of Congress to vote against the Zablocki freeze resolution. As the debate continued that evening, Reagan personally called House Republicans to lobby against the resolution. When some in Congress proved unwilling to switch their votes, Reagan lamented, "They are all buffaloed by the public pressure of the freeze movement."[33]

In the final vote count, the pressure from the administration helped defeat the freeze in the House by the narrowest of margins, 204–202. The vote was largely along party lines: 53 Democrats joined 151 Republicans to support the Broomfield substitute, and 27 Republicans joined 175 Democrats against it. Although the Freeze lost the vote, supporters expressed hope and optimism with an eye toward the 1982 midterm elections. Reagan's "arm-twisting," Congressman Markey proclaimed, would result in "political peril for a large number of congressmen. When we come back here next year, we will have the votes not just to pass a nuclear freeze resolution, but to defeat first-strike destabilizing weapons." Senator Kennedy likewise roared, "The nuclear freeze may have lost in the House of Representatives, but it is winning day by day in the country, and I am confident that it will prevail at the polling stations in November and beyond." Kehler also viewed the vote with optimism, for he believed it demonstrated "the great progress" the campaign had made. But the "real vote," Kehler concluded, "will come this fall, when millions of freeze supporters in thousands of communities across the country assess candidates for Congress on the basis of their stand on the Freeze."[34]

Successes and Divisions

Though a freeze resolution in Congress had been momentarily stifled, the campaign continued to gain traction over the course of the fall. Nuclear freeze referenda were scheduled in ten states: Arizona, California, Massachusetts, Michigan, Montana, New Jersey, North Dakota, Oregon, Rhode Island, and Wisconsin. A freeze referendum was also placed on the ballot in Washington, D.C., while numerous cities and counties had already passed pro-freeze resolutions. The Reagan administration undertook active measures against these various state and local referenda, with a report in the *St. Louis Dispatch* uncovering that the Public Programs Office under the direction of Assistant Secretary of State John Hughes had organized forty-six speaking trips and 168 events between April 1 and September 30, 1982. With an early election on September 14, Wisconsin would be the administration's first battleground in countering a statewide freeze referendum. In a memo to McFarlane, administration public affairs specialist Robert Sims stressed it was "vital" that the "grassroots pro-freeze movement not affect our ability to negotiate arms control agreements, or [to] continue [the] President's re-armament program." The administration must "stimulate and support efforts to counter and defeat freeze resolutions" while still recognizing that local candidates were under immense political pressure to take a stand on the issue. "Regretfully, being *for* arms control and national security and *against* an immediate freeze may not be attractive to most candidates," Sims concluded.[35]

The administration would need a public affairs strategy to combat the Freeze in Wisconsin. An exasperated McFarlane lost track of the countless hours he and administration allies spent putting together "substantive arguments and promotional material necessary" to counter the movement. The material McFarlane and others devised would be coupled with "an aggressive program of sending effective spokesmen throughout the country to publicize the President's arms control policies and counter the freeze proposals in both print and electronic media." Although the material originally met with the approval of Gergen and others, many were having second thoughts, fearing the administration would be perceived as having undertaken "a major effort and not succeeding," given the likelihood that nine states would still pass freeze resolutions. Nevertheless, McFarlane believed the administration "must try to moderate the impact by expanding public awareness of the President's policies so that the movement does not 'by default' become the only game in town." McFarlane contested the idea that the administration would be seen as "having 'failed'" were they to send spokesmen to battle the Freeze only to lose; he contended the administration had "a responsibility to inform the public," for if it did not, by 1983 it would face "new freeze resolutions on the Hill and a much more vocal public favoring the freeze."[36] As the administration expected, the results in Wisconsin did not go their way. By a three-to-one margin, Wisconsin voters passed a nuclear freeze referendum.

But the Freeze campaign was not successful in all its midterm battles. A September Democratic primary election contest in New York's newly created Twenty-Third Congressional District between Samuel Stratton and John Dow was billed by Dow's campaign as "one of the most important contests in the nation," for it would "set the national tone for the November Congressional elections." A twelve-term congressman representing Albany, Samuel Stratton was a hawkish centrist-liberal and a firm proponent of the Vietnam War. Stratton favored larger military budgets, supported Reagan's nuclear arms buildup, and wanted to further expand the nuclear arsenal. Stratton was one of a dozen representatives labeled by Peace PAC as "the doomsday dozen." He was a key vote in the House against the freeze resolution and for funding the MX missile. President Reagan praised Stratton for his support for START and appointed him as a representative to the UN Special Session on Disarmament. When Stratton's constituents presented him with a petition containing over fifteen thousand signatures requesting he support a nuclear weapons freeze, he rejected it, telling them if they disliked his stance, "vote me out." In Congress, Stratton opposed the Kennedy-Hatfield freeze but cosponsored the Jackson-Warner resolution. Stratton's 1982 primary challenger, John Dow, was a former three-term congressman from the middle Hudson Valley. Dow championed a nuclear weapons freeze and was an opponent of US interventionism. He campaigned on his longstanding opposition to nuclear weapons, evidenced by his position on the national board of SANE and his founding of Americans against Nuclear War in 1980. In a radio debate with Congressman Stratton, Dow claimed Stratton was "such an extremist in promoting the belligerence between the United States and Russia that if it continues I think we're all going to be blown to bits."[37]

Although the Freeze campaign was unable to unseat Congressman Stratton, the 1982 midterms amounted to what the *Guardian* called "a messy vote of no confidence" in the administration, boosting both the Freeze campaign and the momentum for a congressional freeze resolution. An estimated 25 percent of the US population voted directly on a nuclear freeze in state referenda one way or the other. Of the ten state referenda, all passed except Arizona's, while pro-freeze resolutions passed in the District of Columbia as well as twenty-nine cities and counties. While the resolutions adopted would have no binding effect, as a confidential British Embassy memo observed, the freeze referenda were "an indication of public feeling, [which] cannot be altogether ignored." Furthermore, the embassy noted, public support for the referenda "may well encourage [Freeze] supporters in Congress to make another attempt to secure the adoption of a resolution calling for a 'freeze.'" The referenda and congressional support would continue to pressure the White House to show progress on arms control, while the Freeze would continue to "serve the very useful purpose of reminding the Administration that concern over nuclear issues is by no means confined to Europe." Although the embassy did not believe the campaign had achieved enough momentum to alter the Reagan administration's negotiating positions, it nevertheless believed there was a "realisation in the

White House" of "the public desire to see some results from current arms negotiations." The memo concluded that domestic political pressures "could become a more important factor as the 1984 election approaches."[38]

Beyond referenda, the 1982 midterms brought serious discussions of the Freeze across political campaigns. In Massachusetts, candidate for lieutenant governor and prominent antiwar Vietnam veteran John Kerry campaigned in support of a freeze, even though the office he was running for had no means of accomplishing the goal. Senator Daniel Patrick Moynihan (D-NY), a neoconservative convert during the late 1970s, now campaigned as "someone specifically committed to a nuclear freeze."[39] With the arms control talks at a stalemate in Geneva and twenty-six new Democrats elected to the House of Representatives (tilting the body more favorably toward a freeze), the Freeze campaign would ride the momentum from the fall campaigns, ensuring another looming congressional freeze battle.

The Freeze campaign once again threw its weight and energy into lobbying Congress. At the December meeting of its national committee, members decided that a congressional freeze resolution was the top priority. Freeze activists debated several options, including reintroducing the Kennedy-Hatfield resolution (verbatim) or the Zablocki freeze resolution (with or without markups); other suggestions included offering a new resolution or even multiple resolutions. Some activists wanted piecemeal legislation that would separate out a freeze and attack specific weapons systems. As a result of the meeting, the Washington national office was instructed to work with congressional cosponsors to introduce a bilateral nuclear freeze "*before* new destabilizing weapons" were deployed by either side, which would include "*all* nuclear weapons—tactical, intermediate-range, intercontinental." As additional rationale for support of an immediate freeze, the committee pointed to the "lack of significant results from the INF and START negotiations."[40]

Following the meeting, Randy Kehler reported to Freeze supporters on Washington's view of the movement since the midterm elections. Kehler observed four perceptions regarding the campaign. First was the perception that "a widespread revolt against the continuing nuclear arms race has taken a firm hold and is growing." "I don't think the politicians understand it," Kehler observed, "but clearly they respect it." Second, in the wake of the House's rejection of the latest proposed basing scheme for the MX missile, Congress perceived that "the Freeze momentum is pulling other related issues into its wake," including defense spending. Third, Kehler reported on questions supporters asked that pertained directly to the heart of the movement: "Can the momentum be sustained? Can Freeze organizers keep the movement from becoming fragmented? . . . Is the Freeze a fad?" Finally, Kehler observed that

among those whom he spoke to, the campaign's next major task was the vote
in the House on a freeze resolution in January. "A successful vote will 'up the
ante' one more notch, paving the way for the next steps toward the actual
achievement of a mutual Freeze," Kehler reported.[41]

Although grassroots activists feared the Democrats were taking control of
the movement, Kehler welcomed their involvement. Likewise, Kehler also believed the campaign should reach out to Republicans as "fellow citizens." "In
treating party affiliation and politics generally as an insignificant condition,"
as David Meyer observes, "Kehler underscored the dramatic depoliticization
the movement was undertaking." As the campaign's focus shifted to Congress,
it likewise changed its slogan from the more populist "The Future Is in Our
Hands" to "The Freeze: Because Nobody Wants a Nuclear War." The new slogan was adopted for future newsletters, buttons, pins, shirts, bumper stickers,
posters, and all other campaign promotions.[42]

FIGURE 7. The Nuclear Weapons Freeze Campaign promoted its message through pins and
buttons, shirts, posters, and bumper stickers. Buttons came in a variety of sizes, shapes, and
colors. They signaled support for local Freeze measures or the Freeze Voter '84 campaign, or
sometimes simply advocated for a nuclear freeze more generally.

Many local and state Freeze activists sought to use the campaign's growing strength to challenge specific weapons programs as they arose within Congress, but the idea of challenging any one system ran counter to the "mutual and bilateral" idea that was central to the campaign's message. As Freeze leaders understood, attacking the MX or Euromissiles specifically would play directly into the charges from the Reagan administration and its allies that the movement sought unilateral disarmament or was "manipulated from abroad"—a particularly sensitive subject among Freeze activists. Outside groups also attempted to insert their agenda into the campaign. A conference at Harvard University's Kennedy School of Government sought to debate the pros and cons of a freeze while strategizing where to go next. The concluding session was "loaded with establishment figures," such as McGeorge Bundy of the Kennedy administration and William Perry of the Carter administration. Indeed, the only leader of the Freeze campaign to participate was Randall Forsberg, who reportedly "had to negotiate her way onto the panel."[43]

While a new nuclear freeze resolution was introduced into the House that January, in early February, the Freeze campaign met for its Third Annual National Nuclear Freeze Conference, in St. Louis, Missouri. Now more than ever, the campaign placed further emphasis on bringing "overwhelming citizen pressure to bear on our elected representatives in Washington," hoping this would cause the US government to "propose a comprehensive, bilateral freeze to the Soviet Union and work towards its immediate bilateral implementation." Until that happened, the campaign would urge Congress to "suspend funding for testing, production and deployment of U.S. nuclear weapons" and call on the Soviet Union to "exercise corresponding restraint." By focusing on passing a freeze resolution in the House, however, the campaign was leaving behind important issues, such as the impending deployment of the Euromissiles. The emphasis on Congress left Pam Solo and like-minded Freeze activists questioning whether the movement was "becoming beholden to Kennedy and Markey." In a memo to Kehler and Forsberg, Solo wondered, "Do we cater too much to what [congressional aides] Jan Kalicki and Doug Waller think our priorities should be?"[44]

To emphasize their commitment to success in Congress, the Freeze campaign organized a massive lobbying effort. "The Citizens' Freeze Lobby," as Freeze coordinators referred to it, would turn out approximately five thousand people in Washington, D.C., on March 7 and 8, 1983, to pressure both the House and Senate to support a nuclear weapons freeze. Reverend Bob Moore (then chair of the New Jersey Nuclear Freeze Campaign) rented twelve buses just for six hundred New Jersey Freeze activists to show up in support. As Moore reflected, "There wasn't a room at the Capitol where our US Senators could meet with all 600 of us, so they had to come to a church in DC to do so." Kehler linked the lobbying turnout (particularly impressive for a weekday) to the strength of the Freeze campaign. At the national conference, Freeze organizers held workshops and training, emphasizing, among other activities, lobbying, House strategy, and preparation for the Freeze lobby. The campaign believed that if it could get a delegation from all congressional districts in the country to come to D.C. for the lobby, it would achieve "an impressive feat."[45]

As the Freeze advanced its congressional strategy, a variety of conservative organizations sought to derail it. Young Americans for Freedom sent a form letter to conservative Republicans who voted for the freeze resolution in the fall, accusing them of becoming "squish" to the threat of the Soviet Union. In a response, Congressman John LeBoutillier (R-NY) denied changing his mind that the Soviets were "evil little SOBs who want to conquer the world." He explained that his support for the freeze resolution was pragmatic, saying, "The resolution is non-binding. It is meaningless. If passed, it would represent nothing more than a statement of opinion from the United States Congress. It cannot be legally enforced." LeBoutillier further distanced himself from the Freeze campaign, confidently explaining that the Soviet Union cannot and would never allow verification—a key tenet of the Freeze. Following this rejection, the public would turn the debate, making the Soviets the "'bad guys' who reject 'world peace.'" LeBoutillier suggested conservatives "stop arguing over a meaningless resolution."[46]

But the most prominent attacks on the Freeze came from defense hawks such as the American Security Council Foundation, which led the "Peace through Strength" coalition (a national organization sponsored by over one hundred conservative and pro-defense organizations that sought both to promote Reagan's nuclear modernization plans and stop the momentum of the Freeze campaign). With the strength and political clout of this coalition, twelve states and the territory of Guam passed joint legislative resolutions endorsing the concept of "peace through strength" throughout fall 1981 and into early winter 1982. Likewise, the House within the Illinois General Assembly passed a Peace through Strength resolution, as did the state senates of Kentucky, Massachusetts, New Hampshire, and Virginia. The campaign relied on several state governors who served as cochairs for the Coalition for Peace through Strength, including the governors of Indiana, Louisiana, North Dakota, South Dakota, Vermont, and Virginia. The coalition had easy access to the highest levels of the Reagan White House, where ASCF president John Fisher met with National Security Advisor Clark on multiple occasions.[47]

To support their actions against the Freeze campaign, the ASCF sought five hundred thousand dollars in emergency funds for immediate actions and five million dollars to sustain the organization's long-term campaign. In a letter to the ASCF membership, Fisher detailed plans to "launch an all-out counter-offensive one week before the radicals get to Washington," in what would be "a clear head-to-head confrontation between the Freeze activists and Peace Through Strength supporters." With these funds, the ASCF planed a "media blitz" in D.C. and fifty other major cities, using television, radio, and newspapers. Through the Peace through Strength coalition, the ASCF would hold a series of press conferences with "prominent business, military and political leaders" and pressure Congress to support a Peace through Strength resolution over a nuclear freeze.[48]

A major partner of the ASCF in carrying out anti-Freeze tasks was the Veterans of Foreign Wars (VFW). In 1982, the nation was just beginning to come to terms with the war in Vietnam, establishing the national Vietnam Veterans Memorial in Washington, D.C., that November. Nevertheless, the progressive Vietnam Veterans Association (VVA) struggled to get recognition, often finding itself blocked by the VFW. In the early 1980s, the VFW was composed mostly of older and more conservative World War II veterans, whose primary concerns were both veterans' benefits and national defense (reflected in the lobbying and support of congressional candidates by its political action committee). While the VVA backed a bilateral nuclear freeze, the VFW leadership viewed it as anti-defense and thus fought the freeze tooth and nail.[49]

In an internal memo, VFW director Phelps Jones framed the freeze debate as a "battle . . . between the 'nuclear freezeniks' and we Peace Through Strength advocates." Although the 1980 election produced "an unmistakable mandate to rearm America in the face of the massive and relentless Soviet military arms buildup," Jones cautioned that the "momentum to achieve this long overdue strengthening of our armed forces was halted" by the lame duck 97th Congress, which "denied the President" production funds for the MX and Pershing II Euromissiles—a by-product of the "nuclear freeze mania plus the well-intentioned, yet deeply hurtful, involvement of the Catholic Bishops in the problems of nuclear deterrence." Enacting a nuclear freeze threatened to "drain off our national will and undercut America's thrust to restore America's military balance." The threat was even more imperative since the 97th Congress barely defeated a freeze resolution and the 98th Congress promised to be "even more Freeze-minded." Meanwhile, Jones warned, "in the real world," the Soviet Union continued to build its "Europe-busting" SS-20 missiles and Backfire bombers in addition to its "U.S.-intimidating" SS-18 and SS-19 "monster missiles," which targeted the "aging Titan and Minuteman missiles," all while the MX lay "stalled, derailed and derided by those charged with providing for the common defense."

But Jones cheerfully reported that "help is on the way." Two "Peace through Strength" resolutions were introduced by "proud recipients" of the VFW's "Congressional Award": Senate Concurrent Resolution 133, introduced by Senator Laxalt, and House Concurrent Resolution 163, introduced by Congressman Stratton. Both bills attracted a large number of cosponsors (54 in the Senate, 251 in the House) and would command support from a majority of the 98th Congress. Helping to lead the charge was Senator Jeremiah Denton (R-AL). In October 1982, Denton, a Vietnam POW, charged supporters (including fellow senators) with giving "aid and comfort to the enemies of this country"—a charge that brought condemnation from Senator Hart and the *New York Times*'s editorial page. In addition to the support of a majority of Congress, the Peace through Strength resolution was supported by President Reagan and the highest levels of his administration. Jones concluded his December memo by urging VFW members to "make this a *NOW* project in every Post in our organization. Nothing we can do during 1983 can be more important." To change the minds of Congress, Jones concluded, "we must change their mail. It's that simple."[50]

Coinciding with the Freeze campaign's lobbying on Capitol Hill, the VFW and the ASCF planned "Peace through Strength" rallies on the steps of every state capital and the District of Columbia. In a call to action to the department commanders of the VFW, Jones strategized that as the "'Freezeniks' are doing their ill-considered 'thing,'" Peace through Strength rallies would be the VFW's "answer." Jones acknowledged he was asking VFW members for "a lot of just plain hard work to get a successful March 8 rally rolling in your state," but "to date, the nuclear 'freezeniks,' with a bonus assist from the Catholic Bishops, have just plain outhustled those of us who, in 1980, got a clear mandate to re-arm." Jones concluded it was "time to put first things first again. 'Peace Through Strength' is the only way to maintain peace with freedom— and I urge my comrades across the country to once again have our VFW lead the way."[51]

As the HFAC met to discuss the Zablocki freeze resolution, nearly five thousand people rallied outside in the rain on the Capitol lawn to demand a nuclear freeze. The activists represented states as far away as California and reflected the diversity of the movement. As the *Los Angeles Times* reported, "the sea of people" gathered in front of the Capitol building wore everything from "clerical collars, to business suits, and university t-shirts" and appeared "related only by their pro-freeze lapel pins." Nearby, members of the Coalition for Peace through Strength rallied, with Congressman Jack Kemp (R-NY) telling several hundred freeze opponents that "a stronger defense will deter war and bring peace."[52]

Freeze activists and opponents descended on Washington, packing the halls of Congress. Of interest to both groups was Senator Moynihan, vice chairman of the Senate Intelligence Committee. During his 1982 reelection campaign, Moynihan ran prominently in favor of a nuclear weapons freeze and called his landslide reelection victory "a mandate on the issue [Freeze activists] brought to Washington." The campaign sought a "clear commitment" from Moynihan, since he was one of eight senators to cosponsor both the Kennedy-Hatfield immediate freeze *and* the Jackson-Warner build-then-freeze resolution. Although Moynihan reiterated his support for a freeze, many activists were unsatisfied and wanted him to go further and renounce support for Jackson-Warner. Acclaimed Broadway and theater actress Colleen Dewhurst of New York believed Moynihan "[owed] it to his state to use his talent and put all his guts behind a freeze." When Senator Alfonse D'Amato (R-NY) was unable to meet with the larger gathering of Freeze activists, a smaller group of fifty activists marched single file to his Senate office and delivered a pro-freeze petition with 280,000 signatures. D'Amato met with this smaller contingent and reiterated his support for "a mutually verifiable reduction in arms."[53]

As pro- and anti-freeze demonstrators rallied outside the Capitol, the HFAC reached a compromise on nuclear freeze legislation. Whereas the resolution initially called for a freeze followed by reductions, an amendment by freshman congressman Ed Zschau (R-CA) modified the language, urging both a freeze and mutual arms reductions. Furthermore, the committee adopted a resolution by Congressman Steven J. Solarz (D-NY) that explicitly stated a freeze resolution would not preclude any other arms control agreement with the Soviet Union. With these compromises in place, the resolution passed the committee overwhelmingly, twenty-nine to seven.[54]

The committee's decision, however, brought with it a plethora of objections from the Reagan administration and congressional freeze opponents. The resolution was passed over the objections of Reagan's INF and START negotiators. Congressman Hyde claimed the resolution "by definition, rejects START and says stop," while a nuclear weapons freeze would furthermore act as a "disincentive to reduction." Given that the resolution was nonbinding, White House spokesman Larry Speakes insisted the resolution would not deter the president "from his goal—that is, serious arms reductions." Congressman Stratton called last-minute hearings in the House Armed Services subcommittee to hear the testimony of administration officials. Stratton questioned the "objectivity and bipartisanship" of the HFAC, redbaited pro-freeze advocates, and insisted the resolution the committee passed was "almost identical to a proposal made by Mr. Brezhnev."[55]

In the days leading up to the vote on the nuclear freeze resolution, Reagan personally met with twenty-five representatives to lobby their votes against it; Secretary of State Shultz spoke against a freeze with the Republican caucus; and Assistant Secretary of Defense for International Security Richard Perle testified before Congress that a nuclear freeze would "undermine the President's ability to negotiate." The news for the Reagan administration, however, was not good. Congressman Michel warned Reagan that a pro-freeze resolution was likely to pass, given the way he read the "tea leaves" on Capitol Hill. Senate Republican leader Howard Baker Jr. also expected a freeze in some form, with "gathering momentum" in the Senate for an alternate resolution favoring "not just a freeze, but a build-down." With no visible "full-court press" from the Reagan administration, Iowa Republican Jim Leach (a cosponsor of the Zablocki freeze resolution) concluded the administration was "recognizing defeat on the House floor" and its main intent now was "to discredit the freeze advocates."[56]

On March 16, 1983, the House took up debate over the freeze resolution once again. Expecting quick and easy passage, many came dressed in tuxedos for St. Patrick's Day parties that evening. But the evening was soon spoiled, as young conservative Republicans took advantage of an error on the part of the Democrats that allowed introduction of the legislation on the floor without restrictions on the number of amendments catching pro-freeze legislators off guard. One such amendment called for a "freeze and/or reductions." Such an amendment would create options for President Reagan, allowing him to negotiate reductions but without necessarily freezing US nuclear modernization plans. While Markey accused his Republican colleagues of "filibuster by amendment," he alienated some allies by appearing too supportive of a unilateral freeze. Likewise, Congressman Zablocki appeared unfamiliar with the full ramifications of the legislation and at one point, over the objection of Freeze activists, claimed a nuclear freeze would not prevent the construction of the B-1 bomber.

The House debate got nasty. Congressman Hyde asked whether the resolution was a "transvestite" because of its alleged inconsistencies. Hyde further ridiculed the resolution, calling it "a semantic mess . . . a political statement reduced to gibberish." Congressman Michel argued a freeze would leave the United States "in a position of strategic vulnerability that could lead to war." He dismissed arguments of nuclear overkill as "naïve and dangerous," while claiming representatives had been "nailed to the cross" by the Freeze movement in the November election.[57]

As the raucous and ugly debate stretched on past midnight and into St. Patrick's Day, with a dozen amendments left to consider, forty Democrats ultimately joined the Republicans in voting for a two-week postponement until after the Easter recess. The delay was a victory for Freeze opponents and gave the Reagan administration breathing room both on arms control and from the pressure of the campaign. It was evident, Congressman Kemp suggested, that the postponement would "slow down the momentum that built up without much debate." Furthermore, Kemp continued, "The Democrats' plan was to sweep [the nuclear freeze resolution] through, get it voted upon and carried in one day." They were unable to accomplish this, however, because "a freeze means too many things to too many people."[58]

The Congressional Freeze Fight Conclusion

Although the legislative battle would be delayed, the debate over a nuclear freeze continued on the editorial pages of major newspapers and in letters to the editors. The *Chicago Tribune*, the *Washington Post*, and the *New York Times* all editorialized against a freeze resolution. The *Tribune* assailed Congress for behaving "so irresponsibly" and called the legislation "pointless, wrong-headed, unenforceable, [and] self-contradictory." The *Post*, contrarily, credited the Freeze movement directly for President Reagan's adjustments on arms control positions and toned-down rhetoric on nuclear war. Nevertheless, the *Post* called the freeze proposal in Congress "bad public policy" that was in spirit "patently unilateralist." The freeze resolution, the *Post* concluded, would undercut President Reagan and Freeze activists by prohibiting an arms control agreement that limited—but did not eliminate entirely—intermediate-range nuclear forces such as the Euromissiles. Like the *Post*, the *New York Times* credited the Freeze with "tempering the belligerency of the Reagan Administration's statements" and paving the way for "reasonable" arms control negotiations. Nevertheless, the *Times* ridiculed claims for a verifiable halt as "nice, but infeasible."[59]

While the major presses editorialized against a freeze resolution, members of congress from across the nation used the break to write for and against a freeze. In a letter to the editor of the *Washington Post*, Congressman Hyde and Congressman James Martin (R-NC) lambasted the *Post*'s coverage of the congressional nuclear freeze debate for omitting "a central development: the freeze supporters disagree among themselves on the meaning of the resolution." Countering Hyde and Martin's letter, Congressman Les AuCoin (D-OR) argued that "the freeze has always been explicit and unambiguous" about distinctions between platforms (e.g., submarines) and weapons (e.g., missiles). For instance, AuCoin noted, "Under the freeze, missile submarines can be repaired, modified or replaced by newer models, provided only that the number of missile tubes is not increased. The weapon to be frozen is the missile. This point was made repeatedly and clearly during the debate on the floor of the House, but the freeze opponents seemed not to hear." In a *New York Times* editorial, Congressman William R. Ratchford (D-CT) heaped praise on the Freeze for bringing out "the best in our people and our government." "Bit by bit," Ratchford observed, "the Freeze movement has forced a reluctant Government to get serious about nuclear arms control. Credit belongs where it is due." Given the movement's impact on the 1982 election, and its presence in the debate over the president's nominee, Kenneth Adelman, as head of ACDA, Ratchford predicted the Freeze movement was sure to become "an entrenched part of American political life."[60]

Conservative forces continued their anti-Freeze attacks. Syndicated conservative columnists Rowland Evans and Robert Novak claimed the "missing ingredient in the Administration's plan to defeat the nuclear freeze resolution in Congress" was the "still-secret case against Soviet violations." If the Reagan administration made public a study of the Soviet violations of SALT, Novak and Evans argued, it would "provide an argument strong enough to cripple the freeze movement, and possibly defeat it in its first test in the House in mid-April." Outside the mainstream press, James R. Currieo (the commander in chief of the VFW) wrote a personal letter to Congress on behalf of the VFW's 2.6 million members calling any resolution passed in favor of a freeze "a propaganda windfall for the Soviet Union" that would further stiffen their "no-give positions" on the Reagan administration's arms control proposals. Furthermore, Currieo argued that a freeze resolution was merely "an exercise in symbolism" since it stood "little chance of passing the Senate and no chance of being signed by the President."[61]

President Reagan continued his full-court press against a nuclear freeze. In a major arms control policy speech to the Los Angeles World Affairs Council, Reagan suggested a freeze "would do more harm than good," would "pull the rug out from under our negotiators," and, if the country appeared divided, might "destroy all hope for an [arms control] agreement." The speech, journalist Lou Cannon noted, "appeared to be directed as much at his domestic political critics as at the Soviets." Furthermore, as Cannon observed, "Reagan's speech was worded carefully so as not to challenge the motives of the freeze advocates," whom Reagan called "well-intentioned" and "concerned about the arms race and the danger of nuclear war."[62]

Following the Easter break, the House would once again resume session amid fierce public debate over the merits of a nuclear freeze. Freeze supporters believed they had the votes for the resolution, had "sharpened and refined" their arguments, and had gained the backing of public opinion. Yet, for the third time in five weeks, Freeze activists were unable to push their resolution through the House. The delay and acrimonious debates left even congressional freeze advocates divided, bitter, and exhausted. Over the course of the debate, Zablocki accepted twenty-five amendments to the legislation in order to speed deliberations. Republican freeze opponents gloated that these amendments and the extended debate forced freeze advocates to "restrict and dilute" the resolution. Debates over freeze amendments continued until they were finally cut off in late April. Voting on the controversial resolution, in addition to other legislation, was delayed considerably, leaving House Speaker O'Neill to criticize the Republicans as "obstructionists bent on stalling everything on the line."[63]

On May 4, 1983, one day after the Catholic bishops made public their final draft of the pastoral letter, the House passed the Zablocki freeze resolution overwhelmingly, 278 to 149. The final resolution, however, divided Freeze activists. An amendment by conservative congressman Elliot Levitas (D-GA) and Congressman Hyde attached a sunset clause that would cancel any nuclear freeze if arms reductions did not occur in a reasonable time. While the clause was vague, upon passage, Freeze opponents hailed it as a defeat for the movement. As Congressman Michel boasted, the amendment was a "victory unthinkable only a few weeks ago," adding that "the pure freeze has lost." Besides the Levitas-Hyde amendment, Freeze activists found the nonbinding nature of the resolution problematic, so it acted more as a symbolic gesture by Congress to prod Reagan on arms control progress than as a congressional mandate for a nuclear weapons freeze. The resolution furthermore did not call on Congress to curtail weapons spending, nor was there any support for preventing deployment of the Euromissiles, save for a compromise that criticized both US and Soviet INF deployments. The resolution left in place vague language such as a "when and how" clause that allowed the United States and Soviet Union to decide for themselves "when and how" they would enact a freeze. The language was so vague that Congressman Leon Panetta (D-CA) claimed, "Whether you are a Hawk or Dove or something in between . . . you can say anything you want about this resolution [to your constituents]."[64]

While freeze opponents boasted that their amendments had gutted the resolution, many activists still believed the congressional resolution was symbolic and a message to the Reagan administration. Congresswoman Barbara Boxer (D-CA), who campaigned in 1982 largely on support for a freeze, believed the House passed "a very decent resolution. We won, but we didn't win totally without a compromise." Indeed, congressional freeze supporters fought off many critical amendments and reached compromise on others. For example, an amendment by Congressman Stratton would have allowed the Reagan administration to continue to modernize nuclear weapons under a freeze. With a compromise, the language was modified to permit "research, development and safety-related improvements." Freeze proponents could also take heart in defeating the build-up-then-freeze amendment the administration backed. That amendment borrowed language from a Senate bill that called for the United States and the Soviet Union to discard two warheads for every one deployed. The House also defeated another amendment that sought mutual reductions before a nuclear freeze. Freeze advocates opposed both amendments on the grounds that they would complicate arms control negotiations while modernization plans would continue the arms race.[65]

The Reagan administration soon spoke out against the resolution. In a prepared statement, President Reagan claimed the resolution was "ambiguous and indeed so internally inconsistent that interpretation is difficult." Although Reagan noted the resolution was "greatly improved," he continued, "it is not an answer to arms control that I can reasonably support." Furthermore, he expressed confidence that if the resolution were debated in the Senate, "the doubts and opposition to a simple freeze . . . will continue to grow."[66]

Despite the weakness of the freeze resolution, the administration nevertheless understood that the public would perceive it as a strike against its arms control proposals. The administration thus sought to lessen the blow in advance. Regarding the controversial INF/Euromissile deployment scheduled for later that year, the president proposed moving away from a pure Zero Option toward a limited deployment in exchange for Soviet cuts to their existing SS-20s. Administration officials also indicated the president would soon endorse a bipartisan Senate proposal that would "establish a U.S.-Soviet crisis center intended to reduce the risk of accidental nuclear war." Moreover, as Cannon reported, Reagan appeared to be offering "an olive branch to Congress on the MX Missile" in order to develop a "national bipartisan consensus" on the controversial weapon. As the *Washington Post* editorialized, "No longer is [Reagan] treating arms control as a trick that wily Soviets play on unwitting Americans. He has adopted it as an endeavor serving the country's vital security interests—not to speak of his own vital political interests."

Furthermore, Reagan sounded more conciliatory than belligerent: "No one gained from this divisiveness: all of us are going to have to take a fresh look at our previous positions." Reagan pledged his own participation on the matter and stressed his personal "determination to assist in forging a renewed bipartisan consensus." Perhaps, as the *Los Angeles Times* editorialized, the Freeze movement had "already accomplished its fundamental purpose of making it politically impossible for the Reagan administration to ignore the importance of arms control." Thus, despite major flaws and loopholes that diminished the value of the freeze resolution, by spring 1983, the pressure of public opinion to curtail the threat of nuclear war had already moved the administration closer to a new détente.[67]

CHAPTER 5

Envisioning the Day After

Fear of the Bomb in 1980s Political
and Popular Culture

Popular culture in the1980s had iconic moments
that helped define the era, from Michael Jackson's moonwalk to Madonna's
white wedding dress. Television series such as *Dynasty* and films such as *Wall
Street* appeared to bask in the decade's greed, but Reagan's America also generated a different subset of pop culture images, one closely linked to the new
conservatism of the era and the increasing Cold War tensions. Popular films
such as the *Rambo* series dealt with themes of veterans' mistreatment in the
first installment of the franchise, while the sequel saw Rambo return to Vietnam to rescue prisoners of war, famously asking, "Do we get to win this time?"
While *Rambo* represented American machismo in the wake of Vietnam, *Red
Dawn* was arguably the quintessential Cold War film of the era. Although originally conceived as an antiwar film, with the success of *Rambo*, the studio
flipped the script and hired John Milius to direct the film. "Renowned for his
fascination with weaponry and advocation of rightwing causes," and further
"emboldened by Reagan's neo-imperial rhetoric," as film historian Tony Shaw
observes, Milius would team up with *Rambo* producer Buzz Feitshans and seek
advice from former secretary of state Alexander Haig. Released amid the Soviet boycott of the 1984 Olympics, *Red Dawn* was one of only two films
throughout the Cold War to feature a direct Soviet invasion of the United
States as a precursor to World War III.[1]

But 1980s popular culture was not all about machismo (*Rambo*) or unfettered greed (*Wall Street*), and Cold War culture of the era did not always reflect Reagan's America. Indeed, a significant strand of the popular culture rejected Reagan's militarism and the Cold War arms race. Comic books of the era often used Reagan's militarism as the basis for World War III, while prominent political cartoonists drew contrasts between Reagan's military spending and his cuts to social programs. Antiauthority, antimilitarism, and anti-Reagan screeds were common themes of the 1980s underground punk scene, while heavy metal artists drew on the imagery of nuclear war in album covers and lyrics. Popular musicians both warned of the dangers of nuclear war and urged diplomacy with the Soviet Union. Hollywood stars and sports celebrities came out directly to support the Freeze campaign, donating their time and waiving salaries for pro-Freeze commercials. Themes of a world destroyed by nuclear weapons saturated cultural media. The threat of a nuclear war between the United States and the Soviet Union became the basis for blockbuster films, box office flops, and a made-for-TV movie viewed by millions.

Beyond the immediate relationship between the Reagan administration and the Freeze campaign, examining the popular culture of the 1980s in relation to the Cold War, diplomacy, and the nuclear question can also provide insights as to why we speak of a Vietnam generation but not a Freeze generation. Unlike the Vietnam antiwar movement, the Freeze movement did not generate protest songs that helped to define the movement and the era. While the June 12 New York City rally featured an array of musicians, it was not a concert or festival in the same way as the Woodstock festival of 1969. Whereas the Freeze campaign peaked over a two-year period, the Vietnam protests stretched out over two administrations and were closely linked to the sixties and the hippie culture. Unlike the 1970s movement against nuclear power, the Freeze campaign did not have a star-packed "No Nukes" concert at Madison Square Garden. Nor was a mutual nuclear weapons freeze an undercurrent theme in major 1980s rock festivals such as Live Aid. Although antinuclear tropes in 1980s popular culture were not always directly related to support for a nuclear freeze, they reflected the unpopularity of Reagan's militarism and furthermore helped build momentum for the campaign.

Just as the Freeze took on new dimensions from its associations with religious communities and political policy circles, it was likewise shaped by popular culture. Indeed, while Catholic bishops brought the movement respectability, and congressional affiliation armed it with political support, popular culture spread the message of the dangers of a continued arms race, influencing the public mind in ways neither religion nor congressional hearings could. These inroads generated further distrust of the Reagan administration's diplomacy, forcing it to take active measures to control the nuclear narrative. A thematic examination of the popular and political culture of the 1980s shows how the Freeze campaign and the broader threat of a nuclear holocaust came to influence society even after the large rallies and political support for the Freeze campaign had come to pass.

Books, Comics, and Cartoon Strips

Between 1980 and 1982, the publication of over one hundred books related to "nuclear fear" was creating a publishing bonanza. The most prominent of these was Jonathan Schell's *The Fate of the Earth*. In the thirty-seven years since the birth of the atomic age, as a *New York Times* review suggested, *The Fate of the Earth* managed to do what no other book had been capable of: compel the nation to "confront the nuclear peril in which we all find ourselves." Originally published in the *New Yorker* as three separate essays on the "Fate of the World," Schell described the cataclysmic effects of a nuclear war in harrowing detail and riveting prose. In bleak contrast to the idea of survivable nuclear war, Schell concluded all that would remain of society would be "a republic of insects and grass." Schell did not outline a solution to the arms race, but the idea was clear: if such a fate was to be avoided, the arms race must not continue.[2]

The Fate of the Earth spent several weeks on the *New York Times* best sellers list and received the *Los Angeles Times* best book prize in 1982. The impact of *The Fate of the Earth* was perhaps best summarized by *Washington Post* columnist James Lardner: "Who would have thought such a dense tome would be offered as a special bargain by the book of the month club, touted as an event by *Time* magazine, entered into the Congressional legislature record more than once (by more than one anxious legislator), extolled on the 'CBS Evening News' and 'Merv Griffin Show,' endorsed by Walter Cronkite, [and] denounced on the editorial pages of *The Wall Street Journal* and *The New York Times*?" Although Schell's argument was "unprovable," Senator Cranston cautioned, "We can't afford to experiment." Helen Caldicott praised Schell's work as "the new bible of our time." Walter Mondale praised it as "mandatory reading." But not everyone had favorable reviews of Schell's essays. The *Wall Street Journal* had critiqued the *New Yorker* for running the original pieces, calling the magazine "a bastion of limousine liberalism" and Schell's articles "destructive of serious thought about how to prevent war and control the spread of nuclear arms." Novelist and columnist George Higgins in the *Boston Globe* criticized the work as "gibble gabble." "Whatever it is," concluded Lardner, "Jonathan Schell's *The Fate of the Earth* has people talking."[3]

While Schell described a nonfictional account of a world destroyed by nuclear war, in the world of comic book fiction, the aftermath of a nuclear war became the basis for some of the decade's most iconic works. In Britain, the comic anthology *Warrior* would include comic writer Alan Moore's future postapocalyptic dystopia *V for Vendetta*. It was set in the United Kingdom during the 1990s in the aftermath of a nuclear war during the 1980s that had devastated the rest of the world, leaving Britain with a fascist government opposed by an anarchist in a Guy Fawkes mask. While *V for Vendetta* would win the United Kingdom's coveted Eagle Awards for best story and best comic writer (Alan Moore) in 1983, the most prominent intersection of comic books and the Cold War nuclear anxiety during the Reagan era was Moore's next project, *Watchmen*. Published by DC Comics in 1986 and 1987, *Watchmen* was set in an alternate 1980s wherein the United States was victorious in Vietnam and Richard Nixon was in his fifth term. Reflecting 1980s Cold War anxieties, the comic opened with the United States and the Soviet Union on the verge of World War III in 1985.

In the early 1980s, the primary source for Americans to get their news was the newspaper, with the first twenty-four-hour news channel, the Cable News Network (CNN), in its infancy. Reagan and elements of the Freeze movement were regular features of the political cartoons of the period, as were critiques of the era's militarism. Cartoonists in 1982 routinely parodied the MX missile while regularly depicting the defense budget as a bloated general (or sometimes Pentagon), in contrast with the starving social needs programs. Herbert Block, a prominent political cartoonist since the Franklin D. Roosevelt administration, depicted Reagan as Senator Joseph McCarthy, holding in one hand *Reader's Digest* and in the other a scrap of paper reading "Charges that nuclear freeze advocates are manipulated by foreign power." Cartoonist Bob Englehardt depicted two Freeze activists standing in a kitchen, watching Reagan as he searched under their refrigerator, with the caption reading, "I just know there's got to be a red under your refrigerator." In the *Baltimore Sun*, Tom Flannery also mocked the Reagan administration's contentions of Soviet involvement in the Freeze campaign, depicting two administration officials wiretapping a church meeting on nuclear freeze and concluding, "Sounds like a sinister foreign movement to me."[4]

Both the Freeze movement and the freeze proposal received largely favorable treatment from the nation's political cartoonists. In the *Fort Worth Star*, Etta Hume depicted two generals walking through a nuclear freeze protest, with the caption, "The beauty of our position is that if they should happen to be right, they won't be around to say 'I told you so.'" In the *Colorado Mountain News*, Ed Stein depicted a world exploding under the strategies of preemptive strike, first strike, and mutual assured destruction, whereas under a nuclear freeze the Earth remained at peace. The Catholic bishops likewise were routinely spotlighted in political cartoons. Whereas the Reagan administration treated the bishops with respect, conservative cartoonists routinely criticized and even mocked the bishops' peace pastoral. Chuck Asay depicted an American fortress blockaded by a cross while a priest (labeled the "Catholic bishops disarmament statement") standing guard outside exclaimed "Peace!" as Native Americans captured women and children, all while Americans behind the fort struggled to pull guns in defense. Likewise, cartoonist Charles Brooks depicted a vandalized Soviet house with civilians pleading for help amid violent attacks, while in contrast a Catholic bishop knocked on the door of a serene home in the United States seeking "peace in the neighborhood."[5]

Although conservative cartoonists could praise Reagan's programs without scandal, in the heated environment of the early 1980s, criticizing Reagan sometimes came with serious consequences, even for popular and established cartoonists. On the eve of the 1980 election, satirical cartoonist Garry Trudeau's popular comic strip *Doonesbury* ran a controversial strip wherein the fictional journalist Roland Burton Hedley III journeys into "dark, deep, neglected territory"—"Reagan's brain." The strip excited critics of Reagan both because of the "sharp accuracy of the satire" and "broad cultural splash," but "Reagan's brain" came under fire from conservative readers and editors, and the strip was subsequently dropped from more than two dozen papers. As a testament to Trudeau and *Doonesbury*'s popularity, however, papers such as the *Indianapolis Star* were obliged to reinstate the strip after the editors received over eight hundred calls in protest. Trudeau's *Doonesbury* continued to lampoon Ronald Reagan and members of his administration throughout the 1980s. In December 1982, just before Trudeau's sabbatical, readers of the strip would find Reverend Scott Sloan publishing a nuclear freeze newsletter as well as mocking an October 1982 *Reader's Digest* piece that suggested Soviet manipulation of the Freeze movement.[6]

Hollywood Fights for a Freeze

Beyond the world of comics and political cartoons, Hollywood and sports luminaries joined the political fracas over the arms race, becoming major allies of the Freeze campaign. These celebrities donated time and money to fight for, and—in some instances—against a bilateral nuclear weapons freeze. In Charlotte, North Carolina, the local SANE chapter received a large grant and used the money on radio spots promoting a nuclear weapons freeze. To help spread the message, SANE sought to enlist local college basketball coaching legend Dean Smith. In 1982, Smith was fresh off coaching the University of North Carolina (UNC) Tar Heels men's basketball team that featured future NBA Hall of Fame stars Michael Jordan and James Worthy to the NCAA Final Four championship. As the head coach of the Tar Heels since 1961 and an assistant coach at UNC for three years before that, Smith had a history of activism, including working to promote desegregation in local restaurants as well as opposing the Vietnam War. Nevertheless, Smith never endorsed political candidates or products. Indeed, as Smith reflected on his opposition to Vietnam, he never wanted to be "a leader on the Vietnam protest or out front at a protest," preferring instead quiet peace vigils and signing petitions.[7]

In North Carolina, "Smith was an almost godlike figure . . . the ideal person to narrate SANE's radio spots," as David Cortright observes, but to SANE activists, Smith's stance on the freeze debate was unknown. As the national director for SANE, Cortright wrote to Smith to request he become a spokesperson for the Freeze campaign. Smith's response came weeks later to the SANE office in the form of a short note: "Coach Smith will be glad to participate in your campaign. Please call to arrange a time to visit." Cortright and the SANE staff were "ecstatic" and saw the recruitment of Smith to the Freeze campaign as "a major coup."[8]

Smith would record two radio spots for SANE. In the first spot, Smith proclaimed, "Winning the national championship was a great thrill. But there is one contest no one wins—the international arms race. We all lose in a nuclear war, and the risk grows greater every day unless we do something about it." Smith concluded the spot by advocating for a bilateral nuclear freeze and encouraging listeners to "take action. Pick up the phone and add your voice to the growing demand for a nuclear freeze." Smith's second radio spot focused on children, calling them "one of life's greatest gifts" but lamenting they were now "an endangered species—because of the arms race." Noting the size of the US and Soviet nuclear arsenals, Smith observed that the two superpowers "together possess over 50,000 nuclear warheads. That's ten tons of explosives for every child on earth. It's insane." At the end of both spots, listeners were directed to an 800 number where they could leave a message in support of a nuclear freeze that would be sent to President Reagan and Soviet general secretary Andropov.[9]

The sixty-second SANE radio spots featuring Smith aired on a dozen radio stations, saturating North Carolina beginning the week of February 7, 1983. Smith's participation in the SANE freeze campaign advertisements created "a sensation," with stories appearing across the major newspapers of the state. The advertisements received wide—and positive—coverage across radio and television platforms, reaching millions of people, while giving a "powerful boost to North Carolina SANE," as Cortright reflected. Smith's alliance brought wide exposure to the peace movement, affiliating SANE and a nuclear freeze with the popular basketball coach in the public mind. "Suddenly," as Cortright reflected, "the peace movement had credibility and access it had not known before." No longer were Freeze advocates "on the fringes"; they were now "part of the mainstream."[10]

With the growth of SANE, particularly in the greater Los Angeles area, the organization revived its older Hollywood for SANE committee after a twenty-two-year absence. In 1983, SANE launched an ad in *Variety* signed by over 250 actors and directors, including Jack Lemmon, James Earl Jones, Ed Asner, and Sally Field, among other Hollywood luminaries. "Hollywood for SANE pledged to make its talents available to all other groups who shared their concern for nuclear disarmament," historian Milton Katz notes, sponsoring several performances of a staged reading, *Handy Dandy, a Comedy but. . . .* The two-person one-act play was an "ironic commentary on the nuclear dilemma," as Cortright notes. The play opened in October 1984 in theaters in New York and London, in addition to fourteen separate theaters in Los Angeles, which featured "twenty-eight of the leading stars of Hollywood." The play was "a media sensation in Los Angeles," with stories across newspapers and broadcast media. All proceeds of *Handy Dandy* directly benefited the Nuclear Weapons Freeze Campaign.[11]

Freeze activists would continue to recruit celebrities into their organizing efforts. To help generate finances for the forthcoming 1984 election campaigns, Freeze activists planned Freeze WALK. On October 8, 1984, over two hundred Freeze groups across the nation would participate in the "1st National FREEZE WALK and Rally," projected to raise anywhere between two hundred thousand and eight hundred thousand dollars. To help raise these sums and draw attention to their efforts, Freeze activists actively sought to involve celebrities. "Well-known figures generate media attention," a Freeze activist noted. Moreover, if the campaign could get celebrity involvement in the action, it would generate both "increased coverage and pre-event publicity." Recruiting celebrities, however, would raise the campaign's budget expenses for the event, since celebrities' participation often required first-class travel. Nevertheless, the Freeze campaign bounced ideas around, such as recruiting actor and activist Paul Newman to walk in one of the fifteen Connecticut Freeze Walks since he lived close by. Ronald Reagan's daughter Patti could participate in the Washington, D.C., event, with the "two kids from [sic] 'WAR GAMES' WALKing near Norad base." The Freeze WALK became a "smashing success," as Randy Kehler reported, with the campaign raising approximately seven hundred thousand dollars.[12]

But the most prominent intersection of policy and popular culture may have been in California, where the California Freeze Campaign sought to pass Proposition 12 (the bilateral nuclear weapons freeze). As journalist Paul Loeb explains, "Because [California] was the nation's largest state, Reagan's home and known—for good or for ill—as a bellwether of shifts in national sentiment, Freeze supporters believed the outcome would echo across the country." The campaign for Proposition 12 became a microcosm of the national Freeze campaign's successes and failures. The origins of the Proposition 12 campaign can be traced to the success of the Massachusetts freeze referendum in 1980. Inspired by the passage of the freeze referendum in conservative counties in Massachusetts, Jo and Nick Seidita of conservative Orange County began organizing within the Unitarian Universalist Society. Backed by the congregation's generous financial support, the Seiditas mounted a campaign that included mailings, phone banking, and visits to organizations and churches to seek endorsements. By August 1981, eighty-four groups were involved in Californians for a Nuclear Weapons Freeze. To gain the required signatures to put the freeze initiative on the ballot across the state, supporters held petition parties, sold the "Freeze Bar" popsicle for a dollar on state beaches, and gathered signatures outside public venues. With over 750,000 names collected, the nuclear freeze question would be put to California voters on the November 1982 ballot.[13]

As diverse as the national Nuclear Weapons Freeze Campaign was, so was California's coalition. As *Nuclear Times* noted, supporters of the freeze initiative ranged from feminists to Roman Catholic bishops, joining "black ministers with corporate lawyers, and Berkeley radicals" alongside Reagan's daughter Patti. A variety of luminaries from the scientific community expressed support, as well as politicians such as California governor Edmund G. ("Jerry") Brown Jr.[14]

Hollywood also played a part. In a commercial supporting Proposition 12 called "First Steps," actors Jack Lemmon and Paul Newman play a game of high-risk poker, as gasoline leaks from a tank on the floor. As the two argue over their poker hands, they begin "splitting off matches from stockpiles in their hands, holding them out to test and threaten," as the leaking gasoline spreads across the floor. With obvious analogies to nuclear stockpiles, Newman shouts, "I got forty-four, how many you got?" "Thirty-six," Lemmon replies. The two strike matches simultaneously, as the screen fills with flames.[15]

Like the national campaign, a strong coalition emerged to challenge Proposition 12, including former civil rights activist and Hollywood luminary Charlton Heston. Heston would appear in a "No on 12" TV advertisement, where he charged that "a freeze wouldn't be honored by the Soviet Union, couldn't be verified, [would] hurt our deterrent ability and would encourage Soviet aggression." After Newman declared that both sides had honored their nuclear weapons treaty obligations, Heston held a press conference from his Beverly Hills tennis court, where he chided Newman as a "good man and a good actor" but someone who needed to "check the facts first." Heston's critiques of Newman were reiterated in an eight-page "Open Letter to Paul Newman," where Congressman Robert K. Dornan (R-CA) listed sixty-seven Soviet treaty violations.[16]

As Newman's biographer Shawn Levy observes, in the coming weeks "a pattern emerged: Newman would appear on some TV or radio show to discuss his support of the nuclear freeze, and Heston would pop up the following day and dismiss whatever Newman had said." While Newman would publicly complain that Heston was "sabotaging" the pro–Proposition 12 campaign, he would soon have a chance to put questions to Heston over the phone on the ABC News show *The Last Word*. While the debate was brief, at Newman's suggestion the two agreed to a real debate on *The Last Word* one week before the 1982 midterm elections. Although Newman prepared extensively for the debate, "throughout the broadcast Heston ran circles around him." Where Newman "alternated between stolid repetition of data and unscripted reactions and even outburst," Heston came across as "a cool customer, referring to his opponent by his first name, calmly provoking Newman with selective points of information, and finally comparing advocates of a nuclear freeze to the Europeans who appeased Hitler."[17]

Newman soon had a falling out with Heston, with the two going their separate ways. Both, however, would continue to use their celebrity activism for and against the arms race. Newman continued to speak out against nuclear proliferation and the militarism of the Reagan administration, publishing letters and opinion pieces in the *New York Times*. Newman narrated a television documentary about "the presumed consequences of a limited nuclear war" and also worked on "a long-gestating film project about the dangers of nuclear weapons." Furthermore, he appeared at benefits for both PSR and the Freeze campaign and was recruited by Randy Kehler for a speaking tour in support of the Freeze in Texas (Newman would decline). Heston ventured further into conservative activism, notably working with the American Security Council Foundation, where he starred in commercials to promote Reagan's Star Wars missile defense program, warning of attempts by "Tip [O'Neill] and his anti-defense friends" to destroy the program, while further imploring viewers to donate money to the ASCF.[18]

The California Campaign for a Nuclear Freeze shows the dilemmas the movement faced as it sought to expand its message. While the power of

Hollywood may have helped the movement reach a wider audience, it left the grassroots activists resentful. Although the actors, writers, and designers donated their services to the pro–Proposition 12 commercials, the California Freeze campaign still spent approximately two million dollars on advertisements. As one activist explained, by spending such amounts of money on advertisements, the campaign failed to nurture "the kind of grass-roots networks that can generate 100 letters at a moment's notice, or generate twenty people to sit in at a congressman's office." Further problems were encountered by the top-down nature imposed on the campaign by financier Harold Willens. Willens used his money and influence to bankroll the California Freeze campaign, though, as *Nuclear Times* noted in 1982, "Willens's mode [of] politics often clashed with the ideas and style of local activists." Willens feared the California Freeze campaign would be captive to "a stupid, silly fringe group whose efforts could be contained in a telephone booth." Seeking to operate the campaign like a business, he made decisions in Los Angeles, then expected everyone else to fall in line—a concept that antagonized northern activists.[19]

Despite the problems that the California Freeze campaign encountered, both internally and from the Reagan administration, the movement succeeded in passing Proposition 12 in California, securing an endorsement from the *Los Angeles Times*. Nationally, with ten separate state freeze referenda and more than one-third of the nation's electorate voting on the freeze question, the state referenda became "the closest this nation has ever come to a national referendum on the nuclear arms race," Douglas Waller notes. While an issue such as handgun control (Proposition 15) in California was soundly defeated, and freeze opponent Republican Pete Wilson would win the Senate seat, Proposition 12 won by a 4 percent margin, 52 percent to 48 percent, showing how the issue could cross party lines.[20]

Rock against Reagan

Although Freeze activists never had a Woodstock moment, many of the most popular pop and rock artists of the 1980s drew on the Cold War tensions, in their lyrics, album covers, and music videos (a platform that reached the height of its popularity in the 1980s with the onset of Music Television, or MTV). Moreover, classically trained musicians formed groups such as Musicians against Nuclear Arms, playing benefit shows for the Freeze, with special guest appearances from Paul Newman, George Kennan, and Helen Caldicott.[21]

Antinuclear and anti-Reagan songs did not always advocate for a nuclear freeze, but they offered a glimpse of opposition to the growing militarism in the country. This was perhaps best exemplified in second-wave, postpunk rock circles. As D.O.A. front man Joey Keithley writes, "A lot of people also hated King Ronnie and what he represented: big business, big military, anti-unionism, big oil." Moreover, as Keithley observed, Reagan may have done more to enhance punk rock in the 1980s than prominent punk rockers such as Jello Biafra of the Dead Kennedys or John Lydon of the Sex Pistols. Reflecting on Reagan's America, Vic Vondi of Chicago's Article of Faith bluntly stated, "It's not morning in America, it's fucking midnight!"[22]

For punk rockers, Ronald Reagan was public enemy number one. Punk bands promoted their shows with anti-Reagan posters, frequently depicting the president with a crudely drawn Adolf Hitler mustache and a swastika on his sleeve, as well as devil horns protruding from his head. Lyrically, bands routinely drew on the fears of a nuclear war between the United States and the Soviet Union, as well as resistance to Reagan's militarism. In the Washington, D.C., hardcore scene, songs by bands such as Scream warned about an unannounced nuclear first strike ("Came without Warning"), while Reagan Youth, an overtly anarchist, socialist, and antiracist punk band, took their name by meshing the name of then-candidate Reagan with Hitler Youth. In the coarse, unambivalent, anti-Reagan tirade "Fucked Up Ronnie," Vancouver-based hardcore act D.O.A. exclaimed, "You're fucked up Ronnie! You're not gonna last, you're gonna die too from a neutron blast!"

Southern California's Orange County was home to the suburban housewives who formed the backbone of the new conservatism of the Reagan era—but it was also home to a festering youth backlash.[23] Inside the famed punk club the Cuckoo's Nest, rebellious teens slam-danced to the music of local acts such as the Adolescents, while teens frequently clashed with police as well as with cowboys from a country bar that shared the same parking lot. Likewise, the broader Los Angeles metropolitan region birthed bands such as TSOL (True Sounds of Liberty), whose debut EP featured songs inspired by French anarchist Pierre-Joseph Proudhon ("Property Is Theft") and songs about refusing a feared return of the military draft ("World War III"), while still other songs, such as "Superficial Love," simply stated, "President Reagan can shove it!" Similar themes against militarism could be found in Bad Religion's debut album and the lyrics of the Minutemen, while Mike Muir of Venice's Suicidal Tendencies, referencing the 1981 assassination attempt on the president, shouted, "I shot Reagan! And I'd shoot him again, and again, and again!"

Punk rock artists were also involved in staging benefit shows and in producing benefit albums. In 1983, Reagan Youth, alongside several other acts, played a series of concerts on a flatbed truck across the country on the "Rock against Reagan" tour, followed by "Rock against Reagan" concerts outside both the 1984 San Francisco Democratic National Convention and the Dallas Republican National Convention. Organized initially by infamous New York City–based peace activists the Yippies, the Rock against Reagan tour sought to mobilize apathetic youth (punk rockers) and register them to vote to defeat Reagan in 1984. Likewise, bands such as MDC routinely played benefit shows throughout the 1980s for various causes and produced a compilation record ("P.E.A.C.E." or "Peace, Energy, Action, Cooperation, Evolution") featuring fifty-two bands, with over ten thousand dollars in proceeds going to US and British antinuclear organizations as well as other progressive causes.[24]

While politics and punk went hand and hand, in the punk scene politics went beyond just anti-Reagan lyrics. Fans routinely wrote passionate letters in the popular fanzine *Flipside* "opposing the national conservative political culture," with some fans urging others to join organizations such as Women Strike for Peace. Even at hardcore shows, progressive and left-wing organizations could be found tabling, while D. Boon of D.C.'s the Minutemen

FIGURE 8. Resistance against nuclear weapons and Ronald Reagan more generally was ubiquitous in 1980s popular culture. In the punk rock scene, Reagan was public enemy number one. Reagan was frequently depicted in punk rock show flyers such as this one from the "Rock against Reagan" tour. Courtesy of Aaron Cometbus Punk and Underground Press Collection #8107, Division of Rare Manuscript Collections, Cornell University Library.

could be found distributing "U.S. OUT OF CENTRAL AMERICA" bumper stickers as well as encouraging fans to "boo Ronald Reagan." Although punk fans could cite a list of progressive-left issues they supported, as historian Martin Bradford observes, punk fans "demonstrated ambiguous attitudes toward politics," displaying a "knee-jerk impulse to reject any interest," perhaps making punk culture more "alternative rather than oppositional." Bradford nevertheless concludes that while 1980s punk lacked a "unified 'Democratic Far Leftist' vision, there was a symbolic fit between its values, lifestyles, musical expressions, and political leanings, which all aligned to resist mainstream society and, frequently, electoral politics."[25]

Although the heavy metal acts of the 1980s did not always share the same overt political stances as their punk rock cousins, besides the glitz and glam of 1980s hair metal, nuclear war was a common motif in lyrics and albums of underground thrash metal bands. Metallica's 1983 album *Ride the Lightning* opened with the track "Fight Fire with Fire," a fast-paced song warning "nuclear warfare shall lay us to rest." Album covers from artists within the genre routinely depicted nuclear war. The cover of Megadeth's 1986 *Peace Sells . . . But Who's Buying?* featured jets racing by in a clouded crimson red sky, as Vic Rattlehead (the band's skeleton mascot) stood beside a "For Sale" sign outside the remains of a bombed out United Nations. Likewise, the cover of Nuclear Assault's debut album, *Game Over*, depicted a population fleeing a large city as a mushroom cloud looms over a fire-lit sky.

The dire consequences of nuclear war were not just themes found in extreme rock acts but were staples of 1980s popular hits. In October 1981, pop-rock artist Prince released his fourth album, *Controversy*, featuring the track "Ronnie Talk to Russia," wherein Prince pleaded with President Reagan, "Ronnie talk to Russia, before it's too late, before they blow up the world." Prince followed this with his 1982 breakout album *1999*, featuring (among other hits) the title track "1999"—a song about refusing to stop dancing in the face of an impending nuclear war. Pop-rock artist Sting's 1985 debut solo album included the single "Russians." "Russians" was a political and social commentary, pleading for the "common sense" of the citizens of the United States and the Soviet Union while disputing ideas of survivable nuclear war. Popular reggae artist Peter Tosh's "No Nuclear War" decried that one superpower deployed the MX and the other the SS, while inflation and social ills plagued society. "Anti-nuclear themes reached the musical hit parade," as historian Philip Jenkins observes, with songs such as "Safety Dance" by Men without Hats, Pink Floyd's "Two Sons in the Sunset," and West German pop band Nena's international dance hit "99 Red Balloons" (or "99 Luftballons" in the original German release).[26]

With the emergence of MTV in the 1980s, music videos became a popular format for promoting a song. Popular parody artist Weird Al Yankovic built his career on music videos that spoofed popular culture and contemporary mainstream acts. His song "Christmas at Ground Zero" spoofed popular ska band Fishbone's "Party at Ground Zero" (itself a song about partying as the world succumbs to nuclear war), while the music video mixed Christmas images with footage of nuclear tests and duck cover drills as a young Ronald Reagan cheerfully—and ambiguously—tells the audience, "The big day is only a few hours away now, I'm sure you're all looking forward to it as much as we are!" In one of the most memorable music videos of the 1980s, Genesis's "Land of Confusion" featured puppets of Ronald and Nancy Reagan going to bed at 5:30 in the afternoon. By the end of the video, Reagan awakes from his nightmare in a pool of sweat but mistakenly hits the button marked "nuke" rather than "nurse."[27]

As in other cultural tropes, musicians and the music of the period challenged the popular ideas of survivable nuclear war while further dissenting against the militarism of the new Cold War. "In dozens of ways, large and small," Cortright reflected, "artists supported the movement to end the arms race." While popular acts and artists did not always explicitly advocate for a nuclear weapons freeze, songs, videos, and imagery about the horror of nuclear war spurred opposition to the arms race and militarism, helping the Freeze campaign reach the apolitical. Although the music from the period did not bring about a response from the Reagan administration, presentation of the antinuclear message in other forms of media would make a critical impact on the president himself.[28]

Television Sitcoms and Major Motion Pictures

The Cold War and the threat of nuclear war played a major role both in film and television plots during the 1980s. Indeed, as the *Wall Street Journal* reported, "Not for two decades . . . has there been so much cinematic activity on the subject." In the eighteen months following Reagan's election, television networks aired "at least three full-length nuclear-bomb scenarios," with at least nine others in production by July 1983. As Michael Fuchs, the president of Time Inc.'s Home Box Office (HBO) entertainment group, told the *Journal*, "We're being pitched stuff on this subject every week. It's *the* creative issue right now."[29]

While studios steadfastly sought to avoid films with a message over entertainment, some films managed to deliver both. In 1983's *WarGames*, Matthew

Broderick played a young computer whiz who tapped into a military computer to play a game of "Thermonuclear Warfare." Although the studio "wanted an entertainment film, not a message film," as executive producer Leonard Goldberg told the *Wall Street Journal*, "they got both." The movie had a clear antinuclear message: the only way to win the game of thermonuclear warfare was to not play it. While the movie enjoyed commercial success, it also caught the attention of Ronald Reagan, who watched a private screening at Camp David during a congressional debate over arms control and the fate of the MX missile. Two days after the screening, as Lou Cannon recounted, Reagan met with "several Democratic congressmen who had backed the MX in exchange for the president's arms control commitment." Reagan began the meeting reading from his tailored cue cards but soon set them aside. His face "lit up," and he asked the congressmen if they had seen *WarGames*. With no immediate response, Reagan "launched into an animated account of the plot," giving an "impromptu review," including critiques of film characters.[30]

WarGames was developed by Lisa Weinstein and executive produced by Paula Weinstein—two sisters with activist pasts. The Weinstein sisters later organized "a glittering Hollywood fundraiser to benefit Freeze Voter '84" (a political action committee seeking to make support for a bilateral nuclear weapons freeze a defining issue during the 1984 elections). Cohosting the Freeze Voter fundraiser were prominent actress Barbara Streisand, Twentieth Century Fox chairman Barry Diller, and Sandy Gallain, manager of country music star Dolly Parton (among other celebrities). As journalist Mark Hertsgard reported in *Mother Jones*, "On a starlit evening" in October 1984, "over 300 writers, agents, actors, producers, and other Hollywood types navigated the steep, twisting road up to Gallain's sumptuous home near the top of Benedict Canyon." The guests that evening listened to Senator Ted Kennedy and Helen Caldicott "talk about the urgency of negotiating a nuclear weapons freeze," inspiring them to donate over one hundred thousand dollars.[31]

Films about nuclear Armageddon were ubiquitous in the popular culture and could be found across genres. Documentaries, such as *The Atomic Café* and *No Place to Hide*, used stock government footage and contemporary films and television shows of the early nuclear age to examine the hysteria around atomic weapons, civil defense drills, and the Cold War in general, showing how "anyone born before 1956 was either deliberately lied to or misled about the facts of nuclear war," as a review in the *Bulletin of the Atomic Scientists* noted. Paramount Pictures' *Testament* (1983) "stressed the horrifying effects of nuclear war on families," as Jenkins writes, with a focus on the death of children, sending the message that "the bomb was the ultimate form of child abuse." Produced in part by the BBC and first airing on British television, *Threads* presented a dark future following a nuclear exchange, depicting, as Toni Perrine observes, "the loss of language, the breakdown of most recognizable forms of social organization and ultimately the end of human reproductive capability."[32]

In the fourth installment of the *Superman* franchise, the United States and the Soviet Union are on the brink of nuclear war, as Superman, addressing the United Nations, promises to rid the world of nuclear weapons. Superman soon rounds up all the world's nuclear weapons, hurling them at the sun. The destruction, however, spawns a new menace, named "Nuclear Man," who is controlled by Superman's arch nemesis Lex Luther. Although widely panned, *Superman IV* was co-written by the star of the franchise, Christopher Reeve. In an interview with *Playgirl* in December 1982, Reeve claimed he "absolutely supported" a "unilateral nuclear freeze" and would further help "lead the movement toward it."[33]

While the administration could not control the message of many of these popular films (or other forms of popular media), it did attempt to limit the reach of specific foreign films. In January 1983, the US Department of Justice (DOJ) ruled an Academy Award–winning Canadian documentary, *If You Love This Planet*, would be listed as "foreign political propaganda." The act of declaring the film propaganda required that the National Film Board of Canada file with the attorney general as an "agent of foreign principal." The film would then have to display a label that identified it as the product of a foreign agent; in addition, the filmmakers would have to file dissemination reports with the DOJ indicating what organizations showed the film and where. The alleged "propaganda" at the heart of the film was a public talk by Helen Caldicott to SUNY Plattsburgh students on the dangers of nuclear war. Although the film was not censored outright, the DOJ charges carried serious consequences. As Edwin Rothschild observed, "The message is unmistakable: the federal government considers the film to be subversive, brands its issuer as the tool of an alien power, questions the patriotism of its users and exhibitioners and regards its viewers as either misled or disloyal." The film never appeared on national television in the United States.[34]

In the world of television, fear of nuclear war and plots around the bomb were common themes. On the 1982 Thanksgiving episode of television sitcom *Family Ties*, ex-hippies Steven and Elyse Keaton are arrested at a rally against nuclear weapons, spoiling Thanksgiving dinner and causing a rift with their young Republican son, Alex P. Keaton. Nuclear fears even found their way into *Mister Rogers' Neighborhood* when a weeklong episode titled "Conflict" featured one character suspected of making bomb parts, which caused another to also build up his stockpile of bomb parts. The theme of nuclear war, however, was not always popular with network executives, and may have brought about the end of the CBS series *Lou Grant*. Toward the end of its fifth season, in 1982, it aired an episode called "Unthinkable," where a confrontation in the Middle East leads to a potential nuclear war between the United States and the Soviet Union. Following its broadcast, network executives canceled *Lou Grant*. Executive producer Allan Burns blamed it on the theme of nuclear war—a view widely shared by cast members and liberal publications alike. According to Burns, CBS "didn't like the theme from the start" and continually asked him, "Can't you do something happy? Balance it, show the good side of self-destruction."[35]

"Unthinkable" received the lowest ratings of the season for *Lou Grant*, even trailing a rerun of TV bloopers, but as a *Mother Jones* investigation alluded to, "This story is so full of holes that even network officials have a hard time sticking to it in private." A spinoff of the popular *Mary Tyler Moore* sitcom of the 1970s, *Lou Grant* popularized progressive ideas on a weekly basis from 1977 to 1982. The star of *Lou Grant*, veteran actor and activist Ed Asner, championed the first amendment, spoke out against the death penalty, supported the striking PATCO air traffic controllers, and, "most explosive of all," spoke out against US involvement in El Salvador's terror campaigns. Like Jane Fonda, Asner was vilified by the Right; however, in a sense, Asner was perhaps "more offensive, more threatening to conservatives than Fonda, because his TV show brought him into American living rooms every week and because his public image was more engaging than Fonda's," *Mother Jones* observed. Although the official line at CBS was "Ratings, not politics, killed *Lou Grant*," the killing was more akin to a "gangland slaying," brought on by an orchestrated pressure campaign by "New Right hitmen like Jerry Falwell, Charlton Heston, Representative John LeBoutillier and Lynn Bouchet, as well as TV advertisers like Kimberly-Clark and the Peter Paul Cadbury company," all of whom "pulled triggers on an assortment of deadly weapons that put *Lou Grant* in the grave." As Burns maintained, CBS was "looking for a reason to cancel us," and an episode about nuclear war gave it to them.[36]

In another instance of television networks' concern over broadcasting films on nuclear war, producer Don Ohlmeyer believed the "explosive content" of his made-for-television movie *Special Bulletin* frightened the NBC network into weakening the show. *Special Bulletin* "centered on an antinuclear terrorist who nonetheless succeeded in blowing up Charleston, South Carolina." The film featured realistic newscasts, which network executives "feared might provoke panic among viewers," as Orson Welles's famous radio broadcast "War of the Worlds" did in 1938. "Rather than risk alarm," as the *Wall Street Journal* reported, "NBC interrupted the show repeatedly with warnings," thus ruining the suspense.[37]

Because network executives feared that nuclear plots made for bad television, Freeze activists urged entertainers to "incorporate [nuclear] issues into their shows." Norman Fleishman, a Los Angeles Freeze activist, had been educating writers, producers, and actors "for years to influence television programming." As the director of Microsecond, an organization that sought "to raise the Hollywood community's awareness about the dangers of nuclear war," Fleishman "orchestrated a series of seminars in prominent entertainers' homes," featuring guest lectures on nuclear issues. For Freeze activists, there was a sense of urgency to get Hollywood to embrace nuclear war in films and television. As Fleishman noted, "The only thing that will work in time to get the planet together is entertainment—everything else is too boring." Fleishman made a pitch for executives: "The nuclear issue can be big business. There's a lot of fear and a lot of anxiety about it. It can get big ratings."[38]

Armageddon Comes to Prime Time

By fall 1983, the Freeze campaign had suffered several setbacks, with losses in the Senate, tempered support from the Catholic bishops, and an escalating Cold War. The Reagan administration still feared, however, that a made-for-television movie called *The Day After* could reignite the antinuclear movement. As ACDA's Kenneth Adelman told *Meet the Press*, the political impact of the film would be "damaging" if viewers came away supporting a nuclear freeze or even unilateral disarmament. "There was a lot of feeling . . . [the film] could . . . be one of those hinge events which changes the nation's mind about itself and its policies," David Gergen later reflected. Because the administration "worried" about the film, Gergen added, it may have "overreacted."[39]

Set in the then present-day Kansas City, Missouri, and neighboring Lawrence, Kansas, *The Day After* followed several families through the grim aftermath of a nuclear strike on the American heartland. Premiering November 20, 1983, on ABC, the film drew nearly one hundred million viewers and was one of the top-rated television shows in the nation's history. As the *Washington Post* reflected, "People protested. People propagandized. People prayed. But everywhere, people watched." School principals sent letters home warning that the film was not just another horror flick. Children were urged not to view it at all, while adults were cautioned not to view it alone. That evening, Americans came together, gathering in churches, schools, and neighbors' homes. Senator Cranston sponsored 136 fund-raising viewing parties across the nation. In Washington, D.C., restaurants closed early that night, while other communities planned "distress workshops" for the following day. In Lawrence,

Kansas, hundreds gathered for a candlelight vigil, but the debate ravaging the nation over nuclear arms continued that crisp fall evening in Lawrence, as local leaders pleaded for nuclear disarmament while counterdemonstrators urged "peace through military strength." *The Day After* was not just a Saturday night sci-fi/horror flick—it was a global event.[40]

The Day After was controversial from the start, costing over seven million dollars to produce and leaving cast members with "nukemares." The visual effects appeared so realistic that a hairdresser ran from the set crying. The film was the vision of ABC Motion Pictures president Brandon Stoddard. The producer of the popular 1970s miniseries *Roots*, Stoddard was further influenced by the 1979 antinuclear power thriller *The China Syndrome*. By the early 1980s, Stoddard sought to create a new film that would highlight the dangers of nuclear war. To direct this task, Stoddard hired Nicholas Meyer, a prominent writer and the director of two previous *Star Trek* films. Meyer, however, was the fourth choice, as three previous directors turned Stoddard down, citing the film as "too depressing." Meyer took on the position as a "civic duty" and began working with a sympathetic screenwriter to make the film as realistic as possible.[41]

Activists began preparing for *The Day After* months in advance. David Cortright and Randy Kehler believed the primary focus of activists should be on "grass roots actions and outreach campaigns" that could be "implemented easily and quickly." These included hosting "house parties," distributing posters alongside sample radio and print advertisements to local groups, and other "feasible activities," such as "tabling and other mass outreach drives." A subgroup of representatives from SANE, Freeze, and the Council for a Livable World would prioritize and establish the criteria for the placement of national advertisements (both broadcast and print). In a joint effort, SANE and Freeze would budget 32,500 dollars for activities.[42]

The SANE-Freeze joint response began with a mailing to thirty thousand local activists alerting them to the ABC broadcast along with suggested local action. The organizations cautioned activists not to watch the film alone since its impact could be "quite devastating." The film, however, offered "an occasion for not only educating millions of Americans about the consequences of nuclear war, but also encouraging them to *act* now to prevent this." Freeze viewing parties, activists explained, could "also help mobilize the 80% of the American public who favor a freeze to take action." With Thanksgiving shopping in full swing following the film's broadcast, Freeze and SANE suggested local activists table in shopping centers, as this would "provide those who have seen the film with a concrete way to *act to prevent nuclear war*." For the Freeze campaign and other antinuclear forces, *The Day After* provided "an excellent

UNTHINKABLE...
NUCLEAR WAR...
APOCALYPSE...THE
END OF THE FAMILIAR...
THE BEGINNING OF
THE END...

THE
DAY
AFTER

FIGURE 9. Promotional poster for ABC television's *The Day After.* Premiering November 20, 1983, over one hundred million viewers watched the made-for-TV movie wherein the residents of Lawrence, Kansas, grappled with the cataclysmic effects of a nuclear exchange. Courtesy of United Archives GmbH/Alamy Stock Photo.

opportunity" for activists to share their concerns over nuclear war with others. Moreover, it offered a "clear, comprehensive, common-sense way of preventing [nuclear war]—a freeze."[43]

While SANE and Freeze worked through their respective activist lists to encourage organizing for a freeze, other national progressive-left organizations organized separate activities around the film. Educators for Social Responsibility sent out a mailing to its membership that included an overview of the film alongside related activities for various ages and grades in order to help students "work through their emotions around this film." Another educational organization, STOP (Student/Teacher Organization to Prevent Nuclear War), encouraged local viewing groups and invited local elected officials to watch the film with the organization while further asking its members to "write to President Reagan right now to ask *him* to watch the movie." The Ground Zero organization would also organize viewing parties across the nation while also preparing a discussion guide to "help groups focus their discussions after the movie."[44]

Besides the national peace and antinuclear organizations, several local groups organized around the film. In Emeryville, California, local activists conceived a project called "The Day Before" out of a concern that "without a way to respond, people could be immobilized rather than mobilized" following a viewing of the film. Emeryville activists sought to remind people "it's *still* the day before . . . there is still time to prevent our annihilation." The Day Before would organize a variety of citizen forums on the eve of the ABC broadcast and saw as its purpose "to provide support, resources, and training to enable more than 100 communities throughout the country to organize, publicize, and facilitate their own public programs." In Kansas City, Missouri, activists formed "Target Kansas City," organizing various candlelight vigils and media events throughout Kansas City and neighboring Lawrence, Kansas. In San Diego, Psychologists for Social Responsibility would hold public gatherings the night after the film's broadcast "for anyone who feels a need to talk about the movie and work through their feelings in response to it." In New York City, Freeze activists created the 800-Nuclear Project, setting up a national 800-number "Nuclear Hotline" for citizens to "receive information about nuclear war and its prevention" in the form of a package that included lists and contact information for antinuclear organizations as well as extensive reading lists. Because the ABC network would not allow the 800 number to air during the broadcast of *The Day After* (or for forty-eight hours after it), Kehler and Cortright expressed reservations about the 800-Nuclear Project. Nevertheless, they still saw its mailing list as a valuable recruitment tool for Freeze organizing.[45]

The ABC network was soon under pressure from the Far Right to cancel the program. Jerry Falwell and Phyllis Schlafly urged sponsors to boycott the film, with both calling it a "2 1/4 hour advertisement for a nuclear arms freeze." Both sought airtime under the fairness doctrine to rebut the film. As historian Lawrence Wittner observes, "enraged American hawks demonstrated outside ABC affiliates," while commercial advertisers dropped out. Pentagon officials who had originally planned to cooperate with ABC reneged after reading the script. A month before the film aired, ABC Motion Pictures president Brandon Stoddard announced, following a screening for reporters, that a line from the film they had just seen would be "deleted by airtime" because it was now considered "too political." The deleted line now made it ambiguous as to who started the war, leaving out a scene wherein deployment of Pershing II missiles to Western Europe became the catalyst for the nuclear attack. In effect,

ABC censored the film following conservative criticism and pressure from the Reagan White House.[46]

The Reagan administration held an advanced screening for members of the State and Defense departments, as well as various secretaries and White House staff. As David Gergen described the audience reaction, "Some of the women were crying and that sort of thing. It seemed to have a real impact on the people who would be closer to the man on the street." After his private screening, President Reagan described the film in his diary as "powerfully done" and "very effective," leaving him "greatly depressed." "Whether it will be of any help to the 'anti nukes' or not I cant [sic] say," Reagan continued, though his own reaction was "one of our having to do all we can to have a deterrent and to see there is never a nuclear war."[47]

Reagan's reaction to The Day After was perhaps unsurprising. As Cannon observes, "Reagan was receptive to the sensory impressions of films, and he was apt to retain what he saw and heard on the screen," adding, "Reagan spent more time at the movies during his presidency than at anything else," in one instance watching The Sound of Music instead of reading through the materials left for him for a major economic summit. But the film's effect on the president should not be underestimated. As Reagan biographer Edmund Morris noted, the diary entry was "the first and only admission I have been able to find in his papers that he was 'greatly depressed.'" Reagan's initial impression, however, would contrast with his later dismissive view of the film as "'anti-nuke' propaganda."[48]

Reagan's private dismissals aside, ABC sought to underscore the importance of the film by airing a one-on-one interview with a high-ranking administration figure immediately following the airing of The Day After. The administration initially wanted Vice President George H. W. Bush to go on the program to speak about "deterrence, arms control and point out that our strategy has worked well for 37 years—offer reassurance." Writing in his diary, President Reagan put it more bluntly: "We're going to take it over and say it shows why we must keep on doing what we're doing." When Bush declined, Secretary of State Shultz agreed to go on the program to defend the administration's arms control policies.[49]

The postmovie program began with ABC news anchor Ted Koppel reminding the audience of the "good news": The Day After was fiction, and their neighborhoods—as well as the communities of Lawrence, Kansas, and Moscow—were still there. Koppel compared The Day After to "a nuclear version of Charles Dickens's A Christmas Carol"—was this "a vision of the future as it will be, or only as it may be? Is there still time?" Koppel then asked Shultz for a response to the question. Shultz calmly asserted that the film did not represent "the future at all" but "a vivid and dramatic portrayal of the fact that nuclear war is simply not acceptable"—a fact Shultz attributed to the "successful policy" of the United States for decades "based on the idea that we do not accept nuclear war." Shultz furthermore stated that the film "says to those who have criticized the President for seeking arms reductions that that is the course to take. . . . What we should be doing is rallying around and supporting [President Reagan]."[50]

The Shultz interview was followed by a roundtable discussion in front of a studio audience. The roundtable was notable for its lack of major figures from the Freeze campaign. In place of Freeze organizers, the roundtable included two administration critics: human rights advocate Elie Wiesel and astrophysicist Carl Sagan, who was now promoting the theory of nuclear winter. The administration's views were represented by former secretary of state and national security advisor Henry Kissinger and conservative columnist and editor of *National Review* William F. Buckley. The panel was rounded out by Lieutenant General Brent Scowcroft (President Ford's national security advisor) and Robert McNamara (who had recently argued in *Foreign Affairs* that NATO should renounce nuclear weapons).

Buckley opened the panel, criticizing Shultz for "missing the point": *The Day After*, Buckley argued, was a deliberate effort to "launch an enterprise that seeks to debilitate the United States." Although Sagan praised ABC for showing the film in the hopes that it would spark a year-long debate, he warned that the aftermath of a nuclear war would be far worse than what the movie depicted. Kissinger suggested the film presented "a simple-minded notion of the nuclear problem" that engaged in "an orgy of demonstrating how terrible the casualties of nuclear war are" without answering important questions about the preservation of freedom in pursuit of security, compatible arms control policies, and how to handle crises. McNamara thought the film showed the need to "avoid the use of these weapons . . . it's stimulating discussion on exactly the issue we ought to be discussing—there's a million times the Hiroshima destruction power out there—we must ensure it not be used!" While Scowcroft elaborated on the importance of deterrence, Wiesel compared the devastation depicted in the film to the Holocaust. "Everybody lives now facing the unknown. We are all in a way helpless. We are talking about nuclear arms, about the Bomb with a capital B, a kind of divinity itself."

The panel discussion following *The Day After* "dramatically demonstrated what happened to the freeze movement in mass media," as David Meyer writes. Nuclear freeze was treated not as a grassroots initiative but as an arms control initiative no different than High Frontier or the "Build-down" proposal. Indeed, for the first forty minutes, the panel's discussion was devoid of any mention of the Freeze campaign. It was not until fifty minutes into the program, during the question-and-answer session, that an audience member raised the issue (addressing it specifically to Sagan, who suggested a nuclear freeze was "a very good first step"). McNamara believed the Freeze movement played a "very positive role in our society" but nevertheless did not "go nearly far enough." "It isn't a freeze we need," suggested McNamara, "it's substantial reductions, an increase in stability, it's a reduction in the risk of use, and the freeze fails to address those issues." Kissinger was—unsurprisingly—less sanguine toward the Freeze movement, believing a nuclear freeze would prevent measures such as de-MIRVing missiles and was "not a solution to the problem" of the arms race.[51]

The Reagan administration sought to immediately control the message surrounding the film. An internal public affairs strategy memo listed twenty-six separate ideas. One such proposal called for contacting the PTA and "various children's [advocacy] groups" to arrange a viewing of the film. These children's advocacy groups would then, in turn, discourage children from watching the film. Other possible responses included the use of high-level administration officials (including President Reagan) on radio and TV talk shows to emphasize the administration's arms control initiatives and deterrence themes. Besides these direct actions, other ideas included having leaders such as President Ford or President Carter speak out in favor of deterrence, while columnists such as George Will could view the film in advance and critique it for violence.[52]

The administration recognized the importance of the film's antinuclear message and sought to co-opt it, both to contain the political fallout and as part of its broader diplomatic efforts with the Soviet Union. In the weeks before the film, the White House began devising plans to "channel peoples' emotional reactions to the film into support for the President's efforts to strengthen deterrence and reduce the threat of nuclear war." As historian William Knoblauch writes, "It was an audacious political pivot." The administration's public affairs strategy included the possibility of the ABC network showing the film to the Soviet leadership. In the event the Soviets turned them down, the memo recommended the "U.S. Embassy in [the] Soviet Union show it to employees and reporters." To further encourage the Soviets to watch the film, President Reagan could "send a hand-written note to Andropov suggesting he watch the program . . . emphasizing RR's desire for arms control." One of the final points of the memo argued that the administration should "suggest to ABC that they not contemplate doing a poll on the nuclear freeze or 'no first use' ideas" since the administration did not see how they applied to "the premise of the film."[53] While the administration's ideas to counter the film were far ranging and varied, it did not seek to counter the film's violent depiction of nuclear war or dismiss fears but sought instead to frame the film's discussion around the question, "How do we prevent a nuclear holocaust?" David Gergen suggested there could only be one correct answer to this question: "Support [Reagan's] policies of deterrence and arms reduction."[54]

After the film aired, the Reagan administration blanketed the media, appearing on twelve television shows ("half national, half major media markets") and fifteen radio talk shows, and providing six op-ed pieces, including a piece by Vice President Bush in the *New York Times*. The talking points developed regarding deterrence and arms control were shared not just with staffers but also with conservative media columnists such as Pat Buchanan and William Safire. A "White House Digest" outlining the "president's views on arms control, [and] current negotiations with the Soviets" was prepared and distributed to administration spokesmen, members of the press, and those in the public who called the White House. Base commanders, defense agencies, and public affairs officers worldwide received a set of "guidance Q and As" indicating the "best ways to respond to the film or questions raised by the public and media." FEMA prepared "letters and a new booklet" that were available to members of the public who requested information on civil defense. The administration used twenty volunteer telephone operators to take calls and answer questions from the public, while a special rotary hotline was set up specifically for "mid-level specialists at the Department of Defense to answer requests from local radio and TV talk shows." The White House's telephones were "literally jammed" following *The Day After*, with one White House operator reporting calls coming in so fast that they could not be counted until the following day.[55]

Government reactions to *The Day After* were not limited to the Reagan administration. In Great Britain, Lord Hugh Thomas sent a letter to Prime Minister Margaret Thatcher warning about what he suspected would be "greatly increased anti-nuclear agitation after the showing of the nuclear war film in this country." To counter this, Thomas advocated revisiting the Acheson-Lilienthal plan of 1946, as it was "still one simple and obvious way the risk of nuclear war could be diminished." While such a plan would come with "great sacrifices," Thomas also saw "great benefits," for if the Soviets rejected the offer, that would create "a propaganda advantage to us." Furthermore, Thomas believed that even if nothing came of the proposal, "it might be helpful to you [Thatcher] politically to propose such an idea; perhaps especially so with the US, if you were to couch the proposal in terms to recall Truman and Acheson-Lilienthal." Thomas concluded the letter by wondering whether he was too cynical—or too naive.[56]

Numerous defense lobbyists held activities to counter *The Day After*. In a memo to the president, David Gergen noted that "Citizens for America sent out packets of talking points and position papers in support of the administration's arms control efforts and deterrence strategy to their chairman in each congressional district where 110 press conferences were held" the morning after the film aired. High Frontier offered a counterfilm that would appear on "at least 40 TV stations," while members of the American Security Council Foundation appeared on talk shows throughout the country to support the administration's policies. In this "renewed debate over nuclear arms," Gergen praised the "first rate job" of the administration and its allies.[57]

In the days to come, however, word leaked about the administration's internal strife. Senior staff members criticized Gergen's handling of *The Day After*, believing he "panicked." Moreover, Shultz's response was ridiculed by conservatives and Freeze proponents alike. In polling data following the film, administration pollster Richard Wirthlin observed that "of those who said it [nuclear war] was a real threat but put it out of their mind, 38% changed their opinion after the show to say that it is not only a real threat but they worry a lot about it."[58]

Although the mainstream press framed *The Day After* as "neither a bonanza for the nuclear-freeze movement nor a political threat to Reagan's re-election," Wirthlin's postfilm polling data found that 44 percent of Republicans, 68 percent of Democrats, and 57 percent of independents favored a mutual nuclear weapons freeze with the Soviet Union as "the best means towards peace." Furthermore, antinuclear organizations that spent money promoting their materials (such as Physicians for Social Responsibility) reported a "big response on the local level," with increased requests for "specific courses of action, and many calls and letters from people eager to learn the basics about the nuclear arms race." While peace organizations such as the Fellowship of Reconciliation did not do as well, in general the antinuclear movement saw *The Day After* as "a rite of passage" that "cut into the culture in a way nothing else could." Following the film's broadcast, a *Washington Post* poll found "support for a nuclear freeze running very high in American public opinion," with 85 percent favoring a freeze and 11 percent against it. Although President Reagan "managed to reassure the American public that he [shared] their horror of nuclear war," as William Schneider observed in the *Los Angeles Times*, "one false step," "one misstatement about our ability to fight and win a nuclear war," and "the Democrats will be home free."[59]

The drama surrounding *The Day After* did not end with its airing on ABC, however. Indeed, the conservative backlash against ABC affected its decision to pursue another television series tackling the subject of nuclear war: Carl

Sagan's *Nucleus*. Because of the wild popularity of both Sagan and his earlier television show *Cosmos*, ABC agreed to develop *Nucleus*, with Sagan as the host. As Sagan's biographer William Poundstone wrote, *Nucleus* would share a "format, intelligence level, and political slant" similar to *Cosmos*. *Nucleus* would "trace the moral and political history of the arms race, skewering the hypocrisy . . . of many of the principals." But with the controversy generated by *The Day After*, Sagan was warned by one network executive that "they did not want people to start thinking of ABC as the Moscow Broadcasting Company." Sagan's refusal to attend dinner with Ronald and Nancy Reagan at the White House made him persona non grata with the Reagans, and "it was even rumored that the Reagan Administration wanted ABC to drop *Nucleus*." As the Cold War escalated in fall 1983, *Nucleus* was put on the "far-back burner," never to come to fruition.[60]

CHAPTER 6

The Perils of Failed Diplomacy

1983 and the Year of Living Dangerously

At the end of 1982, the Freeze campaign rocked the Reagan administration with powerful blows to its defense plans. Public support for the MX missile, defense spending, and administration policy in El Salvador withered. On top of the largest demonstration in US history in June, the second draft of the pastoral letter of the National Conference of Catholic Bishops questioned the morality of deterrence, while the 1982 midterm elections offered a gut check to the administration. Despite defeat of a pro-freeze proposal in Congress that November, with Republican losses in the House, Freeze activists were certain of scoring another political victory over Reagan with a congressionally mandated nuclear freeze resolution by early 1983. At the United Nations that December, over the objections of the West, the UN General Assembly passed two nonbinding resolutions that were expected to strengthen political pressure for a freeze. The first called on the five permanent members of the UN Security Council—the only nations with acknowledged nuclear weapons programs—to stop the production of nuclear weapons and fissionable materials, halt the deployment of nuclear weapons, and ban nuclear tests. The second resolution requested the United States and the Soviet Union "declare an immediate and total freeze on nuclear weapons." In the inaugural issue of the *Journal of European Nuclear Disarmament*, END activist Mary Kaldor proclaimed, "The peace movement is here to stay!"[1]

Despite mounting pressure, the Reagan administration was not out for the count, and when the bell rang for a new round in the battle with the Freeze, the administration came out swinging. This chapter takes a chronological tour through 1983. Having been pushed into the limelight, the Freeze campaign pursued a more moderate and mainstream approach to one of the most controversial issues of the early 1980s: the deployment in Western Europe of intermediate-range Pershing II and cruise missiles (the INF, or Euromissiles). By offering only minor opposition to such a divisive issue, the campaign sowed the seeds of division, both internally and among the broader peace movement. Weak allied support, along with continued efforts for a congressional freeze resolution, left the campaign vulnerable to vicious attacks. The administration and its conservative allies would attempt to link the campaign to the Soviet Union, but when these attacks failed, the administration consciously crafted a strategy to counter perceptions that they were more likely to lead the nation into a full-scale nuclear war. The decision to pursue missile defense led to a continued decline in US-Soviet relations. As millions watched a fictional film depicting the aftermath of a nuclear war in the American heartland, the world was coming dangerously close to the real thing. In a reckless and provocative move, the administration would deploy the Euromissiles in Western Europe. At the ongoing INF talks in Geneva, the Soviet delegation walked out, leaving the United States and the Soviet Union without arms control negotiations for the first time in a decade.

Redbaiting and Discrediting Tactics

Despite the prominence of the Freeze campaign, as historian Lawrence Wittner observes, "the highest levels of the U.S. government remained quarantined from contamination by the antinuclear movement."[2] When Freeze leaders Randall Forsberg and Randy Kehler requested President Reagan meet with a delegation of Freeze supporters from across the country, the Reagan White House rejected it outright, with White House National Security Council staff member Sven Kraemer privately calling Forsberg and Kehler "radical nuclear freeze organizers . . . who have shown no inclination in the past to learn about, or support, the administration's far-reaching arms control efforts." Thus, Kraemer concluded, there was "little to be gained from such a meeting."[3] Although the administration rejected a meeting with Forsberg and Kehler, Freeze activist Helen Caldicott was granted a one-on-one meeting with the president at the behest of Reagan's daughter Patti Davis. On December 6, 1982, President

Reagan would meet with Caldicott for seventy-five minutes. While no official minutes of the meeting were kept and both sides agreed not to talk to the media, Caldicott soon thereafter spoke to a reporter off the record, who then printed her remarks. Caldicott found the meeting frustrating. She read Reagan letters from children who feared the president would start a nuclear war. Reagan, however, "wasn't convinced at all," telling Caldicott, "They've got the wrong teachers." Reagan read from notecards and quoted *Reader's Digest* about the KGB's infiltration of the Freeze but claimed it was from his "intelligence files." "He knew no figures, no data, no technology, no policy decisions, no CIA reports—he was just really out of it," Caldicott reflected. Caldicott offered Reagan backhanded praise: "[Reagan] was a nice old fellow" who "would have made a nice chicken farmer!" Reagan likewise found the meeting frustrating, writing in his diary that Caldicott "seemed like a nice caring person, but she is all steamed up and knows an awful lot of things that aren't true."[4]

While Freeze leaders struggled to get through to Reagan, a bilateral nuclear freeze remained very popular with the public, soaring in the immediate wake of the New York City disarmament rally. A poll by Republican consulting firm Smith and Haroff indicated overwhelming support for a nuclear weapons freeze, with 50 percent indicating they strongly agreed and an additional 30 percent responding they simply agreed with a freeze. Support, however, appeared only an inch deep. When pollsters queried the public whether they still favored a freeze knowing Reagan opposed it, public support was nearly 50 percent; likewise, when asked whether they agreed with Reagan's assessment that strategic nuclear modernization was necessary to negotiate nuclear arms reductions, a majority of the public surveyed "agreed" or "strongly agreed" with the president. In the related case of the controversial MX missile, the majority polled favored its development—but only after pollsters were led to believe the missile would both deter a Soviet attack and increase the likelihood of surviving one. Such leading questions tilted public opinion polls while (perhaps deliberately) confusing the objectives of the Freeze campaign.[5]

To discredit the movement, the US government attempted to establish a link between the Freeze and the Soviet Union. Between 1981 and 1984, the FBI investigated Randall Forsberg as the subject of "foreign counter intelligence inquiries." It tracked Forsberg's speeches and attempted to interview her on multiple occasions. Unable to speak with Forsberg and fearing a confrontation with her prior to the New York City disarmament march would backfire, the FBI attempted to reach her through a "trusted friend." FBI airtel reports, however, indicate Forsberg was "not at all happy with the prospect of a Bureau interview." Forsberg advised the contact that while she and her organization, IDDS, had "nothing to hide, neither did they have anything to discuss with the FBI." On the advice of their informant, the FBI's Boston bureau concluded that any interview with Forsberg "would be, at best, an uncomfortable and hostile exchange." The FBI's investigation of the Freeze movement's ties to the Soviet Union concluded in 1983 after finding no substantive links.[6]

Nevertheless, conservative outlets alongside fringe-right activists regularly charged the campaign was a front for the Soviet Union. A report by Lyndon LaRouche's *Executive Intelligence Review* referred to the hundreds of thousands of participants in the 1981 antinuclear rallies across Europe as "an inflexion-point in an international political-intelligence project featuring the secret services of several disparate nations, designed to create a mass-based fascist movement under the banner of 'peace protests.'" Likewise, it claimed that the Freeze campaign was an outgrowth of the European antinuclear movement, and, like their European counterparts, it was "little concerned with peace, but very concerned with overthrowing the Reagan administration and American constitutional forms of republican self-government."[7] In the *Grants Pass Daily Courier*, the local newspaper in Grants Pass, Oregon, the "Alliance to Halt the Advance of Marxism in the Americas" took out a one-page advertisement asking readers, "Who is the pied piper playing the 'Nuclear Freeze' tune?" The answer, the advertisement explained, was Citizen Action for Lasting Security, an Oregon Nuclear Freeze affiliate whom the Alliance identified as a "COMMUNIST FRONT ORGANIZATION!" As evidence, it listed affiliated "communist front organizations," including SANE, Freeze, Catholic Peace Fellowship, *Mother Jones* magazine, and practically every other major peace organization within the United States.[8]

On the national level, *Reader's Digest* was a regular source of criticism of the Freeze. In June 1982, the magazine published an article calling the proposal "simplistic" and misrepresenting it as unilateral. The following fall, *Reader's Digest* published an article by senior editor John Barron, "KGB's Magical War for 'Peace.'" The article purported to "authenticate in detail" how the movement was "penetrated, manipulated and distorted to an amazing degree by people who have but one aim—to promote communist tyranny by weakening the United States." The article further claimed Freeze activist Terry Provance was a "World Peace Council activist" and a participant in the founding of the "U.S. Peace Council." Provance refuted both allegations. Nevertheless, for Freeze opponents it was proof of "KGB manipulation of the freeze movement." The article caused concerns at the local level, too. Ted Gleichman of the Denver Freeze office worried over "the number of people" who believed the *Reader's Digest* article and feared the average American would believe it if the campaign did not properly respond. Randy Kehler, however, believed the redbaiting was a "predictable, if unfortunate, tactic" but did not feel the campaign should "become defensive and risk changing the focus of the debate from the question of nuclear weapons to the question of patriotic credentials." Although attributed to Barron, the article was largely based on reports by John Rees—a former police informant who turned over reports on Vietnam antiwar activists in Berkeley to then governor Reagan's staff and whom the FBI described as "an unscrupulous, unethical individual" who provided unreliable information.[9]

An avid reader of *Reader's Digest*, President Reagan explained to an Ohio audience that the Freeze movement was "inspired by not the sincere, honest people who want peace, but by some who want the weakening of America and so are manipulating honest people and sincere people." Although Reagan's military audience applauded his speech, it drew accusations of McCarthy-like smears from Freeze activists and was denounced in several major newspaper editorials. British diplomat Michael Pakenham lamented that the comments were "a marked departure from the generally sympathetic tone towards public concern about nuclear issues which the President has adopted since his INF speech" in November 1981. As Pakenham observed, "The moral perhaps is that deep down the President remains as suspicious as ever of arms control 'extremists'; and the pressures of the campaign can still draw from him spontaneous statements less well-considered than the general lines the Administration has adopted on the 'freeze.'"[10]

The FBI, however, continued the Soviet-infiltration narrative. FBI assistant director for the Office of Congressional and Public Affairs Roger Young described Reagan's remarks as both "accurate" and "persistently consistent with what we have learned" (though, like Reagan, Young refused to go into details). Young's remarks brought condemnation from Congressman Don Edwards (D-CA). In a letter to FBI director William H. Webster, Edwards observed that the Freeze debate was "one of the great issues of this era," "similar in importance to the national dialogue over the Vietnam War." Edwards condemned the FBI for "unproved accusations" and for "taking sides by providing secret file information to one side of the debate." In Edwards's firm belief, "Young's statements [violated] the FBI's own rules."[11]

Claims of Soviet infiltration of the Freeze were par for the course for the College Republicans. Foot soldiers in the Reagan Revolution, the College Republicans, led by feisty, later disgraced lobbyist Jack Abramoff, invaded and bullied college nuclear freeze rallies while tarnishing Freeze supporters as Soviet dupes. Abramoff and the College Republicans plastered posters with a picture of Soviet troops in Red Square under the headline: "The Soviet Union Needs You! Support a U.S. '*Nuclear Freeze*.'" Furthermore, the College Republicans funded "truth squads" to bring Freeze opponents to speak on college campuses. Not all Freeze proponents may have been communists, Abramoff explained, but they were "supporting the Kremlin line."[12]

The Freeze movement's alleged Soviet ties fueled attacks from the American Security Council Foundation and the Peace through Strength coalition. The ASCF frequently hyperbolized the dangers of the Freeze by using alarming rhetoric, claiming it was the "biggest anti-defense campaign" in American history. If its supporters did not "take swift action," the movement would "leave America under the shadow of a permanent Soviet thermonuclear superiority." "The outcome of this fight," John Fisher noted, would determine whether the future of the nation was either "phased surrender" or "freedom." To defeat the "freeze-niks," the ASCF created a vast telephone and computer network at a cost of $9.5 million, "the largest budget ever created for a pro-defense organization."[13]

Under the guise of the Peace through Strength coalition, the ASCF updated its promilitarization propaganda films. Whereas in the late 1970s the ASCF propagandized the public with films such as *The SALT Syndrome*, which aimed to defeat SALT II, by the early 1980s they had spent over three hundred thousand dollars creating the film *Countdown for America*—a direct assault on the Freeze campaign. Narrated by Charlton Heston, the film featured cameos by administration figures such as Secretary of Defense Weinberger, who claimed the Soviets favored a nuclear freeze because "it would leave them in a position of permanent security." Likewise, retired Army major general Richard X. Larkin claimed the New York City disarmament march was orchestrated by the KGB and that the Freeze movement itself was under the control of the World Peace Council. The film further made numerous fraudulent claims regarding the nuclear arsenals on both sides.[14]

Another influential and well-connected conservative lobby that fought the Freeze was the American Conservative Union (ACU). The ACU previously fought the SALT treaties and the Panama Canal Accords, had a budget of 3.1 million dollars, and listed among its 325,000 members several Republican congressional members and members of the Reagan administration. On the forty-first anniversary of Pearl Harbor, the ACU launched a one million dollar "peace offensive" to stop the Freeze campaign. ACU chair and congressman Mickey Edwards (R-OK) repeatedly described a nuclear freeze as "unilateral" while vowing never to allow Americans to be caught unprepared again. Alabama senator Jeremiah Denton announced he would chair a national forum to "diffuse the nuclear freeze movement." Echoing Edwards, Denton suggested the movement was "spreading rapidly toward the point of inviting the Soviet Union to deliver another surprise attack on us." To combat the

Freeze, the ACU worked with other conservative and hawkish organizations, in addition to sponsoring television ads in four key test markets, to fight and win "at the local level."[15]

Other Republican operatives and conservative political interest groups devised more surreptitious plans against the Freeze. A sophisticated fake Freeze lobbying scandal was launched by Francis Leonard Holihan, who claimed an extensive past infiltrating left-leaning organizations dating back to the 1960s. By the early 1980s, he had joined Tony Kerpel (a British conservative activist and former assistant to British prime minister Edward Heath) as well as Edward Leigh (a former employee of then British prime minister Margaret Thatcher) in the founding of the Coalition for Peace through Security. Soon after the coalition was established, Holihan attempted to infiltrate an older British antinuclear organization, the Campaign for Nuclear Disarmament. Holihan followed CND members around the United States and was accused of spying on them, first posing as a journalist, then attempting to sell them roller skates.[16]

In an in-depth report on the Coalition for Peace through Security, British journalist Duncan Campbell found links between the organization and their New Right counterparts in the United States. The organization was financed both through its own tactical fundraising efforts and by sympathetic American millionaires. Group communiques shared tips on how to obtain a US passport, conceal money, fly private jets, and open Swiss bank accounts. American conservative political activist and Reagan White House staff member Morton Blackwell was also scheduled to lecture the coalition on direct-mail techniques. The coalition shared many of the extremist views on survivable nuclear war, but these conservative activists operated under the "prevailing assumption" that the early 1980s were the last "1–3 safe years" before a nuclear war started. As libertarian investment adviser Harry Shultz warned the group, if you did not start planning for imminent nuclear war, you were "not serious about surviving."[17]

By spring 1983, Holihan had resigned as director of the coalition and was working for the Global Peace Foundation as chairman of the Counter Freeze Committee. Holihan, alongside Andy Messing of the National Defense Council Foundation, was involved in counterfreeze operations in North Carolina in early March 1983. Indeed, Holihan received personal thanks from prominent lawyer and conservative activist Thomas F. Ellis for the "great service [Holihan] rendered in directing our Anti-Nuclear Freeze Forces." Without the "timely visit" of Holihan and Messing to North Carolina state senator Harold Hardison, "the freeze forces would have had a field day." Ellis thus found it "reassuring to know that there are people like [Holihan] overseas who recognize the Communist scheme to disarm the West and are willing to try to do something about it."[18]

Besides efforts in North Carolina, Holihan's Global Peace Foundation sought to defeat the Freeze by targeting "the actual priority of the freeze movement itself—legislation of the freeze." In fall 1982, Holihan's organization scoped out a "potential nuclear freeze lobby problem" as the Freeze campaign's "weak link." After infiltrating the movement and acquiring documents pertaining to the campaign's lobbying efforts, Holihan's organization orchestrated a "Nuclear Freeze Lobby Scandal." Phyllis Schlafly soon joined Holihan's efforts, writing members of Congress to express her shock that they were on a "'lobbying assignment' hit-list." Schlafly alleged that the Freeze was no grassroots movement but instead a "campaign of manipulation" directed by "a secretive, highly-coordinated nucleus of nuclear-freeze/anti-defense groups known as the 'Monday Group.'" Central to the charges was the tax-exempt status of at least four of the organizations involved in Freeze lobbying. Tax exemption meant the organizations were supposed to be nonpolitical and nonlobbying. Schlafly cited the leaked lobbying plans as evidence that Freeze lobbyists were "part of a well-oiled, professionally orchestrated effort, rather than a movement supported by the American people."[19]

Following Schlafly's efforts, Holihan distributed the material to every congressman and senator "just three days before the Nuclear Freeze vote as an 11th hour effort." This tactic was followed with "intensive phone calling to the so-called 'swing vote' telling them of the other side's legislative hit list targeted against them, and the ensuing Freeze Lobby Scandal or 'Lobby Gate' about to break." In addition, legislators were told "the media may be calling them for a reaction to see if they've been improperly influenced." Holihan's organization then "rang the media" and met with journalists personally to enforce the significance of the scandal, then asked the same journalists to ask Congress about the alleged scandal. Sympathetic representatives and senators were encouraged to "call a press conference" or find "other private ways of using the scandal rumors effectively in the overall counter-freeze strategy." The point of the lobbying scandal, according to Holihan, was "to demonstrate that the Freeze doesn't have the real grassroots support they claim to have and can be beaten by proper planning and perseverance." Furthermore, Holihan claimed, the Freeze campaign's "massive lobbying machine stumbled over the truth, and was not effective over the next few days."[20]

There is, however, reason to doubt the effectiveness of Holihan's elaborate campaign. Beyond the conservative press, the "Freeze Lobby Scandal" did not attract any serious attention. Although conservative activists portrayed the Monday Group meetings as part of a "secret lobbying group," the meetings were open to the public and were attended by many congressional aides. Furthermore, as Douglas Waller recounted, the Monday Group "had been trying to make its operation and methods as public as possible to convince legislators it had clout." Waller was furthermore amused by Schlafly's letter to Congress, while fellow congressional staff members congratulated Waller for making Schlafly's hit list. Moreover, Schlafly's letter may have actually helped the Freeze, since it caught the attention of every senator the campaign targeted.[21]

With the House delaying a vote on freeze legislation, Schlafly continued her attacks on the campaign. In *Human Events*, Schlafly attacked the movement as "anti-American" and ridiculed Freeze advocates for insisting that the nuclear arsenals of both sides were equal. Furthermore, Schlafly contended, nuclear weapons were not inherently evil: "In the hands of the United States, nuclear weapons are the most powerful instrument for peace ever created." Schlafly ridiculed the "moaning and groaning about the horrors of nuclear weapons." She furthermore dismissed verification efforts and insisted the US goal was not arms control but "the preservation of our American freedom and independence."[22]

The Freeze movement's alleged Soviet ties were echoed by the religious right. In direct mailings to members of the Moral Majority, its leader, Jerry Falwell, warned that the "'freez-niks' are hysterically singing Russia's favorite song: a unilateral U.S. nuclear freeze." These "liberal disarmers" were mounting "a massive campaign to cripple President Reagan's defense programs" while attempting to "fool Americans into believing that it is safe to 'freeze' nuclear weapons." Falwell used the Soviet threat to launch an extensive campaign against the Freeze, telling Moral Majority supporters that America and its religious freedom were "in grave danger" because of Soviet aggression and military superiority. A nuclear freeze, Falwell warned, would "lock [the United States] into this dangerous position of inferiority." Falwell furthermore used his Saturday morning television program, *The Old-Time Gospel Hour*, to regularly assault Freeze activists as Soviet pawns and advocates of the "disarming of the United States of America."[23]

To combat the Freeze, Falwell solicited financial support to fund experienced lobbyists, researchers, and analysts to lobby in support of President Reagan's defense proposals and against a nuclear freeze. Subsequent mailings offered a free report that would "shock" and "disturb" the reader. The fourteen-page report, "Special Briefing Opposing an Immediate Nuclear Freeze," claimed its findings were based on those of nuclear defense experts who understood "the dangers inherent in a nuclear freeze" and would "reveal the cold hard truth" about the Freeze. The "experts" Falwell relied on for this "Doomsday Report" were from the neoconservative American Security Council Foundation and contained material given to Falwell directly by the Reagan administration. "If you want to see this country strong and free," Falwell urged his audience to read the report, saying, "This must be in the hands of every American who wants to silence the Freeze-niks!"[24] With the money obtained from mailings, Falwell was able to fund a full-page advertisement that ran across several US newspapers, deriding the "freezeniks," "ultra libs," and "unilateral disarmers" who were after a "president who wants to build up our military strength." At the bottom of Falwell's advertisement ran a three-question "Peace through Strength Ballot," which asked readers to cast a vote on three leading questions regarding the arms race and trusting the Soviets. In subsequent interviews, Falwell went so far as to suggest that the defeat of the Freeze campaign was a bigger issue than both abortion and prayer in school.[25]

Falwell was nevertheless on the fringe of the freeze issue within the evangelical community. As a Gallup Poll showed, evangelical Christians favored a nuclear freeze "by better than 3 to 1." With Falwell's church losing nearly seven million dollars in contributions in 1982, his anti-freeze message appeared to lack resonance among evangelicals. Even President Reagan's own congregation, the Bel Air Presbyterian Church, cosponsored a "Conference on the Church & Peacemaking in the Nuclear Age." Designed as "educational in nature," the conference attracted over two thousand evangelicals, while the agenda promised to place "the issue of peace making in the nuclear age on the agenda of the evangelical community."[26]

While Falwell attacked the Freeze, evangelical minister Billy Graham supported the movement. Within a week of Reagan's swearing-in ceremony, Graham was inducted into the National Religious Broadcasters Hall of Fame, where he spoke to the audience about the dangers of the arms race. Despite his friendship and past spiritual influence over President Reagan, Graham stood against him on the freeze, speaking on behalf of the campaign regularly, and even visiting Moscow for a conference on disarmament in June 1982. Graham's support for the Freeze garnered him much criticism from more conservative elements within the evangelical community, but with other evangelicals following Graham's lead, it was "certain," the *Wall Street Journal* reported, "that soon you will see evangelism fixed atop the banner of the nuclear freeze."[27]

Falwell's opposition and Graham's support of the Freeze were emblematic of the fissure among conservative and moderate evangelicals over the arms race. Alarmed over evangelical support for the Freeze and its political implications, Robert P. Dugan Jr., director of the National Association of Evangelicals (NAE), personally invited President Reagan to speak at the NAE's annual convention, in Orlando, Florida. Although Dugan invited Reagan to speak on "whatever subject you wish," he prodded him to speak on national defense, given that "well-known evangelical voices are attempting to draw evangelical support for a nuclear freeze." Reagan's "persuasive voice," Dugan enthused, could make "a marked impact upon the evangelical community." In a follow-up letter to Reagan's chief of staff, James Baker, Dugan noted the speech could be "strategic politically, were the president to articulate his position on national defense." Noting how the National Council of Churches and the Conference of Catholic Bishops both favored a nuclear freeze, Dugan insisted that the issue had not been settled within evangelical circles. Dugan and the NAE were already privately attempting to influence evangelicals, but, as Dugan cautioned, "the outcome is far from certain." These points were further reiterated to White House speechwriters Tony Dolan and Dana Rohrabacher. Over a steakhouse dinner, NAE vice president Richard Cizik warned the administration that "'the Freezeniks' were making inroads into the evangelical heartland."[28]

Dolan soon began drafting a zealous speech, drawing on earlier drafts of Reagan's speech to the British Parliament wherein the president promised to leave the Soviet Union in the "ash heap of history." Although many in the State Department and others within the administration thought Dolan's speech was troubling and too over the top, many staffers applauded it. "What it says is true and it's not going to lead to World War III, so I don't see any reason to go screaming from the rooftops about it," director of the White House Office of Speechwriting Aram Bakshian argued. Since the speech was a routine domestic policy speech, it did not need clearance from the NSC or approval from the State Department or Defense Department. Despite objections from administration pragmatists, the speech made its way to Reagan.[29]

With a looming congressional freeze battle, the Reagan administration used the foreign policy section of the speech to attack the Freeze and link support for it to Soviet ambitions. Reagan hit on all administration talking points, remarking that an immediate nuclear weapons freeze represented "a very dangerous fraud . . . that is merely the illusion of peace." "I would agree to a freeze," Reagan told evangelicals, "if only we could freeze the Soviets' global desires." Reagan cautioned evangelicals against ignoring "the aggressive impulses of an evil empire" by simply calling the arms race "a giant misunderstanding." The "Evil Empire" speech, as it became known, was praised by defense hawks but received major criticism from the mainstream press. Often portrayed as an example of Reagan's get-tough rhetoric against the Soviets, as journalist James Carroll observed, "what is rarely remarked upon is that [Reagan's] worry on that occasion was not the threat posed by Moscow but the one posed by Randall Forsberg's Freeze movement." Although the Evil Empire speech was aimed at the Freeze, efforts to stop the campaign had not yet peaked.[30]

FIGURE 10.   President Ronald Reagan delivers his famous "Evil Empire" speech at the 41st Annual Convention of the National Association of Evangelicals on March 8, 1983. Although the phrase "Evil Empire" stood out, the speech was delivered to persuade evangelicals not to support the Freeze movement. Photo courtesy of the Ronald Reagan Presidential Library.

Star Wars

With the freeze resolution delayed in Congress and with conservative ally Helmut Kohl and his Christian Democratic Union party securing a narrow victory in the March 1983 federal elections in West Germany, the administration caught some breathing room from the Freeze movement. With the INF talks expected to conclude at the end of March, Reagan would make a major foreign policy speech. A *New York Times* report indicated Reagan was seeking an interim agreement that would limit—but not eliminate—all intermediate-range nuclear weapons in Europe. By backing away from Zero-Zero, the scaled-back plan would lessen the idea that Reagan was uninterested in serious arms control negotiations, but he still had to balance his newer, more moderate proposals with his right-wing constituency and hawkish advisers, who favored a continued arms race.[31]

The prior December, the administration suffered a major setback in its defense modernization plans. Having recently renamed the MX "Peacekeeper," the Reagan administration lobbied for a new basing plan, dubbed "closely spaced basing" or (colloquially) "dense pack." Dense pack would eliminate the previous controversial mobile basing method and substitute it with a scheme that packed the missiles in heavily fortified silos grouped in a line to (theoretically) minimize a first-strike chance. But, as Bud McFarlane recalled, "the 10-warhead MX was a natural target for liberals and nuclear freeze proponents," who "raised a hue and cry over the missile that reverberated loudly on Capitol Hill." With antinuclear activists and the broader coalition against MX pressuring Congress, Reagan's dense pack basing solution was defeated, derailing the centerpiece of the Reagan nuclear buildup.[32]

To salvage the orphaned MX, counter the perceived Soviet threat, and undercut support for the Freeze and antinuclear activism abroad, key advisers to the administration began formulating a plan for a modern ABM system. Retired lieutenant general Daniel O. Graham, a former director of the Defense Intelligence Agency and military adviser to Reagan during his 1976 and 1980 campaigns, founded the High Frontier Society in 1981. High Frontier infused Graham's conceptions for missile defense with scientists who could provide legitimacy to his views. One of those scientists was famed Hungarian physicist Edward Teller. Teller, however, was pushing his own missile defense system, Excalibur. "In theory," writes historian Gregg Herken, "Teller's Excalibur would physically disintegrate space targets at light speed with a focused beam of high-energy x-rays," while Graham's vision for High Frontier relied on "kinetic-kills weapons, which would destroy missiles by colliding with them in space."[33]

Graham and Teller soon parted ways, their missile defense systems rivaling one another. But with the Freeze metastasizing, both Graham and Teller pitched their missile defense visions as ways to undercut its support. In July 1982, Teller wrote Reagan, explaining his Excalibur plan offered "a uniquely effective reply to those advocating the dangerous inferiority implied by a 'nuclear freeze.'" In *Conservative Digest*, Gregory Fossedal of the Heritage Foundation (an early financial backer of the High Frontier Society) wrote of a "secret weapon" under development that would "undercut the freeze crusade," making arms control negotiations "irrelevant." Fossedal boasted that "High Frontier" would "turn the grass-roots nuclear freeze movement inside out." Supporters of High Frontier lobbied Congress around the plan, claiming it would "save us millions of dollars and thousands of hours by defeating antinuke liberals." In a letter to William Clark dated November 9, 1982, Graham warned that the Freeze had a "head of steam built-up" and was "already unraveling the mandate for strong defense and [could] easily become a conservative-devouring monster by 1984." The solution, argued Graham, was "a bold stroke by the Administration" that would "pull the rug out from under these neo-pacifists."[34]

As part of their regular quarterly meeting, Reagan lunched with the Joint Chiefs of Staff. From that meeting came "a super idea": a policy that would usurp deterrence and "protect our people, not avenge them." On March 23, 1983, President Reagan took to the television for a major speech on national defense. After using the first half of the speech to repeat talking points against the Freeze, Reagan concluded by laying out his "vision of the future," in which the nation no longer had to rely on nuclear deterrence but was secure in defense technology that could "intercept and destroy strategic ballistic missiles." That evening, Reagan called on the same scientific community that developed nuclear weapons "to turn their great talents now to the cause of mankind and world peace, to give us the means of rendering these nuclear weapons impotent and obsolete." Pursuing this new program could "pave the way for arms control measures to eliminate the weapons themselves." Reagan concluded optimistically that his vision held the "promise of changing the course of human history."[35]

While the program was devoid of specific arms control proposals, administration officials spoke of an ABM system that would encompass "a full complement of lasers, microwave devices, particle beams and projectile beams." The system would rely on advanced research and technology developments and would furthermore not violate the ABM Treaty of 1973. Although it would take years of research, some administration spokesmen confidently reported that the system would be functional by the end of the century. The program quickly came under attack, however. Senator Kennedy ridiculed the speech for its "redbaiting and reckless Star Wars schemes." The press and critics latched on to Kennedy's witty criticism and labeled the program "Star Wars," since the program had no name and relied on energy beams, which were the main weapon in the 1979 film. Although the administration objected to the label, it would take another year for the program to be officially named the Strategic Defense Initiative (SDI).[36]

The speech surprised many senior members of the administration. To prevent leaks, many high-ranking officials, such as Secretary of State George Shultz, were cut out of the loop. Upon learning of the defense program insert in the speech, Shultz was "aghast." He questioned Reagan's science advisor George Keyworth about the viability of such a shield and its relationship to the ABM Treaty and accused McFarlane and Clark of "leading the president out on a limb" that someone was bound to saw off. "The chiefs should have their necks wrung," Shultz fumed. Shultz attempted to tone down the speech, but when it was returned to him with minimal changes, he lambasted Keyworth as "a lunatic." Unlike Shultz, Reagan truly believed in SDI as a possibility for the elimination of nuclear weapons. As Reagan later told Cannon, he wanted "a defensive screen that could intercept those missiles when they came out of the silos." However, as Cannon writes, "No such screen existed, outside of science fiction."[37]

While SDI appealed to Reagan's imagination, as Cannon notes, Reagan was "susceptible to manipulation by advisors who shared his militant anticommunism but not his distaste for nuclear deterrence." Indeed, McFarlane envisioned SDI as "MX Plus": a bargaining chip for a more favorable arms control agreement with the Soviets and a tool to both "outflank the freeze movement" and gain congressional support for the administration's nuclear buildup. As Richard Smoke observed, "That deterrence was unsatisfactory as a continuing basis for security was precisely the message of Jonathan Schell's *The Fate of the Earth* and of the Catholic Bishops' pastoral letter. From this same premise, however, the movement and the president drew opposite conclusions." SDI offered an alternative answer to solving the threat of nuclear war through future technology, as opposed to the immediate policy solution favored by Freeze activists. If functional, the program would not end the arms race but create a new race for space-based counterweapons.[38]

SDI was immensely controversial for administration friends and foes alike. British ambassador to the United States Oliver Wright derided it as "a chimera" coming from the "dangerous naivety" of the president. Likewise, British prime minister Margaret Thatcher deemed the project a "utopia." Domestically, Paul Warnke derided it as "that great pork barrel in the sky." Freeze activists generally saw SDI as a response to the movement. Helen Caldicott believed "Star Wars" was retaliation by the "military industrial complex," while David Cortright saw the "mounting anti-nuclear ferment" as making "SDI not possible, but necessary."[39]

The Reagan administration's efforts to contain the Freeze, however, did not end with SDI. Soon after the speech, a secret internal public affairs strategy memo drafted by Deputy National Security Adviser John Poindexter outlined the major challenges the campaign presented. "Buoyed by success at the polls last fall," the memo warned, the Freeze campaign was "moving to try to translate its grass-roots popularity into effective political action." With a forthcoming nuclear freeze vote in the House of Representatives expected to pass, the administration worried that the media would portray it as a "vote of no confidence" in their arms control proposals, thus weakening their hand in negotiations, while also fueling antinuclear sentiment in Europe. Furthermore, the administration worried over Freeze activists targeting specific weapons systems as well as their focus on "securing candidates who share their goals in 1984." The administration, Poindexter advised, "must be prepared to deal with the broad concerns that have prompted the Freeze movement, rather than merely explaining the drawbacks of the freeze proposal itself."[40]

Poindexter divided Freeze advocates into three groups: (1) those who saw in the campaign an "emotional desire to end the arms race and reduce the risk of nuclear holocaust"; (2) those who viewed it as "a vehicle for criticizing Administration policies"; and (3) genuine believers who saw the freeze as "a desirable negotiating position for the U.S." The administration prioritized the first and more numerous group. Because of skepticism over its arms control policies and growing concerns over the high military budget, combined with the growing deficit and restraint on domestic social programs, the administration had to show the public they were "pursuing policies to reduce the risk of war and the level of nuclear arsenals." Although public support for a nuclear freeze was high, its depths remained shallow. Nevertheless, the administration had to proceed cautiously. "On the positive side," the memo concluded, "we are not aware of any large-scale anti-nuclear demonstrations in the U.S." such as the New York City demonstration.[41] Going forward, the administration sought to build public support for its arms control proposals while alluding to the dangers a nuclear freeze posed to the national security of the United States.

The House soon passed a nuclear freeze resolution, albeit nonbinding, with several amendments. The week after its freeze vote, however, the House voted to deploy one hundred MX missiles in modified Minuteman missile silos. As Thomas Rochon and David Meyer explain, "[Congressional] support for the freeze was largely a lever to revive the arms control process," whereas support for the MX "was an expression of determination to obtain arms control agreements from a position of strength." Indeed, this allowed moderate nuclear freeze supporters in Congress to justify voting for both a freeze and the MX without acknowledging any contradiction. On May 3, 1983, the Catholic bishops published the final draft of their pastoral letter. Here again, Freeze activists were left hanging, as another significant ally backed away from its previously stronger stance.[42]

By summer 1983, the Freeze movement was waning. In late July, the freeze resolution came before the Senate Foreign Relations Committee, where it received extensive hearings. After an acrimonious discussion, senators tabled the proposal until August by a vote of nine-to-eight along partisan lines. The outcome of the vote was largely due to the efforts of Clark, who assured South Dakota senator Larry Pressler (the Republican chairman of the Senate Foreign Relations Committee's Arms Control Subcommittee) that the administration was working on a "build down proposal," which had "become the channel into which some of the steam behind the nuclear freeze movement has been diverted." With the 1984 election campaign season approaching, senators such as Charles Percy would be placed in an "awkward position" over a vote on the nuclear freeze issue. Although Percy believed the Reagan administration had "dragged its feet on arms control," and he was "sympathetic to the impatience of the freeze movement," he nevertheless saw the "weakness in the freeze proposal" and therefore "tried hard to avoid bringing the issue to a vote." If Percy voted against a freeze, he would alienate the movement in Illinois, which he could "ill afford to do" in the face of a difficult reelection in 1984. Therefore, Percy was hoping the Reagan administration would "come up with a build-down proposal which can credibly be run on the hill as an alternative to the freeze." Despite setbacks, the Freeze movement was, as British Embassy official Stephen Band concluded, "still alive and kicking."[43]

The Year of Living Dangerously

The decision in the spring to pursue missile defense over a freeze, in combination with deep Soviet suspicions of the Reagan administration, allowed US-Soviet relations to continue their downward spiral that summer. Despite private assurances from Reagan that the United States was dedicated to "the course of peace," an ailing and suspicious Soviet general secretary Andropov rejected Reagan's offer for a summit, interpreting it as "duplicity and desire to disorient the Soviet leadership."[44] Abysmal US-Soviet relations would soon reach their nadir in the Reagan era and lead to one of the tensest moments of the Cold War. Indeed, that fall, 1983 became "the year of living dangerously." Before year's end, the world would come perilously close to nuclear Armageddon on three separate occasions.

On September 1, 1983, a Korean Airlines Boeing-747 (KAL-007) veered drastically off course, flying over the Kurile Islands (a strategic part of the Soviet defense perimeter). With the inability of the Soviets to get a clear command of the situation, along with deep suspicions of the Reagan administration, the Soviet operators fired two missiles at what they believed was a US spy plane. Everyone on board flight KAL-007 perished, including Congressman Larry McDonald (a staunch Freeze opponent). In the days to come, the Soviets would publicly deny the accident, while Reagan dubbed the tragedy "the Korean airline massacre."[45] For Freeze opponents, the KAL-007 tragedy was unmistakable proof of Soviet duplicity. In the wake of the tragedy, Reagan's popularity soared. Conservative columnists Robert Novak and Rowland Evans argued that the KAL tragedy gave Reagan "a public mandate from voters of all persuasions to handle the Soviet Union with the toughness he has always said he wanted." With doubts hanging over the MX missile and Freeze activists seeking a delay on the deployment of the Euromissiles, Evans and Rowland suggested such a "grim forecast" was now "outdated," as was any thought of Reagan making concessions for an arms control treaty. "On the contrary," Evans and Rowland suggested, "the path is now open toward a tough new realism in U.S.-Soviet relations of the kind preached by candidate Reagan in 1980, and practiced by President Reagan the first two years in office cast aside of late on the road back to détente."[46]

As the tensions of the fall continued, the world came perilously close to accidental nuclear war when Soviet satellites reportedly detected a US ICBM launch. If the launch was legitimate, the strike-on-warning doctrine required the Soviets to launch their nuclear weapons prior to the incoming attack. But Soviet Air Defense Forces officer Stanislaw Petrov without question saved the world from nuclear catastrophe by ignoring protocol and convincing other officers the warning was a false positive. In October, the United States invaded Grenada over international objections, including a rare rebuke from the British government. The invasion of Grenada would lead the Sandinistas in Nicaragua to fear they were next and the Soviets to fear that they were also on the short list. In parallel to US actions in Grenada, a truck bomb exploded at the US Marine barracks in Lebanon, where the administration was attempting to outmaneuver Syria (a Soviet client state). The explosion killed 241 Americans.[47]

Shortly thereafter, the Republican-controlled Senate took up the Kennedy-Hatfield freeze resolution. In the wake of the KAL-007 tragedy, what was already an uphill battle in the Senate became a mere formality, as Senator Kennedy's proposed freeze amendment—attached as a rider to a Senate bill to increase the federal debt ceiling—was easily defeated by a vote of fifty-eight to forty. While the Senate loss was expected, the Freeze campaign continued to play the game of domestic politics, albeit from a relatively weakened position.[48]

Freeze and antinuclear activists more generally faced a tougher fight when trying to stop NATO's deployment of the Euromissiles in Western Europe, scheduled for that December. The administration's chief INF negotiator, Paul Nitze, feared deploying the Pershing II missiles could "divide the United States and Europe." Moreover, Nitze worried the relationship would sustain considerable damage if "a coalition of working class, environmental, and antinuclear politicians" brought down the "pro-American government in West Germany." If he could get to his Soviet counterpart on his own, however, Nitze believed the two of them could work out a deal. In his famous "walk in the woods," Nitze offered to withdraw deployment of the Pershing II, leaving only the "less menacing" cruise missiles, in exchange for a substantial reduction in Soviet SS-20s. Despite Nitze's efforts, both governments rejected the plan.[49] The INF talks at Geneva soon became "much more formal and generally unproductive," as Nitze concluded. The negotiations went nowhere. The Soviets continued to find the Reagan administration's arms control proposals "unacceptable" and "unrealistic" and accused it of asking for Soviet "unilateral disarmament." Although the Soviets remained open to a summit meeting, Reagan's attached condition that the Soviets approve the Zero-Zero proposal was "not evidence of a serious approach to this question," Andropov said with regret.[50]

Administration hardliners were bent on the Zero-Zero proposal, while moderates such as Shultz considered an intermediate step toward the ultimate goal of zero—an idea Reagan himself was leaning toward. A secret telegram to the Foreign Commonwealth Office (FCO) observed that the administration was "showing an increased realisation of the dangers vis a vis European opinion of appearing to suggest that the zero option is an all or nothing, take it or leave it proposal." Touring the capitals of major European allies in February 1983, Vice President Bush offered more flexibility on the INF negotiations, calling the Zero-Zero proposal "the goal of the U.S. government" but not a "take it or leave it" proposal. Bush further emphasized a determination to "explore in Geneva every opportunity of reaching agreement." The Reagan administration, however, was "anxious not to link Bush's visit publicly with concern about European attitudes to INF deployment," a separate telegram noted. The Reagan administration did not want it known publicly that the visit was "prompted by U.S. concern about the anti nuclear [sic] movement and misconceptions of American policy," which was "likely to be a main theme of Bush's discussions."[51]

The administration continued to face "increasing political pressure to adopt a more forthcoming attitude to arms control," a confidential British telegram reported. Although few Americans saw a true link between arms control and national security, the telegram warned of "public concern at the breakdown of dialogue with the Soviet Union and the apparently indefinite accumulation of nuclear warheads of both sides." The White House was thus "taking an increasingly direct interest in the prospects for nuclear arms control," with the balance within the administration shifting "in favour of those who wish to seriously explore with the Soviet Union the prospects for a new strategic arms agreement."[52] Reagan soon announced changes to the START proposal, relaxing proposed limits on strategic ballistic missiles. Moreover, as Thatcher's private secretary Roger Bone observed, the president had made "an important change in tone," indicating that "the Americans are prepared to negotiate seriously."[53]

To end the impasse over INF, Reagan attempted to intervene directly, writing to Andropov that the two sides had the means to make significant reductions in nuclear weapons, which could "be a first step toward the elimination of all such weapons." A month later, Andropov responded, "We believe a just, mutually acceptable agreement in Geneva, an agreement on the basis of equality, is still possible." But the Reagan administration, Andropov implied, did not seem to recognize or appreciate "how very far" the Soviets had come in agreeing to reduce nearly a third of their medium-range missiles in Europe. "So long as the United States has not begun deploying its missiles in Europe," Andropov cautioned, "an agreement is still possible." After reading Andropov's letter, however, Reagan became "more certain than ever" that his administration must deploy the Euromissiles. Reagan dismissed Andropov's concerns over British and French missiles as "not relevant" and further dismissed Soviet fears over deployment of the Euromissiles. He reiterated the administration's stance: deployment was only to "counter Soviet systems threatening Europe." The two sides remained at an impasse.[54]

In an effort to stop the INF deployment, the Soviet Union, using language directly from the Freeze campaign, proposed a quantitative and qualitative freeze on all nuclear weapons for the five permanent members of the UN Security Council. Under their freeze, the Soviets sought to bar any further deployment of new types and categories of weapons, thus effectively blocking the deployment of the Euromissiles. The Soviet freeze proposal further placed restrictions on replacements of weapons already deployed, called for a moratorium on testing, and advocated that the Soviet Union and the United States become the first two nations to adhere to this, with other nations following thereafter. The proposal emphasized that the Soviet Union did not see a nuclear freeze as an end in itself but rather as "an effective first step on the path to reduction and finally to the complete elimination of all nuclear weapons and . . . the threat of nuclear catastrophe." Foreign Minister Andrei Gromyko underscored these points, calling the proposal "a major and daring step" that was "necessary to stop the arms race before it was too late."[55]

While the Soviet Union hoped each of the four nations to which their proposed freeze was addressed would study it seriously and with care, not one engaged it. The Chinese government called the proposal "a meaningless exercise which would simply serve to perpetuate the existing nuclear superiority of the two superpowers." China, however, noted an important caveat: if the two superpowers were to take the lead and "stop the testing, improvement and production of nuclear weapons and to reduce their existing holdings by fifty percent," they would consider entering into disarmament negotiations. The French government would opt for a low-key response, while the US and British governments would only respond orally to the Soviets "but not to dignify the proposal." Publicly, the British government dismissed the proposal as "entirely self-serving" while reiterating the "dangers" of a nuclear freeze. Soviet deputy ambassador Viktor Komplektov, a noted hardliner, suggested

British support for START and the INF deployment was "perpetuating the arms race" while further jeopardizing its own security by allowing the continuation of the arms race and further proliferation of nuclear weapons.[56]

Just weeks after the Soviet-proposed nuclear freeze, a team of nineteen US House representatives traveled to the Soviet Union for discussions on arms control and other key US-Soviet areas of diplomacy. At the meeting, Soviet officials brought up the rejected "walk in the woods" INF proposal and indicated that if such an offer was made, "it would be negotiated." One congressman on the trip, however, came away with a "slightly different impression." Representative Dick Cheney (R-WY) believed the Soviet response had to be taken in the context of recent belligerent remarks made by Soviet leaders, as well as their unwillingness to yield at the Geneva INF negotiations.[57]

With US-Soviet diplomacy souring in the wake of the KAL-007 incident, the Soviet Union made one final effort to strike a deal that fall, reiterating its call for "a simultaneous, quantitative and qualitative freeze on nuclear weapons" among the five nuclear powers. The Soviets, however, were far from tactful in their diplomacy. In an address to the UN General Assembly, chief Soviet delegate Oleg Troyanovsky placed the onus for an INF agreement on the United States and NATO while accusing the Reagan administration of "whipping up war hysteria" to achieve "military superiority from which they can domineer and issue orders." Outside official channels, the lack of diplomacy and fears that the impending INF deployment would increase the likelihood of nuclear war led activists to begin planning actions to draw attention to the dangers of deployment and to arouse their governments to stop deployment and continue negotiations. The issue carried much weight in Europe, where the missiles were viewed as "public affirmation of American power" and "about who controls European lives," as Mary Kaldor observed. But whereas peace organizations such as CND, END, and IKV rallied Europeans against the Euromissiles, in the United States, peace activists found little public support. In an internal SANE memo, Cortright lamented, "The Euromissiles are seen as a European issue, and it has been unclear how to generate U.S. involvement."[58]

The Freeze campaign nevertheless remained opposed to their deployment. At its national conference in February 1983, the campaign called the deployment "neither a necessary nor legitimate response to [Soviet] SS-20 deployment" and further described deployment as "a dangerous, qualitative escalation of the arms race" that would "jeopardize future arms control negotiations." The campaign called for an arms control agreement that would not deploy the Euromissiles, would reduce the current Soviet deployment of SS-20s and SS-22s, and would freeze future Soviet deployments of such weapons. In an important caveat, the campaign added that if it appeared the two sides could not reach such an agreement by the time of the deployment, the campaign supported "Soviet reductions and a year's delay in the production and deployment" of the Euromissiles.[59]

This caveat drew "strenuous objection" from activists who believed that the proposal would have "serious detrimental consequences for the peace movement in general." This proposal, activists argued, would place the "most visible component of the national grassroots peace movement on record as supporting the threat to deploy U.S. ground-launched cruise and Pershing II missiles in Europe." Likewise, activists saw it as a violation of the spirit of Forsberg's foundational "Call." The concession, activists charged, embraced the "bargaining chip" philosophy that relied on the threat of NATO Euromissile deployment as "a tool to achieve arms control agreements." The proposal further opened the Freeze campaign to potential Soviet or US "veto power," for if Soviet hawks rejected unilateral disarmament of their SS-20s or the Reagan administration delayed signing a treaty (or Congress would not ratify it), the Freeze would be in de facto support of the deployment.[60]

One of the most vocal opponents of the Euromissiles was the Detroit Area Nuclear Weapons Freeze. The Detroit Freeze was not a "spin-off of established left or peace organizations," as they wrote to the national Freeze campaign, but an outgrowth of eight individuals who started the local campaign in their living rooms in 1981 and grew it organically to over five thousand members. These activists were not older peace or political activists but were motivated specifically by concerns about the nuclear arms race: if deployment went forward, it would undermine the campaign and make the goal of a bilateral nuclear freeze nearly impossible. The Detroit Freeze urged the national campaign to focus on deferring the Euromissiles, since that strategy was "less dependent upon Congress alone and allows Freeze supporters to build a massive public movement." A campaign focused on the deployment of the Euromissiles was timely and was not as dependent on generating immediate interest as a test ban would be. "THIS TYPE OF ORGANIZING IS OUR STRENGTH," the letter proclaimed, while encouraging the national campaign to become a "formidable voice" on the issue.[61]

While the national Freeze campaign focused on passing a congressional nuclear freeze resolution, pressure from local activists and European antinuclear organizations, combined with the growing sense that the public viewed Reagan's INF proposals as "a sign of moderation," forced the national campaign to reconsider its overall strategy surrounding the Euromissile deployment. Freeze activists identified and attempted to correct a "wide-spread perception among Freeze supporters around the country" that the campaign's strategy was "too complex, too confusing, too uncertain." The campaign's executive committee nevertheless doubled down on the congressional strategy, seeking legislation to delay the deployment of the Euromissiles *after* the Senate nuclear freeze vote (expected in June 1983). While the national campaign lobbied Congress, local activists were encouraged to "sign petitions, proxies, letters, post cards, etc. urging elected representatives to support the broad position of the Campaign."[62]

Congressional support for cutting off funds for the Euromissiles was not forthcoming, however. In a report on the progress of the Cruise and Pershing Project, its director, Jane Midgley, noted the only member of Congress who was willing to "go after the Euromissiles" was California Democrat Ron Dellums (the first openly socialist member elected to Congress since World War II). Douglas Waller could "count less than 100 House members and almost no Senators willing to tackle the [Euromissiles]." The Euromissiles, Waller writes, were "a far-off concern for most legislators on Capitol Hill" and were considered "a European problem to be settled by the European governments." The congressional Euromissile strategy also suffered from "a lack of people power to do more of the work on the Hill." Stopping the Euromissiles was a major priority for local Freeze groups; however, the national Freeze campaign lacked a director in Washington, D.C., and failed to even issue a press release in support of an amendment delaying deployment. This left other antinuclear activists unclear about "the real commitment of the Campaign" and the commitment among Freeze leaders regarding the Euromissiles. The Freeze campaign would not formally issue its "Call for a Delay" until August.[63]

The Freeze campaign's decision to call for a delay in the deployment of the Euromissiles was endorsed by its Dutch allies, the IKV. This decision to endorse a delay, and not a forthright demand against deployment, drew the wrath of the more radical elements of the peace movement. David McReynolds, a twenty-year veteran peace activist with the War Resisters League, excoriated the IKV. McReynolds was "stunned" that IKV would accept such a modest position and "surprised" to find IKV and other European antinuclear activists so "enchanted by the Freeze," given it did not link nuclear war with conventional war or intervention (be it Afghanistan or Nicaragua), would not unilaterally demand a freeze on deployment of the Euromissiles (or other US first-strike weapons), took no stance on human rights, and opposed civil disobedience. Although the WRL was not an initial signatory to Forsberg's "Call," McReynolds was, and it was McReynolds who brought the WRL into the Freeze coalition. McReynolds was an important voice in the broader peace movement, and his critiques resonated with those who found the Freeze too modest.[64] Randy Kehler later lamented that by not pushing harder against individual weapons systems such as the Euromissiles, the "lost credibility in the disarmament community."[65]

As the deployment date approached that October, the US peace movement, including the Freeze campaign, SANE, AFSC, CALC, FOR, WILPF, and MFS, among three hundred other local and national activist organizations, sponsored demonstrations across the United States. The October Actions were designed not to stop deployment but to "punctuate in a dramatic and timely manner the widespread opposition to the new missiles." From October 21 to 24, 1983, demonstrations across the United States would coincide with widespread demonstrations in Europe and Canada. Although the rallies in the United States did not match the size of the June 1982 demonstrations or their European counterparts, they were nevertheless impressive. In Romulus, New York, eight thousand braved "chill winds" to hear speeches from historian Manning Marble, pediatrician-turned-peace-activist Benjamin Spock, the Catholic bishop of Rochester, and feminist and Women Strike for Peace cofounder Bella Abzug (among others). In Boston, Massachusetts, over eight thousand joined a New England regional rally at the Boston Commons featuring speeches by Barry Commoner, Randy Kehler, Jesse Jackson, Abbie Hoffman, and others. In Greenwich, Connecticut, Freeze activists took two replica cruise missiles around to local shopping centers to collect signatures on petitions against the deployments. A candlelight vigil in Pennsylvania drew fifteen thousand, while between seven hundred fifty and one thousand people attended a rally in Lafayette Park in Washington, D.C., forming a human chain around the White House. Diverse actions took place across the country throughout the weekend, with people braving the weather to attend major rallies, sit-ins at military contractors' offices, and marches in solidarity against the Euromissiles.[66]

Amid the October Actions, NATO announced a decision to unilaterally cut 1,400 tactical nuclear warheads from a range of systems in Western Europe. "Such reductions would be clear evidence of NATO's determination to maintain its security whilst exercising genuine restraint—a policy which can be contrasted sharply with that of the Soviet [Union] and will counter accusations that the West is fueling the arms race," a secret eyes-only memo to Thatcher emphasized. With public pressure against the Euromissiles mounting, it became, as Reagan wrote in a secret letter to Thatcher, "imperative that we explain to our publics our concerted efforts to sustain a credible deterrent force. . . . We will have reduced our arsenal as far as we possibly can on a unilateral basis, and hope that the USSR will exercise similar restraint." Reagan urged Thatcher to join him "in publicly underscoring the importance of these reductions and their contribution to a more stable military balance at the lowest level possible."[67]

Although NATO's decision was based on a four-year study by experts within NATO's capitals and military authorities, given the timing of the announcement, antinuclear activists saw the measure as a political act and as a means of placating concerns over the impending Euromissile deployment. As sociologist Steve Breyman observes, "NATO's naïve hope was that the movement would breathe a sigh of relief, be grateful, forget about the Euromissiles, and go home" or, at a minimum, "put activists on the defensive." But the decision did neither and instead raised doubts among activists that NATO needed more weapons if they could live without nearly a quarter of their battlefield weapons.[68]

The culmination of the October Actions took place Saturday, October 22, 1983, in West Germany, with some eight hundred thousand individuals demonstrating in Bonn, Hamburg, Neu Ulm, Stuttgart, and West Berlin against the Euromissiles. The main rally in Bonn attracted an estimated five hundred thousand and included a keynote speech by Willy Brandt, leader of the West German Social Democratic Party. Activists in Bonn formed a human chain linking the embassies of the world's nuclear powers to the theater square in the nearby city of Bad Godesburg. At the Schwabian Hills near Neu Ulm, approximately two hundred thousand activists gathered to form a human chain that stretched seventy miles under the slogan "Was gilt die Wette, wir schaffen die Kette" ("Fair or rain, we'll build the chain"). As Breyman writes, the chain "linked the headquarters of U.S. forces in West Germany at Stuttgart-Vaihingen to the Wiley barracks near Ulm, encircled the Pershing bases, and was the grand finale of action week."[69]

Demonstrations against the Euromissiles continued throughout October in Austria, Belgium, Denmark, the United Kingdom, and Italy. As prominent West German newspaper *Der Spiegel* observed, "Never before have the governed set themselves so massively against their leaders. Never before has a protest movement put the Establishment under such pressure that the entire system has been put in question." Demonstrations across Europe turned out millions, while an estimated seventy-five thousand protested throughout Canada. In London, thousands demonstrated against the placement of the Euromissiles, including a group marching under the banner "Tories against cruise and Trident." For END's E. P. Thompson, 1983 was the "traumatic year of confrontation."[70]

Despite the outpouring of opposition, Western leaders appeared content to go through with the deployment. At a private luncheon at the Washington offices of the *New Republic*, Richard Perle, Reagan's assistant secretary of defense and the chief overseer of the INF deployment, confided that the missiles "never had much military utility" and were causing far more damage within the NATO alliance than they were worth. Nevertheless, Perle maintained that the NATO deployment must be completed, lest American credibility be "severely damaged."[71]

Inside the British Parliament, ministers sympathetic to the Freeze movement pressed the Thatcher government and the Tories on arms control and support for freeze legislation. Labour Party member and CND backer Lord Hugh Jenkins of Putney rose to ask "her Majesty's government . . . their response to the Warsaw Pact countries' proposal for a nuclear freeze." Paralleling stateside criticisms of a nuclear freeze, Conservative Party member and leader of the House of Lords Baroness Janet Young responded that a freeze at current levels would "perpetuate current imbalances in favour of the Soviet Union and remove the principal incentives for the Russians to agree to reductions." Young further questioned the ability to verify a freeze, concluding it was better to "concentrate on negotiating reductions of nuclear weapons." Lord Jenkins continued to press Young, citing Andropov's offer for the Soviets to scrap and reduce their own INF missiles as part of negotiations (a proposal Young called "a small step in the right direction" but dismissed as one that "did not amount to very much"). Lord Edward Bishop of the Labour Party pressed Young, asking whether, in the wake of the KAL-007 incident, would she not agree that it was now "necessary to stop escalation and bring about a freeze as a first step towards a reduction in weapons on all sides?" Lord Young bluntly responded, "No, my Lords. That is not a view taken by Her Majesty's Government. We believe a freeze in INF at current levels would be unacceptable given the massive Soviet superiority." Young further emphasized that the British government had made it "quite clear" that absent "satisfactory negotiations," NATO would deploy the Euromissiles by the end of 1983.[72]

In the House of Representatives, the Fiscal Year 1984 Defense Department Appropriations Bill (H.R. 4185) contained 247 billion dollars for the Pentagon to purchase the MX, the Pershing II, cruise missiles, and other nuclear weapons. In passing the bill, the US Congress blocked from discussion an amendment by Congressman Martin Sabo (D-MN) requiring that all members vote on whether to delay deployment of the Euromissiles. Sabo's amendment and a similar effort by Congressman David Obey (D-WI) had been defeated in committee two weeks earlier, along with the efforts of Congressman Joseph Addabbo Sr. (D-NY) to cut procurement funds for the Pershing II. As a result of House actions, the path was cleared for the Reagan administration to deploy the missiles in Western Europe. "In my judgment," Congressman Sabo stated, "the deployment of the Pershing II and cruise missiles in Western Europe represents the ultimate failure in diplomacy."[73]

Despite the movement's defeat on the Euromissiles, many activists saw a silver lining. The Cruise and Pershing Project believed lobbying efforts had "definitely produced results." The Sabo amendment was "clearly gaining support and many officers were flooded with calls and letters opposing the Euromissiles." Libby Frank of the WILPF expressed the sentiment of many, telling Ed Glennon of SANE, "We don't consider our work on the Euromissiles completed—not until the decision is reversed." Kaldor observed that US actions against the Euromissiles were giving "new meaning to the concept of alliance solidarity," with European peace organizations reciprocating those actions by adopting freeze resolutions. Antinuclear activists remained firm in their opposition and commitment against the Euromissiles. Financially, however, the actions of the fall left many of the sponsoring stateside organizations scrambling to "clear up the debts."[74]

As millions around the nation tuned in to ABC's *The Day After* to witness a fictional dramatization of nuclear war, US-Soviet tensions that fall nearly led to the real thing. On November 7, 1983, NATO undertook command-post exercise Able Archer 83, a simulated practice exercise for the launch of nuclear weapons. Suspicious of Reagan's hostile rhetoric, the Soviets devised Operation RYaN (a Soviet acronym translating to "Nuclear Missile Attack"). As historian Christopher Andrew and Soviet defector Oleg Gordievsky write, Operation RYaN originated in "a deadly combination of Reagan rhetoric and Soviet paranoia" and existed to "collect military strategic intelligence on the presumed (but non-existent) plans by the United States and NATO between 1981 and 1984 to launch a surprise nuclear first strike on the Soviet Union."[75]

Though this NATO exercise was an annual event, as recently declassified evidence demonstrates, the exercise was far from routine. As Nate Jones observes, the exercise included "multiple non-routine elements—including radio silences, the loading of warheads, reports of 'nuclear strikes' on open radio frequency and a countdown through all DEFCON phases to 'general alert'— that were very similar to actual preparations for a nuclear war." Furthermore, in 1983, the exercise took on a different meaning because of the belief of an increasingly paranoid Soviet Union that the United States had already deployed Euromissiles to West Germany that could potentially reach Moscow within four to six minutes after launch, resulting in a decapitation strike. Moscow responded to this exercise by placing its nuclear-capable bombing forces in East Germany and Poland on call in the event an immediate retaliation was needed. If indeed an attack was imminent, the Soviet launch-on-warning strategy required Moscow to launch their nuclear weapons prior to an incoming US and NATO strike in a "use-it-or-lose-it" scenario. The Soviets waited for conclusive evidence that the United States had indeed launched a first strike, but with no attack incoming, the war scare of 1983 ended without a single casualty.

Relations between the United States and the Soviet Union nevertheless remained "white hot," as one Politburo member described them.[76]

The Able Archer exercise was the closest the United States and the Soviet Union had come to nuclear war since the Cuban Missile Crisis. Upon reading a report on the exercise in June 1984, President Reagan "expressed surprise," describing the events as "really scary." In 1990, a highly classified report by the president's Foreign Intelligence Advisory Board concluded that the Able Archer exercise "may have inadvertently placed our relations with the Soviet Union on a hair trigger." As Jones finds, "the Soviet fear of war during Able Archer 83 was real, not manufactured, and the deployment of Pershing II missiles was a contributing factor to, not an end result of, the war scare."[77]

On November 23, 1983, the Reagan administration's shipment of Pershing II missiles began arriving in West Germany. Citing the missile deployment, the Soviet delegation walked away from the ongoing INF talks at Geneva without committing to a return. Two weeks later, the Soviets walked away from START, while Operation RYaN remained at a heightened alert. For the first time in a decade, there were no arms control negotiations between the United States and the Soviet Union. At the end of 1983, the world remained hostage to the arms race, with fears of a nuclear holocaust reaching new levels. When a blast ripped through a fireworks plant in New York City, witnesses reported seeing a mushroom cloud. Mistaking the cloud and the explosion for the beginning of a nuclear war, residents panicked, drove off in cars, or hid in cellars—just as they had recently witnessed in *The Day After*.[78] With an election year approaching, a bilateral nuclear weapons freeze maintained its popularity in polls, but the Freeze movement itself was becoming further absorbed into the Democratic sphere, causing its independence to appear increasingly evanescent.

CHAPTER 7

Seizing the Peace

The Nuclear Freeze Movement
and the 1984 Election

As 1984 dawned, the Freeze movement looked drained of life and energy. With defeats in the Senate and with Reagan placing Pershing II and cruise missiles in Europe, Freeze activists openly asked, "Where do we go from here?" Antinuclear activist Howard Morland charged that the campaign was haunted by "the specter of unilateralism"—a major distinction between an organization such as END and that of Freeze. Nevertheless, as Pam Solo observed, a "tone of seriousness and energetic determination" motivated activists. At the Fourth Annual National Nuclear Freeze Conference, Freeze activists pledged opposition to future missile deployments and called for the rollback of Euromissiles. Freeze delegates further agreed to a "joint European/US platform campaigning for a worldwide freeze, and the removal of all nuclear forces from foreign soil" and condemned superpower militarism in the affairs of other nations. Nationally, the Freeze would focus its efforts in the political theater by seeking a new congressional resolution, the creation of a political action committee (PAC) to push for a pro-freeze Congress in 1984, and ultimately the defeat of Ronald Reagan. But the new short-term focus of the campaign drew it deeper into the web of the Democratic Party. Subsequently, the Freeze became increasingly partisan, alienating activists and allies of both major political parties.[1]

But not everything was rosy for the administration. Although the economy rebounded from its decade-long doldrums, the decision to play hardball with the Soviets by deploying the Euromissiles left the two sides without negotiations for an arms control treaty for the first time in a decade. Entering an election year, the Reagan administration understood it was vulnerable on foreign policy. With an American electorate overwhelmingly worried that Ronald Reagan would start a nuclear war, the lack of arms control negotiations and poor US-Soviet relations were causes for concern. In an October 1983 memo to William Clark, Republican foreign policy hawk John Carbaugh Jr. observed that the 1984 campaign had the potential to "provide the Democrats with a field day on the alleged 'failure' of the Reagan administration to secure an arms control agreement with the Soviets."[2] To counter this perception, the administration constructed an image and a narrative: America—once vulnerable and in retreat—was now back. Arms control negotiations could begin—as long as the Soviets were willing. Reagan exuded optimism, and his reelection campaign basked in American patriotism. But one significant problem remained for the administration: how to keep the new Reagan from sounding like the old Reagan.

The Freeze and the Democrats

As the 1984 election season dawned, Freeze activists found themselves debating what role, if any, the movement should play in supporting the Democratic challenger to Reagan. Many core activists warned against the movement's involvement in the presidential contest. In a strongly worded comment in *Nuclear Times*, Marcy Darnovsky from the Abalone Alliance warned of the folly of aligning with the lesser of two evils. "It's true Ronald Reagan is the greater of most evils, and it's easier to pressure the Democrats than the Republicans," Darnovsky noted, adding that, nevertheless, "it would be a tragedy and travesty to allow the movements against militarism to be swallowed or sidetracked by the 1984 elections, to let the election circus set the agenda for our movement." Darnovsky warned of an alliance with "spineless" Democrats who voted for a watered-down freeze, then backed the MX and the largest military budget in the nation's history. Given the history of Democrats talking peace and then taking the nation to war, and with no presidential candidate even showing the "tiniest inkling that he would push for the deep structural changes necessary for disarming and dismantling the American empire and the Cold War blocs," Darnovsky urged the movement to seek broader reform rather than simply swapping out Reagan for Reagan lite.[3]

While Darnovsky's views represented a segment of antinuclear activists, the Freeze leadership maintained the importance of the movement in the forthcoming presidential election. "If the freeze and peace movement doesn't get involved in 1984, come January 1985 there'll be no one to blame but ourselves," cautioned SANE activist Mike Mawby. Randall Forsberg saw the 1984 election as a "golden" and "unparalleled" moment, and the "final big test for the freeze movement." If peace activists were to succeed in stopping the arms race and the growth of militarism, Forsberg believed, they "must now take the final step in the democratic process and change the politicians." In a similar vein, David Cortright argued that the "best way to campaign for a nuclear freeze in 1984" was to "work for the defeat of Ronald Reagan and the election of a peace oriented Congress."[4]

But if the movement was to succeed electorally in 1984, it faced a serious challenge. Following the Democrats' languid effort to build support for a strong nuclear freeze resolution within the House, the party's leadership soon turned a cold shoulder to the movement. In a Democratic Party fundraising telethon themed "Come Together Now," Democratic Party chairman Charles T. Manatt cited the major issues of the 1984 campaign as being to "reclaim America for the people," meaning "jobs, housing, education, and Medicare." To the dismay of Freeze activists, the telethon made no mention of securing a bilateral nuclear weapons freeze. The national committee of the Nuclear Weapons Freeze Campaign would shortly thereafter pass a resolution urging the Democratic Party to place a nuclear freeze as a major issue on their agenda.[5]

Although nationally the Democratic Party offered only lukewarm support for a freeze, early favorable results within the Democratic presidential primaries forced the issue into the mainstream of the party. In the June 1983 Wisconsin straw poll, expected front-runner Walter Mondale lost to Senator Alan Cranston. Cranston attributed the victory to his support for a nuclear weapons freeze, believing party leaders, as well as observers and analysts, had "underestimated the deep, deep concerns and apprehensions on the part of the American people about the arms race and the threat of nuclear war." While rivals such as Senator Gary Hart agreed with Cranston's analysis, front-runner Walter Mondale had no explanation other than coming up "short on votes." Mondale, however, soon committed his campaign to support for a freeze. With the earliest primary and caucus contests approaching, Democratic presidential candidates actively courted the support of the Freeze movement. In Iowa, the Cranston campaign held "Peace and Job" rallies, while the Hart campaign held a "freeze walk-a-thon." In New Hampshire, the Mondale campaign canvassed door-to-door in support of a nuclear freeze.[6]

The movement became so integral to capturing the Democratic nomination that by January 1984 all announced candidates supported a freeze. A detailed examination of the candidates in *Nuclear Times*, however, found "substantial differences—some explicit, others subtle" in their support both for a nuclear freeze and for larger peace issues the campaign advocated. While Cranston spoke in favor of a freeze, he promised not an immediate freeze but a unilateral initiative to halt the testing and deployment of nuclear weapons—as long as the Soviets reciprocated. Based on the success of this unilateral initiative, negotiations for a bilateral nuclear freeze would then commence. Other mainstream candidates hesitatingly supported the freeze initiative in the Senate, with Hart, Glenn, and Cranston all favoring the Jackson-Warner build-then-freeze legislation.[7]

A closer examination of the defense issues supported by the Nuclear Freeze campaign would show a clear distinction between those candidates who supported a freeze rhetorically and those who demonstrated a commitment to reversing the arms race. Except for George McGovern, no candidate favored completely stopping the further deployment of Euromissiles or removing those previously deployed. Even Cranston, a favorite among Freeze activists, was cautious about pulling out the Euromissiles and, like most candidates, favored only delaying further deployment. Although no announced candidate offered their support for the preservation of the MX, two candidates supported the development of the B-1 bomber (among them Cranston, who argued that the development of the B-1 was a necessary preservation of US air superiority until a nuclear freeze could be negotiated). When it came to the military budget, only McGovern favored cuts, while other Freeze-friendly candidates spoke only of not increasing it. From the various positions announced, it was clear that Democratic candidates sought to leverage the support of the Nuclear Freeze campaign while attempting to maintain a hard line on national defense. Indeed, except for McGovern, no candidate would even declare that the United States maintained nuclear superiority over the Soviet Union.[8]

Entering the first Democratic primary and caucus contests in January 1984, Mondale remained the front-runner. For Freeze pragmatists, there appeared strong reason to support Mondale. A traditional New Deal Democrat, Mondale opposed production and deployment of the MX, fought against MIRV-ing missiles and ABM deployment as a senator, and, as vice president, supported Carter's controversial appointment of Paul Warnke to ACDA, as well as the ratification of the SALT II Treaty. In a meeting with various arms control organizations, Mondale asserted Reagan was a "radical" on arms control who had "accomplished nothing," which, Mondale chided, "is the good news." Mondale claimed he was the "first presidential candidate to support the freeze" and that as president he would "immediately seek to negotiate a freeze, resume negotiations on a comprehensive test ban, and seek reductions in the strategic arms talks." Mondale clarified that while he might not propose a nuclear freeze on January 21, 1985, he would do so as soon as possible, further praising the idea as "an act of genius."[9]

Despite Mondale's early pronounced coronation, the early Democratic primaries brought no clear front-runner. Although Mondale won the Iowa caucus in January, Senator Hart took the New Hampshire primary in February, while civil rights activist Reverend Jesse Jackson took third place in both contests. With disappointing finishes in Iowa and New Hampshire, Senator Cranston dropped out of the race, with the remaining candidates outside the top three resigning in the weeks to come. Following the New Hampshire primary, the contest for the Democratic nomination, for all practical purposes, was a two-man race between Mondale and Hart.

With Cranston and McGovern out, many Freeze activists gravitated toward Jackson's campaign. Launched in November 1983, Jackson favored a bilateral freeze, opposed any increase in the defense budget, and characterized the arms race as a by-product of "corporate greed." Jackson even sought Randall Forsberg as his campaign's defense adviser as well as David Cortright as a member of his staff (positions both Forsberg and Cortright declined). Jackson and the Rainbow Coalition appealed to a segment of Freeze activists who saw the campaign as an opportunity to push the Democratic Party to the left, but, as Pam Solo observes, "Jackson's anti-Semitic remarks and unwillingness to disassociate from [controversial Nation of Islam leader] Louis Farrakhan made it hard for many Freeze leaders to support his candidacy." The Jackson campaign would remain a distant third to Mondale and Hart throughout the primaries.[10]

As Mondale and Hart campaigned for the nomination, the two regularly attacked each other over who was the greater nuclear freeze-advocate. Mondale attacked Hart for his "weak" support, claiming Hart supported the build-down proposal championed by Senator William Cohen (R-ME), which called on the United States to destroy two warheads for every new warhead added to the arsenal. Hart and his allies rejected these claims. In a letter to Senate Foreign Relations Committee chairman Charles Percy, Hart urged Percy to stop citing him as a proponent of build-down. Furthermore, Hart asserted his support for a freeze, claiming "nothing will have a higher priority in a Hart administration than the negotiation of a mutual and verifiable nuclear freeze that will put us on the path to a world free of nuclear arms." As the first act of his administration, Hart pledged he would "declare a six-month moratorium on the testing or deployment of nuclear weapons." Shortly thereafter, Hart introduced a complementary resolution expressing the sense of the Senate "that the government of the United States propose to the Soviet Union to expand the current START talks to consider ways to prevent the use of nuclear weapons."[11] While the Democratic primaries were far from over, the Freeze campaign could claim modest success in making the issue a factor for the party's nomination. The Democrats, however, only embraced the semantics of nuclear freeze, without a commitment to the radical shift in foreign policy and national security priorities the movement advocated. As Solo writes, nuclear freeze became "common currency—and devalued currency."[12]

With rhetorical support for a nuclear freeze heating up the Democratic primaries, Freeze activists launched a new campaign within Congress to push for a binding nuclear freeze resolution. At their national meeting in December 1983, the Freeze's national committee adopted a new legislative strategy, "The Arms Race Moratorium Act," dubbed the "Quick Freeze." The Quick Freeze expressed the sense of Congress that the president should offer the Soviet Union an immediate moratorium on the testing of new nuclear warheads and on the testing and deployment of ballistic missiles and ABMs, provided the Soviets adhered to the same activities. The crux of the Quick Freeze was that it was "President-proof," relying on the power of the congressional purse strings to enforce. But the new Quick Freeze resolution was not without problems. The legislation would only freeze the testing and deployment of some nuclear weapons, not their production—a fundamental caveat of the original "Call." Allowing production to continue was a cave-in to pressures both from congressional Democrats and from members of the arms control community who were uneasy about passing binding legislation that included a freeze on production. As Solo notes, "Most people within the Freeze believed that it was possible to verify a production freeze, [but] many were afraid that it would be hard to get congressional support for binding legislation that included it."[13]

While SANE lobbied for specific action against the MX, many Freeze activists feared Pyrrhic victories ahead, wherein Congress would reject a system such as the MX only to embrace the Midgetman missile and with it first strike. An exchange between Peter Bergel of Citizen Action for Lasting Security (a Nuclear Freeze affiliate) and Congressman Les AuCoin over the legislation highlights the major concerns over Quick Freeze. In his letter to AuCoin, Bergel observed that the peace movement "has foundered many times on the rocks of opposition to individual weapons systems. . . . [V]ictory is important but a victory we had a few years ago on the B-1 is one I can live without if it's coupled . . . with production of the neutron bomb, and followed a few years later with production of the 'defeated' system after all." Instead, Bergel urged AuCoin to "stand firm for a halt to the qualitative arms race" and "keep our eyes on the real freeze victory we've sought all along: a victory which actually takes us the first meaningful step down the long road to nuclear sanity."

In response, AuCoin sought to clarify the misunderstanding, writing at length of the pros and cons of the Quick Freeze. AuCoin firmly agreed that defeating various individual systems was "worth doing" but could not be the end game, as new systems would emerge that were at least as destabilizing. AuCoin affirmed that a freeze was "our best hope—possibly our only hope— of stopping the qualitative arms race that is taking us inexorably closer to Armageddon" and therefore "must be given precedence over all else." With AuCoin assuring his support for the movement, the conversation turned to one of tactics: "What is the best way to bring the freeze from dream to reality?" Most important to AuCoin was media and public perception. As he put it, "If the freeze is perceived to be gaining strength, this will snowball as media and politicians jump on the bandwagon," while alternatively, "If it's perceived as dying or losing momentum, the bandwagon population will decrease and the freeze will lose its national majority and popular relevance."

AuCoin pointed to several other major considerations with the Quick Freeze. Was a nuclear freeze best achieved by legislation or by executive negotiation? If the White House was "occupied by an intractable arms control opponent for another five years," congressional action might be "the only hope for a freeze before 1989." Yet, any arms control treaty would require "flexible back-and-forth direct negotiating"—a procedure Congress was not equipped for. Should Freeze supporters specify weapons to be quickly frozen? Naming weapons would "distinguish the 'quick freeze' from the entire freeze," as well as eliminate the tiring wait for the negotiation of a complete nuclear freeze. Yet, naming specific systems would complicate the simplicity of the original freeze proposal, throwing arms control negotiations "back into the SALT II framework of haggling over weapons." AuCoin saw this as "a giant step backwards" that was most likely doomed. While a Quick Freeze might allow the movement to further distinguish true freeze supporters from fair-weather supporters, charges of unilateralism could sink it. Although the legislation prohibited both sides from building antisatellite weapons, it allowed unlimited production of Soviet ICBMs while prohibiting US development of next-generation first-strike weapons. As AuCoin saw it, "Perle and Weinberger nearly made the unilateralism charge stick in 1983 when it was a complete lie; if we now give a shred of substance to the charges, they'll use it to murder the freeze—the real freeze."

Several scenarios were considered if the Quick Freeze did not pass. If Congress or the Reagan administration rejected it, AuCoin believed it would still make a statement to the world. Furthermore, Freeze activists were "used to losing," and, if they lost again, they would "just work harder." More problematic was if the Soviets rejected the moratorium cold. Since a Quick Freeze would not stop the production or deployment of the Pershing II or Trident I missiles, there was no reason to believe the Soviets would be eager to agree to the moratorium. If the Soviets rejected the legislation cold, AuCoin believed, Reagan would "exploit the opportunity to discredit the freeze and to deprive it of majority support." AuCoin's hesitations aside, he concluded with hope that the peace movement would "not fracture itself into petty squabbles over 'MX vs. freeze,' or between one organization and another," for if that happened, "Richard Perle will break out the champagne because he will know he'll be heading off defeat on *all* our efforts. In division there is weakness." Although AuCoin believed a vote on the moratorium would lose, he would ultimately get behind the legislation. "We're not in this for political victory," AuCoin proclaimed, "we're in it for a good cause. Win or lose, we have to try."[14]

The movement and the legislation moved forward, with Congressman Edward Markey introducing it in the House along with one hundred cosponsors. In the Senate, Ted Kennedy and Mark Hatfield, along with six others, cosponsored the resolution. Writing on behalf of the national Freeze campaign, Randy Kehler urged reluctant Freeze activists to support the Quick Freeze. Kehler praised the resolution as making "an extremely significant achievement," setting out "a whole new standard for congressional behavior with regard to stopping the threat of nuclear war." The resolution, Kehler enthused, "makes clear that Congress, through its 'power of the purse,' can and must take actions—especially in the absence of presidential initiatives to halt the arms race." Randall Forsberg likewise was "thrilled" with the Quick Freeze, adding that if implemented it would mark "the single greatest step ever taken to halt the nuclear arms race."[15]

The enthusiasm was not shared by the Massachusetts Freeze Campaign, however, which, Solo notes, "persisted in its advocacy for comprehensive legislation." Massachusetts was not an insignificant actor in the movement. The movement's first political victories and its leaders in both houses of Congress were all from Massachusetts. Massachusetts's refusal to advocate for the Quick Freeze allowed the movement to become "seriously divided." While the national campaign lobbied for and backed the Quick Freeze, Massachusetts congressman Nicholas Mavroules (Democrat) introduced competing legislation for a comprehensive nuclear freeze. As a result, the Freeze campaign's legislative strategy became "weakened and confused," creating a "heyday for congressional adversaries of the Freeze and for those sitting on the fence."[16]

Congressional Freeze supporters were also hesitant to back the Quick Freeze. As *Nuclear Times* reported, "Capitol insiders . . . considered the concept of a direct Congressional foreign policy initiative too extreme in an election year." Congressional aides furthermore "fought with the Freeze Campaign over the President-proof principle because they knew it would be difficult to sell on the Hill." Furthermore, the Quick Freeze became victim to the movement's "increasing and unhealthy reliance on Senator Kennedy's office," as David Meyer writes. Kennedy dissuaded Senator Cranston from introducing Quick Freeze legislation and instead introduced more compromised legislation stripped of the words "nuclear freeze" and excised of any references to the Pershing II missiles. When Kehler threatened to withhold support for the legislation, Kennedy's office ignored him. Freeze activists held their noses and supported the legislation, with hopes they could elect a more pro-Freeze Congress in 1984.[17]

The efforts to force a Quick Freeze on the Congress brought mixed results. The House passed only one-third of the bill, supporting a moratorium on antisatellite weapons. Furthermore, as *Nuclear Times* noted, "The moratorium idea was also used in the House effort to table the sea-launched cruise missile" and "became part of the Democratic Party platform and the Mondale campaign." Ultimately, however, the Quick Freeze placed a premium on short-term political victory while further exacerbating divisions within the movement. Furthermore, by stripping the provision supporting a freeze on the production of nuclear weapons, the legislation indirectly abetted the continuation of the arms race and military Keynesianism.[18]

In summer and fall 1983, the campaign began formulating a political action committee, later known as Freeze Voter '84. Established in June 1983 as an outgrowth of an exploratory subcommittee within the national Freeze campaign, Freeze Voter '84 continued its efforts to implement a nuclear freeze by working within the Washington establishment. Freeze Voter had the explicit goal to "elect a President and a Congress who will enact a nuclear weapons Freeze between the U.S. and the U.S.S.R." The Freeze campaign's formation of a PAC to organize and support presidential and congressional candidates committed to a freeze followed the same PAC strategy as other nonprofit arms control organizations, such as SANE (which likewise launched SANE PAC in 1983). Freeze Voter's expressed purpose was to "create such a potent grassroots force that current incumbents and potential challengers at the national level dare not ignore the Freeze issue."[19]

Freeze Voter, however, encountered problems early on. As a 501(c)3 organization, Freeze Voter was allowed to solicit money from the general public in an effort to directly influence the outcome of a federal election. This, however, conflicted with the Freeze campaign's nonprofit, tax-exempt educational status, which forbade it from becoming directly involved in political campaigns. Because of the Freeze campaign's tax-exempt educational status, it had two choices: make Freeze Voter "a separate, freestanding PAC" or "form a PAC as part of the Freeze campaign." The latter approach, while easier, was not feasible, as solicitations could only be made to formal dues-paying members. Unlike SANE, "the Freeze had no membership in that formal sense," writes Solo. Freeze Voter '84 therefore had separate offices, staff, directors, and local networks. Because of Federal Election Commission regulations, communication and coordination between Freeze Voter and the national campaign was forbidden. Scarce resources created a competition for "the same organizers and the same pool of donors," leaving work on the Quick Freeze to wither further.[20]

Because of its independence from the Freeze campaign, Freeze Voter '84 required its own executive director. Through summer and into fall 1983, Freeze Voter searched for an executive director. That November, the PAC's board of directors settled on Bill Curry, a former assemblyman from Connecticut and a failed candidate for Congress in 1982. Curry was "a brilliant speaker and adept at political maneuvering," as Solo reflected, but someone who made for a "much better . . . political candidate than . . . head of Freeze Voter '84." A progressive Freeze supporter, Curry nevertheless had "substantive" conflicts with Randall Forsberg while also clashing with other members of the board. As executive director, Curry was not shy about his support for Mondale. This proved problematic since the PAC would not endorse any candidate for president until after the nominating convention; likewise, it "sent informal signals" to other candidates "that undercut whatever formal strategy the PAC might have liked," Solo observed. The decision not to endorse any candidate until after the nominating convention, however, left the campaign without a "Freeze candidate."[21]

Internal Freeze Voter documents boast of its successes. Within a year of its founding, Freeze Voter was the largest arms control PAC in the nation, claiming twenty thousand Freeze Corps volunteers. Freeze Corps was composed of hundreds of volunteers working for several months across critical states and key congressional races to help sway the outcome in favor of pro-Freeze candidates. Freeze Voter claimed over one hundred Freeze activists working as delegates at the 1984 Democratic National Convention and took credit for the Democrats' adoption of the "strongest arms control plank in the history of either party." While the PAC was in the red through much of 1984, after successfully organizing Freeze Walks and Freeze Voter house parties, the PAC was able to pay off its debts, with statewide and national PAC affiliate offices raising an estimated three million dollars.[22]

Despite the boasting, however, significant doubts about Freeze Voter's efficiency remain. Freeze Voter raised millions of dollars but distributed barely over seventeen thousand dollars to candidates. Of the eight Senate races and thirty-seven House races Freeze Voter was involved in, four pro-Freeze Senate candidates and twenty-five pro-Freeze House candidates won their respective races. While several congressional candidates acknowledged the efforts of Freeze Voter in their reelection campaigns, the "results were hard to evaluate," as Meyer writes. Of the twenty-five House races in which Freeze Voter claimed victory, twenty of the candidates were incumbents in an election in which 96 percent of all incumbents retained their seats; furthermore, of those candidates Freeze Voter endorsed in open elections, only two of six were elected. Likewise, victory in Senate races was not as easy to quantify as the numbers suggest. Of the eight Senate races in which Freeze Voter endorsed a candidate, only one was competitive. In that contest, Illinois Democratic challenger Paul Simon intentionally did not campaign on support for a nuclear freeze in an attempt to move to the center, which his incumbent opponent, Senator Percy, had abandoned. Simon's decision not to emphasize his commitment to peace issues infuriated Freeze activists. As Simon's campaign manager, David Axelrod, recounted, "When we decided to downplay the freeze, the peace activists were furious. Some called to say they hated us. Others quit volunteering."[23]

Freeze Voter further led to the perception that supporting a nuclear weapons freeze was the same as supporting the Democratic Party. As Meyer writes, the Republicans who had supported the Freeze resolution and backed the campaign in 1982 concluded that "the freeze had forgotten them." In Massachusetts's First Congressional District, Freeze Voter endorsed Democratic challenger Marty Wentworth over Republican incumbent congressman Silvio Conte, despite Conte's introduction of the freeze resolution to the House in 1982. In Iowa, Freeze Voter managed to alienate both candidates when it endorsed Republican incumbent and Freeze advocate Jim Leach and his Democratic opponent, Kevin Heady. Freeze Voter proved divisive in Oregon as well, when it waffled over whether to endorse incumbent Republican senator Mark Hatfield, the cosponsor of the Freeze resolution in the Senate. Though the campaign eventually lent its endorsement to Hatfield, it angered Oregon Democrats it relied on for support. Ultimately, Freeze Voter estranged grassroots activists, exacerbated the tensions between the national campaign and the state campaigns, and further contributed to the view that nuclear freeze was a partisan issue.[24]

Reagan's Reversals, Mondale's Stumbles

As the Democrats coalesced around a candidate and the Freeze campaign worked on making its message a defining issue, the Reagan administration began its reelection campaign with a close eye on public opinion and national security issues. Following the intense events of fall 1983, administration pollster Richard Wirthlin delivered an extensive survey of polling data on issues of war and peace to members of the Reagan administration and the Republican National Committee. In a series of polls conducted following the airing of *The Day After*, Wirthlin found that 44 percent of Republicans, 68 percent of Democrats, and 57 percent of independents favored a mutual nuclear weapons freeze with the Soviet Union as "the best means towards peace." Polling data indicated *The Day After* had a major effect on the public perception of the threat of nuclear war. An ABC-Dallas affiliate poll found that prior to *The Day After* 58 percent of respondents thought nuclear war was a real threat but put it out of their mind. Following the show, however, only 38 percent still held that view. Furthermore, Wirthlin reported that six out of ten viewers perceived *The Day After* as "a public service program rather than another television show or just propaganda." "Given these perceptions," a cautious yet relieved Wirthlin reported, "we are fortunate indeed that there was no negative spin-off on the President."[25]

Wirthlin's polling data from the summer demonstrated that the nuclear freeze issue was "the most politically volatile," with "a plurality of Americans (49%)" willing to withdraw their support for a political candidate if that candidate disagreed with the voter's stance on a freeze, even if the voter agreed with the candidate on all other issues. Of the 49 percent, 41 percent favored a nuclear freeze, while an additional 55 percent reportedly opposed it. As Wirthlin reported, "This means one in five Americans favors the freeze, and would vote against a candidate who opposed it. Conversely, 27% of the electorate say they would vote against any candidate who favors the freeze."

Most of the opposition to a nuclear weapons freeze came from the administration's base (identified as base Republican, small business, and Farm Belt states). More problematic for the administration were swing voters: blue-collar workers, senior citizens, women, Catholics, independent leaners, and white Baptists. Although base supporters predictably opposed a freeze, swing groups remained more willing to approve it. Moreover, even when the question was framed to indicate a freeze would be unilateral (and not bilateral as the national Freeze campaign had proposed), the results among swing groups were mixed. Most Catholic voters, for instance, indicated they would not only change their support for a candidate based on the nuclear freeze issue alone but also, unlike other swing constituencies, still favored a nuclear freeze, even if unilateral.[26]

After three years of Reagan's presidency, Wirthlin's polls indicated two-thirds of the American public did not feel the world was any safer than it was prior to Reagan's election. Over half reported the United States was "further from an arms control treaty than at any other time in history." "Not only does disagreement beat out agreement two to one," Wirthlin cautioned, "but the intensity of the disagreement is three times that of the agreement." Moreover, Wirthlin added, "Not even the President's strongest traditional supporters give a plurality—much less a majority—to the agree side." Conversely, Wirthlin's polls found President Reagan still received a slight majority approval rating (52 percent) for his arms control efforts, with over 60 percent believing that "the President supports bilateral reductions for nuclear weapons." "Given the lack of progress most Americans perceive on arms control," Wirthlin found it "surprising" that 52 percent of those polled still approved of the way Reagan was handling the issue. Wirthlin, however, cautioned the administration going forward, noting that polling since November indicated "a four-point drop in Reagan's arms control approval rating and a five-point increase in disapproval, leaving the approval/disapproval ratio at its lowest point since the first half of September 1983."[27]

A report the previous fall from within the Canadian Embassy in Washington, D.C., further underscored the political difficulties the Reagan administration faced on arms control stemming from the "broad spirit of [the] freeze movement." As Richard Luce, minister of state in the British Foreign and Commonwealth Office, observed, the Freeze campaign as a national organization had "finite limits on its usefulness," but those would not apply to the "nuclear freeze in its broadest sense," which instead was a "manifestation of a massive public popular interest in, and even demand for, arms control and disarmament. It is a direct result of growing insecurity in [the] face of an arms race that appears to be out of control and arms control [negotiations] which have failed to produce significant results." Luce underscored the movement's growth in "the incautious, even foolish statements of the [Reagan] Administration in nuclear war fighting" and furthermore the "Reagan agenda for nuclear modernization."

The report further noted how Freeze critics "misunderstood" the campaign and the broader movement, "perhaps intentionally . . . because it is easier to deal with a concrete tactic or specific policy than it is to deal with generalized if undefined demand for significant arms control measures now." The result of this misunderstanding meant that "attempts to undermine [the] Freeze movement as if its primary interest really was in the idea of a freeze are bound to fail." Criticisms that a freeze would leave the United States in a position of inferiority, critiques of its verifiability, or accusations that the movement was a "Communist inspired plot simply miss the point," Luce noted. While such charges might influence congressional support, they would not affect the grassroots basis of the movement, since such critiques did not "diminish concerns . . . or [the] symbolic value of [the] freeze concept." Likewise, while efforts to amend freeze resolutions may "water down their impact," they would not affect the "nature of [the] movement to which specifics of the language are irrelevant." By supporting a freeze, the American public was asking the political establishment for a "tangible commitment to arms control." The Freeze campaign was the US wing of the global peace movement that included CND and END in the United Kingdom, IKV in the Netherlands, the Greens in West Germany, and opposition to cruise missiles in Canada. It would therefore "be a mistake to believe that it is a passing fad" rather than a budding movement. Although freeze as a specific arms control proposal had a "limited life," the movement's size, broad base, and support from both Democrats and Republicans was "a guarantee of its continued life."

As the 1984 election approached, the Freeze made arms control the "single most important item in USA foreign policy." Luce's report tied Reagan's reelection chances "very closely to how [the] public perceives his performance on arms control." Although the movement faced internal divisions and was increasingly seen as a partisan "Democrat position," its "biggest resource" was its grassroots volunteer support. Freeze activists privately admitted Reagan's belligerency and image of opposing arms control kept the organization alive, but if the argument became one about "tactics" or the best way to achieve "meaningful arms control," then it was "most unlikely [the Freeze campaign could] sustain its membership and its cohesion as its various parts [would] then begin to focus on other parts of their agendas." Nevertheless, the movement remained "an important phenomenon," but one that would face difficulties ahead if a "pro–arms control" president got elected. Though the Freeze faced a "cloudy future," Luce concluded, this would not "diminish [the] importance of [the] movement as a whole" since its importance was not in what it accomplished "but in what it is—a massive popular arms control movement with an understandable goal. It treats arms control as a political issue and reflects public opinion that arms control is in [the] national security interest of [the] USA."[28]

Internationally, pressure was mounting for a resumption of arms control talks. In late December 1983, following a meeting with Reagan at the White House, Vatican secretary of state Cardinal Agostino Cassaroli told a group of reporters the Holy See wanted to "mediate" arms control talks, "bringing together the positions and clarifying misunderstandings." Cassaroli's suggestion caused "an explosion amongst the reporters," who "launched into fantasies that saw the Pope in Moscow." The Vatican, however, soon distanced itself from Cassaroli's comments, claiming the cardinal spoke at "a dangerous conjunction of events." The Vatican clarified that it had "no intention of taking an initiative for the resumption of talks on intermediate nuclear weapons" but was "simply making their availability known." The French ambassador to the Vatican reported the Soviet response was "to the effect that it was a pity the offer had been made immediately after the Cardinal's return from the United States."[29]

Within the NATO alliance, fissures began to surface over the deployment of the Euromissiles and the lack of arms control talks. At a joint meeting of the Palme and Brandt Commissions in Rome, Swedish Social Democratic Party leader Olof Palme spoke in favor of a one-year pause on the deployment of nuclear weapons to facilitate a return to arms control talks. Soviet insider Georgi Arbatov praised the proposal, convinced such a measure would "open the way to the resumption of dialogue." Palme's proposal, however, faced strong opposition from the United Kingdom, whose parliament was preparing for a debate later that month over support for a UN resolution calling for a nuclear weapons freeze. In a one-page communiqué, former prime minister Edward Heath of the Conservative Party rose in solitary opposition, countering with a proposal that invited the US and Soviet leaderships to "meet shortly, in order to agree on the purpose and method of future negotiations, and to nominate personal representatives to conduct them." The joint commission rejected Heath's proposal, but Heath successfully blocked Palme's support of a freeze on the deployment of further nuclear weapons. While Heath called Palme's proposal "unacceptable to NATO," Egon Bahr of the West German Social Democratic Party observed that Heath's proposal would be "quite unacceptable to the USSR," a prediction confirmed by angry speeches from Arbatov and Soviet general Mikhail Milstein.[30]

Back in Washington, D.C., just days before his official announcement of his intent to run for reelection, Reagan publicly returned to pursuing détente in all but name. In a speech addressed to the Soviet Union, Reagan offered a heartwarming tale of "Ivan and Anya" sharing a waiting room or a rain shelter with "Jim and Sally." With no language barrier between them, Reagan questioned whether the two couples would "debate the differences between their governments? Or would they find themselves comparing notes about their children and what they did for a living?" Days later, Reagan made another major speech, in which he declared "a new beginning," promising his opponents that what was "good for the people, also turns out is good for the country." The speech, as the *New York Times* noted, was a "celebration of the Reagan Administration itself," with "all the verve needed for a reelection campaign: boastful oratory about its record, self-confident denunciations of the opposition and flag waving on a grand brassy scale." In his 1984 State of the Union Address, Reagan proclaimed, "A nuclear war cannot be won, and must never be fought!" Bewildered by the cool, nonaggressive tone of Reagan's speeches, one staff member wondered, "Who wrote this shit?"[31]

While Reagan was now verbally denouncing nuclear weapons and seeking a return to arms control negotiations, the Soviet Union would once again see a change in leadership. In February 1984, General Secretary Andropov succumbed to his long illness. He was soon succeeded by Konstantin Chernenko, a loyal lieutenant to former general secretary Leonid Brezhnev. At seventy-three years old, Chernenko was suffering from the advanced stages of emphysema. His health issues would force him to rely on Foreign Minister Andrei Gromyko for foreign policy. Despite Chernenko's opposition to the deployment of the Euromissiles, he indicated a willingness to open a dialogue on arms control. Outside the eye of the public, Reagan and Chernenko exchanged a series of letters in early 1984 seeking to defuse the tensions that strained US-Soviet relations. But the honeymoon ended in May, when Chernenko announced that the Soviet Union would boycott the 1984 Olympic Games in Los Angeles. Moscow reiterated that it would not return to the bargaining table until the Euromissiles were removed.[32]

US-Soviet relations appeared mired in gridlock, and the Reagan administration was left without an arms control treaty during an election year. With the economy having recovered, the electoral issue Reagan aides feared most was the "war and peace" issue. To persuade the public that the administration's Soviet diplomacy was not a failure, Reagan positioned himself on the campaign trail that spring as the "champion of dialogue with the Soviet Union." Reagan significantly relaxed the conditions he previously attached to a summit meeting with Chernenko, at one point offering a no-strings-attached meeting. The shift on arms control negotiations prompted Walter Mondale to quip that as president he would "lead [Americans] toward a safer world from the first day . . . in office, and not from the first day that I start my campaign for re-election." Although Reagan told reporters his no-strings-attached offer to meet with Chernenko was not politically motivated, one administration official acknowledged it as "a byproduct of strictly domestic political concerns."[33]

Throughout 1984, several prominent Republicans would privately encourage the Reagan administration to return to arms control negotiations and embrace a nuclear freeze. Jay Harris, the editor of the *Lubbock Avalanche Journal* and a well-connected Republican, sent the president's chief of staff (and fellow Texan) James Baker a four-page peace proposal. To secure world peace, the proposal suggested the United States and the Soviet Union mutually agree to a "complete freeze" on the testing, manufacture, and deployment of nuclear weapons (verified through on-ground inspections). The proposal further advocated for a nuclear weapons free Europe (with all existing nuclear weapons dismantled) and a ban on the sale of weapons to developing nations. Finally, Harris's peace proposal sought to create a World Bank for Human Resources drawing its financial support from funds previously used on armaments. Harris was encouraged to send the peace proposal to the Reagan administration by Congressman Kent Hance (a conservative Texas Democrat) and by former president Gerald Ford. Though Ford was publicly dismissive of a nuclear freeze, he found himself in "substantial agreement" with Harris's peace proposal and pledged to likewise press the Reagan administration to "seriously consider embracing it publicly."[34] The administration, however, dismissed Harris's peace proposal, sticking to official talking points on the problems of verifying a freeze while touting its own arms control proposals for "deep reductions" as a "much better way to secure peace than offered [by] the nuclear 'freeze' proposal."[35]

As Reagan kicked off his reelection campaign unopposed within the Republican primaries, the battle for the Democratic nomination would run through the July Democratic National Convention in San Francisco. Although Gary Hart won more states during the primary battles, Mondale captured the most delegates and would easily win the nomination at the convention. The drawn out and at times bitter primary battle frustrated activists and left Mondale drained of momentum heading into the fall campaign. Indeed, in early June, Mondale trailed Reagan by nineteen points in the polls. While Hart would have made a logical choice as vice presidential nominee, the fledgling Mondale campaign needed a spark. Bypassing Hart, Mondale made a bold move and selected Geraldine Ferraro, the first woman ever nominated to a major party ticket. A former prosecutor, a self-identified feminist, a devout Italian-American Catholic from Queens, New York, and a fervent supporter of a nuclear weapons freeze, Ferraro appealed to a swath of voters while creating a "gender gap" between the Mondale and Reagan campaigns. The "Ferraro factor" soon gave Mondale a two-point edge over Reagan in a Gallup Poll, and the presidential contest of 1984 appeared to be a dead heat.[36]

While Ferraro's nomination initially boosted the languid Mondale campaign, it did not take long for the campaign to begin unraveling. Shortly after Mondale took the stage at the convention to the theme from *Rocky*, he delivered what journalist George E. Condon described as "the most damaging twenty-eight words in the modern history of convention acceptance speeches." Believing voters had to "confront the need to raise revenue," Mondale told voters, "Let's tell the truth . . . Mr. Reagan will raise taxes. And so will I. He won't tell you, I just did." Although Democratic delegates cheered him on, as presidential historian Anthony J. Bennett writes, "It took Mondale only twenty-

FIGURE 11. Former vice president Walter Mondale and running mate Congresswoman Geraldine Ferraro accept the Democratic presidential nomination, flanked by defeated nominees Reverend Jesse Jackson (to Mondale's right) and Senator Gary Hart (to Ferraro's left). Although many activists backed Jackson, the Freeze campaign eventually supported Mondale as the best way to implement a nuclear freeze. Photo courtesy Everett Collection Inc./Alamy Stock Photo.

seven seconds to blunt his momentum and doom his party to a generation of struggle on an issue close to the pocketbooks—and hearts—of most Americans." While Mondale's brutal honesty may have hurt him and the Democratic Party in the long term, in the days immediately following the convention, he maintained his postconvention bump, with Wirthlin's polls placing him within three points of Reagan.[37]

The Mondale campaign, however, soon suffered another setback, when questions over the finances of Ferraro and her husband, John Zaccaro, threatened to engulf it. Married to a successful New York real estate investor, Ferraro had not disclosed her husband's finances in her annual financial disclosure statements to Congress. What was more, questions appeared concerning a potentially illegal campaign contribution from Zaccaro during Ferraro's first campaign for Congress. As these stories began to circulate, new revelations detailing Zaccaro's businesses found he rented to a distributor of sexually explicit magazines. A *New York Times* story found mixed feelings among renters of Zaccaro's properties, with some residents reporting run-down conditions. A story in *New York* magazine alleged one of Zaccaro's companies owned a building that was used as a residence for an organized crime figure between 1963 and 1971.[38]

The hits continued. While Ferraro initially stated she would disclose several years of her and her husband's tax returns, she soon made an about-face on the subject, offering her own income tax returns but not those of her husband, in order to protect his business interests. Since the 1978 Ethics in Government Act, all candidates for president or vice president had been required to fill out a financial disclosure form. By refusing to disclose her husband's tax returns, Ferraro was breaking with the tradition. In so doing, she caught the wrath of Republicans, conservative columnists, and some Democrats. After weeks of controversy, Zaccaro agreed to release six years of tax returns. The returns revealed a family fortune of nearly four million dollars as well as ownership of three homes.[39]

While the issue of tax returns tainted the image of Ferraro as the daughter of a poor Italian immigrant, her status as a pro-choice Catholic created a political wedge that opponents exploited both to diminish her appeal and subsequently neutralize the nuclear issue. A devout Catholic, Ferraro accepted the Church's teachings on abortion. As a public official, however, she could not bring herself to push her own personal religious beliefs on abortion on others. This position brought her into the crosshairs of both Republican and pro-life organizations, which harassed her on the campaign trail. Anti-abortion advocates routinely booed Ferraro, picketed her talks, and held signs calling her a "baby-killer," "murderer," and even an advocate for "experiments on unborn children." As the campaign went on, the signs became personal. At a campaign stop in Texas, Ferraro recalled a sign reading "Dead Democrats Don't Vote." In the Midwest, an anti-abortion activist held up a sign reading "For Gerry's Kids: Rest in Peace" over a drawing of three tombstones. The Secret Service rushed Ferraro away from that crowd, later telling her of a report of three women "cruising the area in a car with a rifle" and another report of a man in the crowd who was "caught carrying a hatchet."[40]

Ferraro had battled with anti-abortion activists since she first ran for Congress, but now the attacks on her pro-choice stance were fueled by open battles with New York archbishop John O'Connor. Although a member of Cardinal Bernardin's war and peace committee, O'Connor did not believe threats over nuclear war trumped the threat to life that abortion posed: "If the unborn in a mother's womb is unsafe, it becomes ludicrous for the bishops to address the threat of nuclear war or the great problems of the homeless or the suffering of the age." O'Connor further puzzled over "how a Catholic of good conscience can vote for an individual expressing himself or herself as favoring abortion." Although he did not mention Ferraro by name, it was widely understood that the remarks were aimed at her, as well as Catholic pro-choice New York Democratic governor Mario Cuomo.[41]

"So began an unprecedented siege between a partisan archbishop and a vice presidential candidate," Ferraro reflected, "the reverberations of which ran through the Church hierarchy nationally, the political hierarchy of the state of New York," and Ferraro's "ever-present antiabortion demonstrators." Archbishop O'Connor soon publicly accused Ferraro of misrepresenting Church doctrine on abortion based on a statement made two years earlier for a fundraiser. In 1982, Ferraro and two other Catholic congresswomen had signed a cover letter inviting other Catholic members of Congress to a breakfast meeting sponsored by Catholics for a Free Choice. Articulating what the briefing would cover, the letter was prefaced with an explanation of the personal struggles of Catholics in Congress, both personally and politically, with "the wrenching abortion issue," which caused all of them to have "experienced moral and political doubt and concern." The controversy surrounded a passage in the letter that suggested "the Catholic position on abortion is not monolithic and that there can be a range of personal and political responses to the issue." As Ferraro emphasized, the letter did not suggest that the teachings of the Catholic Church were not monolithic but that "the Catholic *position* was not monolithic."[42]

Although many pro-choice Catholic allies showed up at rallies to support Ferraro, she nevertheless found herself caught in the crossfire between her pro-choice stance and the attacks of Archbishop O'Connor and other conservative Catholic bishops. Following Bishop O'Connor's comments, James W. Malone, the bishop of Youngstown, Ohio, theologized that Catholics could not draw a line between "personal morality and public policy." The line between church and state became increasingly blurred. In all, eighteen New England bishops signed a statement placing two items at the top of the election in 1984: abortion and nuclear war. For these bishops, the threat of nuclear war and the need to halt the arms race remained important, but it did not trump the "holocaust of abortion." While O'Connor would not directly campaign for Reagan, he did imply that Catholics could not consciously vote for Mondale without opposing Church doctrine. Cardinal Bernardin attempted to find an equilibrium, saying that the bishops were teachers who had a "responsibility to discuss and analyze public policy questions from the point of view of moral principles" but not "to tell people how to vote."[43]

While Ferraro fended off anti-abortion attackers and openly sparred with Archbishop O'Connor, Reagan delivered stump speeches to working-class Catholic audiences. In Hoboken, New Jersey, and Philadelphia, Pennsylvania, Reagan rallied Catholic voters on issues such as abortion and prayer in school and praised the pope as "one of the greatest moral leaders of our time." Reagan's efforts to obtain tax credits for parents with children enrolled in Catholic schools earned him praise from John Cardinal Krol, a Philadelphia bishop who both backed the 1983 pastoral letter and criticized the pro-choice position of Ferraro. Notably missing from Reagan's Catholic stump speeches, however, was any reference to the nuclear freeze or the pastoral letter on war and peace. The Reagan administration carefully shifted the conversation away from disputes on foreign policy to support on issues surrounding tax exemption, prayer in school, and abortion.[44]

Reagan the Peace Candidate

Whatever Ferraro's initial contribution to the Mondale ticket, her battles with Bishop O'Connor and the tax return scandal clearly undercut her value and led some to speculate she was simply taking the fall for Mondale's poor campaign. But what was true in 1980 was still true in 1984: Reagan was his own worst enemy. On August 11, 1984, during a voice check prior to his Saturday radio address, Reagan calmly joked, "My fellow Americans, I am pleased to tell you I have signed legislation that will outlaw Russia forever. We begin bombing in five minutes." The bombing joke was not intended for the public and did not air live, but it was leaked shortly afterward, causing "considerable dismay" within the administration, which feared the joke would tarnish Reagan's new moderate image. For the sake of the campaign, Reagan's staff isolated the president from the media, revving the engines of the Marine helicopters to drown out any of Reagan's further off-script remarks and using the Secret Service as a political screen to keep reporters at bay.[45]

Reagan's off-key bombing remarks elicited no outrage from Mondale, who only insisted the joke was not funny and urged the president to exhibit more caution. While the quip did not make the front page of the major newspapers in the United States, it was front-page news in Europe, where French newspaper Le Monde led with the headline "Gaffe." In West Germany, the Social Democrats and Greens denounced Reagan as "an irresponsible old man." The Soviet Union soon denounced Reagan's bombing joke as "unprecedently hostile" and "dangerous towards the cause of world peace." David Cortright expressed shock over the "supposed joke" about the "annihilation of the human race," declaring Ronald Reagan "a menace to our future!" If Reagan's comments were indeed simply a mocking of the neoconservative hawks within his administration, they were not perceived as such. Reagan's joke only fed the narrative that his antinuclear rhetoric was insincere.[46]

Reagan's microphone gaffe brought a slight boon to Mondale, who in Wirthlin's polls had moved within eight points of the president. But even more worrisome to the administration, Wirthlin's polls showed "an alarming increase in the percentage of Americans who thought Reagan might get the United States into a nuclear war." To assuage Soviet anger and to help restore the image of Reagan as a moderate searching for an end to the arms race, the administration invited Andrei Gromyko to a private meeting with the president at the White House following a meeting of the UN General Assembly. Whereas Gromyko once met regularly with the president, this would be his first meeting with any administration since the Soviet invasion of Afghanistan and, moreover, the first time Reagan had met with anyone in the Soviet leadership.[47]

Reagan's speech to the United Nations that September was, as Frances FitzGerald observes, "conciliatory," uttering "not a word of criticism about the Soviet Union" and making "an almost maudlin plea that the superpowers 'approach each other with ten-fold trust and thousand-fold affection' for the sake of world peace." As the *New York Times* reported, the speech brought Reagan "closer to the position enunciated by past administrations and by Mondale." Although the Soviet Union did not reciprocate the affectionate tone in their UN speech, Reagan's subsequent meeting with Gromyko provided a major boost to his campaign and effectively negated Mondale's charge that Reagan had not yet met with any leader from the Soviet Union.[48]

The Mondale campaign would take the offensive. Based on his own meeting with Gromyko, and the potential paths to halting the arms race, Mondale charged that Reagan's meeting was a failure and a political move on the part of an administration that "for four years has engineered an arms race." Mondale and Ferraro would both soon issue their harshest and most personal attacks against Reagan of the campaign. At a campaign rally in Santa Ana, California, Ferraro accused the administration of "arms control gridlock" and a "failure to grasp the magnitude of the problem that confronts us." She furthermore suggested Reagan did not take the threat from the arms race "seriously" and that neither he nor his administration had "the foggiest idea what needs to be done to reduce the threat of war." At a campaign rally in New Brunswick, New Jersey, Mondale accused Reagan of "having the capacity only to 'dream' of arms control initiatives that are 'doomed' because of his ignorance of the issue and his failure to master Presidential leadership." Mondale further attacked Reagan for his remarks in 1982 that implied a nuclear weapon could be recalled after launch. Even in his harshest attacks on Reagan, however, Mondale insisted the president sincerely wanted peace but simply lacked the knowledge and leadership skills.[49]

Although Mondale and Ferraro attempted to take the fight to Reagan in their campaign rallies, Reagan supporters heckled the Democratic nominees. Anti-abortion activists picketed Ferraro's speeches, while Reagan supporters waved Reagan-Bush placards and drowned out Mondale and Ferraro with shouts of "Reagan, Reagan!" and "Four more years!" After reports surfaced linking the hecklers to the Reagan campaign, Mondale urged the president to put it to a halt. While lamenting the hecklers, the administration disavowed any connections. Because Reagan and Bush kept hecklers far from the staging areas, Freeze activists only rarely heckled them. At a campaign stop in Vermont, two hundred Freeze activists confronted Bush, shouting "No more years!" and "Six more weeks!" Flustered, Bush scrapped his prepared remarks on arms control and addressed the Freeze activists, calling them "out of step" with America.[50]

With the presidential election only a month away, Reagan appeared to have a comfortable lead. Both Wirthlin's internal polls and a Washington Post poll gave Reagan an eighteen-point lead, 55 percent to 37 percent, with the remaining 8 percent undecided. The campaigns agreed to two debates in October. Focusing on domestic issues, the first debate, in Louisville, Kentucky, did not go in the president's favor. The one-time actor gave a poor performance, as he stumbled through statistics. An aggressive yet respectful Mondale criticized Reagan on Social Security, putting the president on the defensive. Fatigue appeared to catch up with the seventy-four-year-old president. Suddenly, Reagan's age was the new issue of the campaign.[51]

The Mondale campaign exited the first debate believing it had created an opening and predicted a tightening of the race. Indeed, a Washington Post / ABC News poll showed a leap of nineteen points in Mondale's personal ratings among voters. Nevertheless, the same poll demonstrated that Mondale's debate victory shaved only three points off Reagan's eighteen-point predebate lead. Wirthlin found "virtually no erosion in Reagan's perceptual strengths," finding Reagan's personal approval and job approval ratings still in place.[52]

But Mondale was not out yet. There was still one more debate between the two, this time with a focus on foreign policy. A day before the second debate, in Kansas City, Missouri, Wirthlin's polls gave Reagan a thirteen-point lead, but on the day of the debate, Mondale entered only eleven points down and with a strong showing could cut into Reagan's lead. This time, however, Reagan came prepared. With sage advice coming from Richard Nixon, and a boost in confidence coming from media consultant Roger Ailes, Reagan entered the second debate poised and confident. Even at the outset of the debate, there was a "night and day difference" between Reagan's appearance (as Mondale later acknowledged) and that of Mondale, who appeared "pasty" because of the light bouncing off the reflective white paper on his podium.[53]

Issues of image aside, Mondale brought a message on defense that appeared to be only Reagan lite. To establish his own hawkish credentials, Mondale insisted that, unlike Reagan, he would not share the technology behind SDI with the Soviets. Furthermore, he even conceded the peace issue, telling Reagan (politely), "I accept your commitment to peace, but I want you to accept my commitment to a strong national defense." When Mondale did attempt to attack Reagan for his 1982 comments about recalling missiles after launch, Reagan responded calmly, insisting the press had distorted his remarks. Instead of coming across as a hawk, Reagan appeared to understand the concerns voters had over nuclear war, saying, "How anyone could think that any sane person would believe you could call back a nuclear missile, I think is as ridiculous as the whole concept has been." Reagan's response brought laughter from the audience, and it appeared to journalist and Reagan biographer Lou Cannon that "Reagan was indeed himself again."[54]

The crux of the debate, however, may have come when Reagan was questioned whether his age and his health would prove detrimental in circumstances such as those President Kennedy faced during the Cuban Missile Crisis. Reagan denied his age would negatively impact his performance in the event of a crisis, adding, "I will not make age an issue of this campaign. I am not going to exploit, for political purposes, my opponent's youth and inexperience." Hysteria broke out in the audience, and even Mondale chuckled. The lighthearted dismissal of an issue Reagan was surely vulnerable on was perhaps the fatal dagger into the heart of the Mondale campaign. Within days of the conclusion of the second debate, Reagan was back up to a seventeen-point lead.[55]

Reagan's reelection appeared certain. In Seattle, as SANE activists canvassed for a nuclear freeze, they preferred talking about local candidates. "Trying to get people upset about Reagan is like beating your head against a wall," noted one SANE activist. Even conservative voters feared nuclear war and were apprehensive of Reagan as commander in chief. Nevertheless, the abstract threat of nuclear war did not amount to a reason to vote for Mondale over Reagan. As one voter explained, "I'd vote for Mondale, but I'm afraid he'd return to the social programs that cost too damn much." Others who were planning to vote against Reagan did so for reasons unrelated to defense issues, such as Reagan's assault on the unions. One local Democratic Party official identified "a defeatist attitude" among Mondale supporters: "No one believes, deep down inside, that we're going to get rid of Reagan."[56]

Public opinion polls routinely showed nuclear war was the number one concern in the 1984 campaign—and seemingly everyone had an opinion on the issue. New York City slumlord Donald J. Trump talked "nonstop about the threat of nuclear war." Based on the advice of his friend and lawyer, Roy Cohn, Trump boasted to the *Washington Post* about how he could negotiate better arms control agreements than Reagan: "It would take an hour-and-a-half to learn everything there is about missiles. . . . I think I know most of it anyway."[57] Although the stinging critiques of Reagan's ignorance on arms control and the dangers of a continued arms race spoke to public anxieties, they appeared to lack resonance with voters as a reason to dump Reagan. "By any normal mathematical equation this would add up to a landslide for Mondale," observed syndicated columnist Ellen Goodman, but in the "new math of this election, the No. 1 negative—fear of war—is less important than the No. 1 positive—an improved economy." While the threat of nuclear war terrified voters, there was "no concrete solution up for a vote." Washington pundits declared the Freeze "on the ropes, if not actually on the floor," with Americans more interested in the start of football season.[58]

Nevertheless, Freeze advocates attempted to maintain optimism and stressed the importance of defeating Reagan. In mid-October, the Freeze campaign organized major rallies across the United States, combined with voter registration drives. SANE cochairs Seymour Melman and William Winpisinger appealed directly to members to make an "extraordinary effort" to get out the vote, warning that "four more years of Reagan promises a procession of Central American war and heightened risk of nuclear war." Acknowledging the flaws in the Democratic Party and its shallow support for a nuclear weapons freeze, Melman and Winpisinger still pleaded with SANE members to make a "national effort" to turn out "at least 2,000,000 pro-peace, anti-Reagan voters on election day." The Freeze campaign dubbed November 6 "Turn out Tuesday" and urged activists to take the day off work to help efforts to get out the vote. In all, volunteers targeted five hundred precincts, where they hoped to canvas 250,000 voters. Just days before the election, Helen Caldicott took out a full-page advertisement in several newspapers urging voters to read her book *Missile Envy* before they even read their ballot, urging, "It could be the most important thing you can do for yourself, your family and your country."[59]

On Tuesday, November 6, 1984, voters went to the polls to cast their ballots. With unemployment down, the stock market up, and US-Soviet tensions relaxing, Americans reveled in Reagan's optimistic vision. Reagan soared to reelection, trouncing Mondale, carrying forty-nine states and garnering 59 percent of the popular vote and 525 Electoral College votes. It was one of the most lopsided electoral triumphs in US presidential history. While Reagan hesitated to call his victory a "mandate," he quickly vowed to resume arms control negotiations with the Soviets, repeating in his second inaugural address that a nuclear war "cannot be won and must never be fought."[60]

Reagan's triumphant reelection caused the Freeze campaign irreparable damage. Freeze activists tried to remain optimistic, but a sense of defeat and pessimism hung over much of the campaign. Grassroots Freeze activists lamented that "nuclear freeze" was "no longer a dynamic label," having become "corrupted in the 1984 presidential race." Randall Forsberg later reflected on how "tremendously disappointed and frustrated" grassroots Freeze activists were over the "shock" of the 1984 election. Indeed, Reagan's victory left Freeze activists "reeling." Unless the peace movement gathered its strength and voted in a pro-Freeze Congress in 1986, Caldicott predicted dark days ahead for humanity. At the Freeze campaign's Fifth Annual National Nuclear Freeze Conference, delegates were told the November elections "made it clear that a majority of Americans do not consider the nuclear freeze a high priority." Even major congressional allies such as Alan Cranston appeared apprehensive going forward, with Cranston stating he had "no plans to introduce new freeze legislation."[61]

Although a nuclear weapons freeze remained popular with the public at large, voters found no contradiction in supporting a freeze and voting for Ronald Reagan. A *New York Times* Election Day survey found 46 percent of voters still favored an immediate freeze, while a *Los Angeles Times* poll found arms control and defense the most important issue among both Republicans and Democrats. Contradicting the campaign's message, both polls also found most voters believed in Reagan's message that America needed to strengthen its military muscle. Furthermore, polling results demonstrated a clear partisan split on support for a freeze, with 82 percent of Mondale voters favoring an immediate nuclear freeze, contrasted with a mere 17 percent of Reagan voters. Thus, "nuclear freeze" became seen less as a nonpartisan message about stopping the arms race and more as a partisan idea to express opposition to Reagan.[62]

The Freeze campaign lost in 1984 not because its ideas were unpopular but because of the lack of commitment from its supposed political allies. Randy Kehler later regretted that the alignment with Senator Kennedy did not produce real allies for the campaign but instead individuals who signed on only as an expression of their dissatisfaction with Reagan. During the 1984 vice presidential debate, Ferraro was unable to even articulate how a freeze could be verified. Nevertheless, Kehler thought the movement was successful: "The Ronald Reagan elected in 1984 was quite different from the Ronald Reagan of 1980, a leader promising moderation and arms negotiations with the Soviets."[63]

Freeze activists found little to celebrate in Walter Mondale. His support for the Trident II missile and for increased military budgets angered Freeze activists, who "got into the posture . . . of pressuring the Democrats," noted Freeze Voter's Bill Curry. At times, Curry explained, Freeze activists were more critical of Mondale than of Reagan.[64] Freeze activists wanted Mondale to make the arms race and support for a freeze the focal point of his campaign. "Mondale was a real idiot," noted Forsberg, who called the alliance with the Mondale campaign "very painful." Likewise, Caldicott called Mondale "a dumb man," to whom the Freeze handed the election "on a silver plate."[65] The grassroots resentment toward Mondale was evident from activists within the Pennsylvania chapter of the Nuclear Weapons Freeze Campaign who candidly asserted that he "did more to destroy Freeze in 1984 than Ronald Reagan ever could have."[66] Mondale's lackluster campaign left volunteers to joke, "Vote for Mondale; at least you'll *live* to regret it."[67]

By the end of 1984, the Freeze was left smoldering in the ashes of the failed Mondale campaign. It had become "reduced to a symbolic expression of public sentiment, no longer a political force behind a serious policy proposal," as Solo reflected. That December, in a decision pressured by funders, media, and congressional leadership, but resented by grassroots activists, the campaign moved its offices from St. Louis, Missouri, to Washington, D.C. At the Freeze clearinghouse in St. Louis, many staff members refused to relocate, while local activists sought "to resist the decision and reclaim our movement." Resistance, however, proved futile. The "fire in the belly" that propelled the grassroots and created the largest political demonstration in US history just two years prior was now extinguished.[68] Although the Freeze would soon "melt away," as journalist Frances FitzGerald writes, soon so would the Cold War that gave rise to and fueled the movement.[69]

Epilogue
Bedtime for the Bomb

At an antinuclear rally at Berkeley in 1983, historian and activist E. P. Thompson remarked that "most social movements [only] have a life span of about six years. If they do not make an impact within this 'window of opportunity,' they will have little effect on the larger political structures they hope to transform."[1] The Freeze campaign operated within a very limited "window," fueled both by Reagan's bellicosity and by the growing nuclear threat. Its rapid rise combined with its political naiveté allowed both the Reagan administration and the Democrats to co-opt the movement for their own political ends. This co-optation prevented grassroots elements from building and sustaining the infrastructure necessary to force stronger congressional legislation or lessen the damage from co-optation. Boxed in by the history of the US Cold War and the limitations of its foundational "Call" for a bilateral nuclear weapons freeze, the movement could not condemn NATO deployment of the Euromissiles outright without acquiescing to the McCarthyite charge that it supported unilateral disarmament. The Freeze Voter '84 campaign, along with the push for Quick Freeze legislation, continued a flawed and divisive strategy that essentially turned the movement into a caucus of the Democratic Party.

At the campaign's Fifth Annual National Nuclear Freeze Conference, in December 1984, Randy Kehler advocated a new strategy, calling for both an "inward" and "downward" turn to revitalize the movement. Inwardly, the campaign would build a "mature nationally-organized movement that has the long-term staying power, goals, and commitment to achieve a Freeze"; downwardly, the campaign would "refocus on the grassroots, re-localize the Freeze." It would, however, prove "impossible to recapture the original momentum," as sociologist Robert Kleidman lamented. Kehler resigned as national coordinator, leaving a strife-ridden organization to his successor, Jane Gruenebaum. Without Kehler's fundraising skills and established relationships, the Freeze experienced its first decline in funding in 1985. Although initially the decline was small, big foundations and major donors soon cut support in response to "a perceived lack of national coordination" and having already provided seed money. By 1987, the national campaign's total budget had dropped to 79,000 dollars from its peak of 571,000 dollars in 1983. The lack of funds meant layoffs to the national staff, some of whom had been with the campaign since its beginning. By 1986, campaign staff dropped from twenty-five employees to twelve. The Freeze executive committee soon forced Gruenebaum's resignation, replacing her with regional Freeze leader Carolyn Cottom.[2]

With continued dwindling finances, the Freeze campaign sought a merger with SANE. Because the term "merger" raised defenses among activists, however, Cortright referred to the meetings between Freeze and SANE as "Unity Talks." Leading figures of SANE and Freeze formed the SANE / Freeze Unity Committee to discuss key philosophies and programs, and structural considerations, and to determine a process going forward. The committee concluded that SANE and Freeze were "moving toward a broader political program" and "not focusing exclusively on the freeze or the nuclear arms race." Several meetings would take place throughout 1986 to resolve outstanding merger issues, including dealing with rumors and speculation of a "SANE takeover." Likewise, the two organizations faced questions over how to maintain the diversity of the membership, their relationship to other peace organizations, the relationship of Freeze Voter and SANE PAC to the organization, and whether to encourage or allow local groups to merge prior to the national SANE / Freeze merger. As the talks continued, they further postponed discussion of long-range political and strategic goals of the movement.[3]

The Freeze campaign grew rapidly between 1981 and 1983, gaining endorsements from numerous organizations across the political spectrum, "but when the time came to convert those endorsements to political power (money and people)," as Freeze activist Ben Senturia observed, "few groups beyond the disarmament community were willing to make the Freeze a priority." Senturia found the fault lay with the Freeze's one-sided organizing around the "Make the Freeze the Issue" campaign. Although the Freeze sought alliances with "labor unions, religious groups, environmental organizations, people of color, and others," as Kehler lamented, the campaign "never got traction." Senturia recollected a meeting with a labor leader who had learned to avoid meeting with peace activists since the conversations revolved around "What can you do to help pass a Freeze?" and not "How can we help each other?" This "narrow strategy of focusing exclusively on the Freeze made it difficult to have the broader two-way conversations that might have yielded stronger, more complex connections," Senturia regretted.[4]

By 1985, antinuclear activists were branching out, seeking new directions and tactics. One controversial tactic was the use of civil disobedience at the Nevada Test Site. At the Fifth Annual National Nuclear Freeze Conference, Freeze delegates voted against endorsing civil disobedience, leading to grassroots criticism that the national campaign was committed only to "tactics acceptable to the nonradical American majority." More radical activists concluded the campaign was "not moving with the times and was no longer on the cutting edge of the peace issue." The vote against civil disobedience, and the consolidation of offices in Washington, D.C., pushed a group of activists to split from the Freeze and form American Peace Test to specifically oppose the testing of nuclear weapons at the NTS, including by means of civil disobedience.[5]

Freeze and SANE had separate but sometimes overlapping agendas. While the Freeze campaign focused on one goal—a bilateral nuclear freeze—SANE had a broader agenda, which included support for a freeze but also opposition to US interventionism, including US aid to the death squads of El Salvador. But SANE and Freeze also had significant differences. Freeze was more grassroots, while SANE recruited members by going door-to-door and through mass mailings. Moreover, there was a "clash of cultures." Many older SANE activists who had been with the organization since its inception in 1957 believed the Freeze was too narrow in its focus, missing the links between militarism, capitalism, and other intertwining forces that produced the arms race. Freeze activists in turn saw SANE as "too centralized," with its leadership too divorced from and not sufficiently committed to grassroots organizing. Although SANE attempted to change its elitist image, by 1984, the organization's strategies still focused heavily on flooding the general public and policymakers with detail-oriented advertising, while other mainstream antinuclear organizations stuck to "image and simple rhetoric." To create the harmonious "unity" between Freeze and SANE, the two organizations would have to set aside differences and begin working toward common goals.[6]

Throughout 1986, the SANE / Freeze Unity Committee worked tirelessly to resolve differences and solve issues surrounding the merger, including drafting and revising a credo statement. Members of SANE and Freeze moreover respectively participated in nearly one hundred onsite "listening sessions" and numerous in-depth phone conservations across thirty-nine states to hear responses and assess the proposed merger. Across the sessions, activists sought to broaden the political agenda. Although being single issue attracted newcomers and may have helped with lobbying efforts in Congress, activists conversely noted the approach hampered speaking about other related issues that limited inclusion of natural allies (people of color and labor); likewise, it was not possible to speak of limiting the arms race without also addressing the interconnected issues of interventionism and military Keynesianism. Grassroots distrust of the "national" Freeze emerged as yet another point of disagreement. Thus, to create a "democratic, dynamic, and vibrant organization," activists sought to hold organizations and leaders accountable for following structures and pursuing agreed on political goals.[7]

The question of whether to merge SANE with Freeze was put to members at the national Freeze conference in December 1986 and the SANE national board meeting in January 1987. Freeze members voted overwhelmingly for a "Three-Way Unity Proposal" that would unite Freeze, Freeze Voter, and SANE while merging SANE and Freeze in a legal sense. Although there was "strong hope of a legal merger with Freeze Voter," the proposal passed only called for "maximum cooperation." Fearing that the merged organization did not have the resources to sustain it, Freeze Voter would remain an independent peace PAC solely committed to electing pro-freeze candidates through the 1988 election. Freeze Voter nevertheless pledged its continued cooperation with SANE / Freeze.[8]

Unity negotiations, however, soon deadlocked, when a dispute arose over who would head the new organization: SANE's Cortright, with his "mainstream, 'bureaucratic'" approach, or Freeze's Cottom, with her "facilitative, networking style"? The "old rivalries threatened to derail the peace movement," as Bruce Ferguson recounted. But the unity committee "found a conciliator par excellence in the Reverend William Sloane Coffin." A noted civil rights and Vietnam antiwar activist, Coffin's involvement with the Freeze dated to its inception. Furthermore, he was instrumental in building support, with the founding of the Riverside Church disarmament program (one of the original national organizations to endorse Forsberg's "Call"). In January 1988, Coffin would become president of SANE / Freeze, while Cortright and Cottom would stay on as codirectors. With a new, broader focus for peace and opposition to militarism, the organization changed its name to "SANE / Freeze: Campaign for Global Security." In the years to come, as both the public desires for a freeze and the Cold War tensions that fueled the campaign faded, SANE /

Freeze changed its name again, to Peace Action, transitioning into the current nonprofit peace and social justice organization it is today.[9]

What ultimately drove Reagan's victory over the Freeze movement in 1984 cannot just be attributed to the failures of the Mondale campaign. Nor can the Freeze campaign's own internal struggles fully explain why the issue became moot. Instead of direct assaults and unsubstantiated accusations against the campaign, the Reagan administration moved away from the neoconservatives who influenced the early rhetoric. In so doing, they reinvented the president's diplomacy and image. The administration's public relations campaigns (capped by SDI) proved successful in capturing the war and peace issue. SDI usurped the moral high ground on deterrence from the Catholic bishops' pastoral letter, while its timing undercut the House freeze debate. As a defense research project that would take decades to complete, it would more than replace the lost capital of the orphaned MX missile while expanding the warfare state into the realms of outer space. By claiming to eliminate the threat of nuclear war, SDI offered a fantastical and optimistic solution that appealed to Reagan's personal distaste for deterrence but in reality offered only a rhetorical usurping of the Freeze. Although SDI could assuage public fears over nuclear war, it would not end the arms race, only foster it into new dimensions. It is a tragic legacy that in advocating a freeze on offensive weapons, the Freeze movement inadvertently opened the door to the pursuit of space-based missile defense. These "defensive" programs were funded at the cost of billions of dollars throughout the Reagan and George H. W. Bush administrations and into the administration of Bill Clinton. Although conclusive tests of SDI were later found to have been staged, the continued folly of searching for missile defense led to the US withdrawal from the ABM Treaty under the George W. Bush administration while opening the door to a new arms race.[10]

Reagan may have privately expressed his hatred for nuclear weapons, but not until after the Freeze campaign emerged as a political threat did the administration change course on nuclear diplomacy. With the 1984 campaign just over the horizon, Reagan became a dove, dropping conditions for an arms control summit. When the Soviets walked out of the INF negotiations, they inadvertently gave the Reagan administration a major public relations gift, allowing it to blame them for the lack of arms control negotiations. After Reagan's "joke" about bombing the Soviets, his staff took extra precautions on the campaign trail to ensure the president would not speak off-the-cuff and destroy the moderate image his staff had worked to create. Television advertisements popped with patriotism and zinged of the strength to confront the mythical "bear in the woods." Reagan used his charm, wit, and optimism to full effect during stump speeches, all while skillfully ducking the tag of "nuclear risk-taker." Through successful marketing and image control, Reagan's campaign sold him as the peace candidate in 1984, at a time when voters overwhelmingly feared nuclear Armageddon. As a result, Reagan never had to advocate for a freeze in order to win reelection. Reagan's new, moderate image prevented Freeze activists from turning the election based on the abstract dangers a second term posed.

Reagan's new approach to diplomacy helped erase his image as a reckless cowboy. Once skeptical Western Europeans now looked optimistically on the prospects for a second Reagan term, given both the improved US economy and the more conciliatory tone in US-Soviet relations. Political allies, such as former French prime minister Raymond Barre, praised Reagan for reestablishing "the frontier spirit" and restoring faith in America, while skeptics, such as British Labour Party leader Neil Kinnock, questioned, "Is this the real Reagan? Or will he lose his spots and go back to the 'Evil Empire' speech?" With the departure of hawks and Reagan rebuffing hardliners from the Pentagon, West German officials expressed optimism for the future of US-Soviet relations and, by extension, rapprochement between East and West Germany.[11]

Though the Freeze campaign appeared to be at its nadir, founder Randall Forsberg remained optimistic. Over the next five years, Forsberg envisioned an even wider peace movement that would reject military Keynesianism and empire, pressuring both the United States and the Soviet Union to give up third world interventions, mutually make deep cuts in conventional forces, and, finally, "get the Soviets to give up their hegemony in Eastern Europe." Forsberg's vision was not on a four-year plan, or even a ten-year plan, but might take a hundred years. "Many people will say this is hopeless, this is too much, this is too big, it's too hard," Forsberg cautiously explained, but if left unchecked, militarism and the arms race would "go on forever," with three hundred billion dollar defense budgets and with continued proliferation of nuclear weapons beyond the twenty-five thousand that already existed. Forsberg's peace vision appeared a pipe dream, but so did the end of the Cold War just a year earlier.[12]

As the Freeze campaign began its thaw in 1985, so did the Cold War. Just months after Reagan's reelection, Konstantin Chernenko became the third Soviet leader to die while Reagan was in office. The Politburo soon selected Mikhail Gorbachev as the next general secretary of the Communist Party. Gorbachev, however, inherited a Soviet system that resembled, as historian Walter LaFeber described it, "a science-fiction movie's huge gray blob that looked threatening but moved ever more slowly." Rampant alcoholism, food shortages, bread lines, and "horrid hospital facilities" plagued Soviet society. Compounding these domestic problems was a "runaway military budget" and an endless, costly war in Afghanistan.[13]

Born in 1931, Gorbachev was significantly younger than previous Soviet leaders and represented a new generation of Soviets (those born after the October Revolution). From the outset, there was a clear difference between Gorbachev and his predecessors in both style and substance. Whereas prior Soviet leaders claimed only socialists would survive a nuclear war, Gorbachev insisted that in a nuclear war not even the socialists would survive. As LaFeber writes, "Gorbachev and this new class demanded what they soon called 'new thinking'—not because they feared Reagan's military buildup but because they understood that the Soviet system could not keep up with, and adjust to, the technological changes . . . that were revolutionizing Western societies." To save the Soviet Union, Gorbachev offered radical reforms: "glasnost" (political openness) and "perestroika" (restructuring of the economy). For Gorbachev's reforms to succeed, he needed to end the arms race. Gorbachev thus bargained with the one chip he had left: nuclear weapons.[14]

In summer 1985, Gorbachev unilaterally implemented a moratorium on the testing of nuclear weapons—one of the original components of Forsberg's "Call." The moratorium was scheduled to last until January 1, 1986, but Gorbachev extended it through February 1987. Believing nuclear testing was "vital to the U.S. nuclear weapons program," Reagan dismissed the moratorium as a "propaganda ploy" and refused to join, but the administration soon came under pressure from the House of Representatives, which passed a resolution calling for reopening test ban negotiations. Backed by public opinion polls and the broader antinuclear movement, resolutions favoring a test ban passed in five states and over a hundred communities. By May 1986, dissident antinuclear scientists from the United States began installing seismic monitors on Soviet test sites, over opposition from the Reagan administration. These actions proved that cooperative verification measures were possible and had a rippling effect across the political scene, domestically and internationally. Under domestic political pressure from "the arms control community, the Congress, and the press," the administration felt the need to "do something," as ACDA's Ken Adelman confessed. The administration soon introduced a measure at the United Nations that would reduce both the number of tests and their yield. While the final Comprehensive Test Ban Treaty would not come until 1996, antinuclear activists helped lay its groundwork.[15]

Antinuclear activism not only played a role in US domestic politics and arms control diplomacy but likewise influenced Soviet decisions. Under pressure from arms control organizations, Gorbachev became convinced there was more security in an arms builddown than in an arms race. Moreover, the

European antinuclear movement profoundly influenced Gorbachev. Mary Kaldor recounted a meeting with Gorbachev's speechwriter, Alexei Pankini. Pankini explained to Kaldor how Gorbachev subscribed to the *Journal of European Nuclear Disarmament*, "even though it was forbidden." Gorbachev's speechwriters furthermore dissected pieces in the journal and then added them to Gorbachev's speeches. "In other words," as LaFeber writes, "private peace groups were perhaps more important than Reagan's military buildup in convincing Gorbachev to wind down the arms race."[16]

In his second inaugural address, in 1985, President Reagan made a dramatic shift in tone. Reagan proclaimed that the United States did not just seek to "reduce" the number of nuclear weapons in the world but aimed for "the total elimination . . . of nuclear weapons from the face of the Earth"—a far cry from the rhetoric that dominated the administration's first years. Phrases such as this did not reflect the administration's nuclear weapons policies. As Reagan's director of speechwriting Aram Backshian observed, "Very few of the people who were writing [Reagan's] speeches would have pushed it in that direction," adding that the line could have been Reagan's "own formulation" or a "repetition of something he'd gotten from the outside." The new Reagan came across as a peacemaker—a concept First Lady Nancy Reagan "obviously thought . . . would be a great thing" for the president.[17]

With Gorbachev's commitment to reforming the Soviet Union and determination for rapprochement, Reagan could further neutralize his domestic opponents by agreeing to an arms control summit in Geneva at the end of November 1985—the first summit meeting in six years between the president of the United States and the general secretary of the Soviet Union. The overtures from the peace movement found a willing listener in Gorbachev. Prior to the summit, Gorbachev met for forty-five minutes with a delegation from the US peace movement that included Cortright (SANE), Gruenebaum (Freeze), and Jesse Jackson (Rainbow Coalition). The delegation presented Gorbachev with a petition to freeze the arms race, signed by over 1.1 million Americans. As Reagan and Gorbachev began negotiations in Geneva, over five hundred summit vigils occurred stateside. Although Reagan and Gorbachev did not agree to a freeze, and further failed to agree to a nuclear test ban, the summit meeting did end with an agreement in principle on a 50 percent cut in strategic forces and a reopening of cultural exchange programs.[18]

In October 1986, with midterm elections just one month away, Reagan met Gorbachev again for a dramatic summit at the Hofdy House in Reykjavik, Iceland. They were accompanied separately by delegations from SANE, Freeze, and Women for a Meaningful Summit, who traveled to Reykjavik to "demand progress towards peace." Over the course of two days, Reagan and Gorbachev tangled over a score of issues with nearly earthshaking consequences. Reagan proposed eliminating all ballistic missiles on the condition that the United States would reserve the right to deploy SDI to counter any further perceived threats. Gorbachev countered, suggesting the two sides agree to eliminate all nuclear weapons by the year 2000—as long as SDI remained confined to laboratory testing during the ten-year period. Reagan refused to budge, falsely believing such restrictions would devastate the program. The two sides left without an agreement. While Secretary of State Shultz boasted over Reagan's rejection of Gorbachev's proposal, Ambassador Jack Matlock Jr. felt "crushed," believing the United States missed the chance for a "world-transforming arms control agreement."[19]

In the wake of the summit, Reagan faced criticism from across the political spectrum. Conservatives criticized him for meeting with Gorbachev and were shocked that he had "almost given away the store," while arms control advocates believed he had missed "a golden opportunity." Shortly after the failures at Reykjavik, however, the Iran-Contra scandal broke, marring the administration. In the Soviet Union, Gorbachev was still searching for an exit from the "bleeding wound" in Afghanistan. Although SDI undercut the Reykjavik summit, Gorbachev soon realized the program was far from workable, and he offered to restart arms control discussions. Needing relief from Iran-Contra, Reagan jumped at Gorbachev's offer. Building on the substantial progress made at Reykjavik, the two sides came to an agreement on the text for the INF Treaty in September 1987.[20]

SANE / Freeze remained cautiously optimistic. While the agreement would result in some "real reduction," thousands of nuclear weapons remained. But SANE / Freeze could not remain aloof. The organization sent letters to all major Democratic candidates, urging them to back the INF Treaty. SANE / Freeze further sought to create a national INF ratification campaign. The campaign proposed a range of ideas, including working with peace, labor, environmental, race, gender, and minority progressive organizations, consulting with arms control allies within the Senate to ensure the treaty's passage, and sponsoring an INF conference in Washington in 1988 that would include representatives from Europe to discuss the next steps in arms control after INF. SANE / Freeze outlined the campaign's agenda, created print ads with slogans such as "2,000 down, 42,000 to go," and even sketched out a television advertisement ("INF: A Taste for Disarmament") wherein popular actor Danny DeVito would eat a new Ben & Jerry's ice cream flavor, "I Scream for Peace."[21]

On December 8, 1987, Gorbachev traveled to Washington, D.C., for the INF Treaty signing ceremony. The treaty eliminated an entire class of missiles, including the highly controversial Euromissiles, as well as their Soviet counterparts, the SS-20s. The landmark treaty in effect bound the two superpowers to the idea that European antinuclear activists had championed a decade earlier: zero intermediate-range nuclear weapons in Europe. Reagan and Gorbachev would embrace following its signing, but the INF Treaty faced a full-on revolt within the Republican Party. Among Republican presidential candidates, only Vice President Bush would go on the record in support of it. A friend of Reagan's before either was in politics, Senator Jesse Helms (R-NC) warned the president not to "discard those people who brought you to the dance." Republican foreign policy heavyweights opposed the treaty, with Richard Nixon privately urging Reagan to "be more hawkish in dealing with Gorbachev." The young and politically ambitious Senator Dan Quayle (R-IN) broke with Reagan, repeatedly denounced the treaty, and warned in the *Wall Street Journal* about the threat to Europe once the missiles were withdrawn. In the conservative press, columnist George Will complained of the "cult of arms control," while *National Review* dedicated an entire issue to "Reagan's Suicide Pact." The ASCF mailed out 110,000 letters urging members to "barrage the Senate" to defeat the INF Treaty. Likewise, the Conservative Caucus mailed out 175,000 letters

FIGURE 12. President Reagan and Soviet general secretary Gorbachev sign the Intermediate-Range Nuclear Forces (INF) Treaty on December 8, 1987. The treaty was a milestone in ending the Cold War. It bound the two superpowers to the idea that European antinuclear activists championed a decade earlier: zero intermediate-range nuclear weapons in Europe. Photo courtesy of the Ronald Reagan Presidential Library.

opposing it, while circulating five thousand cassettes of former supreme commander of NATO General Bernard Rogers attacking the treaty.[22]

The INF Treaty was nevertheless popular with the American public. In an internal memo, Reagan's director of communications, Thomas Griscom, argued the administration should "emphasize the key words that tested well with the public: 'movement' and 'peace.'" Reagan would further prod critics as seeking war. Opponents such as Quayle took the bait and denounced Reagan's comments on the Senate floor, opening the door for Reagan to portray them as "warmongers and himself as a man of peace," as James Mann writes. Ultimately, as Adelman observed, Republicans in the Senate "could not turn down the most conservative president in the postwar era on an accord he had proposed six years before." Likewise, with arms control at the top of the Democrats' "international wish list . . . they had to cheer." As opposition crumbled, the Senate subsequently ratified the INF Treaty in May 1988 by a vote of ninety-three to five.[23]

Reagan soon traveled to Moscow on a goodwill trip. When asked by a reporter about his 1983 "evil empire" remarks, Reagan disavowed them: "You are talking about another time, another era." Although Reagan and Gorbachev could not come to a final arms control treaty, the United States, Reagan assured, could now look "with optimism on future negotiations." By April 1989, a *New York Times* editorial proclaimed, "The cold war of poisonous Soviet-American feelings, of domestic political hysteria, of events enlarged and distorted by East-West confrontation, of almost perpetual diplomatic deadlock is over." But who deserved the credit? During his 1988 presidential campaign, George H. W. Bush insisted the Reagan administration taught its "liberal critics" a lesson: "peace through strength works." Bush insisted his opponent, Massachusetts governor Michael Dukakis, supported members of the "radical left" who wanted a "unilateral freeze" that would "restrain us, not the Soviet Union." After distorting the objective of the Freeze, a grateful Bush remarked, "Thank God we didn't listen to them."[24]

But the Freeze movement should not be so easily dismissed nor lost in the shadows of great leader diplomacy. It instilled the idea that arms control was not just a subject for the "nuclear priesthood," as Kehler observed. The campaign brought millions of ordinary people from across the globe without extensive background in the details of nuclear weaponry into a direct conversation with world leaders and policymakers over sensitive national security issues. Furthermore, Freeze and the broader antinuclear activism of the era helped transform the political dialogue on arms control and nuclear weapons. As Paul Warnke suggested, the movement "changed the political rhetoric . . . you don't find people talking about 'limited nuclear war' anymore." Even Adelman acknowledged the Freeze was "helpful in sensitizing individuals about the need for real arms control of nuclear weapons."[25]

The Freeze campaign made a hardline approach to diplomacy and arms control politically unacceptable. "The heat was kept on the Administration to keep doing something in this area," Les Janka observed, adding, "Knowing the characters involved . . . these people were not arms controllers down deep. They were doing it only because of a sense of having to do something on public pressure. They were far more concerned with building up the military than building it down. Public concern about arms control and then especially the pressure from Congress . . . forced [the Reagan Administration] to pay more attention to [the Freeze] than their instincts would have led them to." Likewise, White House NSC staffer Robert Kimmit believed public opinion was "a key factor" throughout the Reagan years and for Gorbachev. "I think the freeze movement told us something," Reagan's science adviser George Keyworth confessed, that "the public is frightened. . . . I think the president was sensing and fearing the public's concern."[26]

The Freeze campaign's rapid rise was tied to public fears of a nuclear conflict; when the threat of a nuclear war seemed lessened, the objective need for an activist solution to the arms race no longer appeared necessary. With the campaign's decline, Gorbachev stepped into the space the movement was vacating, implementing its ideas. Though historians continue to argue whether Reagan or Gorbachev deserves more credit for the peaceful end of the Cold War, this ignores the pressures US and Soviet leaders faced from grassroots antinuclear activists. In a global sense, the Cold War had multiple end points, but the return of détente between the United States and the Soviet Union, and the subsequent ending of the arms race, had little to do with the unrestrained militarism and hawkish rhetoric of the Reagan administration. While Reagan and Gorbachev both deserve credit for standing up to the hawks, the peace of the late 1980s was made possible by public demand and the political pressures of antinuclear activism.

The cause championed by peace and Freeze activists of the 1980s remains important, for the threat of nuclear war remains omnipresent. Thanks to the arms control treaties of the late Cold War, the stockpile of US and Russian nuclear arsenals is much smaller than in 1980. But when it comes to the "good faith . . . measures relating to the cessation of the nuclear arms race . . . and to nuclear disarmament," as Article VI of the binding Non-proliferation Treaty states, the progress has been minimal. Indeed, as of this writing, the United States plans to spend four hundred billion dollars over the next decade and 1.2 trillion dollars over the next thirty years to modernize its nuclear arsenal— while it and the world's other nuclear powers boycott a UN treaty to ban nuclear weapons. With the withdrawal from the INF Treaty in 2019 under the Donald J. Trump administration, a new arms race beckons.

Toward the end of his career, prominent revisionist historian William Appleman Williams reflected on the trajectory of the American empire and its entanglement with the American "way of life." Williams offered readers a stark warning: "Empire as a way of life will lead to nuclear death."[27] Today the nuclear sword of Damocles dangles ever closer. Strategically obsolete ICBMs—a relic of the Cold War and a by-product of military Keynesianism—remain on hair-trigger alert, creating the potential for accidental nuclear war. This threat to the survival of the human species is compounded both by the refusal of successive US administrations to rule out a potential first strike and by the continued vesting of sole authority to launch a nuclear weapon in the president of the United States. For modern peace activists, the Freeze campaign may demonstrate the failures of working within the political establishment and the ease of political and rhetorical co-optation by friends and enemies alike. But the history of the Freeze should also demonstrate that even through direct and short-term failures, it is still possible to pressure even the most hardline governments to turn back the Doomsday Clock.

Acknowledgments

This project began as an idea early in graduate school with my own interests in peace and antiwar activism and its relationship to US foreign policy. I began writing about the Freeze movement and the Reagan administration in Tom Maddux's seminars at Cal State University, Northridge. When I began studying for the PhD at UC Santa Barbara, I picked up the project more in-depth in seminars with Salim Yaqub and Nelson Lichtenstein. It soon became my dissertation topic, and, with significant revisions, the present book.

Along the way I received significant financial support from various institutions. This project was supported by grants from the American Institute of Physics, the Cushwa Center for the Study of Catholicism at Notre Dame University, the Philip and Aida Siff Foundation, the History Department and the History Associates at UCSB, as well as the Center for Cold War Studies and International History and the Center for the Study of Work, Labor, and Democracy. Likewise, I received two dissertation completion fellowships from the Institute of Global Conflict and Cooperation (IGCC) at UC San Diego that relieved me of teaching obligations and gave me the time and financial support for research and writing. I am grateful to both IGCC and the Nuclear Science and Security Consortium at UC Berkeley for their support and to Toshi Hasegawa for bringing their fellowships to my attention and encouraging me to apply. In fall 2016, I was the Agnese N. Haury post-doctoral fellow at the Center for the Study of the United States and the Cold War at Tamiment Library, New York University. It was an invaluable experience that allowed me to spend extensive time in the archives at both NYU and the Swarthmore College Peace Collection in Swarthmore, Pennsylvania.

A project that relies as much on archival work as this obviously does not happen without the assistance of librarians and archivists pulling books and boxes and offering suggestions on where else to look. I would like to thank the staff and archivists of the Ronald Reagan Presidential Library, especially Kelly Barton, Leo Belleville, and Martha Huggins for pulling countless boxes and helping me file Mandatory Declassification Reviews for thousands of documents (many of which as of this writing—sadly—still remain classified) and to Michael Pinckney for answering nagging questions about permissions and photos. At the Chicago Archdiocese, I would like to thank vice chancellor John Treanor for granting me permission to use the War and Peace papers of Joseph Bernardin, as well as Meg Hall and the staff for all their assistance. At Swarthmore College, I'm deeply grateful to Wendy Chmielewski, Mary Sigado, and Anne Yoder. At NYU, I'd like to thank Michael Koncewicz and the rest of the staff for the many opportunities and great times in the Big Apple. Anyone working on this topic owes a debt of gratitude to Larry Wittner. I am personally grateful to him for sharing with me his interview transcripts with both Freeze activists and Reagan Administration officials. I benefited from email exchanges with peace/Freeze activists David Cortright, Steve Ladd, Libby Frank, Bob Moore, and Terry Provance. For photos, I'm grateful to the Edward M. Kennedy Foundation, Rick Reinhard, and the family of the late Ray Pinkson. Permission to quote from Howard Zinn's *The Politics of History* obtained from the Zinn Estate via Anthony Arnove. My many intellectual debts can be found in the footnotes and bibliography.

I received fantastic feedback at various stages of this project, presenting at conferences such as the UCSB-LSE-GWU Cold War Conference, the Boston University Graduate Student Political History Conference, the Annual Conference of the Society of Historians of American Foreign Relations (SHAFR), and several other venues. Andy Johns and Mitch Lerner invited me to be a part of the SHAFR Summer Institute for the Intersection of Domestic Politics and Foreign Policy in Columbus, Ohio, in 2015; I'm grateful for their feedback and from my exchanges and formed friendships with the other participants. I learned a great deal from my participation in both the Summer Institute on the Conduct of Archival Research at George Washington University and the Public Policy and Nuclear Threats Summer "Boot Camp" at UC San Diego.

At UCSB, I'm especially indebted to Nelson Lichtenstein and Salim Yaqub for their advice over the years, their readings and feedback on draft after damn draft, and their encouragement to "think big" and be bold. At the dissertation stage, Laura Kalman offered great feedback and was a model teacher. At Cornell University Press, I have been fortunate to work with Michael McGandy who believed in the project from the beginning and went to bat for it. Likewise, Clare Jones helped me navigate permissions, fair use, and all the other ins-and-outs of books they never teach you about in graduate school. I received substantial blind peer review feedback that greatly helped me think through my revisions and helped shape the book for the better. In the final stages of production, I had the pleasure of working with Michelle Witkowski and Westchester Publishing Services who oversaw the copyediting and typesetting of the book. It should go without saying, but any faults in this book are obviously my own. Special thanks to Jim O'Brien for the thorough index and helpful corrections.

Writing acknowledgments is a bit like giving an Oscar's speech: there are many who need to be thanked and only so much time before you are played off. That being said, I was fortunate to have many sharp colleagues in and out of seminars throughout graduate school. I'm grateful to the CSUN History crew: Anne Alman, Bojan Bosanac, Brittany Bounds, Jon Eckel, Jarrod Kellogg, Brian Kovalesky, Shane Peterson, Rob Shafer, and Jeff Shettler. My countless friends and colleagues from UCSB made life less stressful and more pleasant: Kashia Arnold, Paul Baltimore, Jill Briggs, Steve Campbell, Abby Dowling, Roger Eardley-Pryor, Mashsa Fedorova and Paul Warden, Eric Fenrich, Joe Figliulo-Rosswurm, Cheryl Jimenez Frei, Brian Griffith, Paul Hirsch, Ken Hough, Hanni Jalil, Janiene Langford and Abraham Mendoza, Sunny Lim, Regina Longo, Brian Lovato, Nikki Luthy, Eric Massie, Patrick Mooney, Nicole Pacino, Chichi Peng, Jason Saltoun-Ebin, Travis Seifman, Jeb Sprague, Jason Stohler, Will Thompson, Sarah Watkins, Rachel Winslow, Peninah Wolpo, Nathan York and Kristen Bryant, and Jason and Aurora Zeledon. In the broader profession, I've benefitted from friendships and feedback from David Atkinson, Tom Balcerski, Scott

Bennett, Andrea Chiampan, Tom Devine, Zach Fredman, Andrew Higgins, Jonathan Hunt, Nate Jones, Martin Klimke, Tom Maddux, Jorge Rivera Marin, Alex Marino, Patrick McCray, Asa McKercher, Mary McPartland, Jamie Miller, Aaron Coy Moulton, Michelle Paranzino, Jason Parker, Joe Parrott, Nat Powell, Andrew Preston, Erika Rappaport, Ben Todd, Bob Tomlinson, David Wight, and numerous others. I made many close friends from my involvement with UAW 2865 and AWDU, especially Anne Kelly, and Robert Wood and Kathleen Johnson. Sincere thanks to Liz Soskin, a close friend since my undergraduate days at UCSD who accompanied me on several research trips and helped me to see more of the world than just dusty library archives.

Finally, I would like to thank my family for all the generous support in this project: my cousins Margaret and Sarah who always took me out on my many trips to Swarthmore; my Uncle Matt, Aunt Terry, and Frs. Matthew and Richie; the Doheny family and the New York Maar clan; my parents Margie and Hank Maar; my sister Laura Maar; my brother and sister-in-law Michael and Kristi Maar; my cat McDreamy and the late-great Buster dog. This book is dedicated to the Maar Family and to the memory of Tom Layton (a beloved and inspirational teacher, exemplary mentor, and dear family friend).

NOTES

Introduction

1. Works that argue more overtly for a "Reagan victory school" include John Lewis Gaddis, *The United States and the End of the Cold War: Implications, Reconsiderations, Provocations* (New York: Oxford University Press, 1992); Jay Winik, *On the Brink: The Dramatic Behind the Scenes Saga of the Reagan Era and the Men and Women Who Won the Cold War* (New York: Simon and Schuster, 1996); Peter Schweizer, *Victory: The Reagan Administration's Secret Strategy That Hastened the Collapse of the Soviet Union* (New York: Atlantic Monthly Press, 1996); Peter Schweizer, *Reagan's War: The Epic Story of His Forty Year Struggle and Final Triumph over Communism* (New York: Doubleday, 2002); Richard C. Thornton, *The Reagan Revolution I: The Politics of U.S. Foreign Policy* (Victoria: Trafford, 2003); Paul Kengor, *The Crusader: Ronald Reagan and the Triumph over Communism* (New York: Regan, 2006); Steven F. Hayward, *The Age of Reagan: The Conservative Counterrevolution, 1980–1989* (New York: Crown Forum, 2009); Francis H. Marlo, *Planning Reagan's War: Conservative Strategists and America's Cold War Victory* (Dulles, VA: Potomac Books, 2012). A second subset that focuses more on Reagan's personal antinuclear instincts as the defining outcome of the Cold War includes Beth A. Fischer, *The Reagan Reversal: Foreign Policy and the End of the Cold War* (Columbia: University of Missouri Press, 1997); Paul Lettow, *Ronald Reagan and His Quest to Abolish Nuclear Weapons* (New York: Random House, 2005); Martin Anderson and Annelise Anderson, *Reagan's Secret War: The Untold Story of His Fight to Save the World from Nuclear Disaster* (New York: Three Rivers Press, 2009).

2. Archie Brown, *The Gorbachev Factor* (New York: Oxford University Press, 1996). See also Walter LaFeber, *America, Russia, and the Cold War, 1945–2002*, updated 9th ed. (Boston: McGraw-Hill, 2004); Campbell Craig and Fredrik Logevall, *America's Cold War: The Politics of Insecurity* (Cambridge, MA: Belknap Press of Harvard University Press, 2009).

3. Melvyn Leffler, *For the Soul of Mankind: The United States, the Soviet Union, and the Cold War* (New York: Hill and Wang, 2007); James Mann, *The Rebellion of Ronald Reagan: A History of the End of the Cold War* (New York: Penguin Group, 2010); James Graham Wilson, *The Triumph of Improvisation: Gorbachev's Adaptability, Reagan's Engagement, and the End of the Cold War* (Ithaca, NY: Cornell University Press, 2013). An earlier line to this argument is Don Oberdorfer, *From the Cold War to a New Era: The United States and the Soviet Union, 1983–1991*, updated ed. (Baltimore: Johns Hopkins University Press, [1991] 1998).

4. Works that support an effective Freeze movement include David Meyer, *A Winter of Discontent: The Nuclear Freeze in American Politics* (New York: Praeger, 1990); David Cortright, *Peace Works: The Citizen's Role in Ending the Cold War* (Boulder, CO: Westview Press, 1993); Lawrence S. Wittner, *The Struggle against the Bomb, Vol. 3: Towards Nuclear Abolition; a History of the Nuclear Disarmament Movement, 1971–Present* (Stanford, CA: Stanford University Press, 2003). Works arguing against the effectiveness of the Freeze movement include Adam Garfinkle, *The Politics of the Nuclear Freeze* (Philadelphia: Foreign Policy Research Institute, 1984); J. Michael Hogan, *The Nuclear Freeze Campaign: Rhetoric and Foreign Policy in the Telepolitical Age* (East Lansing: Michigan State University Press, 1994); Christian Peterson, *Ronald Reagan and Antinuclear Movements in the United States and Western Europe, 1981–1987* (Lewiston, NY: Edwin Mellin Press, 2003). More recent substantial works on the Freeze (in whole or in part) include Bradford Martin, *The Other Eighties: A Secret History of America in the Age of Reagan* (New York: Hill and Wang, 2011); Kyle Harvey, *American Anti-nuclear Activism, 1975–1990: The Challenge of Peace* (New York: Palgrave Macmillan, 2014); William M. Knoblauch, *Nuclear Freeze in a Cold War: The Reagan Administration, Cultural Activism, and the End of the Arms Race* (Amherst: University of Massachusetts Press, 2017); Paul Rubinson, *Rethinking the American Antinuclear Movement* (New York: Routledge, 2018); Natasha Zaretsky, *Radiation Nation: Three Mile Island and the Political Transformation of the 1970s* (New York: Columbia University Press, 2018).

5. J. Michael Hogan, Review of *Coalitions and Political Movements: The Lessons of the Nuclear Freeze*, ed. Thomas R. Rochon and David S. Meyer, *Rhetoric and Public Affairs* 2, no. 1 (Spring 1999): 156–159.

6. Noam Chomsky, *Turning the Tide: US Intervention in Latin America and the Struggle for Peace* (Boston: South End Press, 1985), 178. Chomsky further criticized the antinuclear and disarmament movements for missing the larger Cold War structures that plagued the third world in the present: "For the peasants of Guatemala, or the people of Afghanistan or Timor, the effects of nuclear bombardment are of secondary matter . . . since they are already suffering something similar." See Letter, Noam Chomsky to Beverly Woodward (International Seminars on Training for Nonviolent Actions), circa December 1981, National Nuclear Weapons Freeze Campaign Records, box 1, folder 25, Thomas Jefferson Library, Western Manuscript Collection, University of Missouri, St. Louis (hereafter UMSL).

7. Thomas Bailey, *The Man in the Street: The Impact of Public Opinion on Foreign Policy* (New York: MacMillan, 1948), 1.

8. See Richard Perlstein, *Nixonland: The Rise of a President and the Fracturing of America* (New York: Scribner, 2008), 418–421. Historian and diplomat George Kennan likewise dismissed public opinion as a "poor and inadequate guide for national action." See George Kennan, *American Diplomacy*, expanded ed. (Chicago: University of Chicago Press, [1951] 1984), 99–100.

9. David S. Meyer, "How Social Movements Matter," *Contexts* 2, no. 4 (Fall 2003): 31.

10. Paul Boyer, *By the Bomb's Early Light: American Thought and Culture at the Dawn of the Atomic Age* (Chapel Hill: University of North Carolina Press, 1985), 183.

11. Milton S. Katz, *Ban the Bomb: A History of SANE, the Committee for a Sane Nuclear Policy, 1957–1985* (New York: Greenwood Press, 1986), 2–5; Lawrence S. Wittner, *The Struggle against the Bomb, Vol.1: One World or None; a History of the World Nuclear Disarmament Movement through 1953* (Stanford, CA: Stanford University Press, 1992), 66.

12. Wittner, *One World or None*, 61; FAS, "Survival Is at Stake," in *One World or None: A Reporting to the Public on the Full Meaning of the Atomic Bomb*, ed. Dexter Mathers and Katherine Way (New York: New Press, 2007), 218.

13. Boyer, *By the Bomb's Early Light*, 62.

14. Wittner, *One World or None*, 251.

15. Wittner, *One World or None*, 253.

16. Katz, *Ban the Bomb*, 15–16.

17. Thomas Judt, *Greening the Red, White, and Blue: The Bomb, Big Business, and Consumer Resistance in Postwar America* (New York: Oxford University Press, 2014), 77; Jeffrey W. Knopf, *Domestic Society and International Cooperation: The Impact of Protest on US Arms Control Policy* (New York: Cambridge University Press, 1998), 113.

18. Katz, *Ban the Bomb*, 1.

19. Katz, *Ban the Bomb*, 24.

20. Katz, *Ban the Bomb*, 39–44.

21. Marian Mollin, *Radical Pacifism in Modern America: Egalitarianism and Protest* (Philadelphia: University of Pennsylvania Press, 2006), 73–74, 83.

22. Katz, *Ban the Bomb*, 49–64. SDS would later advocate nuclear disarmament over arms control and deterrence in its famous Port Huron Statement.

23. Katz, *Ban the Bomb*, 65–66, 70; John F. Kennedy, Address to the United Nations General Assembly, September 25, 1961, transcript at https://www.jfklibrary.org/Asset-Viewer/DOPIN64xJUGRKgdHJ9NfgQ.aspx.

24. Katz, *Ban the Bomb*, 77–80. The Kennedy administration also privately agreed to remove missiles from Turkey at a later date.

25. Allen Pietroban, "The Role of Norman Cousins and Track II Diplomacy in the Breakthrough to the 1963 Limited Test Ban Treaty," *Journal of Cold War Studies* 18, no. 1 (Winter 2016): 63–73.

26. Pietroban, "Norman Cousins and Track II Diplomacy," 74–77.

27. Paul Boyer, "From Activism to Apathy: The American People and Nuclear Weapons, 1963–1980," *Journal of American History* 70, no. 4 (March 1984): 821–844.

28. Walter LaFeber, *The Deadly Bet: LBJ, Vietnam, and the 1968 Election* (Lanham, MD: Rowman and Littlefield, 2005), 131–133; Larry Berman, *No Peace, No Honor: Nixon, Kissinger, and Betrayal in Vietnam* (New York: Free Press, 2001), 32–35.

29. Thomas A. Halstead, "Lobbying against the ABM, 1967–1970," *Bulletin of the Atomic Scientists* 27, no. 4 (April 1971): 23–28.

30. "A Numb Society: The Real Threat," *SANE World* 8 no. 6 (June 1969): 1; Ernest J. Yanarella, *The Missile Defense Controversy: Technology in Search of a Mission*, revised and updated ed. (Lexington: University Press of Kentucky, 2010), 147. For a larger discussion on Nixon, domestic politics, and arms control, see Henry R. Maar III, "Subtraction by Addition: The Nixon Administration and the Domestic Politics of Arms Control," in *The Cold War at Home and Abroad: Domestic Politics and US Foreign Policy since 1945*, ed. Andrew L. Johns and Mitchell B. Lerner (Lexington: University Press of Kentucky, 2018), 123–145.

31. Conversation between Richard Nixon and Henry Kissinger, March 16, 1971, in Douglas Brinkley and Luke A. Nichter, eds., *The Nixon Tapes, 1971–1972* (New York: Houghton Mifflin Harcourt, 2014), 44.

32. Conversation between Richard Nixon, Bob Haldeman, and Henry Kissinger, April 23, 1971, in Brinkley and Nichter, eds., *The Nixon Tapes, 1971–1972*, 99.

33. Conversation between Richard Nixon, Bob Haldeman, and Henry Kissinger, April 17, 1971, in Brinkley and Nichter, eds., *The Nixon Tapes, 1971–1972,* 76.

34. Richard Smoke, *National Security and the Nuclear Dilemma: An Introduction to the American Experience* (Reading, MA: Addison-Wesley, 1984), 153.

35. Nina Tannenwald, *The Nuclear Taboo: The United States and the Non-use of Nuclear Weapons since 1945* (Cambridge: Cambridge University Press, 2007), esp. 241–293.

Chapter 1. The Lost Years

1. This chapter appeared in an earlier form in Henry Richard Maar III, "The Lost Years: The American Peace Movement from Vietnam to Nuclear Freeze," *Peace and Change* 44, no. 3 (July 2019): 386–411.

2. William Appleman Williams, *Empire as a Way of Life* (New York: Oxford University Press, 1980; reprint (Brooklyn: IG Publishing, 2007), 6.

3. David Cortright interview by Lawrence Wittner, June 29, 1987 (transcript in author's possession).

4. Charles Chatfield with Robert Kleidman, *The American Peace Movement: Ideals and Activism* (New York: Twayne, 1992), 148–150.

5. Meyer, *A Winter of Discontent,* 147.

6. Nick Kotz, *Wild Blue Yonder: Money, Politics, and the B-1 Bomber* (Princeton, NJ: Princeton University Press, 1988), 93.

7. Kotz, *Wild Blue Yonder,* 91–97.

8. Kotz, *Wild Blue Yonder,* 110–120; Pam Solo, *From Protest to Policy: Beyond the Freeze to Common Security* (Cambridge: Ballinger, 1988), 29–30; "Supersonic Swing-wing Swindle," e-mail from Terry Provance to the author, November 9, 2020.

9. "What Is Peace Conversion? [draft]," February 7, 1974. Clergy and Laity Concerned, DG 120, box 227, series III, Swarthmore College Peace Collection (hereafter SCPC).

10. "What Is Peace Conversion? [draft]," February 7, 1974; *Stop the B-1 Bomber / National Peace Conversion Campaign Newsletter,* no. 3, February 1974, Clergy and Laity Concerned, DG 120, box 227, series III, SCPC.

11. Kotz, *Wild Blue Yonder,* 141–142; *Stop the B-1 Bomber / National Peace Conversion Campaign Newsletter,* no. 1, November 1973, Clergy and Laity Concerned, DG 120, box 227, series III, SCPC.

12. This is only a partial list of activists involved in organizing for the Stop the B-1 / National Peace Conversion Campaign. Names were found on documents within the CALC papers at Swarthmore College. Biographical details were found in various obituaries and on websites. See Terry Provance interview by Lawrence Wittner, July 20, 1999 (transcript in author's possession). Provance would later become a founding member of the Freeze campaign and chairperson for the Nuclear Freeze International Task Force. Additional biographical details for Provance are from "Nuclear Disarmament Speaker, Terry Provance," NWFC Records, box 8, folder 245, UMSL; Tom Hayden, *Hell No: The Forgotten Power of the Vietnam Peace Movement* (New Haven, CT: Yale University Press, 2017), 2.

13. Provance interview by Wittner, July 20, 1999.

14. Minutes of the Joint National Coordinating Committee, May 20, 1974; *Stop the B-1 Bomber / National Peace Conversion Campaign Newsletter*, no. 4, March 1974, Clergy and Laity Concerned, DG 120, box 227, series III, SCPC.

15. Minutes of the Joint National Coordinating Committee, May 20, 1974; *Stop the B-1 Bomber / National Peace Conversion Campaign Newsletter*, no. 5, April 1974; AFSCME flyer, Clergy and Laity Concerned, DG 120, box 227, series III, SCPC.

16. Stefan Ostrich, "Labor: The B-1's First Victim," *The Nation* 222, no. 22 (June 5, 1976), Clergy and Laity Concerned, DG 120, box 227, series III, SCPC.

17. Minutes of Meeting of Concerned Organizations to Discuss Strategy to Defeat B-1 Weapons System, March 4, 1975, Clergy and Laity Concerned, DG 120, box 227, series III, SCPC.

18. Kotz, *Wild Blue Yonder*, 145.

19. John W. Finney, "House Approves Funds for Production of $21 Billion B-1 Bomber," *New York Times*, April 9, 1976, 12; Stop the B-1 Bomber / National Peace Conversion Campaign, news release, April 1976, Clergy and Laity Concerned, DG 120, box 227, series III, SCPC.

20. Minutes, B-1 Staff Meeting, April 14, 1976, Clergy and Laity Concerned, DG 120, box 227, series III, SCPC. Emphasis in original. Although the minutes attribute "bringing the war home" to Terry Provance, according to Provance, the phrase was likely inserted by Jamie Lewontin to represent Provance's words, per e-mail from Terry Provance to the author, November 5, 2020.

21. Minutes, 1976 Stop the B-1 Bomber /National Peace Conversion Campaign Conference, June 29–July 1, Clergy and Laity Concerned, DG 120, box 227, series III, SCPC.

22. Minutes, 1976 Stop the B-1 Bomber / National Peace Conversion Campaign Conference, June 29–July 1, Clergy and Laity Concerned, DG 120, box 227, series III, SCPC.

23. Barry R. Schneider, "Is the B-1 Still Flying or Was It Shot Down This Summer?," *Bulletin of the Atomic Scientists* 32, no. 8 (October 1976): 7; Kotz, *Wild Blue Yonder*, 139–144. Jackson was often mocked as the "Senator from Boeing" because of his extensive support for defense systems.

24. Cortright interview by Wittner, June 29, 1987; Wittner, *Towards Nuclear Abolition*, 28; "SANE Message at Inaugural," *SANE World* 16, no. 2 (February 1977): 1; e-mail, Terry Provance to the author, November 9, 2020.

25. Laura Kalman, *Right Star Rising: A New Politics, 1974–1980* (New York: W. W. Norton, 2010), 178; "Carter Urges Freeze on New A-Weapons," *Los Angeles Times*, October 15, 1976, A5, 12–13.

26. Letter, President Carter to Soviet general secretary Brezhnev, January 26, 1977, in *Foreign Relations of the United States, 1977–1980: Volume VI, Soviet Union*, ed. Melissa Jane Taylor (Washington, DC: US Government Printing Office, 2013), 1–3; "The Carter Watch (I): The Appointments," *SANE World* 16, no. 3 (March 1977): 1–4.

27. Paul C. Warnke, "Apes on a Treadmill," *Foreign Policy*, Spring 1975, 12–29; "The Warnke Nomination: Dress Rehearsal for SALT II, *SANE World* 16, no. 4 (April 1977): 1, 3; J. Peter Scoblic, *U.S. vs. Them: How a Half Century of Conservatism Has Undermined America's Security* (New York: Viking, 2008), 101–104.

28. Paul H. Nitze with Ann M. Smith and Steven L. Rearden, *From Hiroshima to Glasnost: At the Center of Decision—a Memoir* (New York: Grove Weidenfeld, 1989), 355; "The Warnke Nomination," 1, 3; Scoblic, *U.S. vs. Them*, 101–104; "The Carter Watch (I)," 2. Nitze further privately questioned Warnke's knowledge of military affairs and his capabilities as a negotiator while urging the Senate to reject him for both appointments. See letter, Paul Nitze to John Sparkman, February 7, 1977, Papers of Paul H. Nitze, box 64, folder 2, Manuscripts Division, Library of Congress (hereafter LOC).

29. "The Warnke Nomination," 3.

30. "Carter Watch II: Tentative First Hundred Days," *SANE World* 16, no. 5 (May 1977): 1; Christopher S. Wren, "In Moscow, Harsh Words," *New York Times*, April 1, 1977, 45; Bernard T. Feld, "Let's Not Panic Prematurely," *Bulletin of the Atomic Scientists* 33, no. 5 (May 1977): 8–9; Raymond L. Garthoff, *Détente and Confrontation: American-Soviet Relations from Nixon to Reagan*, revised ed. (Washington, DC: Brookings Institution Press, 1994), 626–627; Kalman, *Right Star Rising*, 281.

31. Mary McGrory, "Payday for Peace Workers," *New York Post*, March 8, 1977, in Nitze Papers, box 64, folder 2, LOC.

32. Letter, Jeanne Kaylor and Rick Boardman (CALC) to Opponents of the B-1 Bomber, May 1977; letter, Jeanne Kaylor to "Stop the B-1" supporters, Clergy and Laity Concerned, DG 120, box 227, series III, SCPC.

33. Letter, Jeanne Kaylor to "Stop the B-1" supporters, Clergy and Laity Concerned, DG 120, box 227, series III, SCPC; e-mail from Terry Provance to the author, November 6, 2020.

34. Kotz, *Wild Blue Yonder*, 171–172; Provance interview by Wittner, July 20, 1999; letter, National Campaign to Stop the B-1 Bomber to friends, December 20, 1977, Clergy and Laity Concerned, DG 120, box 227, series III, SCPC.

35. Len Ackland, *Making a Real Killing: Rocky Flats and the Nuclear West*, updated ed. (Albuquerque: University of New Mexico Press, 1999), 170; Solo, *From Protest to Policy*, 30–31.

36. Sidney Lens, *Unrepentant Radical: An American Activist's Account of Five Turbulent Decades* (Boston: Beacon Press, 1980), 401–402; Wittner, *Towards Nuclear Abolition*, 30. Although peace activist David Dellinger cofounded MFS, he did not have a prominent leadership role. With leftist publications folding in the mid-1970s, Dellinger preferred spending time on his new biweekly magazine, *Seven Days*. See Andrew E. Hunt, *David Dellinger: The Life and Times of a Nonviolent Revolutionary* (New York: New York University Press, 2006), 252.

37. Solo, *From Protest to Policy*, 31–32; "Task Force Meeting, Nuclear Transportation Project," July 22–23, 1978, TAM 127, box 1, "American Friends Service Committee," Tamiment Library and Robert F. Wagner Archives, New York University (hereafter Tamiment). For a wider discussion on the actions at the 1979 UN Special Session on Disarmament, see Vincent J. Intondi, *African Americans and the Bomb: Nuclear Weapons, Colonialism, and the Black Freedom Movement* (Stanford, CA: Stanford University Press, 2015,) 90–92.

38. Solo, *From Protest to Policy*, 32–33, 191fn2; Harvey, *American Anti-nuclear Activism*, 17.

39. Associated Press, "Trident Foes to Continue," *Spokane Daily Chronicle*, May 23, 1978, 6; Associated Press, "Protest Hits Trident Base," *Spokane Daily Chronicle*, October 29, 1979, 6; Associated Press, "Police Arrest Nuke Protesters by Busload," *Gadsden*

Times, October 30, 1979, 7; Associated Press, "Connecticut Protests," *New York Times*, October 30, 1979, D5; Dorothy Nelkin, "Anti-nuclear Connections: Power and Weapons," *Bulletin of the Atomic Scientists* 37, no. 4 (April 1981): 38–40.

40. Francis Farley, quoted in Cortright, *Peace Works*, 134; John Edwards, *Superweapon: The Making of MX* (New York: W. W. Norton, 1982), 207, 209, 211–212.

41. Kalman, *Right Star Rising*, 318–319; "Human Security Program Update," CALC, April 12, 1979, TAM 127, box 1, "CALC: Clergy and Laity Concerned," Tamiment.

42. Nick Lewer, *Physicians and the Peace Movement: Prescriptions for Hope* (New York: Routledge, 1992), 74.

43. Helen Caldicott, *A Desperate Passion: An Autobiography* (New York: W. W. Norton, 1997), 171–172; Helen Caldicott interview by Lawrence Wittner, February 27, 1999 (transcript in author's possession).

44. Patricia McCullough, "How the Freeze Campaign's Unifying Idea Empowered Us," *Peace Action: Past, Present, Future*, ed. Glen Harold Strassen and Lawrence S. Wittner (Boulder, CO: Paradigm Publishers, 2007), 60; Solo, *From Protest to Policy*, 33–34, 43.

45. Randall Forsberg interview by Lawrence Wittner, July 7, 1999 (transcript in author's possession); Carol Slacker, "A Fighter for Arms Control," *Boston Globe*, November 6, 1981, 62, 64.

46. Caldicott interview by Wittner, February 27, 1999; Forsberg interview by Wittner, July 7, 1999. For arguments in favor of unilateral disarmament, see Alfred Bingham, "A Case for Unilateral Disarmament," *SANE World* 19, no. 12 (December 1980): 2–3.

47. Forsberg interview by Wittner, February 27, 1999; McCullough, "How the Freeze Campaign's Unifying Idea Empowered Us," 60; e-mail, Bob Moore to the author, November 12, 2020.

48. Randall Forsberg, "Call to Halt the Nuclear Arms Race—Proposal for a Mutual U.S.-Soviet Nuclear-Weapon Freeze," reprinted in *The Nuclear Predicament: A Sourcebook*, ed. Donna Gregory (New York: St. Martin's Press, 1986), 259–265.

49. Meyer, *A Winter of Discontent*, 160; Solo, *From Protest to Policy*, 46.

50. Meyer, *A Winter of Discontent*, 158–159; Richard J. Barnet, "America and Russia: The Rules of the Game; U.S.-Soviet Relations: The Need for a Comprehensive Approach," *Foreign Affairs* 57, no. 4 (Spring 1979): 779–795.

51. "Declaration on the Arms Race," December 20, 1977, in Owen Chamberlain Papers, "Committee of Concerned Scientists," BANC MSS 2002/345 Z15, Bancroft Library, University of California, Berkeley (hereafter BANC). Emphasis in original. The list of signees included prominent physicists such as Hans Bethe and Owen Chamberlain, politicians such as Eugene McCarthy, former presidential science advisers James R. Killion Jr. and Jerome Weisner, and numerous economists, biologists, and former members of ACDA.

52. Solo, *From Protest to Policy*, 44–45.

53. CALC memo, June 4, 1980, MFS, TAM 127, box 1, "CALC: Clergy and Laity Concerned," Tamiment.

54. Solo, *From Protest to Policy*, 47.

55. Ted Glick, "People's Alliance Coordinator's Update," 4–5, February 22, 1980, Leslie Cagan Papers, TAM 138, box 3, "Coalition for a People's Alternative, formation of, founding conference, Youngstown, OH, 1980," Tamiment; "Survival Summer," *CALC Report* 6, no. 4 (June 1980): 12, MFS, TAM 127, box 1, "CALC: Clergy and Laity Concerned," Tamiment; e-mail, Moore to the author, November 12, 2020.

56. Virginia Witt, "Exit Warnke, Enter Seignious," *SANE World* 18, no. 1 (January 1979): 1; "Testimony of David Cortright Before the Senate Foreign Relations Committee Hearings on the Appointment of Gen. George M. Seignious II as Director of ACDA," January 26, 1979, SANE Records, National Office (DG 58), box 18, series G, SCPC.

57. Smoke, *National Security and the Nuclear Dilemma*, 168–169.

58. Smoke, *National Security and the Nuclear Dilemma*, 188–191; Frank Brodhead and Mark Niedergang, "60,000 in Germany Rally against NATO Missiles as Disarmament Movement Grows," *Freeze Newsletter* 1, no. 2 (July 1981): 7.

59. Vladislav M. Zubok, *A Failed Empire: The Soviet Union in the Cold War from Stalin to Gorbachev* (Chapel Hill: University of North Carolina Press, 2007), 260–263.

60. Presidential Directive 59, "Nuclear Weapons Employment Policy," http://www.fas.org/irp/offdocs/pd/pd59.pdf, accessed August 16, 2017.

61. Anthony Austin, "Soviet Calls the U.S. Strategy Shift on Nuclear War an 'Ominous' Sign," *New York Times*, August 8, 1980, A6; Mike Mawby, "SANE Condemns Nuclear War Policy and MX Missile," August 7, 1980, SANE Records (DG 58), box 64, series G, Files of D. Cortright, SCPC; News release, Federation of American Scientists, "PD-59: An Evolutionary Step Backwards," August 20, 1980, SANE Records (DG 58), box 64, series G, Files of D. Cortright, SCPC; Oswald Johnston, "'New' U.S. Nuclear Policy: Just a Footnote in Politics?," *Los Angeles Times*, September 10, 1980, B1, B10–11.

62. Bernard T. Feld, "The Hands Move Closer to Midnight," *Bulletin of the Atomic Scientists* 36, no. 1 (January 1980): 1–3; David Cortright, "Moving Closer to Midnight," *SANE World* 19, no. 2 (February 1980): 1.

63. Timothy Stanley, *Kennedy vs. Carter: The 1980 Battle for the Democratic Party's Soul* (Lawrence: University of Kansas Press, 2010), 124–125.

64. Richard Bergholz, "Carter Hits Reagan Fantasy," *Los Angeles Times*, August 15, 1980, 1, 15.

65. Richard Wirthlin interview by Larry Wittner, October 6, 1999 (transcript in author's possession).

66. Timothy D. Schellhardt, "Carter Strikes Hard at Reagan, by Name, Claiming Nuclear Arms Race Threatened," *Wall Street Journal*, September 3, 1980, 4; Edward Walsh, "Carter to Return to the 'Peace or War' Issue," *Washington Post*, September 28, 1980, A2.

67. Martin Schram, "War or Peace, an Issue Reagan Created," *Washington Post*, October 19, 1980, A1, A7; Steven R. Weismann, "Carter Assails Reagan over Arms Control," *New York Times*, October 3, 1980, A19; Richard E. Meyer, "Bush Charges He Was Misquoted," *Los Angeles Times*, September 11, 1980, 11; Robert Scheer, *With Enough Shovels: Reagan, Bush, and Nuclear War* (New York: Random House, 1982), 29.

68. Kalman, *Right Star Rising*, 360; Beth Baker, "A Sane View of the 1980 Election," *SANE World* 19, no. 10 (October 1980): 2; Coleman McCarthy, "War and Peace on the Campaign Trail," *Washington Post*, October 5, 1980, H7.

69. "The Political War over Peace," *New York Times*, September 28, 1980, E20; Kalman, *Right Star Rising*, 362.

70. Eugene Rostow, "Remarks at the Annual Dinner of the Board Members of the Committee on the Present Danger," November 6, 1980, Committee on the Present

Danger Records, box 337, Hoover Institution Archives, Stanford University, Palo Alto, CA (hereafter HIA).

71. Jon Margolis, "Reagan Plays It Safe in the Northeast," *Chicago Tribune*, October 2, 1980, 2; Eleanor Randolph, "Reagan Rally in Northridge Draws Backers, Hecklers," *Los Angeles Times*, October 11, 1980, C3; Steve Neal, "Reagan Proposes SALT III, Rebuts 'Warmaker' Charge," *Chicago Tribune*, October 20, 1980, 8; Stanley, *Kennedy vs. Carter*, 189.

72. Sharon Erickson Nepstad, *Religion and War Resistance in the Plowshares Movement* (New York: Cambridge University Press, 2008), 31–33.

73. Richard Severo, "Scientists Say Nuclear Blast in City Would Kill 2 Million," *New York Times*, September 27, 1980, 27; Associated Press, "Medical Group Expects Nuclear War in 20 Years," *Washington Post*, September 28, 1980, A8; Seymour Melman, "No Time for Retreat," *SANE World* 19, no. 12 (December 1980): 1–2.

74. David A. Schmidt, *Citizen Lawmakers: The Ballot Initiative Revolution* (Philadelphia: Temple University Press, 1989), 159–160.

75. Schmidt, *Citizen Lawmakers*, 160; "Arms Race Referendum," *SANE World* 20, no. 1 (January 1981): 3.

Chapter 2. Igniting a Movement

1. On the Team B report, see, among others, Scoblic, *U.S. vs. Them*, 92–98.

2. Bernard T. Feld, "The Hands Move Closer to Midnight," *Bulletin of the Atomic Scientists* 7, no. 1 (January 1981): 1; Paul V. Valentine, "Groups to Protest against Reagan," *Washington Post*, January 18, 1981, B1, B4.

3. Gergen quoted in Knopf, *Domestic Society and International Cooperation*, 205. Several studies pointing out the folly of conflating defense spending with job creation are listed in Colman McCarthy, "Haig, He's Wrong for the Job," *The Bulletin* [Bend, Oregon, daily], January 26, 1981, 6; and "Pentagon Budget Cuts Jobs," *SANE World* 14, no. 5 (May 1975): 1.

4. David Stockman, *The Triumph of Politics: Why the Reagan Revolution Failed* (New York: Harper and Row, 1986), 290–291; Meyer, *A Winter of Discontent*, 53–54.

5. George C. Wilson, "Weinberger Calls for Even Bigger Buildup," *Washington Post*, July 19, 1981, A5.

6. Michael Sherry, *In the Shadow of War: The United States since the 1930s* (New Haven, CT: Yale University Press, 1995), 384; Don Oberdorfer, "Kennan Urges Halving of Nuclear Arsenals," *Washington Post*, May 20, 1981, A1, A14. Excerpts from Kennan's acceptance speech were printed as editorials in the nation's major newspapers.

7. Michelle Stone and Beth Baker, "Who's Behind the New Cold War? The Same Old Faces," *SANE World* 20, no. 2 (February 1981): 1–2. The ASCF later moved its headquarters to Washington, D.C.

8. Scoblic, *U.S. vs. Them*, 72–73; ASCF details in Interchange, "Anti-Freeze File, Report no. 2, Coalition for Peace through Strength," January 20, 1983, NWFC Records, box 5, folder 140, UMSL.

9. Stone and Baker, "Who's Behind the New Cold War?," 1–2.

10. Ronald Powaski, *Return to Armageddon: The United States and the Nuclear Arms Race, 1981–1999* (New York: Oxford University Press, 2000), 15.

11. Scheer, *With Enough Shovels*, 40.

12. The list of CPD members within the Reagan administration would include Secretary of State George Shultz and ACDA director Ken Adelman. See Scheer, *With Enough Shovels*, 39–43, and 145–146, fn 1; Colin S. Gray and Keith Payne, "Victory Is Possible," *Foreign Policy*, no. 39 (Summer 1980): 14–27.

13. Thornton, *The Reagan Revolution I*, 56–58; "Introducing Our New Secretary of State," *SANE World* 20, no. 18 (February 1981): 3; Scheer, *With Enough Shovels*, 90.

14. "The President's News Conference, January 29, 1981," The Public Papers of President Ronald W. Reagan, Ronald Reagan Presidential Library, Simi Valley, CA (hereafter RRPL), https://www.reaganlibrary.gov/research/speeches/12981b.htm; James Reston, "The Reagan Show," *New York Times*, February 1, 1981, E21; "Excerpts from an Interview with Walter Cronkite of CBS News, March 3, 1981," The Public Papers of President Ronald W. Reagan, RRPL, https://www.reaganlibrary.gov/research/speeches/30381c; Congressional Quarterly, *U.S. Foreign Policy: The Reagan Imprint* (Washington, DC: Congressional Quarterly, 1986), 7; George P. Shultz, *Turmoil and Triumph: My Years as Secretary of State* (New York: Charles Scribner's Sons, 1993), 4–5.

15. Strobe Talbott, *Deadly Gambits: The Reagan Administration and the Stalemate in Nuclear Arms Control* (New York: Alfred A. Knopf, 1984), 209; Meyer, *A Winter of Discontent*, 72.

16. "Brezhnev and Reagan on Atom War," *New York Times*, October 21, 1981, A5; US Embassy in Oslo to Info Secstate WashDC, USMission USNATO, AmEmbassy Bonn, AmEmbassy Copenhagen, AmEmbassy Helsinki, AmEmbassy London, AmEmbassy Reykjavik, AmEmbassy Stockholm, NSC cable, October 21, 1981, folder "NATO-meetings: Briefs in arms control," box 90556, box 9, Sven F. Kraemer Files, RRPL.

17. United States Congress, Senate Committee on Foreign Relations, *Nomination of Alexander M. Haig, Jr. Hearings Before the Committee on Foreign Relations, United States Senate, Ninety-seventh Congress, First Session, on the Nomination of Alexander M. Haig, Jr., to be Secretary of State, January 9, 10, 12, 13, 14, 15, 1981* (Washington, DC: US Government Printing Office, 1981), 70; Department of State, "Document 168, Testimony of Secretary of State Before the Senate Foreign Relations Committee, November 4, 1981 (Extract),"*American Foreign Policy Current Documents 1981* (Washington, DC: Department of State, 1981), 480; Scoblic, *U.S. vs. Them*, 126. Prior to his nomination, Haig had infamously suggested there were "more important things than peace."

18. Robert Scheer, "U.S. Could Survive War in Administration's View," *Los Angeles Times*, January 16, 1982, A1; Scheer, *With Enough Shovels*, 18–26.

19. Knopf, *Domestic Society and International Cooperation*, 209; Dan Smith, "American 'Freeze' Helping to Thaw Cold War," *END Bulletin*, no. 10, July–August 1982, 27.

20. Richard Halloran, "Pentagon Draws Up First Strategy for Fighting a Long Nuclear War," *New York Times*, May 30, 1982, 1, 12; Richard Halloran, "Weinberger Confirms New Strategy on Atom War," *New York Times*, June 4, 1982; Richard Halloran, "Weinberger Denies U.S. Plans for 'Protracted' War," *New York Times*, June 21, 1982, A5; Richard Halloran, "Weinberger Defends His Plan on a Protracted Nuclear War," *New York Times*, August 10, 1982, A8; Robert Scheer, "Pentagon Plan Aims at Winning Nuclear War," *Los Angeles Times*, August 15, 1982, 1, 12.

21. Fred Kaplan, "The Neutron Bomb: What It Is, the Way It Works," *Bulletin of the Atomic Scientists* 37, no. 8 (October 1981): 6–7; Leslie H. Gelb, "Reagan Orders Pro-

duction of 2 Types of Neutron Arms for Stockpiling in the U.S.," *New York Times*, August 9, 1981, 1; "Neutron Bomb Gets Green Light: SANE Launches Opposition Campaign," *SANE World* 8, no. 6 (September 1981): 1, 4; "Texas Catholic Bishops Reject the Neutron Bomb," *New York Times*, September 13, 1981, A37.

22. Russell Peterson et al., Letter to President Reagan Opposing MX, case file Begin-016566, ND 018, box 1, WHORM Subject File, RRPL; J. Roy Bardsley, "Utahns Support Reagan in Handling of Duties," *Salt Lake Tribune*, August 9, 1981, case file 039938 (1 of 3), ND 017 box 1, WHORM Subject File, RRPL; Daniel E. Gorski, "Changed Mind about MX? Not So," *Deseret News*, May 15–16, 1981, 4A.

23. George Raine, "Catholic Bishop Chastises MX Missile, Arms Race," *Salt Lake Tribune*, April 9, 1981, B-1, B-9; "LDS First Presidency Issues Statement on MX," *Deseret News*, May 5, 1981, 1; Associated Press, "MX Opposition Soars since LDS Statement," *Deseret News*, May 25–26, 1981, B2; David E. Campbell, John C. Green, and J. Quin Monson, *Seeking the Promised Land: Mormons and American Politics* (Cambridge: Cambridge University Press, 2014), 146–147.

24. Matt Evangelista, "Europeans Say 'No' to NATO Nuclear Weapons," *Freeze Newsletter* 1, no. 1 (March 1981): 8; Frank Brodhead and Mark Niedergang, "60,000 in Germany Rally against NATO Missiles as Disarmament Movement Grows," *Freeze Newsletter* 1, no. 2 (July 1981): 6. Italy was an outlier, seeing little opposition, as the Communist Party did not organize opposition around the Euromissiles.

25. Dan Ebner, "The Day After," Strategy Development Meeting, November 5, 1980, MFS, TAM 127, box 9, "Nuclear Freeze Campaign," Tamiment.

26. Memo, "Nuclear Freeze Campaign," Dana Naparsteck to Steering Committee Members, November 20, 1980, MFS, TAM 127, box 9, "Nuclear Freeze Campaign," Tamiment. On the Freeze campaign's failure to pay staff, see memo, Dana Naparsteck to Nuclear Freeze Steering Committee, December 5, 1980, MFS, TAM 127, box 9, "Nuclear Freeze Campaign," Tamiment.

27. Notes found in MFS, TAM 127, box 9, "Nuclear Freeze Campaign," Tamiment. Emphasis in original.

28. Dan Ebner, "Freeze: For Disarmament Activists," *The Mobilizer* 2, no. 1 (Winter 1982): 11. Emphasis in original.

29. Invitation, "US-USSR Nuclear Weapons Freeze Campaign," December 12, 1980, MFS, TAM 127, box 9, "Nuclear Freeze Campaign," Tamiment.

30. Memo, Gordon Faison and Randy Kehler to Active Participants in the Nuclear Weapon Freeze Campaign, July 22, 1981, Catholic Peace Fellowship Records, box 44, folder 13, Archives of the University of Notre Dame (hereafter AUND).

31. Alex Brummer, "N-campaigners Make for Middle America," *The Guardian*, March 24, 1982, 6; "Call for a Nuclear Weapons Freeze, USA-USSR," First Annual Freeze Conference, March 20–22, 1981, MFS, TAM 127, box 9, "Nuclear Freeze Campaign," Tamiment; "Structure Proposal for First Year of Freeze Effort," undated, box 44, folder 13, Catholic Peace Fellowship Records, AUND.

32. "Call for a Nuclear Weapons Freeze, USA-USSR," First Annual Freeze Conference, March 20–22, 1981, MFS, TAM 127, box 9, "Nuclear Freeze Campaign," Tamiment.

33. "Call for a Nuclear Weapons Freeze, USA-USSR," First Annual Freeze Conference, March 20–22, 1981, MFS, TAM 127, box 9, "Nuclear Freeze Campaign," Tamiment.

34. "Call for a Nuclear Weapons Freeze, USA-USSR," First Annual Freeze Conference, March 20–22, 1981, MFS, TAM 127, box 9, "Nuclear Freeze Campaign," Tamiment.

35. "April 25th Actions Protest Nuclear Arms Race," *Freeze Newsletter* 1, no. 2 (July 1981): 11; Robert E. Tomasson, "Corpus Christi Launched in Groton as 1,000 Protest Sub and Its Name," *New York Times*, April 26, 1981, 44.

36. "Petitioning Campaigns Take Off," *National Freeze Campaign Monthly Update*, June 1981.

37. "Freeze Wins in Mass., Oregon Legislatures; NY State Assembly," *Freeze Newsletter* 1, no. 2 (July 1981): 1.

38. "Freeze Wins in Mass., Oregon Legislatures; NY State Assembly," 12.

39. Memo, Gordon Faison and Randy Kehler (Trappock Peace Center) to Active Participants in the Nuclear Weapons Freeze Campaign, July 22, 1981, Catholic Peace Fellowship Records, box 44, folder 13, AUND.

40. "Endorsers of a Bilateral Nuclear-Weapon Freeze," listed under the "Call to Halt the Nuclear Arms Race," MFS, TAM 127, box 9, "Nuclear Freeze Campaign," Tamiment.

41. Wittner, *Towards Nuclear Abolition*, 102; Lee Lescaze, "Reagan Still Sure Some in New Deal Espoused Fascism," *Washington Post*, December 24, 1981, A7.

42. David Gergen interview by David Cortright, October 8, 1990, David Cortright Papers (DG 101), box 2, SCPC; Alexander M. Haig Jr., *Caveat: Realism, Reagan, and Foreign Policy* (New York: Macmillan, 1984), 229.

43. Minutes from cabinet meeting, in Anderson and Anderson, *Reagan's Secret War*, 65–67.

44. Anderson and Anderson, *Reagan's Secret War*, 65–71; Haig, *Caveat*, 229.

45. Goodby quoted in Knopf, *Domestic Society and International Cooperation*, 229–230.

46. The distinction between a "medium" and a "heavy" missile is based on a missile's throw weight (the measure of the total weight of a missile, including its payload, reentry vehicles, guidance systems, and penetration aids). See Powaski, *Return to Armageddon*, 21–22.

47. Ronald Reagan, *An American Life* (New York: Simon and Schuster, 1990), 550; Meyer, *A Winter of Discontent*, 71; Gaddis, *The United States and the End of the Cold War*, 121–122; Robert Chesshyre, "Reagan Gives Arms Deal Headache to Shultz," *The Guardian*, January 16, 1983, 16; Strobe Talbott, "Time to START, Says Reagan," *Time* 119, no. 20 (May 17, 1982): 43; Sherry, *In the Shadow of War*, 404.

48. Robert Shogan, "Nuclear Freeze Movement Emerges as Political Test," *Los Angeles Times*, April 17, 1982, A1; "Ferocious Mr. Reagan and the Freeze," *New York Times*, March 16, 1982, A22; Barry Sussman and Robert G. Kaiser, "Survey Finds 3-to-1 Backing for A-Freeze," *Washington Post*, April 29, 1982, A1; "A New Outcry over Nukes," *Newsweek*, March 29, 1982, 18–20.

49. ABC News / *Washington Post* survey, April 21–24, 1982, Papers of Edwin Meese, box 685, HIA.

50. Harris Survey Poll no. 48, June 17, 1982, Papers of Edwin Meese, box 685, HIA; Richard Wirthlin interview by Lawrence Wittner, October 6, 1999 (transcript in author's possession); Mary McGrory, "Reagan's Latest Boost for a Nuclear Freeze," *Washington Post*, April 4, 1982, C1.

51. Robert Shogan, "Nuclear Freeze Movement Emerges as Political Test," *Los Angeles Times*, April 17, 1982, A1, 9–10; Jeremy J. Stone and Herbert F. York, "The Freeze

Is Not a Joke," *Washington Post*, March 19, 1982, A23; James J. Kilpatrick, "Where Are the Conservatives on the Nuclear Danger?," *Los Angeles Times*, March 22, 1982, C5.

52. George F. Will, "A Nuclear Freeze Would Leave America in the Cold," *Los Angeles Times*, March 18, 1982, F11; David H. Petraeus, "What Is Wrong with a Nuclear Freeze?," *Military Review*, November 1983, 49–64, Committee on the Present Danger Records, box 30, HIA.

53. "The Answer to Freeze Is SALT," *New York Times*, March 21, 1982, E20.

54. Krauthammer's *New Republic* article quoted in Robert D. Benford and Scott A. Hunt, "Intersectional Dynamics in Public Problems Marketplaces," in, *Challenges and Choices: Constructionist Perspectives on Social Problems*, ed. James Holstein and Gale Mille (New York: Walter de Gruyter, 2003), 165; Charles Krauthammer, *Things That Matter: Three Decades of Passions, Past Times, and Politics* (New York: Crown Books, 2010), 13.

55. Barack Obama, "Breaking the War Mentality," *Sun Dial*, March 10, 1983, 2–5.

56. All quotations in Boris Aldonov, *The Human Predicament: The Secular Ideologies, Volume 1* (New Delhi: Vikas, 1988), 23.

57. Letter, Rod Morris to Randy Kehler and Randall Forsberg, March 15, 1982, and *Nightline* transcript, March 10, 1982, in NWFC Records, box 1, folder 8, UMSL.

58. Howell Rainess, "Reagan Again Asks to Meet Brezhnev," *New York Times*, April 21, 1982, A7; Knopf, *Domestic Society and International Cooperation*, 228–229.

59. "Reagan Sympathetic to Nuclear Demonstrators," *Los Angeles Times*, April 21, 1982, B11. Memo, Diana Lozano to Elizabeth H. Dole, April 13, 1982, folder "Nuclear Freeze (Jan.–June) (1982) [2 of 3]," series I, Subject Files 1981–1983, box 26, OA 6390, Elizabeth H. Dole Files, RRPL.

60. Judith Miller, "Opinions Are Mixed on Antinuclear Drive's Impact," *New York Times*, April 25, 1982, B10; memo, William Clark to the Secretary of State, the Secretary of Defense, the Director, Arms Control and Disarmament Agency, the Director, International Communication Agency, April 26, 1982, and memo, William Clark to James A. Baker III, April 26, 1982, both in folder "Nuclear [Freeze] [1 of 8]," series 3, Daily Files, box 4, OA1529, David Gergen Files, RRPL.

61. Memo, William Clark to Edwin Meese III, James A. Baker III, and Michael Deaver, April 22, 1982, folder "Nuclear [Freeze] [1 of 8]," Series OA1529, box 4, David Gergen Files, RRPL.

62. Memo, Red Cavaney to Michael Deaver, April 16, 1982, "Nuclear Freeze (Jan.–June) (1982) [1 of 3]," series I, Subject Files 1981–1983, OA9421, 9422, box 26, Elizabeth H. Dole Files, RRPL.

63. Memo, David Gergen to William P. Clark and Jim Baker, March 30, 1982, "Nuclear Freeze/Nuclear Policy (1)," RAC box 12, box 3, John Poindexter Files, RRPL; memo, James Cicconi, March 30, 1982, folder "Nuclear [Freeze] [3 of 8]," series II, Subject File OA 9421, 9422, box 7, David Gergen Files, RRPL.

64. Memo, David Gergen to Jim Baker, May 28, 1982, folder "Nuclear [Freeze] [4 of 8]," series 3, Daily Files, OA 10529, box 4, David Gergen Files, RRPL; Robert C. McFarlane with Zofia Smardz, *Special Trust* (New York: Cadell and Davies, 1994), 198.

65. Memo, Cavaney to Deaver, April 16, 1982, RRPL.

66. Judith Miller, "72% in Poll Back Nuclear Halt If Soviet Union Doesn't Gain," *New York Times*, May 30, 1982, 1–22; "Will the Real Freeze Please Stand Up?," *National Review* 34, no. 12 (June 25, 1982): 741; Judith Miller, "Despite Foes and Skeptics, Administration Presses Ahead on Civil Defense," *New York Times*, June 10, 1982, B20.

67. Clyde Sanger, "MPs Call for an Immediate Freeze on Nuclear Arsenals," *The Guardian*, June 7, 1982, 7; Steven R. Weismann, "Reagan, at U.N., Lectures Soviet in Arms Speech," *New York Times*, June 18, 1982, A1, A16.

68. "Rallying for Disarmament: June Actions a Major Success," *SANE World* 21, no. 7 (July–August 1982): 1; Steering Brief [Confidential], Foreign and Commonwealth Office (hereafter FCO) and Telegram Number 1978, Nicholas Henderson to Immediate FCO, "Visit by President Reagan: Briefing for the Prime Minister," June 1, 1982, FCO 82/1230, National Archives, Kew, London, United Kingdom (hereafter TNA); "Message From Europe," *END Bulletin*, no. 10, July–August 1982, 3.

69. Leslie Cagan, "June 12th: A Look Back, a Look Ahead," *The Mobilizer* 2, no. 3 (September 1982): 1, 9–10; "Media Information," June 12th Rally Committee, MFS, TAM 127, box 9, "Nuclear Freeze Campaign," Tamiment; "Puerto Ricans Rally for Disarmament," *Daily World*, June 5, 1982, 10.

70. Cagan, "June 12th," 1, 9–10.

71. "Rallying for Disarmament: June Actions a Major Success," *SANE World* 21, no. 7 (July–August 1982): 1; Cagan, "June 12th," 1, 9–10.

72. "Rally program" and press release, Dentures Art Club, "Thousands to Participate in Disarmament Rally Balloon Release June 12th in Central Park," June 11, 1982, MFS, TAM 127, box 9, "Nuclear Freeze Campaign," Tamiment.

Chapter 3. From the Streets to the Pulpit

1. Robert Sims interview by David Cortright, December 21, 1990, David Cortright Papers (DG 101), box 2, SCPC.

2. John Tracy Ellis, "American Catholics and Peace: A Historical Sketch," reprinted in James S. Rausch, ed., *The Family of Nations: An Expanded View of Patriotism; a New Dedication to Humanity* (Huntington, IN: Our Sunday Visitor, 1970), 17; Giuseppe Alberigo, *A Brief History of Vatican II*, trans. Matthew Sherry (Maryknoll, NY: Orbis Books, 2006), 112.

3. James Hitchcock, "A Single Issue," *National Catholic Register*, December 5, 1982, folder "Nuclear Freeze [3 of 10]," Series I Subject File OA 9079, box 8, Morton Blackwell Files, RRPL.

4. All numbers come from an internal memo from within the Reagan administration: memo, Elizabeth Dole to Edwin Meese III, James A. Baker III, Michael Deaver, undated, folder "Catholic Strategy [1 of 3]," Series II Subject File OA 1241, box 2, Robert Reilly Files, RRPL. Of Carter's 11 percent drop, 5 percent went to Reagan, while the other 6 percent went to independent candidate John B. Anderson.

5. Jim Castelli, "President Reagan and Catholics: Is the Love Affair Ending?," *Visitor*, November 8, 1981, 3, folder "Catholics Miscellaneous (6)," Series IV General Subject File OA 9747, box 1, Jack Burgess Files, RRPL; Thomas J. Gumbleton and Bryan J. Hehir, "Is SALT Worth Supporting?," *Commonweal*, 106, no. 4 (March 2, 1979), 105–110; "SALT Debate: Readers React," *Commonweal*, 106, no. 7 (April 13, 1979), 226.

6. Address of P. Francis Murphy, auxillary bishop of Baltimore, Maryland, at the UN Panel on "The Moral Imperative of Halting the Arms Race," United Nations, New York, June 19, 1980, found in box 2, folder 4, PAX Christi USA Records, AUND.

7. "Peace Group Urges Restoration of Friday Abstinence, Halt to Arms Race," *Vermont Catholic Tribune*, October 24, 1980, 9, in box 2, folder 4, PAX Christi USA Records,

AUND. The statement further urged the Catholic Church to restore "the Friday rule of abstinence from meat" as a symbolic sharing with the world's poor.

8. Letter, Mary Evelyn Jergen (National Coordinator, Pax Christi USA) to Randy Forsberg, January 2, 1981, box 2, folder 29, PAX Christi USA Records, AUND; "Declaration of Pax Christi International on Disarmament and Security," May 31, 1981, box 16, folder 2, PAX Christi USA Records, AUND.

9. The Reagan administration formally established diplomatic relations with the Vatican in January 1984—a move Senator Richard Lugar (R-IN) had urged the administration to undertake in order for the president to "reap political benefits with Catholic voters." Memo, Peter R. Sommer to Robert C. McFarlane, November 15, 1983, folder "Vatican 1983–1984 (3 of 3)," RAC box 7, box 5, European and Soviet Affairs Directorate: Records, RRPL.

10. Paul Kengor, "Reagan's Catholic Connections," *Catholic Exchange*, June 11, 2004, http://catholicexchange.com/reagans-catholic-connections.

11. Kenneth A. Briggs, "Religious Leaders Objecting to Nuclear Arms," *New York Times*, September 5, 1981, A1, A20; "Texas Catholic Bishops Reject the Neutron Bomb," *New York Times*, September 13, 1981, A37; Jim Castelli, *The Bishops and the Bomb: Waging Peace in a Nuclear Age* (New York: Doubleday, 1983), 58; Mike Cochran, "Bishop's Bombshell Has City Up in Arms," *Victoria Advocate*, August 8, 1982, 10B.

12. Castelli, *The Bishops and the Bomb*, 58.

13. "Catholics Get Appeal to Ban Nuclear Arms," *New York Times*, October 3, 1981, A4.

14. Statement by Roger Mahoney on the Arms Race, December 30, 1981, untitled folder, EXEC/N0930/41, Executive Records—USCCB Committee and Council Files, Cardinal Joseph Bernardin, War and Peace Papers, 1/1/1981–12/31/1983, Archdiocese of Chicago, Joseph Cardinal Bernardin Archives and Records Center, Chicago, IL(hereafter ARC).

15. Vincent A. Yzermans, "A Catholic Revolution," *New York Times*, November 14, 1981, A23; Kenneth A. Briggs, "The Bishops Take a Risk, New 'Peace' Positions Sure to Ignite Dissent," *New York Times*, November 23, 1981, B10.

16. John T. McGreevy, *Catholicism and American Freedom: A History* (New York: W. W. Norton, 2003), 284–285; Eugene Kennedy, *Bernardin: Life to the Full* (Chicago: Bonus Books, 1997), 228; James E. Dougherty, *The Bishops and Nuclear Weapons: The Catholic Pastoral Letter on War and Peace* (Hamden, CT: Archon Books, 1984), 118–119.

17. Castelli, *The Bishops and the Bomb*, 78–83; letter, Eugene Rostow to Joseph Bernardin, May 26, 1982, untitled folder, EXEC/N0930/41, Executive Records—USCCB Committee and Council Files, Cardinal Joseph Bernardin, War and Peace Papers, 1/1/1981–12/31/1983, ARC.

18. Letter, Joseph Bernardin to Father J. Bryan Hehir, March 17, 1982, "Correspondence, etc.," EXEC/N0930/41, Executive Records—USCCB Committee and Council Files, Cardinal Joseph Bernardin, War and Peace Papers, 1/1/1981–12/31/1983, ARC.

19. Memo, Thomas Patrick Melady to James A. Baker III, April 13, 1982, folder "Nuclear Freeze (January–June) (1982) [1 of 3]," Series I Subject Files OA 6390, 1981–1983, box 26, Elizabeth H. Dole Files, RRPL.

20. A. O. Sulzberger Jr., "Reagan Says Ban on Abortion May Not Be Needed," *New York Times*, March 7, 1981, A11; "Remarks at a White House Ceremony in Observance of National Day of Prayer, May 6, 1982," The Public Papers of President Ronald W.

Reagan, RRPL, https://www.reaganlibrary.gov/research/speeches/50682c; "Presidential Pen," *Time*, 121, no. 19 (May 9, 1983): 36.

21. Castelli, *The Bishops and the Bomb*, 87, 91, 99; letter, Sisters of Charity of Nazareth to Joseph Bernardin, "Correspondence, etc.," EXEC/N0930/41, Executive Records—USCCB Committee and Council Files, Cardinal Joseph Bernardin, War and Peace Papers, 1/1/1981–12/31/1983, ARC; "Morality and the Church," *Daily World*, August 10, 1982, 6.

22. Castelli, *The Bishops and the Bomb*, 95; "Message of His Holiness Pope John Paul II to the General Assembly of the United Nations," June 10, 1982, http://www.vati can.va/holy_father/john_paul_ii/speeches/1982/june/documents/hf_jp-ii_spe _19820607_disarmo-onu_en.html.

23. Letter to J. Bryan Hehir from Thomas Gumbleton, August 14, 1982, box 43, folder 1, Thomas J. Gumbleton Papers, AUND.

24. "Remarks at the Centennial Meeting of the Supreme Council of the Knights of Columbus in Hartford, Connecticut, August 3, 1982," The Public Papers of President Ronald W. Reagan, RRPL, https://www.reaganlibrary.gov/research/speeches/80382a; Steven R. Weisman, "Reagan Calls on Catholics in U.S. to Reject Nuclear Freeze Proposal," *New York Times*, August 4, 1982, A1.

25. Bruce Shapiro, "Trident Protesters Sentenced," *Nuclear Times* 1, no. 2 (November–December 1982): 12–13.

26. Letter from National Association of Catholic Bishops to Reagan administration, October 13, 1982, case file 104643–108250, ND 018, box 7, WHORM Subject File, RRPL; United Press International, "Church Stops Paying Tax in Protesting Arms Race," *Bulletin-Journal* (Cape Girardeau, MO), December 14, 1982, 3.

27. Letter, William Clark to Clare Booth Luce, July 30, 1982, folder "National Conference of Catholic Bishops," Series II Subject File OA 12419, box 3, Robert Reilly Files, RRPL.

28. Memo, Red Cavaney to Bill Triplett, October 26, 1982, folder "Nuclear Freeze (2)," Series II Subject File OA 12419, box 3, Robert Reilly Files, RRPL.

29. Richard Halloran, "Proposed Catholic Bishops' Letter Opposes First Use of Nuclear Arms," *New York Times*, October 26, 1982, A1, A22.

30. Rowland Evans and Robert Novak, "Will the Pope Stop 'Nuclear Heresy?,'" *Washington Post*, November 7, 1982, A15.

31. Kennedy, *Bernardin*, 229–230; "No Pressure, Bishops Say," *Los Angeles Times*, November 15, 1982, B2.

32. "The President's News Conference, November 11, 1982," The Public Papers of President Ronald W. Reagan, RRPL, http://www.reagan.utexas.edu/archives/spee ches/1982/111182g.htm.

33. Memo, Jack Burgess to Red Cavaney and Archbishop Phillip M. Hannan, "Table Letter on Nuclear War," *New Orleans Clarion Herald*, November 11, 1982, 6, folder "Nuclear Freeze (January–June) (1982) [2 of 3]," Series I Subject File OA 6390, 1981–1983, box 26, Elizabeth H. Dole Files, RRPL.

34. Memo, Red Cavaney to Bud McFarlane, April 30, 1982, folder "Nuclear Freeze (January–June) (1982) [1 of 3]," Series I Subject File OA 6390, 1981–1983, box 26, Elizabeth H. Dole Files, RRPL.

35. Memo, Cavaney to McFarlane, "Nuclear Freeze (January–June) (1982) [1 of 3]"; Hannan, "Table Letter on Nuclear Arms," 6. Archbishop Hannan made these same

objections to the pastoral letter in a personal letter to then archbishop Joseph Bernardin. See letter, Philip Hannan to Joseph Bernardin, July 10, 1982, untitled folder, EXEC/N0930/41, Executive Records—USCCB Committee and Council Files, Cardinal Joseph Bernardin, War and Peace Papers, 1/1/1981–12/31/1983, ARC.

36. Letter, William Clark to Archbishop Bernardin, November 16, 1982, folder "National Conference of Catholic Bishops," Series II Subject File OA 12419, box 3, Robert Reilly Files, RRPL.

37. John Lehman, "The U.S. Catholic Bishops and Nuclear Arms," *Wall Street Journal*, November 15, 1982, 28.

38. Memo, Dana Rohrabacher to William B. Clark, December 10, 1982, folder "Chron—November 1982 (McFarlane)(7)," RAC box 4, box 2, Robert C. "Bud" McFarlane Files, RRPL.

39. Letter, James Rowny to Joseph F. Fogarty Jr., January 18, 1983, and letter, Archbishop James Hickey to Joseph F. Fogarty Jr., "Correspondence, etc.," EXEC/N0930/41, Executive Records—USCCB Committee and Council Files, Cardinal Joseph Bernardin, War and Peace Papers, 1/1/1981–12/31/1983, ARC.

40. Anonymous memo to Reagan administration, December 14, 1982, folder "Nuclear Freeze (4 of 10)," box 8, OA 9079, Morton Blackwell Series I Subject File, RRPL.

41. Hitchcock, "A Single Issue."

42. Castelli, *The Bishops and the Bomb*, 108; Michael Novak, "American Bishops and Nuclear Disarmament," *Wall Street Journal*, January 14, 1982, 29; Memo, Bud McFarlane to Sven Kramer, November 12, 1982, folder "Chron—November 1982 (McFarlane) (7)," RAC box 4, box 2, Robert C. "Bud" McFarlane Files, RRPL.

43. James L. Franklin, "Politics & Religion; US Catholic Bishops Raise Nuclear Alarm," *Boston Globe*, November 14, 1982, 1.

44. "The Bishops and the Nuclear Freeze," *Phyllis Schlafly Report* 16, no. 6 (January 1983), sec. 1; letter, Kathleen Sullivan, Northern Illinois Coordinator for Eagle Forum, February 1983, "War and Peace: Correspondence," EXEC/N0930/38, Executive Records—USCCB Committee and Council Files, Cardinal Joseph Bernardin, War and Peace Papers, 1/1/1981–12/31/1983, ARC; Andrew Preston, *Sword of the Spirit, Shield of Faith: Religion in American War and Diplomacy* (New York: Alfred A. Knopf, 2012), 592–593.

45. The Lady of Fatima had reputedly promised in 1929 that if Russia were consecrated to the Immaculate Heart, many souls would be saved and the world would know peace. If, however, people continued to offend God, the Lady of Fatima forewarned that God would punish the world through famine and war, and Russia would continue to "spread her errors throughout the world, causing wars and persecutions of the Church." See Lucia dos Santos, *Fatima in Lucia's Own Words*, ed. L. Kondor, trans. the Dominican Nuns (Fatima: Postulation Center, 1975), 162.

46. Letter, Robert Harrington to Joseph Bernardin, November 16, 1982, "War and Peace, 1983, Alphabetical G–H," EXEC/N0930/38, Executive Records—USCCB Committee and Council Files, Cardinal Joseph Bernardin, War and Peace Papers, 1/1/1981–12/31/1983, ARC.

47. Letter, Frances M. Ahern to Joseph Bernardin, January 6, 1983, and Joseph Bernardin's reply, January 25, 1983, "Remarks: 1983 Cardinal Bernardin," EXEC/N0930/38, Executive Records—USCCB Committee and Council Files, Cardinal Joseph Bernardin, War and Peace Papers, 1/1/1981–12/31/1983, ARC.

48. Ann Landers, "Fervent Pleas for Peace," (undated clipping) and letter, Mrs. M. N. Ockey to Ann Landers (CC, Ronald Reagan), November 17, 1982, case file 116000–116499, ND 018, box 8, WHORM Subject File, RRPL.

49. Letter, Rev. John Khmech to Ronald Reagan, and President Reagan's reply, case file 122040–122999, ND 018, box 8, WHORM Subject File, RRPL.

50. Letter, Ronald Reagan to Ambassador Earl T. Smith, in Kiron Skinner, Martin Anderson, and Annelise Anderson, eds., *Reagan: A Life in Letters* (New York: Free Press, 2003), 392.

51. Memo, Bud McFarlane to William Clark, January 10, 1983, and memo, Bud McFarlane to Dick Boverie, January 11, 1983, folder "Chron–January 1983 (McFarlane) (2)," RAC box 5, box 2, Robert C. "Bud" McFarlane Files, RRPL.

52. "Informal Consultation on Peace and Disarmament," January 18–19, 1983, box 43, folder 7, Thomas J. Gumbleton Papers, AUND. All conference quotations are from this document unless otherwise noted.

53. Confidential memorandum, Cardinal Bernardin to Archbishop Roach, Bishop Gumbleton, Bishop Fulcher, Bishop O'Connor, Bishop Reilly, Msgr. Hoye, and Father Hehir, February 9, 1983, box 43, folder 7, Thomas J. Gumbleton Papers, AUND.

54. For details of the bishops' deliberations over "freeze," see Castelli, *The Bishops and the Bomb*, 134–149.

55. Douglas C. Waller, *Congress and the Nuclear Freeze: An Inside Look at the Politics of a Mass Movement* (Amherst: University of Massachusetts Press, 1987), 186; Castelli, *The Bishops and the Bomb*, 140; letter, Francis Ebil to Joseph Bernardin, April 6, 1983, "War and Peace Alphabetical E–F," EXEC/N0930/38, Executive Records—USCCB Committee and Council Files, Cardinal Joseph Bernardin, War and Peace Papers, 1/1/1981–12/31/1983, ARC.

56. "Statement by Archbishop Roach, president, and Joseph Cardinal Bernardin, Chairman of the Ad Hoc Committee on War and Peace, Regarding Third Draft of National Conference of Catholic Bishops Pastoral on War and Peace," April 10, 1983, "Remarks: 1983 Cardinal Bernardin," EXEC/N0930/38, Executive Records—USCCB Committee and Council Files, Cardinal Joseph Bernardin, War and Peace Papers, 1/1/1981–12/31/1983, ARC.

57. "Statement by Archbishop Roach, president, and Joseph Cardinal Bernardin, Chairman of the Ad Hoc Committee on War and Peace, Regarding Third Draft of National Conference of Catholic Bishops Pastoral on War and Peace"; correspondence between the bishops after the second draft of the Pastoral Letter, "Amendments 90–9," Amendments to 3rd Draft, Cardinal Joseph Bernardin, War and Peace Papers, 1/1/1981–12/31/1983, ARC.

58. John Garvey, "The Ambiguous Pastoral," *Commonweal* 110, no. 9 (May 6, 1983): 264–265; "Bishops Cross Wire," *Nuclear Times* 1, no. 7 (May 1983): 3–4; Kenneth A. Briggs, "Roman Catholic Bishops Toughen Stance against Nuclear Weapons," *New York Times*, May 3, 1983, A1.

59. "Bishops Cross Wire," 4; Cortright, *Peace Works*, 51–52.

60. Letter, Tom Hayden to Joseph Bernardin, May 27, 1983, "War and Peace, 1983, Alphabetical G–H," EXEC/N0930/38, Executive Records—USCCB Committee and Council Files, Cardinal Joseph Bernardin, War and Peace Papers, 1/1/1981–12/31/1983, ARC.

61. Letter, A. Miller to Joseph Bernardin, May 5, 1983, "War and Peace 'Thank-You' Letters," EXEC/N0930/44, Executive Records—USCCB Committee and Council Files, Cardinal Joseph Bernardin, War and Peace Papers, 1/1/1981–12/31/1983, ARC.

62. Mailgram from Father Roy Bourgeois, April 6, 1983, "Remarks: 1983 Cardinal Bernardin," EXEC/N0930/38, Executive Records—USCCB Committee and Council Files, Cardinal Joseph Bernardin, War and Peace Papers, 1/1/1981–12/31/1983, ARC.

63. Philip Berrigan interview (undated newspaper clipping, no publication information listed), folder 18, box 7, group 1696, series II, Coalition to Stop Trident Records (MS 1696), Manuscripts and Archives, Yale University Library, New Haven, CT.

64. Memo, Elliot Abrams to William Clark, case file 151682–151793, ND 018, box 12, WHORM Subject File, RRPL; letter, Phillip Lawler to Nazalee Shortly, May 9, 1983, folder "Catholic Conference," Series II Subject File OA 12418, box 1, Robert Reilly Files, RRPL; "Question-and-Answer Session with Reporters on Domestic and Foreign Policy Issues, May 4, 1982," The Public Papers of President Ronald W. Reagan, RRPL, https://www.reaganlibrary.gov/research/speeches/50483d.

Chapter 4. With Friends Like These

1. Les Janka interview by David Cortright, August 23, 1990, David Cortright Papers (DG 101), box 2, SCPC.

2. Waller, Congress and the Nuclear Freeze, 12–13.

3. Juan de Onis, "Lobbying Body to Push Congress for a Nuclear Edge over Soviet," New York Times, January 6, 1981, A11; George C. Wilson, "Weinberger, in His First Message, Says Mission Is to 'Rearm America,'" Washington Post, January 23, 1981, A3; James Reston, "Reagan Is Prepared to Hold Arms Talks if Soviet Is Sincere," New York Times, February 3, 1981, A1, A13; Clayton Fritchey, "Whatever Happened to SALT III?," Washington Post, April 27, 1981, A19.

4. "Structure Proposal for First Year of Freeze Effort," University of Notre Dame Catholic Peace Fellowship (CPF), box 44, Nuclear Freeze 1981–1984, AUND; Waller, Congress and the Nuclear Freeze, 58; Meyer, A Winter of Discontent, 224.

5. Waller, Congress and the Nuclear Freeze, 45–48; Cortright, Peace Works, 22–23.

6. Waller, Congress and the Nuclear Freeze, 48–49.

7. Waller, Congress and the Nuclear Freeze, 53–57.

8. Waller, Congress and the Nuclear Freeze, 58–59; Meyer, A Winter of Discontent, 224; letter, Steve Ladd to Randy Kehler, March 4, 1982, NWFC Records, box 1, folder 25, UMSL.

9. Waller, Congress and the Nuclear Freeze, 61.

10. Margot Hornblower, "Bipartisan Resolutions Urge U.S.-Soviet Nuclear Weapons Freeze," Washington Post, March 11, 1982, A3; Waller, Congress and the Nuclear Freeze, 60; Meyer, A Winter of Discontent, 224; Hatfield-Kennedy resolution in Waller, Congress and the Nuclear Freeze, 309–310.

11. Hornblower, "Bipartisan Resolutions Urge U.S.-Soviet Nuclear Weapons Freeze"; Waller, Congress and the Nuclear Freeze, 67. Although Kennedy and Hatfield were listed as coauthors, the book was actually written by staff. See Meyer, A Winter of Discontent, 226.

12. Waller, *Congress and the Nuclear Freeze*, 59; Cortright, *Peace Works*, 23–24; Solo, *From Protest to Policy*, 76; Meyer, *A Winter of Discontent*, 224.

13. Waller, *Congress and the Nuclear Freeze*, 65–66.

14. Margot Hornblower, "House Members Stage 'Historic' Debate on Nuclear Arms Freeze," *Washington Post*, March 31, 1982, A9.

15. George Skelton, "Reagan Rejects Call for Nuclear Arms Freeze," *Los Angeles Times*, March 16, 1982, B1, B13; Hornblower, "Bipartisan Resolutions Urge U.S.-Soviet Nuclear Weapons Freeze"; Judith Miller, "Effort to 'Freeze' Nuclear Arsenals Spreads in U.S.," *New York Times*, March 15, 1982, B12.

16. John Maclean and Storer Rowley, "Hawks Find Flaws in Reagan Strategy," *Chicago Tribune*, March 29, 1982, 1, 8.

17. Margot Hornblower, "House GOP Freshmen on Verge of Rebellion," *Washington Post*, March 1, 1982, A1–A2.

18. Robert G. Kaufman, *Henry M. Jackson: A Life in Politics* (Seattle: University of Washington Press, 2000), 421–422; Waller, *Congress and the Nuclear Freeze*, 92; Judith Miller, "58 Senators Back Alternative Plan on Nuclear Arms," *New York Times*, March 31, 1982, A1, A7.

19. Alex Brummer, "Reagan Will Back Call for 'Delayed' Arms Freeze," *The Guardian*, March 31, 1982, 7; Miller, "58 Senators Back Alternate Plan on Nuclear Arms."

20. Miller, "58 Senators Back Alternate Plan on Nuclear Arms"; Bernard Gwertzman, "Reagan, Under Pressure on Arms, Now Favors Freeze After Buildup," *New York Times*, March 30, 1982, A1, A6.

21. George Skelton, "Reagan 'Favorable' toward New Arms Freeze Proposal," *Los Angeles Times*, March 31, 1982, SD18; Jack Nelson, "Reagan Urges Nuclear Freeze," *Los Angeles Times*, April 1, 1982, 1, 6; Hedrick Smith, "The Nuclear Freeze: Reagan Starts Fighting a Groundswell against Buildup of American Arsenal," *New York Times*, April 1, 1982, A23; "The President's News Conference, March 31, 1982," The Public Papers of President Ronald W. Reagan, RRPL, https://www.reaganlibrary.gov/research/speeches/33182d.

22. Memo, William Clark to the President, March 27, 1982, folder "Nuclear Freeze (03/10/82–03/28/82)," Executive Secretariat box 20, NSC Subject File, RRPL; Norman Podhoretz, "The Neo-conservative Anguish over Reagan's Foreign Policy," *New York Times*, May 2, 1982, 96–97.

23. Waller, *Congress and the Nuclear Freeze*, 110–129.

24. Adam Clymer, "Democrats Cheer Call for Freeze on Nuclear Arms," *New York Times*, June 25, 1982, A16; Jon Margolis, "Ted's Rouser Ends Convention," *Chicago Tribune*, June 28, 1982, A2; Adam Clymer, "Democrats Open Parley by Assailing Reagan," *New York Times*, June 26, 1982, 11; Waller, *Congress and the Nuclear Freeze*, 110.

25. Adam Clymer, "Democrats Offer Job Plan Financed by Cap on Tax Cut," *New York Times*, June 27, 1982, 2, 30; Waller, *Congress and the Nuclear Freeze*, 110.

26. Pat Towell, "House Panel Adopts Nuclear Freeze Measure," *Congressional Quarterly*, June 26, 1982, 1515, folder "Arms Control/Nuclear Freeze (4)," RAC box 1, box 4, Robert C. "Bud" McFarlane Files, RRPL.

27. Memo, Robert McFarlane to Dick Boverie and Bob Kimmit, July 16, 1982, folder "Arms Control/Nuclear Freeze (4)," RAC box 1, box 4, Robert C. "Bud" McFarlane Files, RRPL; memo, Clark to the President, March 27, 1982.

28. Letter, Edward L. Rowny to Congressman William S. Broomfield, August 2, 1982, folder "Arms Control/Nuclear Freeze (4)," RAC box 1, box 4, Robert C. "Bud" McFarlane Files, RRPL; Knopf, *Domestic Society and International Cooperation*, 223–224; David Gergen interview by David Cortright, David Cortright Papers (DG 101), box 2, SCPC.

29. Waller, *Congress and the Nuclear Freeze*, 144–145; Herbert H. Denton, "Reagan Urges House to Stop A-Freeze Bid," *Washington Post*, July 27, 1982, A1, A3.

30. Waller, *Congress and the Nuclear Freeze*, 151–153.

31. Waller, *Congress and the Nuclear Freeze*, 154–156.

32. Margot Hornblower, "Alternate A-Freeze Plan Passes," *Washington Post*, August 6, 1982, A1, A10.

33. Hornblower, "Alternate A-Freeze Plan Passes"; Reagan quoted in Wittner, *Towards Nuclear Abolition*, 259.

34. Hornblower, "Alternate A-Freeze Plan Passes"; Kennedy and Kehler quoted in Robert Subrug, *Beyond Vietnam: The Politics of Protest in Massachusetts, 1974–1990* (Amherst: University of Massachusetts Press, 2009), 156.

35. Letter, Reuben McCornack (Washington Freeze spokesman) to John Hughes, October 21, 1982, box 5, folder 139, NWFC Records, UMSL; memo, Robert Sims to Bud McFarlane, August 12, 1982, folder "Arms Control/Nuclear Freeze (6)," RAC box 1, box 4, Robert C. "Bud" McFarlane Files, RRPL. Emphasis in original.

36. Memo, Bud McFarlane to Judge William Clark, August 28, 1982, folder "Arms Control/Nuclear Freeze (4)," RAC box 1, box 4, Robert C. "Bud" McFarlane Files, RRPL.

37. John Dow for Congress Committee, "For a Nuclear Weapons Freeze Now, Vote Dow," July 15, 1982, SANE Records, National Office (DG 58), box 15, series G, SCPC; Jane Perlez, "It's Hawk versus Dove in Stratton-Dow Battle," *New York Times*, September 8, 1982, B1, B5.

38. "A Messy Vote of No Confidence," *The Guardian*, November 4, 1982, 14; memo, Robin Renwick to John Weston, "U.S. Mid-term Elections: Nuclear 'Freeze,'" November 10, 1982, FCO 46/3144, "U.S. Views on Nuclear Arms Control (Inc. INF and Start)," TNA.

39. Brian C. Mooney, "John Kerry: Candidate in the Making," *Boston Globe*, June 19, 2003, A1; Jane Perlez, "1,000 Ask Moynihan to Help Get a Nuclear Freeze," *New York Times*, March 9, 1983, A21.

40. "Minutes, National Committee Meeting," December 3–5, 1982, SANE Records, National Office (DG 58), box 152, series G, Files of Mike Mawby, SCPC. Emphasis in original.

41. "Message from the National Coordinator," December 1982, SANE Records, National Office (DG 58), box 152, series G, Files of Mike Mawby, SCPC.

42. Meyer, *A Winter of Discontent*, 189.

43. Walter Pincus, "Nuclear Freeze Movement Split on What Steps to Take Next," *Washington Post*, January 5, 1983, A2.

44. "Decisions Made by the Third National Conference of the Nuclear Weapons Freeze Campaign," St. Louis, Missouri, February 4–6, 1983, SANE Records, National Office (DG 58), box 152, series G, Files of Mike Mawby, SCPC; Meyer, *A Winter of Discontent*, 228–229.

45. E-mail, Bob Moore to the author, November 13, 2020; "Decisions Made by the Third National Conference of the Nuclear Weapons Freeze Campaign" and "Message

from the National Coordinator," SANE Records, National Office (DG 58), box 152, series G, Files of Mike Mawby, SCPC.

46. John LeBoutillier to Alfred Salzberg, September 2, 1982, NWFC Records, box 5, folder 137, UMSL.

47. Peace through Strength information obtained from several coalition documents found in "Nuclear Freeze (3 of 16)," Series I Subject File Nuclear Freeze, box 15, Morton Blackwell Files, RRPL.

48. Letter, John Fisher to ASCF Membership, January 28, 1983, NWFC Records, box 5, folder 140, UMSL.

49. Vietnam Veterans against the War, "VVA and 'The Temple of . . . ,'" http:// www.vvaw.org/veteran/article/?id=2675, accessed August 16, 2017; E. R. Shipp, "Younger V. F. W. Members Rising," New York Times, August 24, 1984, A8. The American Legion would also later back a nuclear weapons freeze. See Jane Gross, "At American Legion Posts, Veterans of Vietnam Fan the Winds of Change," New York Times, May 16, 1986, B1–B2.

50. "Indecent Debate," New York Times, October 6, 1982; Memo, Phelps Jones to National Officers, National Council of Administration, Past-Commanders-in-Chief, Department Commanders, Department Adjutants, Department Publications, National Security Committee, National Legislative Committee, "'Peace through Strength' in the 98th Congress," December 23, 1982, folder "Nuclear Freeze (3 of 16)," Series I Subject File Nuclear Freeze, box 15, Morton Blackwell Files, RRPL.

51. Memo, Phelps Jones to Department Commanders (VFW), February 10, 1983, folder "Nuclear Freeze (3 of 16)," Series I Subject File Nuclear Freeze, box 15, Morton Blackwell files, RRPL.

52. Adam Clymer, "Reagan in the Pulpit," New York Times, March 9, 1983, A18; Gary Geispel, "5,000 Rally in Capital to Urge Nuclear Freeze," Los Angeles Times, March 9, 1983, A7; Perlez, "1,000 Ask Moynihan to Help Get a Nuclear Freeze."

53. Perlez, "1,000 Ask Moynihan to Help Get a Nuclear Freeze."

54. Gerald F. Seib, "Urged by House Foreign Panel in 27–9 Vote," Wall Street Journal, March 9, 1983, 2.

55. UPI, "A-Freeze Likely to Pass, Michel Advises Reagan," Los Angeles Times, March 9, 1983, A2.

56. Margot Hornblower and Juan Williams, "President Lobbies on Freeze Measure," Washington Post, March 16, 1983, A2; UPI, "A-Freeze Likely to Pass."

57. Martin Tolchin, "House Action on Arms Freeze Postponed 2 Weeks," New York Times, March 18, 1983, A30; Margot Hornblower, "Nuclear Freeze Supporters Plan Lobbying Drive," Washington Post, March 18, 1983, A3; Dorothy Colin, "GOP Delays A-Freeze, but Can't Melt It," Chicago Tribune, March 17, 1983, 1–2.

58. Tolchin, "House Action on Arms Freeze Postponed 2 Weeks."

59. "The Pro-Nuclear Resolution," Chicago Tribune, March 20, 1983, A6; "The Freeze Debate," Washington Post, March 20, 1983, C6; Leslie H. Gelb, "Aides Say Reagan Is Ready to Offer Arms Compromise," New York Times, March 23, 1983, A1. Reagan at the time was contemplating a limited-INF proposal regarding Zero-Zero.

60. Henry J. Hyde and James G. Martin, "Disagreement in the Freeze Ranks," Washington Post, March 23, 1983, A24; Les AuCoin, "The Nuclear Freeze Debate," Washington Post, April 2, 1983, A14; William R. Ratchford, "Resolution on Arms Race Is Democracy in Action," New York Times, March 27, 1983, CN26. The freeze

debate started by Hyde and Martin in the *Washington Post* continued in letters to the editor over the month of April. See Robert R. Denny, "The Freeze Won't Work," *Washington Post*, April 9, 1983, A17, and Congressman Thomas J. Downey's response to Denny, "Bears, Blackjacks and B52s (Cont'd.)," *Washington Post*, April 19, 1983, A20.

61. Rowland Evans and Robert Novak, "Reagan's Anti-Freeze: Soviet Cheating," *Washington Post*, April 4, 1983, A15; letter, James R. Currieo to Members of the 98th Congress, April 22, 1983, folder "Nuclear Freeze (3 of 16)," Series I Subject File Nuclear Freeze, box 15, Morton Blackwell File, RRPL.

62. Steven R. Weisman, "Reagan Calls Nuclear Freeze Dangerous," *New York Times*, April 1, 1983, A8; Lou Cannon, "President Pushes Arms Proposals, Criticizes Freeze," *Washington Post*, April 1, 1983, A1, A6.

63. Mary McGrory, "Why Did the Congress Steal April?," *Washington Post*, April 24, 1983, C1, C3; Steven V. Roberts, "O'Neill Criticizes G.O.P. over Delays," *New York Times*, May 4, 1983, B7.

64. Robert C. Toth and Ellen Hume, "House Votes Freeze with a Time Limit," *Los Angeles Times*, May 5, 1983, A7, A15; Cortright, *Peace Works*, 23–25; Meyer, *A Winter of Discontent*, 231; Randy Kehler, "Doing the Freeze Better," *Nuclear Times* 1, no. 8 (July 1983): 17.

65. "Capitol Roll Call," *Los Angeles Times*, April 24, 1983, V4; Waller, *Congress and the Nuclear Freeze*, 241–243; Toth and Hume, "House Votes Freeze with a Time Limit."

66. "President Criticizes Nuclear Arms Freeze Urged by the House," *Wall Street Journal*, May 6, 1983, 3.

67. Judith Miller, "In the Heat of House Debate on Nuclear Freeze," *New York Times*, April 23, 1983, 8; "Speaking of Arms Control," *Washington Post*, April 1, 1983, A14; Cannon, "President Pushes Arms Proposals, Criticizes Freeze"; Lou Cannon and Walter Pincis, "Effort Pledged by Reagan," *Washington Post*, May 6, 1983, A1, A12; "The Meaning of the Freeze," *Los Angeles Times*, May 9, 1983, C4.

Chapter 5. Envisioning the Day After

1. Reagan and Haig moreover used *Red Dawn* to "disparage the Democrats' stance on foreign policy." See Tony Shaw, *Hollywood's Cold War* (Amherst: University of Massachusetts Press, 2007), 269–276.

2. Kai Erickson, "A Horror beyond Comprehension [review of Jonathan Schell, *The Fate of the Earth*]," *New York Times*, April 11, 1982, BR3; Jonathan Schell, *The Fate of the Earth* (New York: Alfred A. Knopf, 1982), 22–23.

3. Philip M. Boffey, "Contemplating the Heart of the Nuclear Darkness," *New York Times*, March 28, 1982, E9; James Lardner, "The Bomb Schell: The Media Fallout After 'The Fate of the Earth' Schell Shock," *Washington Post*, April 22, 1982, C1.

4. Herb Block, cartoon, *Washington Post*, November 17, 1982, 39, and Bob Englehardt, cartoon, *St. Louis Post-Dispatch*, November 14, 1982, both in NWFC Records, box 8, folder 245, UMSL; Tom Flannery, cartoon, in Charles Brooks, ed., *Best Editorial Cartoons of the Year, 1983* (Gretna, LA: Pelican, 1983), 37.

5. Etta Hume and Ed Stein, in Brooks, *Best Editorial Cartoons of the Year, 1983*, 38; Chuck Asay and Charles Brooks, in Charles Brooks, ed., *Best Editorial Cartoons of the Year, 1984* (Gretna, LA: Pelican, 1984), 38.

6. Kerry D. Soper, *Garry Trudeau: Doonesbury and the Aesthetics of Satire* (Jackson: University Press of Mississippi, 2007), 40–41; G. B. Trudeau, *Doonesbury*, December 13–15, 1982, December 24–25, 1982 (Rev. Sloan's newsletter) and December 26, 1982 (mocking the idea that the Freeze was a Soviet plot).

7. Cortright, *Peace Works*, 61; Dean Smith with John Kilgo and Sally Jenkins, *A Coach's Life: My Forty Years in College Basketball* (New York: Random House, 1999), 114, 257.

8. Cortright, *Peace Works*, 61.

9. Cortright, *Peace Works*, 62.

10. Cortright, *Peace Works*, 63.

11. Katz, *Ban the Bomb*, 155–156; Cortright, *Peace Works*, 67.

12. Letter, Richard Zeichik to National Freeze Voter PAC Board [budget estimates], August 23, 1983; letter, Richard Zeichik to Kathy Wright [celebrity involvement], August 12, 1983; and letter, Randy Kehler to Richard Zeichik, Shelly Green, and Diane Brown, October 7, 1983, all in NWFC Records, box 8, folder 240, UMSL.

13. Paul Rogat Loeb, *Hope in Hard Times: America's Peace Movement in the Reagan Era* (Lexington, MA: Lexington Books, 1987), 68–71; "Of Millionaires and Militants," *Nuclear Times* 1, no. 1 (October 1982): 13; William Endicott, "Brown Backs Nuclear Arms Freeze," *Los Angeles Times*, April 17, 1982, A23; Cathy Cevoli, "Antinuclear Stars Come Out," *Nuclear Times* 1, no. 8 (June 1983): 27–28.

14. Loeb, *Hope in Hard Times*, 69–70; Cevoli, "Antinuclear Stars Come Out," 27–28.

15. Loeb, *Hope in Hard Times*, 72.

16. Lee Dembart, "Heston, in Political Role, Hits Newman's Pro-freeze Stance," *Los Angeles Times*, October 15, 1982, B3; Endicott, "Brown Backs Nuclear Arms Freeze"; Lee Dembart, "Foes of Nuclear Freeze Initiative Will Seek Free TV Time for Ads," *Los Angeles Times*, October 19, 1982, A3; Shawn Levy, *Paul Newman: A Life* (New York: Three Rivers Press, 2009), 331.

17. Levy, *Paul Newman*, 331–332.

18. Levy, *Paul Newman*, 332; Emile Raymond, *From My Cold Dead Hands: Charlton Heston and American Politics* (Lexington: University Press of Kentucky, 2006), 221; letter, Paul Newman to Randy Kehler, September 28, 1983, NWFC Records, box 8, folder 234, UMSL.

19. Loeb, *Hope in Hard Times*, 72–73, 77; "Of Millionaires and Militants," 13–14.

20. "Nuclear Freeze: Yes on 12," *Los Angeles Times*, October 24, 1982, F4; "For Special Attention," *Los Angeles Times*, November 1, 1982, C4; Waller, *Congress and the Nuclear Freeze*, 163.

21. Concert program, "Musicians against Nuclear Arms—in Concert," October 24, 1983, NWFC Records, box 4, folder 114, UMSL.

22. Joey Keithley, *I, Shithead: A Life in Punk* (Vancouver: Arsenal Pulp Press, 2003), 86; Mark Baumgarten, *Love Rock Revolution: K Records and the Rise of Independent Music* (Seattle: Sasquatch Books, 2012), 73; Ben Nadler, *Punk in NYC's Lower East Side 1981–1991*, Scene History Series 1 (Portland, OR: Microcosm, 2014), 19; Vic Vondi quoted in Steven Blush and Paul Rachman, *American Hardcore*, directed by Paul Rachman (Culver City, CA: Sony Pictures, 2006).

23. On Orange County's connection to the conservative movement, see Lisa McGirr, *Suburban Warriors: The Origins of the New American Right* (Princeton, NJ: Princeton University Press, 2001).

24. Dave Dictor, *MDC: Memoir from a Damaged Civilization* (San Francisco: Manic D. Press, 2016), 87.

25. Martin, *The Other Eighties*, 104–107.

26. Philip Jenkins, *Decade of Nightmares: The End of the Sixties and the Making of Eighties America* (New York: Oxford University Press, 2006), 222.

27. The puppets used in "Land of Confusion" were borrowed from the British television show *Spitting Image*, wherein Reagan was routinely depicted as lacking a brain and nearly starting a nuclear war.

28. Cortright, *Peace Works*, 68.

29. Jane Mayer, "Hollywood Is Hoping Nuclear Drama Isn't a Box Office Bomb," *Wall Street Journal*, July 19, 1983, 1, emphasis in original.

30. Mayer, "Hollywood Is Hoping Nuclear Drama Isn't a Box Office Bomb," 1; Cannon, *Role of a Lifetime*, 38.

31. Mark Hertsgaard, "Lights, Camera, Activism!" *Mother Jones* 10, no. 4 (May 1985): 8–9.

32. John Dowling, "Films," *Bulletin of the Atomic Scientists* 39, no. 4 (April 1983): 37; Jenkins, *Decade of Nightmares*, 222; Toni A. Perrine, *Film and the Nuclear Age: Representing Cultural Anxiety* (New York: Garland, 1998), 238.

33. Reeve further lambasted Reagan for "absolutely raping poor people" in the United States while "provoking the Russians in a terrifying way." See Christopher Reeve, *Playgirl* interview (December 1982), http://chrisreevehomepage.com/sp-playgirl1982interview.html. Reeve's costar in the *Superman* franchise, Margot Kidder, was also a major supporter of the Freeze campaign.

34. Edwin A. Rothschild, "If You Love These Films," *Bulletin of the Atomic Scientists* 39, no. 6 (June–July 1983), 39; Wittner, *Towards Nuclear Abolition*, 266.

35. "No Nukes Is Good Nukes," *Family Ties*, season 1, episode 8, original air date November 24, 1982; "There Goes the Neighborhood," *Nuclear Times* 1, no. 10 (August–September 1983): 4; Marcia Dunn, "A Little War in the Neighborhood," *Pittsburgh Post-Gazette*, November 28, 1983, 23; Mayer, "Hollywood Is Hoping Nuclear Drama Isn't a Box Office Bomb," 1.

36. Mark Dowie and David Talbot, "Asner: Too Hot for Medium Cool," *Mother Jones* 7, no. 7 (August 1982): 6, 10–11.

37. Mayer, "Hollywood Is Hoping Nuclear Drama Isn't a Box Office Bomb," 18.

38. Mayer, "Hollywood Is Hoping Nuclear Drama Isn't a Box Office Bomb," 18; Dowie and Talbot, "Asner," 13.

39. Hedrick Smith, "Shultz Reaffirms Atomic Arms View," *New York Times*, November 21, 1983, A1, A19; Gergen interview by Cortright, David Cortright Papers (DG 101), box 2, SCPC.

40. Peter J. Boyer and John J. Goldman, "'The Day After' Airs amid Debate, Fear, Intense Hype," *Los Angeles Times*, November 21, 1983, 1, 18.

41. Cortright, *Peace Works*, 72–73; Mayer, "Hollywood Is Hoping Nuclear Drama Isn't a Box Office Bomb," 1; Knoblauch, *Nuclear Freeze in a Cold War*, 62–63.

42. Letter, David Cortright and Randy Kehler to Ed Lawrence, September 23, 1983, NWFC Records, box 2, folder 35, UMSL.

43. Letter, Pam McIntyre to Local Freeze Supporters, undated [circa October 1983], NWFC Records, box 2, folder 35, UMSL. Emphasis in original.

44. Memo, "Other Activity on the Film, 'The Day After,'" undated [circa October 1983], and letter, McIntyre to Local Freeze Supporters, both in NWFC Records, box 2, folder 35, UMSL. Emphasis in original.

45. Memo, Pam McIntyre to Randy Kehler, "Memo Regarding 'The Day After,'" October 7, 1983; memo, Cortright and Kehler to Lawrence, September 23, 1983; memo, "Other Activity on the Film, 'The Day After,'" all in NWFC Records, box 2, folder 35, UMSL. Emphasis in original.

46. Wittner, *Towards Nuclear Abolition*, 187; Knoblauch, *Nuclear Freeze in a Cold War*, 65; Jay Sharbutt, "Mixed Views to Follow 'Day After,'" *Los Angeles Times*, November 17, 1983, L1, L5; newspaper clipping, Clarke Taylor, "ABC Still Tinkering with 'Day,'" NWFC Records, box 2, folder 35, UMSL.

47. David Gergen quoted in Cortright, *Peace Works*, 71; Ronald Reagan, October 10, 1983, in *The Reagan Diaries, Volume 1, January 1981–October 1985*, ed. Douglas Brinkley (New York: HarperCollins, 2007), 273.

48. Cannon, *Role of a Lifetime*, 36, 127; Edmund Morris, *Dutch: A Memoir of Ronald Reagan* (New York: Modern Library, 1999), 498; Reagan, November 18, 1983, *The Reagan Diaries, Volume 1*, 290.

49. "Ideas for Public Affairs Strategy: 'The Day After,'" folder "ABC's The Day After 11–20 [3]," White House Office of Media Relations OA 9118, box 15, Karna Small-Stringer Files, RRPL; Reagan, November 18, 1983, *The Reagan Diaries, Volume 1*, 290.

50. Smith, "Shultz Reaffirms Atomic Arms View," A1, A19; Michael Getler, "Shultz Says Movie Is Not 'the Future,'" *Washington Post*, November 21, 1983, A1–A2.

51. Meyer, *A Winter of Discontent*, 132.

52. "Ideas for Public Affairs Strategy: 'The Day After.'"

53. Knoblauch, *Nuclear Freeze in a Cold War*, 66; "Ideas for Public Affairs Strategy: 'The Day After.'"

54. Memo, David Gergen to Ronald Reagan, November 21, 1983, folder "ABC's The Day After 11–20 [1]," White House Office of Media Relations OA 9118, box 15, Karna Small-Stringer Files, RRPL.

55. Memo, Gergen to Reagan, November 21, 1983; Boyer and Goldman, "'The Day After' Airs amid Debate, Fear, Intense Hype."

56. Letter, Hugh Thomas to Margaret Thatcher, "Nuclear Disarmament," November 22, 1983, PREM 19/973, TNA.

57. Memo, Gergen to Reagan, November 21, 1983.

58. Steven R. Weisman, "Among the Staff, the Mood Is Testy," *New York Times*, November 28, 1983, B6; Richard Wirthlin, Memo: "QUBE Results on 'The Day After,'" November 28, 1983, box 686, Edwin Meese Papers, HIA.

59. Wirthlin memo: "QUBE Results on 'The Day After,'"; Renata Rizzo, "'Day After' Aftermath: Movement Recruits," *Nuclear Times* 2, no. 3 (January 1984): 18; William Schneider, "ABC Film Has Little Impact, but Public Still Wants a Freeze," *Los Angeles Times*, November 27, 1983, 1, 3.

60. William Poundstone, *Carl Sagan: A Life in the Cosmos* (New York: Henry Holt, 1999), 292, 306.

Chapter 6. The Perils of Failed Diplomacy

1. Jane Rosen, "UN Overrides West in Vote for Freeze," *The Guardian*, December 15, 1982, 7; Mary Kaldor, "Editorial," *Journal of European Nuclear Disarmament*, no. 1 (December 1982–January 1983): 2.

2. Wittner, *Towards Nuclear Abolition*, 260.

3. Letter, Randall Forsberg and Randy Kehler to President Ronald Reagan, November 15, 1982 and Memo, Sven Kraemer to William P. Clark, December 9, 1982, case file 108251–109957, ND 018, box 7, WHORM Subject File, RRPL.

4. Wittner, *Towards Nuclear Abolition*, 260; Helen Caldicott interview by Lawrence Wittner, February 27, 1999 (transcript in author's possession). Reagan also met with California Nuclear Weapons Freeze Campaign organizer Harold Willens at the behest of Patti Davis, but the meeting was of no value to Freeze activists.

5. Smith and Harnoff Poll, "Nuclear Freeze / Arms Control," July 8–15, 1982, folder "Nuclear Freeze / Arms Control," OA 1122–11227, box 4, Michael Baroody Files, RRPL.

6. Airtel from Boston to FBI, August 4, 1982, obtained via FBI FOIA request; George Lardner Jr., "Soviet Role in Nuclear Freeze Limited, FBI Says," *Washington Post*, March 26, 1983, A7; Leslie Maitland, "F.B.I. Rules Out Russian Control of Freeze Drive," *New York Times*, March 26, 1983, 1. Although the FBI report was widely reported, an FOIA request to the FBI for the official report came back with no records returned.

7. "Who Controls the International 'Peace' Movement," *Executive Intelligence Review*, May 1, 1982, 22–24.

8. Advertisement, Alliance to Halt the Advance of Marxism in the Americas, *Grants Pass Daily Courier*, April 21, 1982, letter, Linda Friedman (CALS) to Mary Jean Amideus, May 7, 1982, and letter, Susan Delles to Nuclear Freeze Campaign, June 4, 1982, all in NWFC Records, box 5, folder 137, UMSL. CALS regarded the advertisement as libelous and had their attorney send a cease and desist letter.

9. William E. Griffith, "Perspective on the Peace Movement I: Ban Whose Bomb?," *Reader's Digest*, June 1982; John Baron, "The KGB's Magical War for 'Peace,'" *Reader's Digest*, October 1982, 206–259; letter, Terry Provance to editor of *Reader's Digest*, September 30, 1982, letter, John M. Fisher (American Security Council Foundation) to Ned Crosby, memo to Randy Kehler, September 30, 1982, and letter, Randy Kehler to Local Freeze Organizers, October 11, 1982, all in NWFC Records, box 5, folder 135, UMSL; Seth Rosenfeld, *Subversives: The FBI's War on Student Radicals and Reagan's Rise to Power* (New York: Farrar, Straus and Giroux, 2012), 494.

10. "Remarks in Columbus to Members of Ohio Veterans Organizations, October 4, 1982," The Public Papers of President Ronald W. Reagan, RRPL; "Indecent Debate," *New York Times*, October 6, 1982, A26; letter, Michael Pakenham to Richard Gozney, "President Reagan and the Nuclear Freeze Movement," October 8, 1982, FCO 46/3144, "U.S. Views on Nuclear Arms Control (Inc. INF and Start)," TNA.

11. Leslie Maitland, "Sources Are Cited for Charge of Soviet Tie to Arms Freeze," *New York Times*, November 13, 1982, 7; letter, Don Edwards to William H. Webster, November 17, 1982, Mary McGrory Papers, box 56, folder 1, LOC.

12. Nina J. Easton, *Gang of Five: Leaders at the Center of the Conservative Crusade* (New York: Simon and Schuster, 2000), 151–155 (emphasis in original); Allan J. Lichtman,

White Protestant Nation: The Rise of the American Conservative Movement (New York: Atlantic Monthly Press, 2008), 360–361.

13. Letter, Adm. Thomas H. Moorer (ASC) to Ned Crosby, September 3, 1982, NWFC Records, box 5, folder 137, UMSL; form letter, John Fisher to Arne Moore, November 20, 1982, NWFC Records, box 5, folder 140, UMSL.

14. Robert D. Benford and Lester R. Kurtz, "Performing the Nuclear Ceremony: The Arms Race as a Ritual," in *A Shuddering Dawn: Religious Studies and the Nuclear Age,* ed. Ira Chernus and Edward Tabor (Albany: SUNY Press, 1989), 79; Wittner, *Towards Nuclear Abolition,* 189, 262; John Dowling, "Film: Reviews," *Bulletin of the Atomic Scientists* 39, no. 9 (November 1983): 47.

15. Ron Corday, "2 Groups Launch Anti-freeze Efforts," *Washington Times,* December 8, 1982; background on ACU from memo, Kris Jacobs (Interchange), December 9, 1982, NWFC Records, folder 140, box 5, UMSL.

16. Duncan Campbell, "Fruitcake Right," *New Statesman,* March 12, 1982, 11–13; Wittner, *Towards Nuclear Abolition,* 136–137, 281–282.

17. Campbell, "Fruitcake Right"; Wittner, *Towards Nuclear Abolition,* 262–263.

18. Letter, Thomas F. Ellis to Leonard Holihan, March 4, 1983, folder "Nuclear Freeze (1 of 16)," Series I Subject File Nuclear Freeze, box 15, Morton Blackwell Files, RRPL.

19. Letter, Phyllis Schlafly to Senate, March 10, 1983, folder "Nuclear Freeze (1 of 16)," Series I Subject File Nuclear Freeze, box 15, Morton Blackwell Files, RRPL.

20. Leonard Holihan and James S. Bell Jr., "Nuclear Freeze Lobby Scandal, a Project by the Counter Freeze Committee in cooperation with the Global Peace Foundation and J. S. Bell and Associates," undated (circa March 1983), folder "Nuclear Freeze (1 of 16)," Series I Subject File Nuclear Freeze, box 15, Morton Blackwell Files, RPPL.

21. Waller, *Congress and the Nuclear Freeze,* 188. For additional discussion regarding the impetus for the Monday Group, see Cortright, *Peace Works,* 142.

22. Phyllis Schlafly, "Six Fatal Fallacies of the Nuclear-Freezers," *Human Events* 43, no. 26 (June 25, 1983): 17.

23. Wittner, *Towards Nuclear Abolition,* 190; Jerry Falwell/Moral Majority, "I Have Campaigned for Peace through Strength" (direct mailing), undated, and letter, Jerry Falwell/Moral Majority, June 17, 1982, both in People for the American Way collection of conservative political ephemera, BANC MSS 2010/152 C77, BANC; "The Bomb and Jerry Show," *Nuclear Times* 1, no. 10 (August–September 1983): 25.

24. Jerry Falwell/Moral Majority, "I Have Campaigned for Peace through Strength"; letter, Jerry Falwell/Moral Majority, June 17, 1982; Jerry Falwell/Moral Majority, "Special Briefing Opposing an Immediate Nuclear Freeze," June 1983, in People for the American Way collection of conservative political ephemera, BANC MSS 2010/152 C77, BANC.

25. "An Open Letter from Jerry Falwell on the Nuclear Freeze," *Los Angeles Times,* March 28, 1983, E8; "Reagan and Falwell," *St. Petersburg Times,* March 16, 1983, 20A; Frances FitzGerald, *The Evangelicals: The Struggle to Shape America* (New York: Simon and Schuster, 2017), 322.

26. Marjorie Hyer, "Poll Shows Evangelicals Support Nuclear Freeze," *Washington Post,* July 8, 1983, A5; Jim Brenneman [Conference on the Church and Peacemaking

in the Nuclear Age] to Morton Blackwell, May 4, 1983, folder "Nuclear Freeze [3 of 16]," Series I Subject File Nuclear Freeze, box 15, Morton Blackwell Files, RRPL; John Dart, "Church Conservatives Swamped on Question of Arms Buildup," *Los Angeles Times*, May 28, 1983, B6.

27. David Brand, "Russian Doves," *Wall Street Journal*, June 21, 1982, 1; Susanne Garment, "U.S. Evangelicals Begin to Emerge on the Left," *Wall Street Journal*, May 14, 1982, 24. Graham discusses the trip in his memoir, *Just as I Am: The Autobiography of Billy Graham* (New York: HarperCollins, 1997), 499–510; FitzGerald, *The Evangelicals*, 223.

28. Letter, Robert P. Dugan Jr. to Ronald Reagan, December 3, 1982, and letter, Robert P. Dugan Jr. to James A. Baker III, December 3, 1982, folder "National Assn. of Evangelicals, Orlando, Fl., 3/8/83," Speech Writing, box 86, White House Research Office, 1981–1989, RRPL; Robert Schlesinger, *White House Ghosts: Presidents and Their Speechwriters* (New York: Simon and Schuster, 2008), 328.

29. Schlesinger, *White House Ghosts*, 328.

30. "Remarks at the Annual Convention of the National Association of Evangelicals in Orlando, Florida, March 8, 1983," The Public Papers of President Ronald W. Reagan, RRPL, https://www.reaganlibrary.gov/research/speeches/30883b; letter, John Fisher to ASC Members, April 19, 1983, NWFC Records, box 5, folder 141, UMSL. For criticism of the speech in the press, see "The Lord and the Freeze," *New York Times*, March 11, 1983, A30; James Carroll, *House of War: The Pentagon and the Disastrous Rise of American Power* (New York: Houghton Mifflin, 2006), 389.

31. Leslie H. Gelb, "Aides Say Reagan Is Ready to Offer Arms Compromise," *New York Times*, March 23, 1983, A1, A9.

32. McFarlane, *Special Trust*, 223; Smoke, *National Security and the Nuclear Dilemma*, 208.

33. Gregg Herken, *Cardinal Choices: Presidential Science Advising from the Atomic Bomb to SDI* (Stanford, CA: Stanford University Press, [1992] 2000), 333fn59.

34. Edward Teller to Ronald Reagan, July 23, 1982, folder "Nuclear Freeze," C0A 415, box 3, Edwin Meese Files, RRPL; letter, Burt Hurlbert to Jack Kemp, January 18, 1983, box 107, folder 4, Jack Kemp Papers, LOC; Gregory Fossedal quoted in "Spaced Out," *Nuclear Times* 1, no. 1 (October 1982): 5; Daniel Graham to William Clark, November 9, 1982, case file ND 018 119150–120099, ND 018 box 8, WHORM Subject File, RRPL.

35. Schlesinger, *White House Ghosts*, 330; "Address to the Nation on Defense and National Security, March 23, 1982," The Public Papers of President Ronald W. Reagan, RRPL.

36. Storer Rowley, "High-Tech Defense Proposed by Reagan," *Chicago Tribune*, March 24, 1983, 1, 16; Lou Cannon, "President Seeks Futuristic Defense against Missiles," *Washington Post*, March 24, 1983, A1, A13. The administration would later unsuccessfully try to dub the program "Peace Shield." See Smoke, *National Security and the Nuclear Dilemma*, 237–238.

37. Frances FitzGerald, *Way Out There in the Blue: Reagan, Star Wars and the End of the Cold War* (New York: Simon and Schuster, 2000), 205–206; Lou Cannon, *President Reagan: The Role of a Lifetime* (New York: Touchstone/Simon and Schuster, [1991] 2000), 249–250, 278.

38. Cannon, *Role of a Lifetime*, 250, 287; Donald R. Baucom, *The Origins of SDI, 1944–1983* (Lawrence: University Press of Kansas, 1992), 182; Smoke, *National Security and the Nuclear Dilemma*, 237.

39. Oliver Wright and Margaret Thatcher quoted in Ralph L. Dietl, *The Strategic Defense Initiative: Ronald Reagan, NATO Europe, and the Nuclear and Space Talks, 1981–1988* (Lanham, MD: Lexington Books, 2018), 45; Warnke quoted in William Hartung, "Star Wars Pork Barrel," *Bulletin of the Atomic Scientists* 3, no. 4 (January 1986): 20; Solo, *From Protest to Policy*, 134; Caldicott, *A Desperate Passion*, 251; Cortright, *Peace Works*, 160.

40. John Poindexter to Bob Sims, "Nuclear Freeze: Public Affairs Strategy," undated, folder "Nuclear [Freeze] (8 of 8)," series II, Subject File OA9421, 9422, box 7, David Gergen Files, RRPL.

41. Poindexter to Sims, "Nuclear Freeze: Public Affairs Strategy."

42. Thomas R. Rochon and David S. Meyer, "Introduction: Nuclear Freeze in Theory and Action," in *Coalition and Political Movements: The Lessons of the Nuclear Freeze*, ed. Thomas R. Rochon and David S. Meyer (Boulder, CO: Lynne Rienner, 1997), 12. For details on the House nuclear freeze resolution, see chapter 4 of the present work.

43. Letter, Stephen Band to Richard Gozney, August 9, 1983, FCO 46/3607, "Proposals for Freezing Nuclear Weapon Levels," TNA.

44. Zubok, *A Failed Empire*, 273–274.

45. Zubok, *A Failed Empire*, 274.

46. Rowland Evans and Robert Novak, ". . . A Mandate to Talk Tough," *Washington Post*, September 5, 1983, A17.

47. Zubok, *A Failed Empire*, 274.

48. Waller, *Congress and the Nuclear Freeze*, 290–291.

49. Nicholas Thompson, *The Hawk and the Dove: Paul Nitze, George Kennan, and the History of the Cold War* (New York: Henry Holt, 2009), 285–290. Nitze's efforts were kept from the public until they were leaked following the administration's firing of ACDA's Eugene Rostow.

50. Nitze, *From Hiroshima to Glasnost*, 389; telegram no. 121, Moscow to Immediate FCO, February 3, 1983, PREM 19/973, TNA.

51. Nitze, *From Hiroshima to Glasnost*, 389; telegram no. 302, Washington to Immediate FCO, February 4, 1983, "Vice-President Bush's Visit to London: INF," and telegram no. 074, Rome to Immediate FCO, "Visit of Vice President Bush," February 8, 1983, Prime Minister's Office Files (PREM) 19/973, TNA; telegram no. 4030, Washington to Priority FCO, December 23, 1982, FCO 46/3144, "U.S. Views on Nuclear Arms Control (Inc. INF and Start)," TNA.

52. Telegram no. 1612, Washington to Priority FCO, June 10, 1983, PREM 19/973, TNA.

53. Memo, Roger Bone to John Coles, June 10, 1983, PREM 19/973, TNA.

54. Letter, Reagan to Andropov, circa July 8, 1983, in Skinner, Anderson, and Anderson, *A Life in Letters*, 742–743; Reagan, *An American Life*, 576–581.

55. Gromyko quoted in telegram no. 671, British Moscow Embassy to Immediate FCO, June 22, 1983, and telegram no. 667, "Soviet Proposal for Freeze of Nuclear Forces," both in FCO 46/3607, "Proposals for Freezing Nuclear Weapon Levels," TNA.

56. Telegram no. 666, British Moscow Embassy to Immediate FCO, June 21, 1983, "Soviet Proposal for Freeze of Nuclear Forces"; telegram no. 623, Peking to

Priority FCO, July 4, 1983, "Soviet Proposal for Freeze of Nuclear Forces"; telegram no. 793, British Moscow Embassy to Immediate FCO, July 15, 1983; memo, P. J. Weston to Mr. Cartledge and Mr. Wright, July 6, 1983, "Soviet Proposal for Freeze of Nuclear Forces"; telegram no. 1003, June 17, 1983, "Supreme Soviet Call for Nuclear Freeze by all Powers," all in FCO 46/3607, "Proposals for Freezing Nuclear Weapon Levels," TNA.

57. Dusko Doder, "Soviets Hint Shift on Missile Talks," *Washington Post*, July 8, 1983, A1.

58. Ari L. Goldman, "Soviet in U.N. Calls for an Arms Freeze," *New York Times*, October 5, 1983, 3; Mary Kaldor, "A Strategy for 1983," *Journal of European Nuclear Disarmament*, no. 2 (February–March 1983): 2; David Cortright, "Opposing Cruise and Pershing II Missile Deployments in Europe," November 9, 1982, SANE Records, National Office (DG 58), box 70, series G, Files of David Cortright, SCPC.

59. "The Nuclear Weapons Freeze Campaign's Position on the Pershing II and Cruise Missiles," no date, circa 1983, SANE Records, National Office (DG 58), box 134, series G, Files of Ed Glennon, SCPC.

60. Letter, Howard Morland to Freeze Strategy Committee, May 9, 1983, SANE Records, National Office (DG 58), box 135, series G, Files of Ed Glennon, SCPC.

61. Letter, Debbie Hejl (Detroit Area Nuclear Weapons Freeze coordinator) to Nuclear Weapons Freeze Campaign Task Force, April 28, 1983, SANE Records (DG 58), box 64, series G, Files of D. Cortright, SCPC.

62. Memo, Barbara Roche to National Committee Members, June 3, 1983, and memo, Randy Kehler to National Committee Members, June 3, 1983, both in SANE Records, National Office (DG 58), box 135, series G, Files of Ed Glennon, SCPC.

63. Waller, *Congress and the Nuclear Freeze*, 171; memo, Jane Midgley to Executive Committee, Cruise and Pershing Project, SANE Records, National Office (DG 58), box 135, series G, Files of Ed Glennon, SCPC.

64. Letter, David McReynolds (WRL) to Wim Bartels (IPCC), August 26, 1983, SANE Records, National Office (DG 58), box 134, series G, Files of Ed Glennon, SCPC.

65. Kehler quoted in Ben Senturia in consultation with Randy Kehler, *Peace Action*, ed. Strassen and Wittner, 70.

66. Pam Solo, "October Actions to Stop Euromissiles," no date, circa September 1983, and "Summary of Euromissile Demonstrations," October 1983, SANE Records, National Office (DG 58), box 134, series G, Files of Ed Glennon, SCPC.

67. "Briefing Notes for Ministers: Reductions in NATO's Nuclear Stockpile," November 22, 1983; Secret UK Eyes memo, Council of Defence to Margaret Thatcher, October 21, 1983; and letter, Ronald Reagan to Margaret Thatcher, undated, circa October 24, 1983, all in PREM 19/973, TNA.

68. Steve Breyman, *Why Movements Matter: The West German Peace Movement and U.S. Arms Control Policy* (Albany: State University of New York Press, 2001), 191–192.

69. Breyman, *Why Movements Matter*, 193–196.

70. *Der Spiegel* quoted in Breyman, *Why Movements Matter*, 196; "Tories against Cruise and Trident," quoted in "Nuclear Freeze Proposals," House of Lords, vol. 444, no. 22, October 24, 1982, 7, FCO 46/3607, "Proposals for Freezing Nuclear Weapon Levels," TNA; E. P. Thompson quoted in Kaldor, "A Strategy for 1983."

71. Perle quoted in Fred Kaplan, "Official: Missile Decision a Mistake," *Boston Globe*, June 2, 1983, 1, 12.

72. "Nuclear Freeze Proposals," House of Lords, vol. 444, no. 22, October 24, 1982, 5–8, FCO 46/3607, "Proposals for Freezing Nuclear Weapon Levels," TNA.

73. Cruise and Pershing Project, "Legislative Update," November 11, 1983, SANE Records, National Office (DG 58), box 135, series G, Files of Ed Glennon, SCPC.

74. Cruise and Pershing Project, "Legislative Update," November 11, 1983; Libby Frank (WILPF) to Ed Glennon (SANE), December 23, 1983, "Not Until the Decision Is Reversed," and letter, Mike Jendrzejczyk (FOR) to Ed Glennon (SANE), December 21, 1983, "Clear Up the Debts," SANE Records, National Office (DG 58), box 134, series G, Files of Ed Glennon, SCPC; Mary Kaldor, "Twin Track for Peace: Nuclear Freeze Plus Roll Back," *The Guardian*, November 28, 1983, 10.

75. Christopher Andrew and Oleg Gordievsky, *Comrade Kryuchkov's Instructions: Top Secret Files on KGB Foreign Operations 1975–1985* (Stanford, CA: Stanford University Press, 1993), 67.

76. Nate Jones, ed., *Able Archer 83: The Secret History of the NATO Exercise That Almost Triggered Nuclear War* (New York: New Press, 2016), 26; Andrew and Gordievsky, *Comrade Kryuchkov's Instructions*, 74; Murrey Marder, "The U.S.-Soviet War of Words Escalates: A 'White Hot' Confrontation," *Washington Post*, November 21, 1983, A1, A13. For a wider overview see Marc Ambinder, *The Brink: President Reagan and the Nuclear War Scare of 1983* (New York: Simon and Schuster, 2018) and Taylor Downing, *1983: Reagan, Andropov, and a World on the Brink* (New York: Da Capo Press, 2018). Several scholars contend the dangers of the Able Archer incident have been overstated. See, among others, Vojtech Mastny, "How Able Was 'Able Archer'? Nuclear Trigger and Intelligence in Perspective," *Journal of Cold War Studies* 11, no. 1 (Winter 2009): 108–123, and Simon Miles, "The War Scare That Wasn't: Able Archer 83 and the Myths of the Second Cold War," *Journal of Cold War Studies* 22, no. 3 (Summer 2020): 86–118.

77. Jones, *Able Archer 83*, 3, 11.

78. "2 Are Killed and 24 Hurt as Blasts Rip through L.I. Fireworks Plant," *New York Times*, November 27, 1983, 1.

Chapter 7. Seizing the Peace

1. David Cortright, "Where Do We Go from Here: Next Steps for the Peace Movement," *SANE Action* 2, no. 7 (December 2, 1983): 1–4; Howard Morland, "Unilateralism and the Freeze," 1984, European Nuclear Disarmament, Records, 19/17, London School of Economics, Archives Division, London, England; Pam Solo, "Freeze Summit," *Journal of European Nuclear Disarmament*, no. 8 (February–March 1984). On the similarities and differences between the US and European antinuclear movements, see Mary Kaldor's interview with Randy Kehler and Mient Jan Faber (IKV), "Learning from Each Other," *Journal of European Nuclear Disarmament*, no. 2 (February–March 1983): 22–23.

2. Letter, John Carbaugh to William Clark, case file 182654–183499, ND 018, box 14, WHORM Subject File, RRPL.

3. Marcy Darnovsky, "Dangerous Illusions," *Nuclear Times* 3, no. 3 (January 1984): 14–15.

4. David Cortright, "Where Do We Go from Here: Next Steps for the Freeze/Peace Movement," SANE Records, National Office (DG 58), box 152, series G, Freeze Campaign Files of Mike Mawby, 1982–1984, SCPC.

5. Tom Shales, "Bombing Out for the Bottom Line," *Washington Post*, May 30, 1983, D1, D11; Nuclear Weapons Freeze Campaign, "Resolution," undated, SANE Records, National Office (DG 58), box 152, series G, Freeze Campaign files of Mike Mawby, 1982–1984, SCPC.

6. Howell Raines, "Cranston Beats Mondale in Wisconsin Democratic Straw Poll," *New York Times*, June 12, 1983, 22; Martin Schram, "Touting Freeze, Cranston Scores Straw Poll Upset in Wisconsin," *Washington Post*, June 12, 1983, 5; "Candidates Vie for Peace Votes," *Nuclear Times* 3, no. 4 (February 1984): 7–8.

7. "Where They Stand," *Nuclear Times* 3, no. 4 (February 1984): 8.

8. "Where They Stand," 8.

9. Robert W. Merry, "Mondale Jabs Hart from Both Sides," *Wall Street Journal*, March 20, 1984, 58; "Meeting of Walter F. Mondale with Representatives of Arms Control Groups," January 23, 1984, transcript in SANE Records, National Office (DG 58), box 143, series G, Files of Beth Baker, 1980–1985, SCPC.

10. Meyer, *A Winter of Discontent*, 247; "Where They Stand," 8; Solo, *From Protest to Policy*, 156.

11. Letter, Gary Hart to the Honorable Charles Percy, March 4, 1984, in SANE Records, National Office (DG 58), box 143, series G, Files of Beth Baker, 1980–1985, SCPC.

12. Solo, *From Protest to Policy*, 156.

13. Solo, *From Protest to Policy*, 158.

14. Letter, Peter Bergel to Les AuCoin, March 8, 1984, and Les AuCoin to Peter Bergel, March 21, 1984, SANE Records, National Office (DG 58), box 173, series G, Files of Jerry Hartz, SCPC. Emphasis in original.

15. Memo, Randy Kehler to Freeze Supporters, April 6, 1984, SANE Records, National Office (DG 58), box 173, series G, Files of Jerry Hartz, SCPC.

16. Solo, *From Protest to Policy*, 162–163; Douglas Lavin, "Quick Freeze Falters," *Nuclear Times* 3, no. 1 (October–November 1984): 7.

17. Meyer, *A Winter of Discontent*, 237.

18. Lavin, "Quick Freeze Falters," 7.

19. Solo, *From Protest to Policy*, 148.

20. Solo, *From Protest to Policy*, 149.

21. Solo, *From Protest to Policy*, 156.

22. "History of Freeze Voter '84," Freeze Voter Records (DG 158), box 1, series A, SCPC.

23. Solo, *From Protest to Policy*, 169; Meyer, *A Winter of Discontent*, 244–246.

24. Meyer, *A Winter of Discontent*, 246.

25. Memo, Richard B. Wirthlin, November 28, 1983, box 686, Edwin Meese Papers, HIA.

26. Memo, Richard B. Wirthlin to Edwin Meese III, James A. Baker III, and Michael K. Deaver, August 31, 1983, box 686, Edwin Meese Papers, HIA.

27. Memo, Richard B. Wirthlin to Republican National Committee, January 27, 1984, box 686, Edwin Meese Papers, HIA.

28. Telegram, Richard Luce to Erik Deakins, September 28, 1983, FCO 46/3607, "Proposals for Freezing Nuclear Weapon Levels," TNA.

29. Associated Press, "Mediation Offer by Vatican," *The Times* [London], December 5, 1983, in FCO 33/7049, "Vatican Attitude towards Nuclear Weapons," TNA.

30. Memo, Stuart Jack to Richard Gozney, January 26, 1984, "Notices on Questions and Motions," January 23, 1984, no. 82, "Freeze on Nuclear Weapons [390]," and memo, confidential, Rome to Immediate Foreign and Commonwealth Office, January 23, 1984, both in FCO 46/4164, "Proposals for Freezing Nuclear Weapon Levels," TNA.

31. Francis X. Clines, "President's Team Celebrates Itself," *New York Times*, January 21, 1984, 1; John Lewis Gaddis, *The Cold War: A New History* (New York: Penguin Books, 2005), 228.

32. Oberdorfer, *From the Cold War to a New Era*, 79–83.

33. Steven R. Weisman, "Light Workouts for the Reagan Campaign," *New York Times*, June 24, 1984, A1.

34. Charlotte Curtis, "Ford's Glamour," *New York Times*, August 31, 1982, 8.

35. Letter, Jay Harris to James Baker, October 16, 1984; letter, James A. Baker III to Jay Harris, October 31, 1984; and letter, Gerald R. Ford to Jay Harris, July 30, 1984, case file 269000–319999, Peace PC, box 2, WHORM Subject File, RRPL. Rep. Hance changed his party affiliation to Republican in 1985.

36. Norman D. Atkins, "Poll Puts Mondale Even with Reagan," *Washington Post*, July 23, 1984, A3; Barry Sussman, "Presidential-Preference Polls Are Disagreeing More Than Usual," *Washington Post*, July 24, 1984, A7.

37. Condon quoted in Anthony J. Bennett, *The Race for the White House from Reagan to Clinton: Reforming Old Systems, Building New Coalitions*, The Pursuit of the Presidency, vol. 1 (New York: Palgrave Macmillan, 2013), 67; Walter F. Mondale with David Hage, *The Good Fight: A Life in Liberal Politics* (New York: Scribner, 2010), 296.

38. United Press International, "Husband, Panel Paid Fine for '78 Ferraro Race," *Washington Post*, July 15, 1984, A17; Ralph Blumenthal, "Rep. Ferraro's Financial Status Starts to Emerge," *New York Times*, July 18, 1984, A20; Charles Babcot and Margaret Hornblower, "Porn Firm Said Tenant of Zaccaro," *Washington Post*, July 26, 1984, A5; Rick Atkinson, "Zaccaro Agrees to Release Six Years of Tax Returns," *Washington Post*, August 18, 1984, A5.

39. Atkinson, "Zaccaro Agrees to Release Six Years of Tax Returns," *Washington Post*, A1, A5; Bennett, *The Race for the White House*, 70.

40. Geraldine A. Ferraro with Linda Bird Francke, *Ferraro: My Story*, new ed. (Evanston, IL: Northwestern University Press, 2004), 218, 236.

41. Ferraro, *Ferraro*, 215–222.

42. Ferraro, *Ferraro*, 222–225, emphasis Ferraro's.

43. Ellen Goodman, "Bishops as Bosses," *Washington Post*, September 11, 1984, A23; Bruce Buursma, "Bernardin Joins Debate over Religion, Politics," *Chicago Tribune*, September 16, 1984, 12.

44. Weisman, "Light Workouts for the Reagan Campaign"; Steven R. Weisman, "Roman Catholic Shrine Is Site for Reagan Rally," *New York Times*, September 10, 1984, B9.

45. Cannon, *Role of a Lifetime*, 473–475; Maureen Dowd, "Women Assess Impact of Mondale Loss," *New York Times*, November 14, 1984, A22.

46. Paul Taylor, "Mondale Says President's Joke Wasn't Funny," *Washington Post*, August 14, 1984, A6; Celestine Bohlen, "Soviets Formally Denounce Reagan's Joke," *Washington Post*, August 16, 1984, A32; Hedrick Smith, "Reagan's Gaffe," *New York Times*, August 14, 1984, A4; David Cortright/SANE PAC, letter to SANE members, undated, box 839, folder 2, Carl Sagan Papers, LOC.

47. Cannon, *Role of a Lifetime*, 473; FitzGerald, *Way Out There in the Blue*, 240.

48. FitzGerald, *Way Out There in the Blue*, 240; Bernard Gwertzman, "A Reagan Pledge on Peace Efforts," *New York Times*, September 23, 1984, 11.

49. Francis X. Clines, "Mondale Assails Reagan on Arms Control," *New York Times*, October 2, 1984, A22; Bob Drogin, "Ferraro Harshly Attacks Reagan Arms Policies," *Los Angeles Times*, September 22, 1984, A6.

50. Cannon, *Role of a Lifetime*, 475; Marglene Cimons and Bob Drogin, "Mondale Urges Reagan to Curb Rowdy Hecklers," *Los Angeles Times*, September 21, 1984, 1, 13; Jane Perlez, "Bush, in Vermont, Confronts Antinuclear Hecklers," *New York Times*, September 24, 1984, B13.

51. Cannon, *Role of a Lifetime*, 475.

52. David S. Broder and Barry Sussman, "Mondale's Ratings Improve," *Washington Post*, October 11, 1984, A1, A10.

53. Cannon, *Role of a Lifetime*, 485–486.

54. Cannon, *Role of a Lifetime*, 483–485; "Transcript of the Reagan-Mondale Debate on Foreign Policy," *New York Times*, October 22, 1984, B4.

55. Cannon, *Role of a Lifetime*, 486–487; "Transcript of the Reagan-Mondale Debate on Foreign Policy."

56. Paul Taylor, "Presidency Not Focus of Nuclear Fear," *Washington Post*, October 2, 1984, A1, A8.

57. Trump quoted in Lois Ramano, "Donald Trump Holding All the Cards," *Washington Post*, November 15, 1984, D1, 10–11. Cohn is perhaps best remembered as Joseph McCarthy's chief counsel during the Army-McCarthy hearings.

58. Ellen Goodman, "Fearing Nuclear War They'll Vote for . . . Reagan!," *Los Angeles Times*, October 2, 1984, C5; Jean Stead, "How the Cold Warrior Outgunned the Freeze Movement," *The Guardian*, October 15, 1984, 15.

59. Seymour Melman and William Winpisinger, "One for Twenty, Twenty for All: An Appeal to Every Member of SANE," *SANE World* 23, no. 9 (October 1984): 1; Cathy Cevolli, "Peace Issues Pick Up Steam," *Nuclear Times* 3, no. 1 (October–November 1984): 12–14; Douglas Lavin, "Try 'Til November," *Nuclear Times* 3, no. 1 (October–November 1984): 16–17; "Display Ad 22," *New York Times*, November 2, 1984, A23.

60. Julian Zelizer, *Arsenal of Democracy: The Politics of National Security—from World War II to the War on Terrorism* (New York: Basic Books, 2010), 330; FitzGerald, *Way Out There in the Blue*, 259. Although Reagan won the most votes in the Electoral College in 1984 (525), Franklin Roosevelt's 1936 electoral victory over Alfred Landon received a higher percentage of Electoral College votes.

61. "Backers of Nuclear Freeze Seek to Broaden Base," *New York Times*, December 10, 1984, A20; Meyer, *A Winter of Discontent*, 253; "Cranston Cool on Freeze?," *Nuclear Times*, 3, no. 4 (March 1985): 3.

62. "Arms Freeze Advocates Count on 1986 Races," *New York Times*, November 18, 1984, A26.

63. Randy Kehler interview by Lawrence Wittner, August 20, 1999 (transcript in author's possession); Randy Kehler, *Freeze Focus*, December 1984, David Cortright Papers (DG 101), box 2 of 8, SCPC.

64. Cevolli, "Peace Issues Pick Up Steam."

65. Forsberg interview by Wittner, July 7, 1999; Caldicott interview by Wittner, February 27, 1999.

66. Pennsylvania Nuclear Weapons Freeze Campaign, "A Freeze-PAC: In Whose Interest?" (no date, circa 1985), Nuclear Weapons Freeze Campaign (CDG-A), Freeze Campaigns (State and Local), Ohio–West Virginia, box 2 of 2, SCPC.

67. "Mondale, with Tears," *Nuclear Times* 3, no. 1 (October–November 1984): 17, emphasis in original.

68. Solo, *From Protest to Policy*, 151; Senturia with Kehler, "The Freeze Grassroots Strategy," 70–73.

69. FitzGerald, *Way Out There in the Blue*, 259.

Epilogue

1. E. P. Thompson speech quoted from Robert Korstad and Nelson Lichtenstein, "Opportunities Found and Lost: Labor, Radicals, and Civil Rights," *Journal of American History* 75, no. 3 (December 1988): 811.

2. Robert Kleidman, *Organizing For Peace: Neutrality, the Test Ban, and the Freeze* (Syracuse, NY: Syracuse University Press, 1993), 161–165; Solo, *From Protest to Policy*, 176; Bruce Ferguson, "Different Agendas, Styles, Shape SANE/Freeze," *Bulletin of the Atomic Scientists* 5, no. 3 (April 1988): 27.

3. Solo, *From Protest to Policy*, 176; David Cortright, "Notes of Freeze, SANE Unity Meeting," March 18, 1986, and minutes, FREEZE/SANE Commission, July 30–31, 1986, in SANE Records, National Office (DG 58), SANE Strategy, 1986–1988, Transition to SANE/FREEZE 1986–1987, box 20A, series G, SCPC.

4. Senturia with Kehler, "The Freeze Grassroots Strategy," 70–73.

5. "Disarmament Groups Seek Rallying Point After Faltering on Atom Freeze," *New York Times*, August 18, 1985, 22; Ferguson, "Different Agendas, Styles, Shape SANE/Freeze," 27.

6. Kleidman, *Organizing for Peace*, 166–167; Harvey, *American Anti-nuclear Activism*, 53.

7. Pam Baker and Gene Carroll, "Listening Project," November 17, 1986, SANE Records (DG 58), box 87, series G, Files of D. Cortright, SCPC.

8. "Key Aspects of Merger Decisions from the 7th Annual National Freeze Conference, December 5–7, 1986," January 28, 1987, SANE Records, National Office (DG 58), SANE Strategy, 1986–1988, Transition to SANE/FREEZE 1986–1987, box 20A, series G, SCPC; Memo, Freeze Voter Board of Directors to Freeze-Sane Transition Team, "Board Position on Possible Merger," March 15, 1987, Freeze Voter '84 Records (DG156), box 3, SCPC.

9. Ferguson, "Different Agendas, Styles, Shape SANE/Freeze," 27; David Cortright, *Peace: A History of Movements and Ideas* (New York: Cambridge University Press, 2008), 142; Kleidman, *Organizing for Peace*, 166.

10. On the fraud of SDI and BMD, moreover, see William J. Perry and Tom Z. Collina, *The Button: The New Nuclear Arms Race and Presidential Power from Truman to Trump* (Dallas: BenBella Books, 2020), 149–166.

11. Keith Love, "Democrats Take Hard Look at the Election," *Los Angeles Times*, November 11, 1984, 1, 14; William Drozdiak, "Reagan Gains Favor in W. Europe," *Washington Post*, October 5, 1984, A1, A28.

12. Ellen Goodman, "Toward Peace on Earth," *Washington Post*, December 18, 1984, A19.

13. LaFeber, *America, Russia, and the Cold War*, 332–333, 337.

14. LaFeber, *America, Russia, and the Cold War*, 334–335, 338.

15. Wittner, *Towards Nuclear Abolition*, 384–388. The Comprehensive Test Ban Treaty unfortunately was never ratified by the US Senate. See Perry and Collina, *The Button*, 194–198.

16. Mary Kaldor interview by Lawrence Wittner, June 7, 1999 (transcript in author's possession); LaFeber, *America, Russia, and the Cold War*, 338–339.

17. Aram Backshian interview by David Cortright, July 16, 1990, David Cortright Papers (DG 101), box 2, SCPC.

18. Memo, National Freeze Staff to Local Organizers, November 22, 1985, SANE Records, National Office (DG 58), box 173, series G, Files of Jerry Hartz, SCPC; David Cortright, "SANE at the Summit—Report from Geneva," *SANE World* 25, no. 1 (January–February 1986): 1–2. The candlelight vigils were part of "Turning on Lights for Peace," an initiative by leaders of the National Council of Churches of Christ, the World Council of Churches, and the US Catholic Conference calling on citizens everywhere to "light porchlights, candles and other lights . . . from dusk to dawn" during the Geneva Summit to "openly display their desire for world peace." Proclamation of South Carolina Governor Richard W. Riley, no date, circa October 1985, case file 360591, PC (Peace), box 2, WHORM Subject File, RRPL. Numerous other governors from across the US also issued similarly-worded proclamations.

19. Jack F. Matlock Jr., *Reagan and Gorbachev: How the Cold War Ended* (New York: Random House, 2004), 237–239.

20. Cortright, *Peace Works*, 175; William Taubman, *Gorbachev: His Life and Times* (New York: W. W. Norton, 2017), 274; Mann, *The Rebellion of Ronald Reagan*, 231–232; LaFeber, *America, Russia, and the Cold War*, 341.

21. "INF: A Taste for Disarmament," no date, circa 1987, "Zero Option: An Opportunity and Challenge," May 28, 1987, and David Cortright and Carolyn Cottom, "Proposal for a National INF Campaign," circa 1987, all in SANE Records (DG 58), box 87, series G, Files of D. Cortright, SCPC.

22. Hedrick Smith, "The Right against Reagan," *New York Times Magazine*, January 17, 1988, SM36; Frederick Kempe and Tim Carrington, "White House Is Criticized for Rushing to Reach Arms Pact That May Leave Europe Vulnerable," *Wall Street Journal*, April 10, 1987, 1; Dan Quayle, "INF Treaty's Dangerous Vagueness," *Wall Street Journal*, February 8, 1988, 24; Mann, *The Rebellion of Ronald Reagan*, 233, 264.

23. Mann, *The Rebellion of Ronald Reagan*, 265–266; Kenneth L. Adelman, *The Great Universal Embrace: Arms Summitry—a Skeptic's Account* (New York: Simon and Schuster, 1989), 248–249.

24. LaFeber, *America, Russia, and the Cold War*, 339; Stanley Meisler, "Reagan Recants 'Evil Empire' Description," *Los Angeles Times*, June 1, 1988, B1; "The Cold War Is Over," *New York Times*, April 2, 1989, E30; Gerald M. Boyd, "Hailing Arms Pact, Bush Attacks Foe," *New York Times*, September 9, 1988, A15.

25. Kehler interview by Wittner, August 20, 1999; Warnke and Adelman quoted in Mike Feinsilber, Associated Press, "Does Movement to Force Nuclear Weapons Freeze Have Future?," *The Telegraph*, April 21, 1984, 29.

26. Les Janka interview by David Cortright, August 23, 1990, and Robert Kimmit interview by David Cortright, December 20, 1990, both in David Cortright Papers (DG 101), box 2, SCPC. Keyworth quoted in Hartung, "Star Wars Pork Barrel," *Bulletin of the Atomic Scientists*, 20.

27. Williams, *Empire as a Way of Life*, 199.

BIBLIOGRAPHY

Archival Collections

Official

United Kingdom

The National Archives, Kew, London (TNA)
    Foreign and Commonwealth Office Files (FCO)
    Prime Minister's Office Files (PREM)

United States

Ronald Reagan Presidential Library, Simi Valley, CA (RRPL)
    White House Office of Records Management, Subject File (WHORM)
    White House Staff and Office Files

Personal and Organizational Collections

United Kingdom

London School of Economics, Archives Division, London, England
    European Nuclear Disarmament, Records

United States

Archdiocese of Chicago, Joseph Cardinal Bernardin Archives and Records Center,
    Chicago, IL (ARC)
    Bernardin, Joseph Cardinal, War and Peace Papers, Executive Records—United
        States Conference of Catholic Bishops (USCCB) Committee and Council Files
Bancroft Library, Special Collections, University of California, Berkeley, Berkeley,
    CA (BANC)
    Chamberlain, Owen, Papers
    People for the American Way, collection of conservative political ephemera
Hesburgh Library, Special Collections, Archives of the University of Notre Dame,
    University of Notre Dame, South Bend, IN (AUND)
    Catholic Peace Fellowship, Records (CPF)
    Gumbleton, Thomas J., Papers
    PAX Christi USA, Records
Hoover Institution Archives, Stanford University, Palo Alto, CA (HIA)
    Committee on the Present Danger, Records
    Meese, Edwin, Papers

Library of Congress, Manuscripts Division, Washington, DC (LOC)
    Kemp, Jack, Papers
    McGrory, Mary, Papers
    Nitze, Paul H., Papers
    Sagan, Carl, Papers
Swarthmore College Peace Collection, Swarthmore, PA (SCPC)
    Clergy and Laity Concerned, Records
    Cortright, David, Papers
    Freeze Campaigns [State and Local] Collected Records, 1980–1989
    Freeze Voter, Records
    SANE, Inc., Records, National Office, Series G
Tamiment Library and Robert F. Wagner Archives, New York University, New York, NY
    Cagan, Leslie, Papers
    Mobilization for Survival, Records (MFS)
Thomas Jefferson Library, Western Manuscript Collection, University of Missouri, St. Louis, MO (UMSL)
    National Nuclear Weapons Freeze Campaign (NWFC), Records
Yale University Library, Manuscripts and Archives, New Haven, CT
    Coalition to Stop Trident, Records

Government Documents

Department of State. *American Foreign Policy Current Documents 1981.* Washington, DC: Department of State, 1981.

Forsberg, Randall. FBI file.

Reagan, Ronald. *Public Papers of the Presidents of the United States: Ronald Reagan, 1981–1988.* 9 vols. Washington, DC: US Government Printing Office, 1990

Taylor, Melissa Jane, ed. *Foreign Relations of the United States, 1977–1980, Volume VI: Soviet Union.* Washington, DC: US Government Printing Office, 2013.

United States Congress, Senate Committee on Foreign Relations. *Nomination of Alexander M. Haig, Jr. Hearings Before the Committee on Foreign Relations, United States Senate, Ninety-Seventh Congress, First Session, on the Nomination of Alexander M. Haig, Jr., to Be Secretary of State, January 9, 10, 12, 13, 14, 15, 1981.* Washington, DC: US Government Printing Office, 1981.

Print Media

Boston Globe
The Bulletin [Bend, OR]
Bulletin-Journal [Cape Girardeau, MO]
Chicago Tribune
Cincinnati Enquirer
Daily World
Deseret News
Gadsden Times

Grants Pass Daily Courier
The Guardian
Los Angeles Times
New York Post
New York Times
Salt Lake Tribune
Spokane Daily Chronicle
St. Louis Post-Dispatch
St. Petersburg Times
The Times [London]
Wall Street Journal
Washington Post

Periodicals

Bulletin of the Atomic Scientists
CALC Report
Commentary
Commonweal
Congressional Quarterly
Conservative Digest
END Bulletin
Executive Intelligence Review
Foreign Affairs
Foreign Policy
Freeze Newsletter
Human Events
Journal of European Nuclear Disarmament
Military Review
The Mobilizer
The Nation
National Catholic Register
National Freeze Campaign Monthly Update
National Review
New Statesman
Newsweek
Nuclear Times
Reader's Digest
SANE Action
SANE World
Phyllis Schlafly Report
Stop the B-1 Bomber / National Peace Conversion Campaign Newsletter
Sun Dial
Time
Visitor

Interview Transcripts

Wittner, Lawrence. Interviews with Reagan administration officials and antinuclear activists.

Primary Sources (Print)

Adelman, Kenneth L. *The Great Universal Embrace: Arms Summitry—a Skeptic's Account*. New York: Simon and Schuster, 1989.

Brinkley, Douglas, and Luke A. Nichter, eds. *The Nixon Tapes, 1971–1972*. New York: Houghton Mifflin Harcourt, 2014.

Caldicott, Helen. *A Desperate Passion: An Autobiography*. New York: W. W. Norton, 1996.

Congressional Quarterly. *U.S. Foreign Policy: The Reagan Imprint*. Washington, DC: Congressional Quarterly, 1986.

Cortright, David. *Peace Works: The Citizen's Role in Ending the Cold War*. Boulder, CO: Westview Press, 1993.

Dictor, Dave. *MDC: Memoir from a Damaged Civilization*. San Francisco: Manic D. Press, 2016.

Dos Santos, Lucia. *Fatima in Lucia's Own Words*. Ed. L. Kondor, trans. the Dominican Nuns. Fatima: Postulation Center, 1975.

Ferraro, Geraldine A., and Linda Bird Francke. *Ferraro: My Story*. New ed. Evanston, IL: Northwestern University Press, 2004. Original edition New York: Bantam Books, 1985.

Graham, Billy. *Just as I Am: The Autobiography of Billy Graham*. New York: Harper-Collins, 1997.

Gregory, Donna, ed. *The Nuclear Predicament: A Sourcebook*. New York: St. Martin's Press, 1986.

Haig, Alexander M., Jr. *Caveat: Realism, Reagan, and Foreign Policy*. New York: Macmillan, 1984.

Jones, Nate, ed. *Able Archer 83: The Secret History of the NATO Exercise That Almost Triggered Nuclear War*. New York: New Press, 2016.

Keithley, Joey. *I, Shithead: A Life in Punk*. Vancouver: Arsenal Pulp Press, 2003.

Kennedy, John F. Address to the United Nations General Assembly, September 25, 1961, Transcript at https://www.jfklibrary.org/Asset-Viewer/DOPIN64xJUGRKgdHJ9NfgQ.aspx.

Krauthammer, Charles. *Things That Matter: Three Decades of Passions, Pastimes, and Politics*. New York: Crown Books, 2010.

Lens, Sidney. *Unrepentant Radical: An American Activist's Account of Five Turbulent Decades*. Boston: Beacon Press, 1980.

Mathers, Dexter, and Katherine Way, eds. *One World or None: A Reporting to the Public on the Full Meaning of the Atomic Bomb*. New York: New Press, 2007.

Matlock, Jack F., Jr. *Reagan and Gorbachev: How the Cold War Ended*. New York: Random House, 2004.

McFarlane, Robert C., with Zofia Smardz. *Special Trust*. New York: Cadell and Davies, 1994.

Mondale, Walter F., and Dave Hage. *The Good Fight: A Life in Liberal Politics*. New York: Scribner, 2010.

Nitze, Paul H., with Ann M. Smith and Steven L. Rearden. *From Hiroshima to Glasnost: At the Center of Decision—a Memoir*. New York: Grove Weidenfeld, 1989.

Obama, Barack. "Breaking the War Mentality." *Sun Dial*, March 10, 1983, 2–5.

Reagan, Ronald. *An American Life*. New York: Simon and Schuster, 1990.

——. *The Reagan Diaries, Volume 1, January 1981–October 1985*, edited by Douglas Brinkley. New York: HarperCollins, 2007.

Schell, Jonathan. *The Fate of the Earth*. New York: Alfred A. Knopf, 1982.

Shultz, George P. *Turmoil and Triumph: My Years as Secretary of State*. New York: Charles Scribner's Sons, 1993.

Skinner, Kiron K., Martin Anderson, and Annelise Anderson, eds. *Reagan: A Life in Letters*. New York: Free Press, 2003.

Smith, Dean, with John Kilgo and Sally Jenkins. *A Coach's Life: My Forty Years in College Basketball*. New York: Random House, 1999.

Solo, Pam. *From Protest to Policy: Beyond the Freeze to Common Security*. Cambridge: Ballinger, 1988.

Stockman, David. *The Triumph of Politics: Why the Reagan Revolution Failed*. New York: Harper and Row, 1986.

Strassen, Glen Harold, and Lawrence S. Wittner, eds. *Peace Action: Past, Present, Future*. Boulder: Paradigm, 2007.

Waller, Douglas. *Congress and the Nuclear Freeze: An Inside Look at the Politics of a Mass Movement*. Amherst: University of Massachusetts Press, 1987.

Secondary Sources (Books, Articles, and Chapters)

Ackland, Len. *Making a Real Killing: Rocky Flats and the Nuclear West*. Updated ed. Albuquerque: University of New Mexico Press, 1999.

Alberigo, Giuseppe. *A Brief History of Vatican II*. Translated by Matthew Sherry. Maryknoll, NY: Orbis Books, 2006.

Aldonov, Boris. *The Human Predicament: The Secular Ideologies, Volume 1*. New Delhi: Vikas, 1988.

Ambinder, Marc. *The Brink: President Reagan and the Nuclear War Scare of 1983*. New York: Simon and Schuster, 2018.

Anderson, Martin, and Annelise Anderson. *Reagan's Secret War: The Untold Story of His Fight to Save the World from Nuclear Disaster*. New York: Three Rivers Press, 2009.

Andrew, Christopher M., and Oleg Gordievsky. *Comrade Kryuchkov's Instructions: Top Secret Files on KGB Foreign Operations, 1975–1985*. Stanford, CA: Stanford University Press, 1993.

Bailey, Thomas A. *The Man in the Street: The Impact of Public Opinion on Foreign Policy*. New York: Macmillan, 1948.

Barnet, Richard J. "America and Russia: The Rules of the Game; U.S.-Soviet Relations: The Need for a Comprehensive Approach," *Foreign Affairs* 57, no. 4 (Spring 1979): 779–795.

Baucom, Donald R. *The Origins of SDI, 1944–1983*. Lawrence: University Press of Kansas, 1992.

Baumgarten, Mark. *Love Rock Revolution: K Records and the Rise of Independent Music*. Seattle: Sasquatch Books, 2012.

Benford, Robert D., and Scott A. Hunt. "Intersectional Dynamics in Public Problems Marketplaces." In *Challenges and Choices: Constructionist Perspectives on Social Problems*, ed. James Holstein and Gale Mille, 153–186. New York: Walter de Gruyter, 2003.

Benford, Robert D., and Lester R. Kurtz. "Performing the Nuclear Ceremony: The Arms Race as a Ritual." In *A Shuddering Dawn: Religious Studies and the Nuclear Age*, ed. Ira Chernus and Edward Tabor, 69–90. Albany: SUNY Press, 1989.

Bennett, Anthony J. *The Race for the White House from Reagan to Clinton: Reforming Old Systems, Building New Coalitions*. Vol. 1, *The Pursuit of the Presidency*. New York: Palgrave Macmillan, 2013.

Berman, Larry. *No Peace, No Honor: Nixon, Kissinger, and Betrayal in Vietnam*. New York: Free Press, 2001.

Boyer, Paul. *By the Bomb's Early Light: American Thought and Culture at the Dawn of the Atomic Age*. Chapel Hill: University of North Carolina Press, 1985.

——. "From Activism to Apathy: The American People and Nuclear Weapons, 1963–1980." *Journal of American History* 70, no. 4 (March 1984): 821–844.

Breyman, Steve. *Why Movements Matter: The West German Peace Movement and U.S. Arms Control Policy*. Albany: State University of New York Press, 2001.

Brooks, Charles, ed. *Best Editorial Cartoons of the Year, 1983*. Gretna, LA: Pelican, 1983.

——. *Best Editorial Cartoons of the Year, 1984*. Gretna, LA: Pelican, 1984.

Brown, Archie. *The Gorbachev Factor*. New York: Oxford University Press, 1996.

Campbell, David E., John C. Green, and J. Quin Monson. *Seeking the Promised Land: Mormons and American Politics*. Cambridge: Cambridge University Press, 2014.

Cannon, Lou. *President Reagan: The Role of a Lifetime*. New York: Touchstone / Simon and Schuster, 1991; reprint New York: PublicAffairs, 2000.

Carroll, James. *House of War: The Pentagon and the Disastrous Rise of American Power*. New York: Houghton Mifflin, 2006.

Castelli, Jim. *The Bishops and the Bomb: Waging Peace in a Nuclear Age*. New York: Doubleday, 1983.

Chatfield, Charles, with Robert Kleidman. *The American Peace Movement: Ideals and Activism*. New York: Twayne, 1992.

Chomsky, Noam. *Turning the Tide: US Intervention in Latin America and the Struggle for Peace*. Boston: South End Press, 1985.

Cortright, David. *Peace: A History of Movements and Ideas*. New York: Cambridge University Press, 2008.

Craig, Campbell, and Fredrik Logevall. *America's Cold War: The Politics of Insecurity*. Cambridge, MA: Belknap Press of Harvard University Press, 2009.

Dietl, Ralph L. *The Strategic Defense Initiative: Ronald Reagan, NATO Europe, and the Nuclear and Space Talks, 1981–1988*. Lanham, MD: Lexington Books, 2018.

Dougherty, James E. *The Bishops and Nuclear Weapons: The Catholic Pastoral Letter on War and Peace*. Hamden, CT: Archon Books, 1984.

Downing, Taylor. *1983: Reagan, Andropov, and a World on the Brink*. New York: Da Capo Press, 2018.

Easton, Nina. *Gang of Five: Leaders at the Center of the Conservative Crusade*. New York: Simon and Schuster, 2000.

Edwards, John. *Superweapon: The Making of MX*. New York: W. W. Norton, 1982.

Ellis, John Tracy. "American Catholics and Peace: A Historical Sketch." Reprinted in *The Family of Nations: An Expanded View of Patriotism; a New Dedication to Humanity*, ed. James S. Rausch, 13–39. Huntington, IN: Our Sunday Visitor, 1970.

Evangelista, Matthew. *Unarmed Forces: The Transnational Movement to End the Cold War*. Ithaca, NY: Cornell University Press, 1999.

Federation of American (Atomic) Scientists. "Survival Is at Stake." In *One World or None: A Reporting to the Public on the Full Meaning of the Atomic Bomb*, ed. Dexter Mathers and Katherine Way, 215–220. New York: New Press, 2007.

Fischer, Beth A. *The Reagan Reversal: Foreign Policy and the End of the Cold War*. Columbia: University of Missouri Press, 1997.

FitzGerald, Frances. *The Evangelicals: The Struggle to Shape America*. New York: Simon and Schuster, 2017.

——. *Way Out There in the Blue: Ronald Reagan, Star Wars, and the End of the Cold War*. New York: Simon and Schuster, 2000.

Gaddis, John Lewis. *The Cold War: A New History*. New York: Penguin Press, 2005.

——. *The United States and the End of the Cold War: Implications, Reconsiderations, Provocations*. New York: Oxford University Press, 1992.

Garfinkle, Adam. *The Politics of the Nuclear Freeze*. Philadelphia: Foreign Policy Research Institute, 1984.

Garthoff, Raymond L. *Détente and Confrontation: American-Soviet Relations from Nixon to Reagan*. Revised ed. Washington, DC: Brookings Institution Press, 1994.

Gray, Colin S., and Keith Payne. "Victory Is Possible." *Foreign Policy*, no. 39 (Summer 1980): 14–27.

Harvey, Kyle. *American Anti-nuclear Activism, 1975–1990: The Challenge of Peace*. New York: Palgrave Macmillan, 2014.

Hayden, Tom. *Hell No: The Forgotten Power of the Vietnam Peace Movement*. New Haven, CT: Yale University Press, 2017.

Hayward, Steven F. *The Age of Reagan: The Conservative Counterrevolution, 1980–1989*. New York: Crown Forum, 2009.

Herken, Gregg. *Cardinal Choices: Presidential Science Advising from the Atomic Bomb to SDI*. Stanford, CA: Stanford University Press, 2000. Originally published New York: Oxford University Press, 1992.

Hogan, J. Michael. Review of *Coalitions and Political Movements: The Lessons of the Nuclear Freeze*, ed. Thomas R. Rochon and David S. Meyer, *Rhetoric and Public Affairs* 2, no. 1 (Spring 1999): 156–159.

——. *The Nuclear Freeze Campaign: Rhetoric and Foreign Policy in the Telepolitical Age*. East Lansing: Michigan State University Press, 1994.

Hunt, Andrew E. *David Dellinger: The Life and Times of a Nonviolent Revolutionary*. New York: New York University Press, 2006.

Intondi, Vincent J. *African Americans and the Bomb: Nuclear Weapons, Colonialism, and the Black Freedom Movement*. Stanford, CA: Stanford University Press, 2015.

Jenkins, Philip. *Decade of Nightmares: The End of the Sixties and the Making of Eighties America*. New York: Oxford University Press, 2006.

Johns, Andrew L., and Mitchell B. Lerner, eds. *The Cold War at Home and Abroad: Domestic Politics and US Foreign Policy since 1945*. Lexington: University Press of Kentucky, 2018.

Judt, Thomas. *Greening the Red, White, and Blue: The Bomb, Big Business, and Consumer Resistance in Postwar America*. New York: Oxford University Press, 2014.

Kalman, Laura. *Right Star Rising: A New Politics, 1974–1980*. New York: W. W. Norton, 2010.

Katz, Milton S. *Ban the Bomb: A History of SANE, the Committee for a Sane Nuclear Policy, 1957–1985*. New York: Greenwood Press, 1986.

Kaufman, Robert G. *Henry M. Jackson: A Life in Politics*. Seattle: University of Washington Press, 2000.

Kengor, Paul. *The Crusader: Ronald Reagan and the Triumph over Communism*. New York: Regan, 2006.

——. "Reagan's Catholic Connections." *Catholic Exchange*, June 11, 2004. https://catholicexchange.com/reagans-catholic-connections.

Kennan, George. *American Diplomacy*. Expanded ed. Chicago: University of Chicago Press, [1951] 1984.

Kennedy, Eugene. *Bernardin: Life to the Full*. Chicago: Bonus Books, 1997.

Kleidman, Robert. *Organizing for Peace: Neutrality, the Test Ban, and the Freeze*. Syracuse, NY: Syracuse University Press, 1993.

Knoblauch, William K. *Nuclear Freeze in a Cold War: The Reagan Administration, Cultural Activism, and the End of the Arms Race*. Amherst: University of Massachusetts Press, 2017.

Knopf, Jeffrey W. *Domestic Society and International Cooperation: The Impact of Protest on US Arms Control Policy*. New York: Cambridge University Press, 1998.

Korstad, Robert, and Nelson Lichtenstein. "Opportunities Found and Lost: Labor, Radicals, and Civil Rights." *Journal of American History* 75, no. 3 (December 1988): 786–811.

Kotz, Nick. *Wild Blue Yonder: Money, Politics, and the B-1 Bomber*. Princeton, NJ: Princeton University Press, 1988.

LaFeber, Walter. *America, Russia, and the Cold War, 1945–2002*. Updated 9th ed. Boston: McGraw-Hill, 2004.

——. *The Deadly Bet: LBJ, Vietnam, and the 1968 Election*. Lanham, MD: Rowman and Littlefield, 2005.

Leffler, Melvyn. *For the Soul of Mankind: The United States, the Soviet Union, and the Cold War*. New York: Hill and Wang, 2007.

Lettow, Paul. *Ronald Reagan and His Quest to Abolish Nuclear Weapons*. New York: Random House, 2005.

Levy, Shawn. *Paul Newman: A Life*. New York: Three Rivers Press, 2009.

Lewer, Nick. *Physicians and the Peace Movement: Prescriptions for Hope*. New York: Routledge, 1992.

Lichtman, Allan J. *White Protestant Nation: The Rise of the American Conservative Movement*. New York: Atlantic Monthly Press, 2008.

Loeb, Paul Rogat. *Hope in Hard Times: America's Peace Movement in the Reagan Era.* Lexington, MA: Lexington Books, 1987.

Maar, Henry R., III. "The Lost Years: The American Peace Movement from Vietnam to Nuclear Freeze," *Peace and Change* 44, no. 3 (July 2019): 386–411.

——. "Subtraction by Addition: The Nixon Administration and the Domestic Politics of Arms Control." In *The Cold War at Home and Abroad: Domestic Politics and US Foreign Policy since 1945*, ed. Andrew L. Johns and Mitchell B. Lerner, 123–145. Lexington: University Press of Kentucky, 2018.

Mann, James. *The Rebellion of Ronald Reagan: A History of the End of the Cold War.* New York: Penguin Group, 2010.

Marlo, Francis H. *Planning Reagan's War: Conservative Strategists and America's Cold War Victory.* Dulles, VA: Potomac Books, 2012.

Martin, Bradford D. *The Other Eighties: A Secret History of America in the Age of Reagan.* New York: Hill and Wang, 2011.

Mastny, Vojtech. "How Able Was 'Able Archer'? Nuclear Trigger and Intelligence in Perspective." *Journal of Cold War Studies* 11, no. 1 (Winter 2009): 108–123.

McGirr, Lisa. *Suburban Warriors: The Origins of the New American Right.* Princeton, NJ: Princeton University Press, 2001.

McGreevy, John T. *Catholicism and American Freedom: A History.* New York: W. W. Norton, 2003.

Meyer, David. "How Social Movements Matter." *Contexts* 2, no. 4 (Fall 2003): 30–35.

——. *A Winter of Discontent: The Nuclear Freeze in American Politics.* New York: Praeger, 1990.

Miles, Simon. "The War Scare That Wasn't: Able Archer 83 and the Myths of the Second Cold War." *Journal of Cold War Studies* 22, no. 3 (Summer 2020): 86–118.

Mollin, Marian. *Radical Pacifism in Modern America: Egalitarianism and Protest.* Philadelphia: University of Pennsylvania Press, 2006.

Morris, Edmund. *Dutch: A Memoir of Ronald Reagan.* New York: Modern Library, 1999.

Nadler, Ben. *Punk in NYC's Lower East Side 1981–1991.* Volume 1, Scene History Series. Portland, OR: Microcosm, 2014.

Nepstad, Sharon Erickson. *Religion and War Resistance in the Plowshares Movement.* New York: Cambridge University Press, 2008.

Oberdorfer, Don. *From the Cold War to a New Era: The United States and the Soviet Union, 1983–1991.* Updated ed. Baltimore: Johns Hopkins University Press, 1998. Originally published 1991.

Perlstein, Richard. *Nixonland: The Rise of a President and the Fracturing of America.* New York: Scribner, 2008.

Perrine, Toni A. *Film and the Nuclear Age: Representing Cultural Anxiety.* New York: Garland, 1998.

Perry, William J., and Tom Z. Collina. *The Button: The New Nuclear Arms Race and Presidential Power from Truman to Trump.* Dallas: BenBella Books, 2020.

Peterson, Christian. *Ronald Reagan and Antinuclear Movements in the United States and Western Europe, 1981–1987.* Lewiston, NY: Edwin Mellin Press, 2003.

Pietroban, Allen. "Norman Cousins and Track II Diplomacy in the Breakthrough to the 1963 Limited Test Ban Treaty." *Journal of Cold War Studies* 18, no. 1 (Winter 2016): 60–79.

Poundstone, William. *Carl Sagan: A Life in the Cosmos.* New York: Henry Holt, 1999.

Powaski, Ronald. *Return to Armageddon: The United States and the Nuclear Arms Race, 1981–1999.* New York: Oxford University Press, 2000.

Preston, Andrew. *Sword of the Spirit, Shield of Faith: Religion in American War and Diplomacy.* New York: Alfred A. Knopf, 2012.

Raymond, Emilie. *From My Cold Dead Hands: Charlton Heston and American Politics.* Lexington: University Press of Kentucky, 2006.

Rochon, Thomas R., and David S. Meyer. "Introduction: Nuclear Freeze in Theory and Action." In *Coalition and Political Movements: The Lessons of the Nuclear Freeze*, eds. Thomas R. Rochon and David S. Meyer, 1–21. Boulder, CO: Lynne Rienner, 1997.

Rosenfeld, Seth. *Subversives: The FBI's War on Student Radicals and Reagan's Rise to Power.* New York: Farrar, Straus and Giroux, 2012.

Rubinson, Paul. *Rethinking the American Antinuclear Movement.* New York: Routledge, 2018.

Scheer, Robert. *With Enough Shovels: Reagan, Bush, and Nuclear War.* New York: Random House, 1982.

Schlesinger, Robert. *White House Ghosts: Presidents and Their Speechwriters.* New York: Simon and Schuster, 2008.

Schmidt, David A. *Citizen Lawmakers: The Ballot Initiative Revolution.* Philadelphia: Temple University Press, 1989.

Schweizer, Peter. *Reagan's War: The Epic Story of His Forty Year Struggle and Final Triumph over Communism.* New York: Doubleday, 2002.

——. *Victory: The Reagan Administration's Secret Strategy That Hastened the Collapse of the Soviet Union.* New York: Atlantic Monthly Press, 1996.

Scoblic, J. Peter. *U.S. vs. Them: How a Half Century of Conservatism Has Undermined America's Security.* New York: Viking, 2008.

Shaw, Tony. *Hollywood's Cold War.* Amherst: University of Massachusetts Press, 2007.

Sherry, Michael. *In the Shadow of War: The United States since the 1930s.* New Haven, CT: Yale University Press, 1995.

Smoke, Richard. *National Security and the Nuclear Dilemma: An Introduction to the American Experience.* Reading, MA: Addison-Wesley, 1984.

Soper, Kerry D. *Garry Trudeau: Doonesbury and the Aesthetics of Satire.* Jackson: University of Mississippi Press, 2007.

Stanley, Timothy. *Kennedy vs. Carter: The 1980 Battle for the Democratic Party's Soul.* Lawrence: University of Kansas Press, 2010.

Subrug, Robert. *Beyond Vietnam: The Politics of Protest in Massachusetts, 1974–1990.* Amherst: University of Massachusetts Press, 2009.

Talbott, Strobe. *Deadly Gambits: The Reagan Administration and the Stalemate in Nuclear Arms Control.* New York: Alfred A. Knopf, 1984.

Tannenwald, Nina. *The Nuclear Taboo: The United States and the Non-use of Nuclear Weapons since 1945.* Cambridge: Cambridge University Press, 2007.

Taubman, William. *Gorbachev: His Life and Times.* New York: W. W. Norton, 2017.

Thompson, Nicholas. *The Hawk and the Dove: Paul Nitze, George Kennan, and the History of the Cold War*. New York: Henry Holt, 2009.

Thornton, Richard C. *The Reagan Revolution I: The Politics of U.S. Foreign Policy*. Victoria: Trafford, 2003.

Williams, William Appleman. *Empire as a Way of Life: An Essay on the Causes and Character of America's Present Predicament, along with a Few Thoughts about an Alternative*. New York: Oxford University Press, 1980; reprint Brooklyn: IG Publishing, 2007.

Wilson, James Graham. *The Triumph of Improvisation: Gorbachev's Adaptability, Reagan's Engagement, and the End of the Cold War*. Ithaca, NY: Cornell University Press, 2013.

Winik, Jay. *On the Brink: The Dramatic Behind the Scenes Saga of the Reagan Era and the Men and Women Who Won the Cold War*. New York: Simon and Schuster, 1996.

Wittner, Lawrence S. *The Struggle against the Bomb, Vol.1: One World or None, a History of the World Nuclear Disarmament Movement through 1953*. Stanford, CA: Stanford University Press, 1992.

——. *The Struggle against the Bomb, Vol. 3: Towards Nuclear Abolition, a History of the Nuclear Disarmament Movement 1971–Present*. Stanford, CA: Stanford University Press, 2003.

Yanarella, Ernest J. *The Missile Defense Controversy: Technology in Search of a Mission*. Revised and updated ed. Lexington: University Press of Kentucky, 2010.

Zaretsky, Natasha. *Radiation Nation: Three Mile Island and the Political Transformation of the 1970s*. New York: Columbia University Press, 2018.

Zelizer, Julian E. *Arsenal of Democracy: The Politics of National Security—from World War II to the War on Terrorism*. New York: Basic Books, 2010.

Zubok, Vladislav M. *A Failed Empire: The Soviet Union in the Cold War from Stalin to Gorbachev*. Chapel Hill: University of North Carolina Press, 2007.

Films

Blush, Steven, and Paul Rachman. *American Hardcore*. Directed by Paul Rachman. Culver City, CA: Sony Pictures, 2006.

INDEX

CPSIA information can be obtained
at www.ICGtesting.com
Printed in the USA
LVHW092313110322
713256LV00014B/349/J

9 781501 760884